Im
Great Priest Imhotep

9

MAKOTO
MORISHITA

Great Priest Imhotep

SCROLL 32: LAST SUMMER

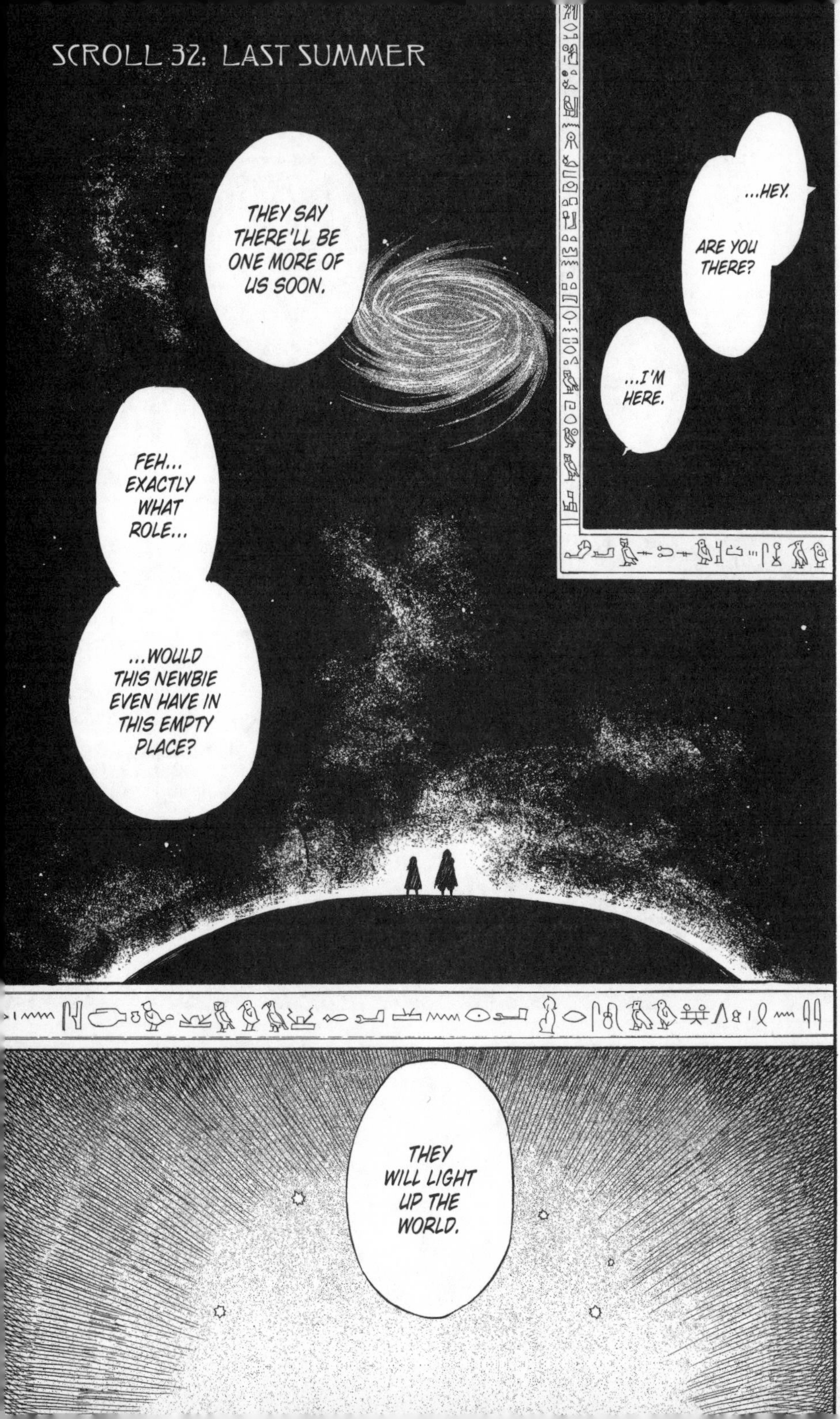
...HEY.
ARE YOU THERE?
...I'M HERE.
THEY SAY THERE'LL BE ONE MORE OF US SOON.
FEH... EXACTLY WHAT ROLE...
...WOULD THIS NEWBIE EVEN HAVE IN THIS EMPTY PLACE?
THEY WILL LIGHT UP THE WORLD.

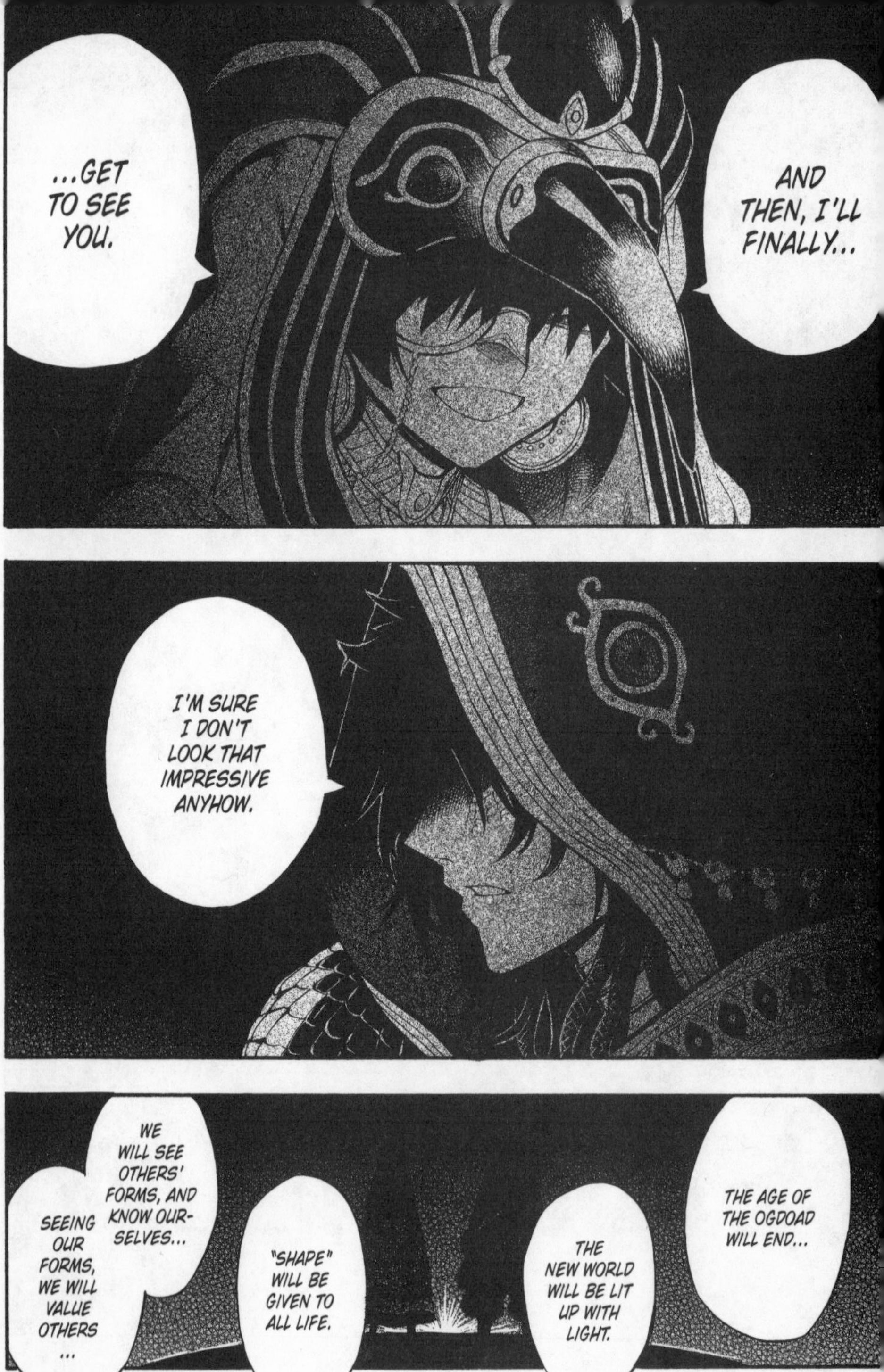
AND THEN, I'LL FINALLY...
...GET TO SEE YOU.
I'M SURE I DON'T LOOK THAT IMPRESSIVE ANYHOW.
THE AGE OF THE OGDOAD WILL END...
THE NEW WORLD WILL BE LIT UP WITH LIGHT.
"SHAPE" WILL BE GIVEN TO ALL LIFE.
WE WILL SEE OTHERS' FORMS, AND KNOW OUR-SELVES...
SEEING OUR FORMS, WE WILL VALUE OTHERS ...

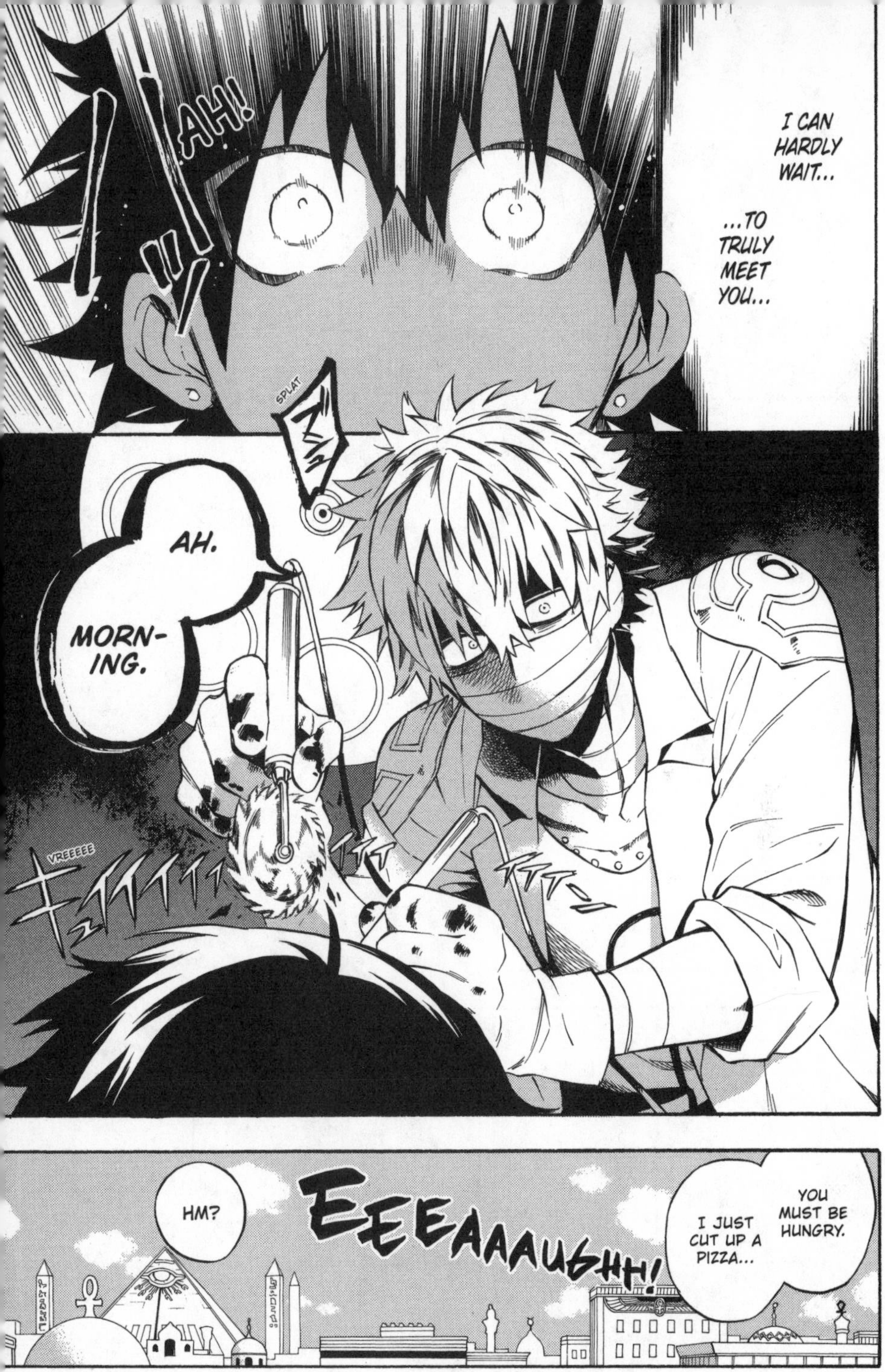
I CAN HARDLY WAIT...
...TO TRULY MEET YOU...
AH!
SPLAT
AH. MORNING.
VREEEEE
YOU MUST BE HUNGRY.
I JUST CUT UP A PIZZA...
EEEAAAAUGHH!
HM?

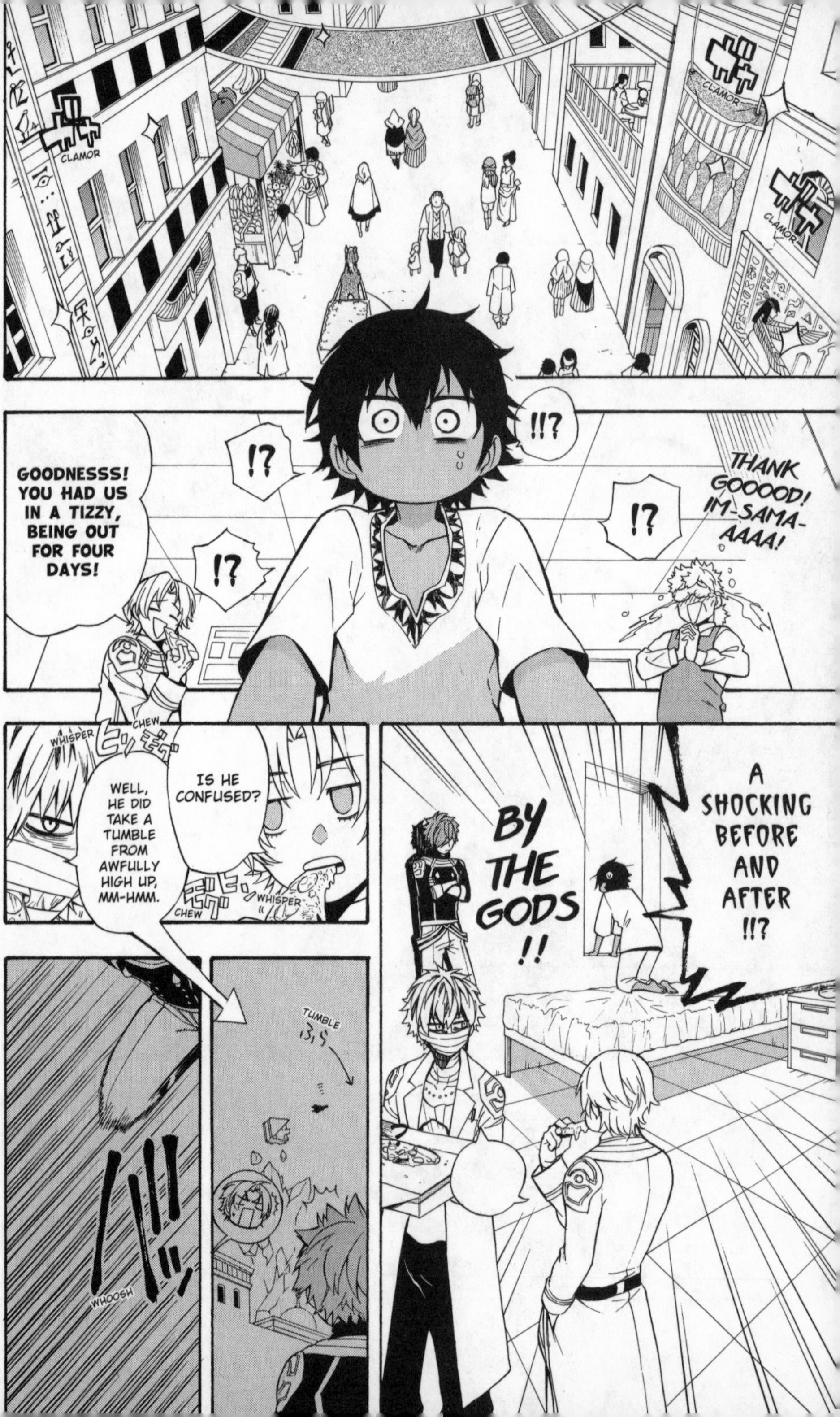
CLAMOR
CLAMOR
CLAMOR
THANK GOOOOD! IM-SAMA-AAAA!
!?
!!?
!?
!?
GOODNESSS! YOU HAD US IN A TIZZY, BEING OUT FOR FOUR DAYS!
A SHOCKING BEFORE AND AFTER !!?
BY THE GODS !!
IS HE CONFUSED?
CHEW
WHISPER
WELL, HE DID TAKE A TUMBLE FROM AWFULLY HIGH UP, MM-HMM.
WHISPER
CHEW
TUMBLE
WHOOSH

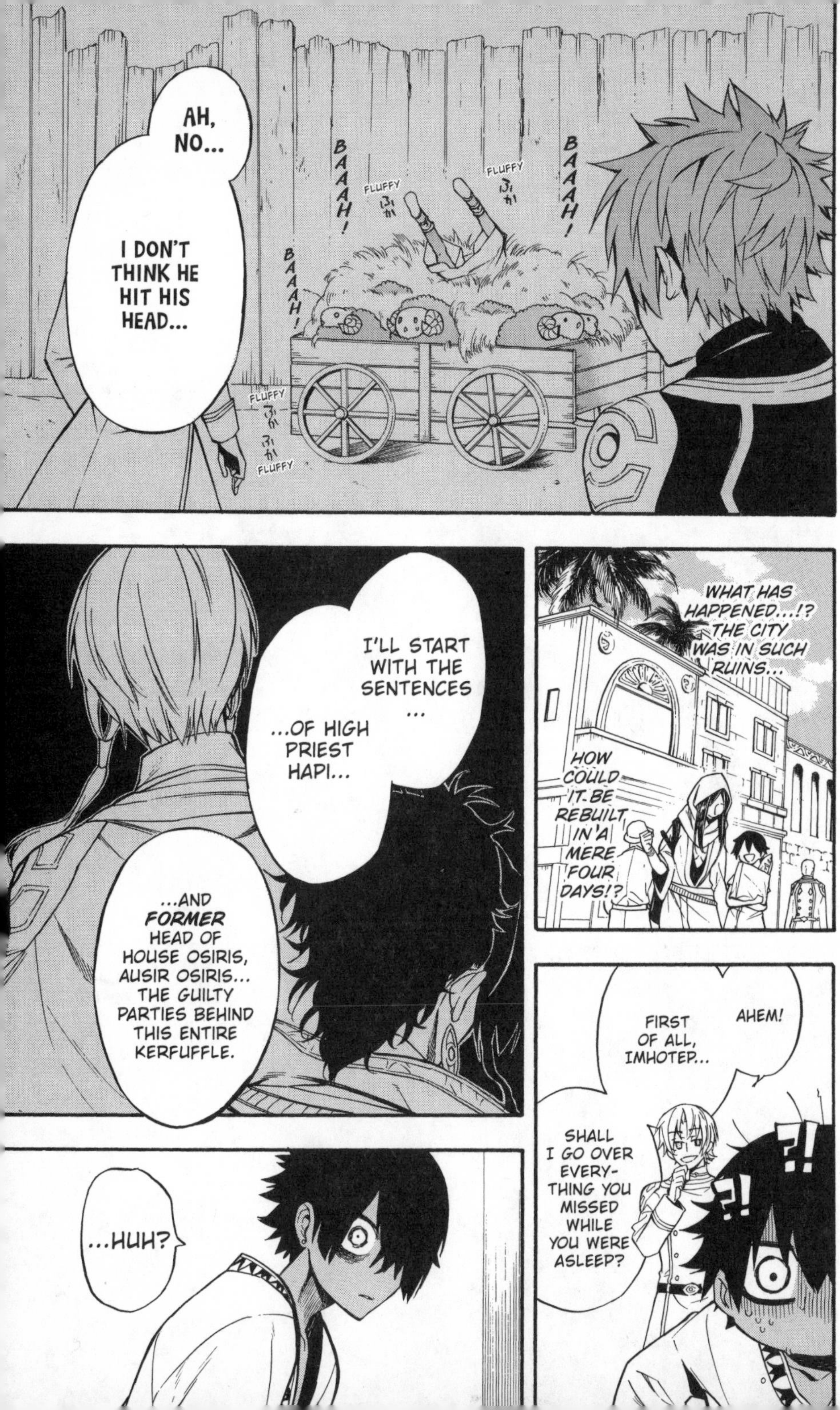

BAAAH!
FLUFFY ふか
BAAAH!
FLUFFY ふか
BAAAH!
AH, NO...
I DON'T THINK HE HIT HIS HEAD...
FLUFFY ふか
ふか FLUFFY
WHAT HAS HAPPENED...!? THE CITY WAS IN SUCH RUINS...
HOW COULD IT BE REBUILT IN A MERE FOUR DAYS!?
I'LL START WITH THE SENTENCES...
...OF HIGH PRIEST HAPI...
...AND *FORMER* HEAD OF HOUSE OSIRIS, AUSIR OSIRIS... THE GUILTY PARTIES BEHIND THIS ENTIRE KERFUFFLE.
AHEM!
FIRST OF ALL, IMHOTEP...
SHALL I GO OVER EVERY-THING YOU MISSED WHILE YOU WERE ASLEEP?
?!
?!
...HUH?

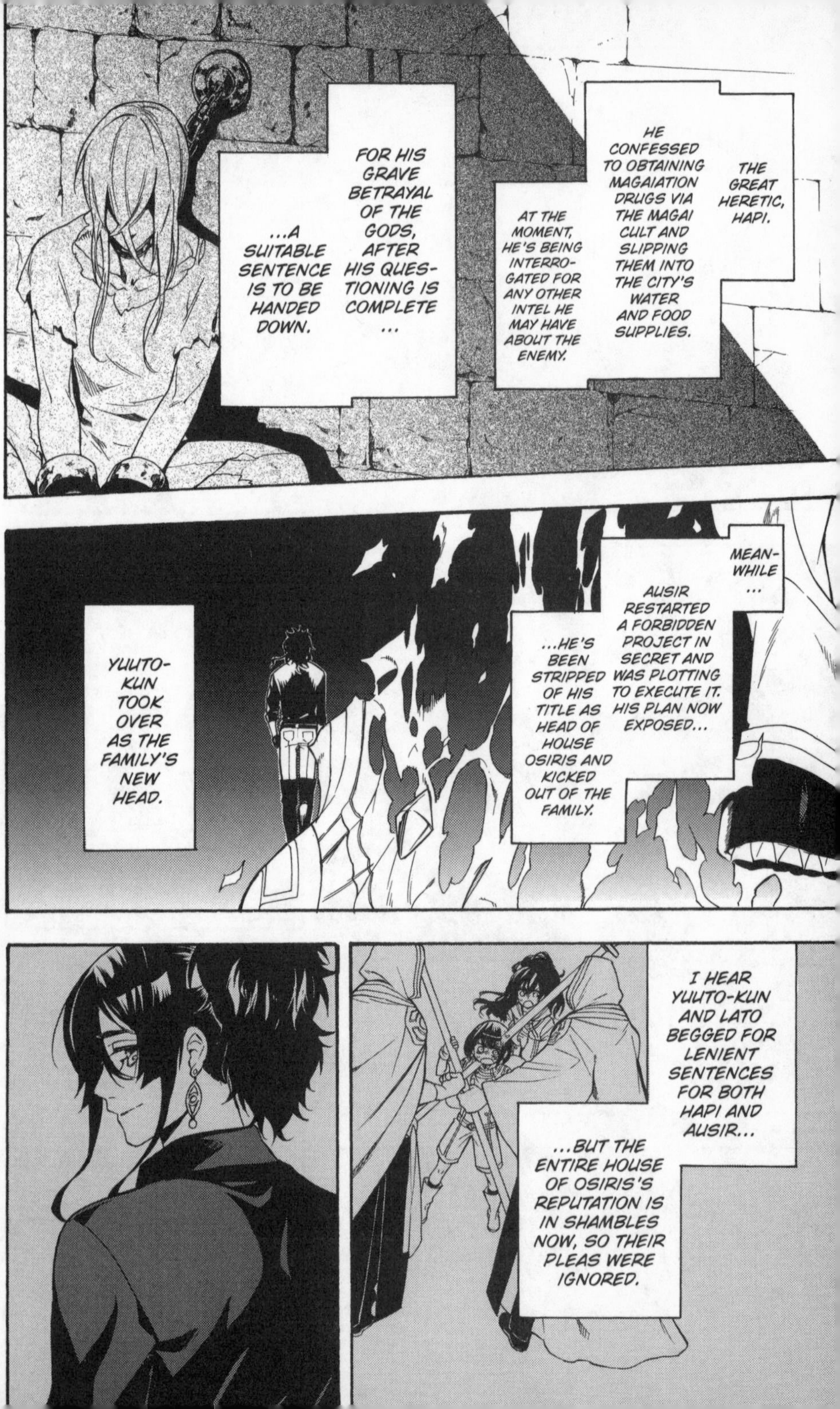
THE GREAT HERETIC, HAPI.
HE CONFESSED TO OBTAINING MAGAIATION DRUGS VIA THE MAGAI CULT AND SLIPPING THEM INTO THE CITY'S WATER AND FOOD SUPPLIES.
AT THE MOMENT, HE'S BEING INTERRO-GATED FOR ANY OTHER INTEL HE MAY HAVE ABOUT THE ENEMY.
FOR HIS GRAVE BETRAYAL OF THE GODS, AFTER HIS QUES-TIONING IS COMPLETE ...
...A SUITABLE SENTENCE IS TO BE HANDED DOWN.
MEAN-WHILE ...
AUSIR RESTARTED A FORBIDDEN PROJECT IN SECRET AND WAS PLOTTING TO EXECUTE IT. HIS PLAN NOW EXPOSED...
...HE'S BEEN STRIPPED OF HIS TITLE AS HEAD OF HOUSE OSIRIS AND KICKED OUT OF THE FAMILY.
YUUTO-KUN TOOK OVER AS THE FAMILY'S NEW HEAD.
I HEAR YUUTO-KUN AND LATO BEGGED FOR LENIENT SENTENCES FOR BOTH HAPI AND AUSIR...
...BUT THE ENTIRE HOUSE OF OSIRIS'S REPUTATION IS IN SHAMBLES NOW, SO THEIR PLEAS WERE IGNORED.

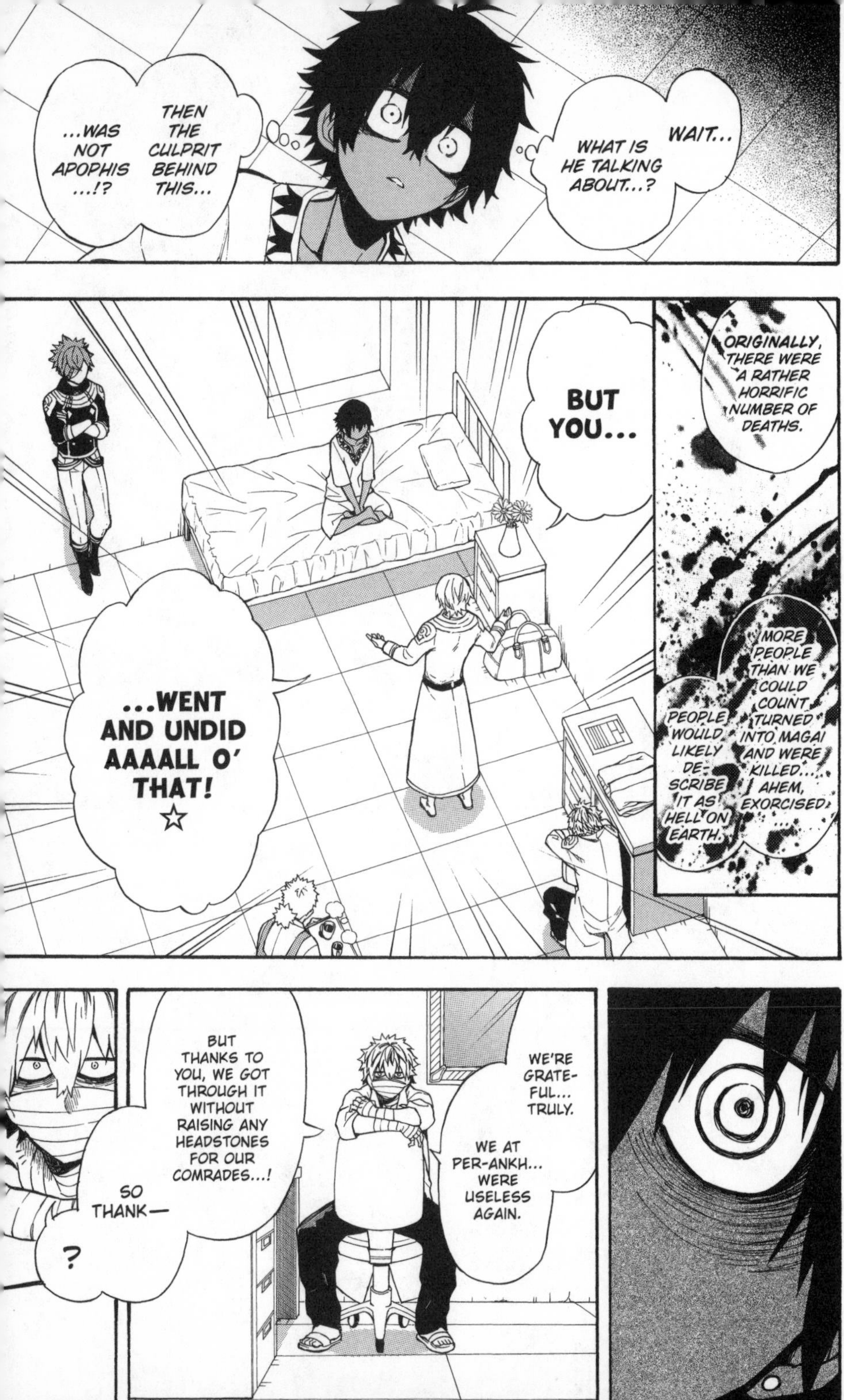
WAIT...
WHAT IS HE TALKING ABOUT...?
THEN THE CULPRIT BEHIND THIS...
...WAS NOT APOPHIS ...!?
ORIGINALLY, THERE WERE A RATHER HORRIFIC NUMBER OF DEATHS.
MORE PEOPLE THAN WE COULD COUNT TURNED INTO MAGAI AND WERE KILLED... AHEM, EXORCISED...
PEOPLE WOULD LIKELY DE-SCRIBE IT AS HELL ON EARTH.
BUT YOU...
...WENT AND UNDID AAAALL O' THAT! ☆
WE'RE GRATE-FUL... TRULY.
WE AT PER-ANKH... WERE USELESS AGAIN.
BUT THANKS TO YOU, WE GOT THROUGH IT WITHOUT RAISING ANY HEADSTONES FOR OUR COMRADES...!
SO THANK—
?

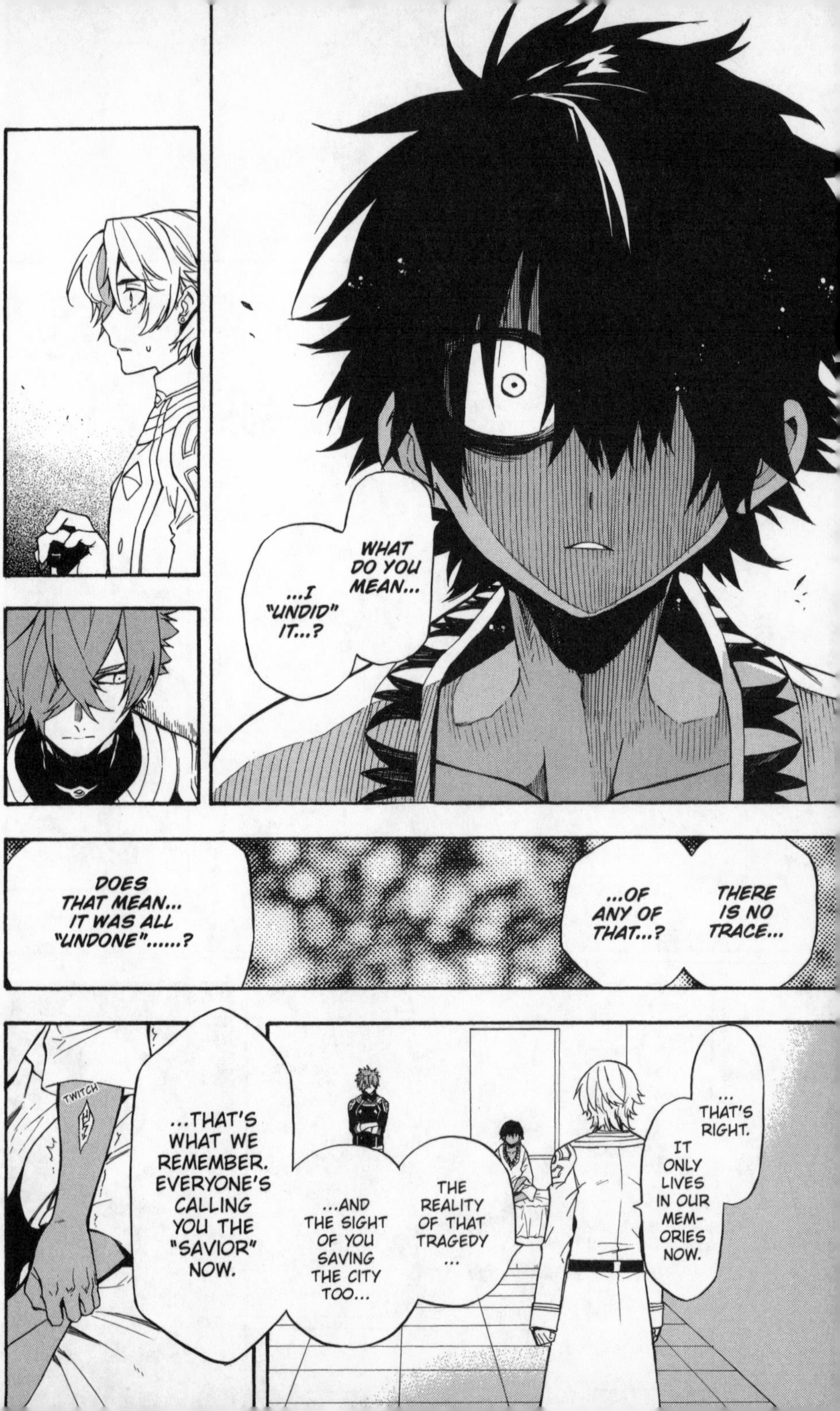
WHAT DO YOU MEAN...
...I "UNDID" IT...?
THERE IS NO TRACE...
...OF ANY OF THAT...?
DOES THAT MEAN... IT WAS ALL "UNDONE"......?
...THAT'S RIGHT.
IT ONLY LIVES IN OUR MEM-ORIES NOW.
THE REALITY OF THAT TRAGEDY...
...AND THE SIGHT OF YOU SAVING THE CITY TOO...
...THAT'S WHAT WE REMEMBER. EVERYONE'S CALLING YOU THE "SAVIOR" NOW.
TWITCH

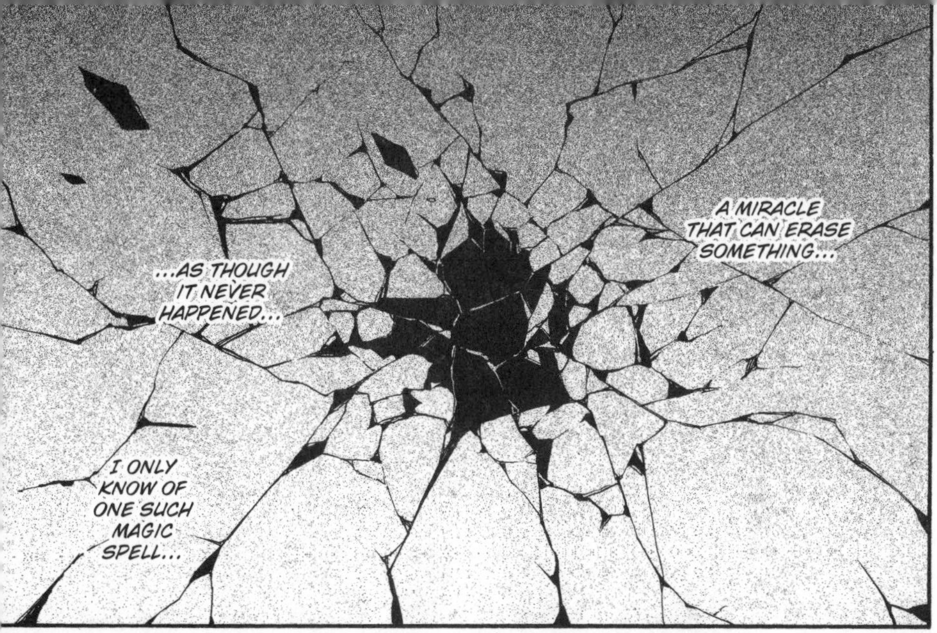
A MIRACLE THAT CAN ERASE SOMETHING...
...AS THOUGH IT NEVER HAPPENED...
I ONLY KNOW OF ONE SUCH MAGIC SPELL...

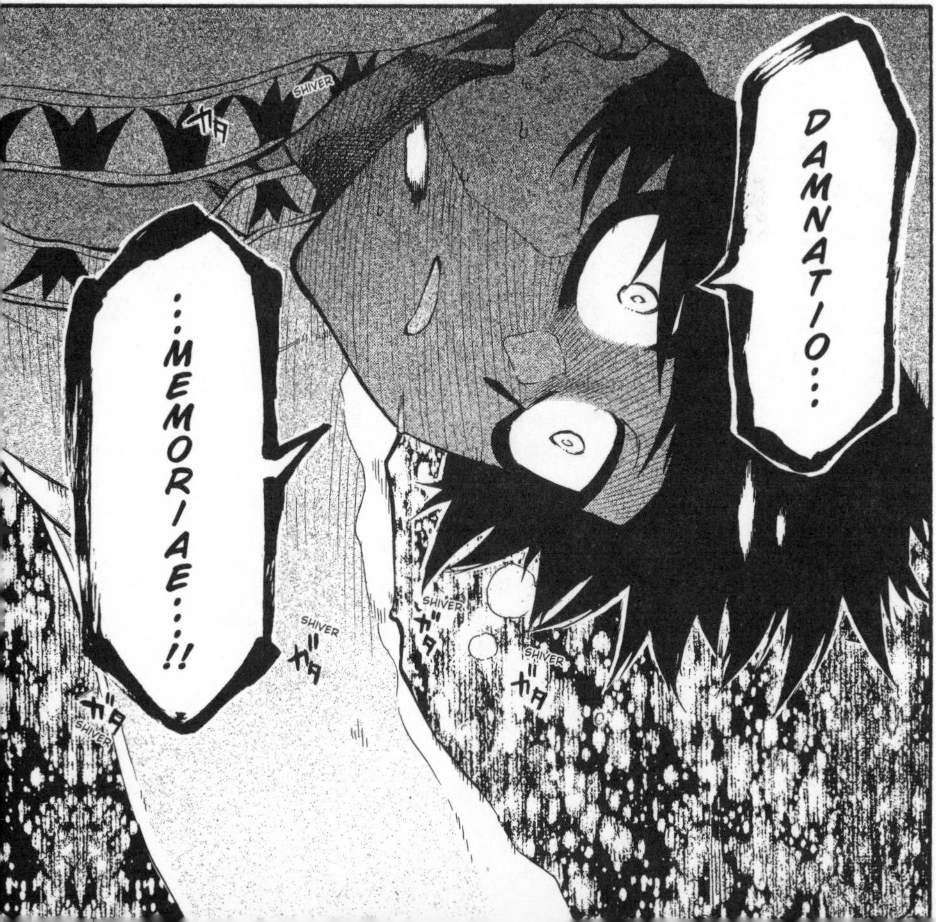
SHIVER
DAMNATIO...
...MEMORIAE...!!
SHIVER
SHIVER
SHIVER
SHIVER

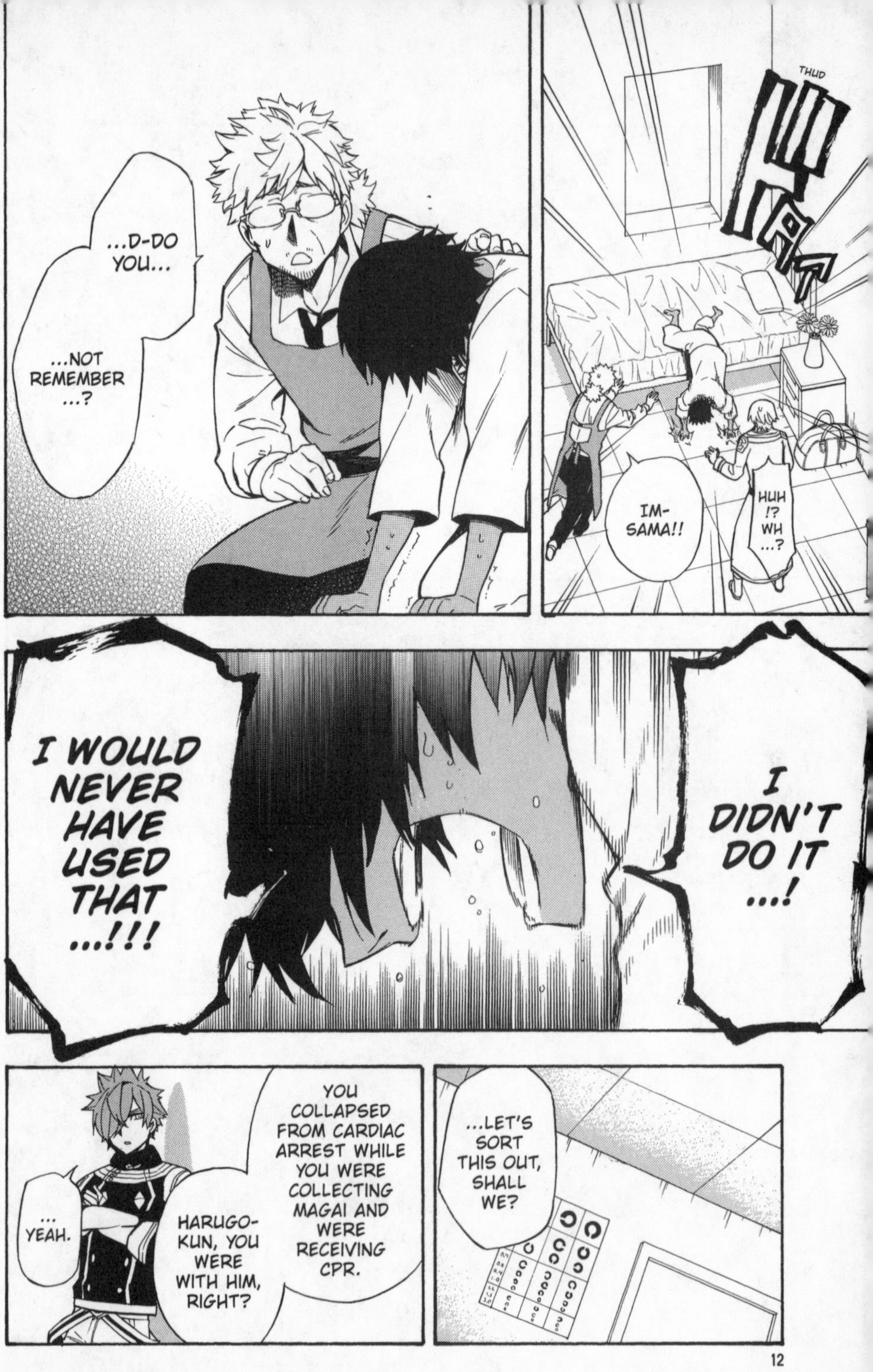
THUD
IM-SAMA!!
HUH!? WH...?
...D-DO YOU...
...NOT REMEMBER...?
I DIDN'T DO IT...!
I WOULD NEVER HAVE USED THAT...!!!
...LET'S SORT THIS OUT, SHALL WE?
YOU COLLAPSED FROM CARDIAC ARREST WHILE YOU WERE COLLECTING MAGAI AND WERE RECEIVING CPR.
HARUGO-KUN, YOU WERE WITH HIM, RIGHT?
...YEAH.

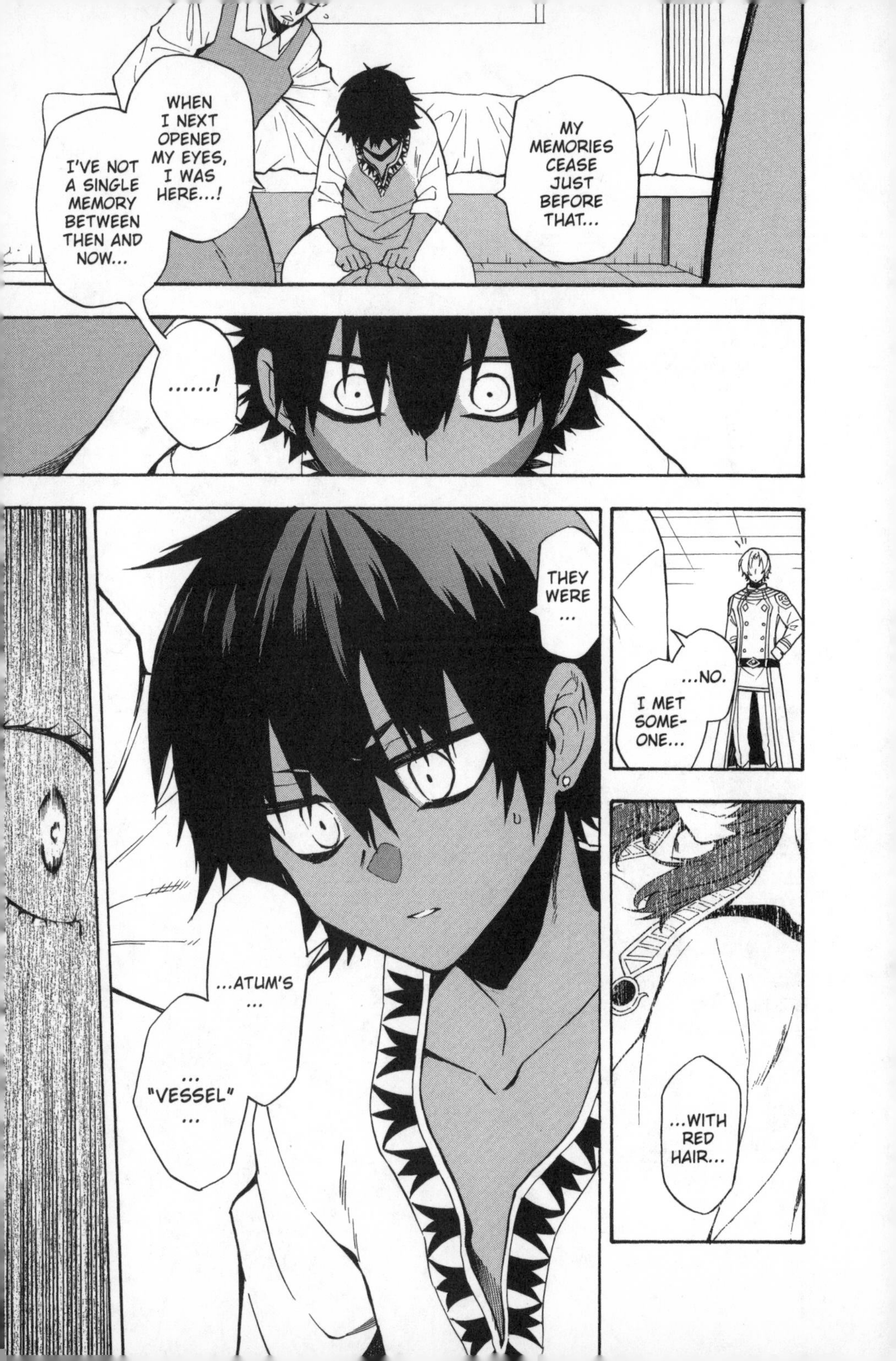
MY MEMORIES CEASE JUST BEFORE THAT...
WHEN I NEXT OPENED MY EYES, I WAS HERE...!
I'VE NOT A SINGLE MEMORY BETWEEN THEN AND NOW...
......!
...NO. I MET SOME-ONE...
...WITH RED HAIR...
THEY WERE ...
...ATUM'S ...
... "VESSEL" ...

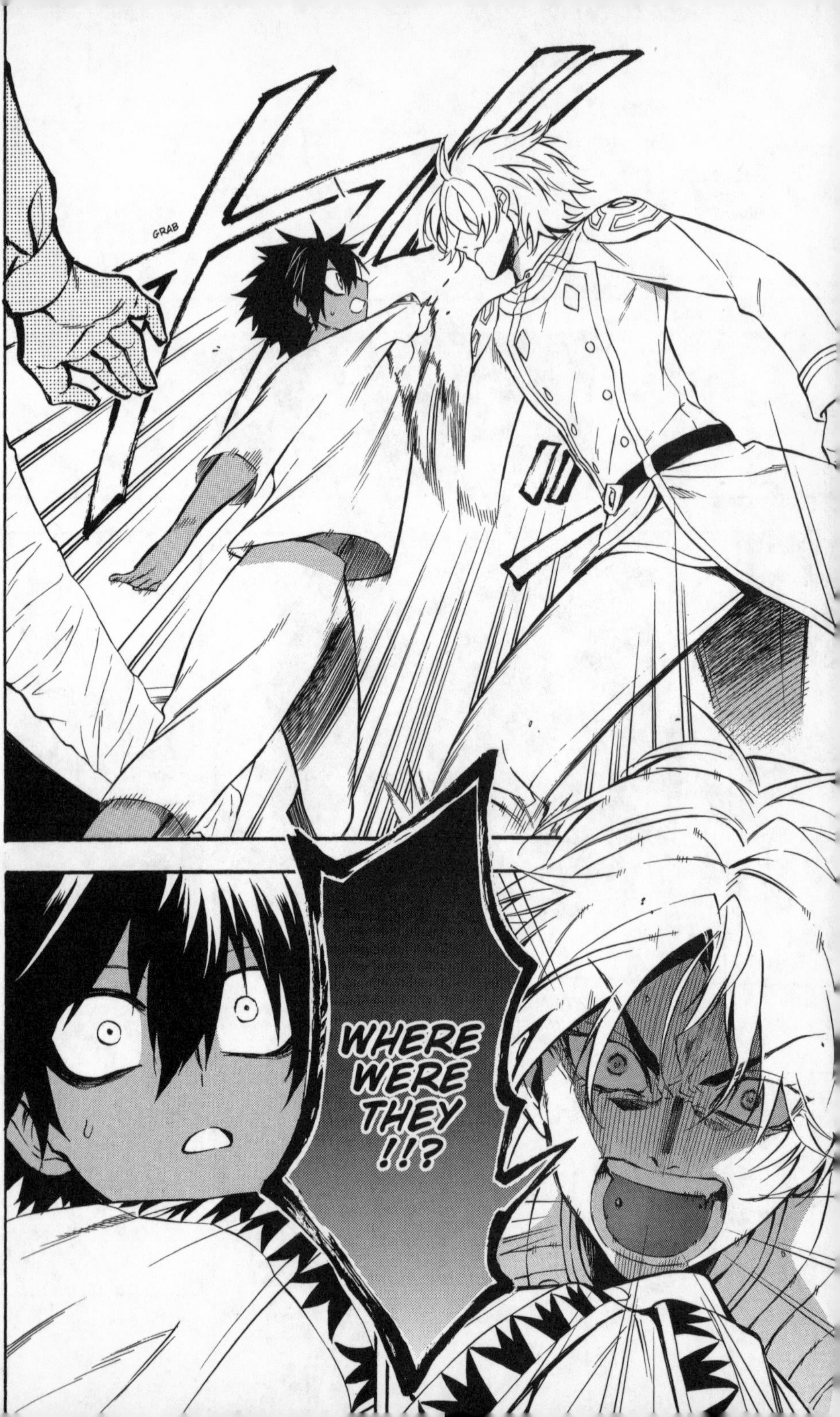
GRAB
WHERE WERE THEY!!?

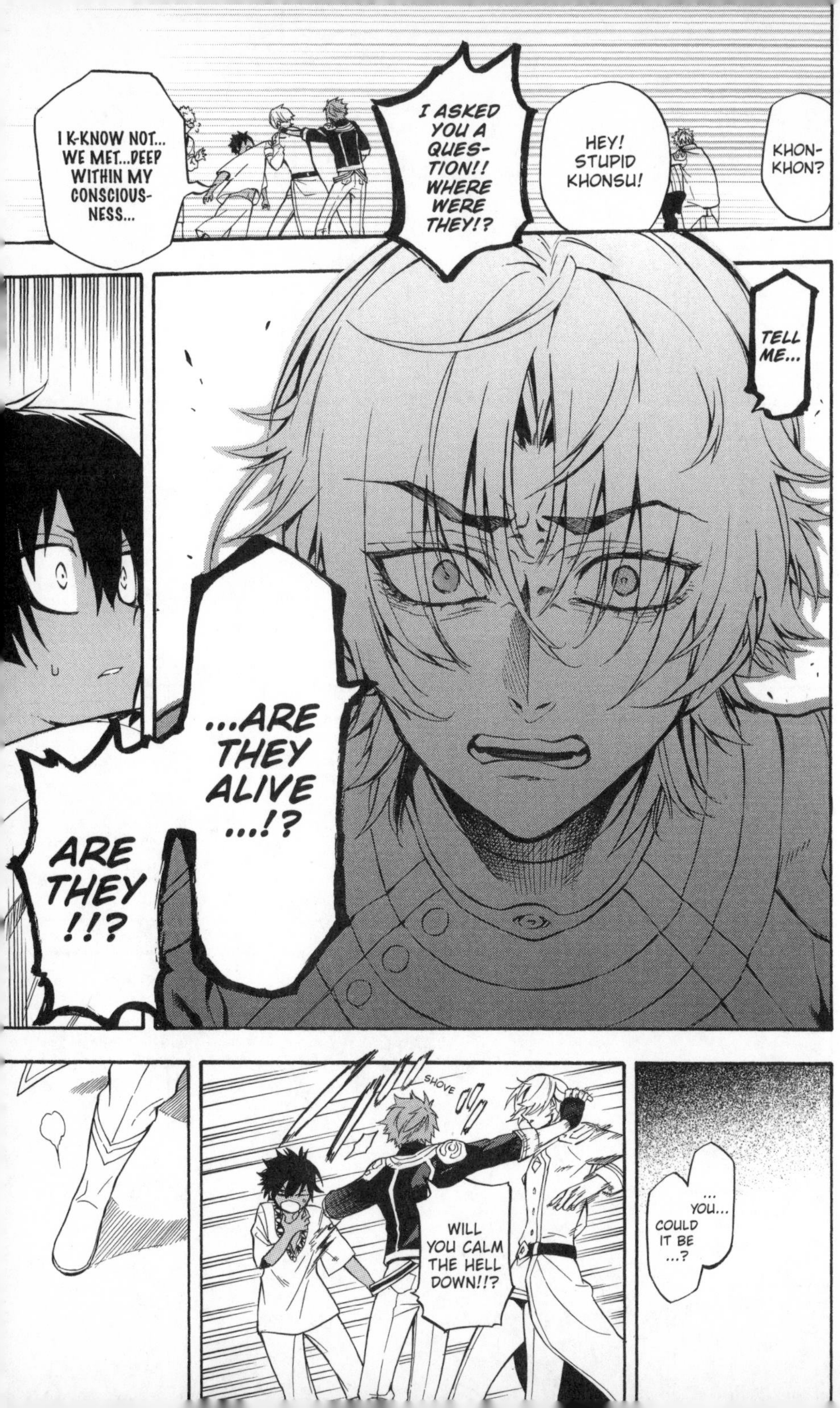
KHON-KHON?
HEY! STUPID KHONSU!
I ASKED YOU A QUES-TION!! WHERE WERE THEY!?
I K-KNOW NOT... WE MET...DEEP WITHIN MY CONSCIOUS-NESS...
TELL ME...
...ARE THEY ALIVE ...!?
ARE THEY !!?
... YOU... COULD IT BE ...?
SHOVE
WILL YOU CALM THE HELL DOWN!!?

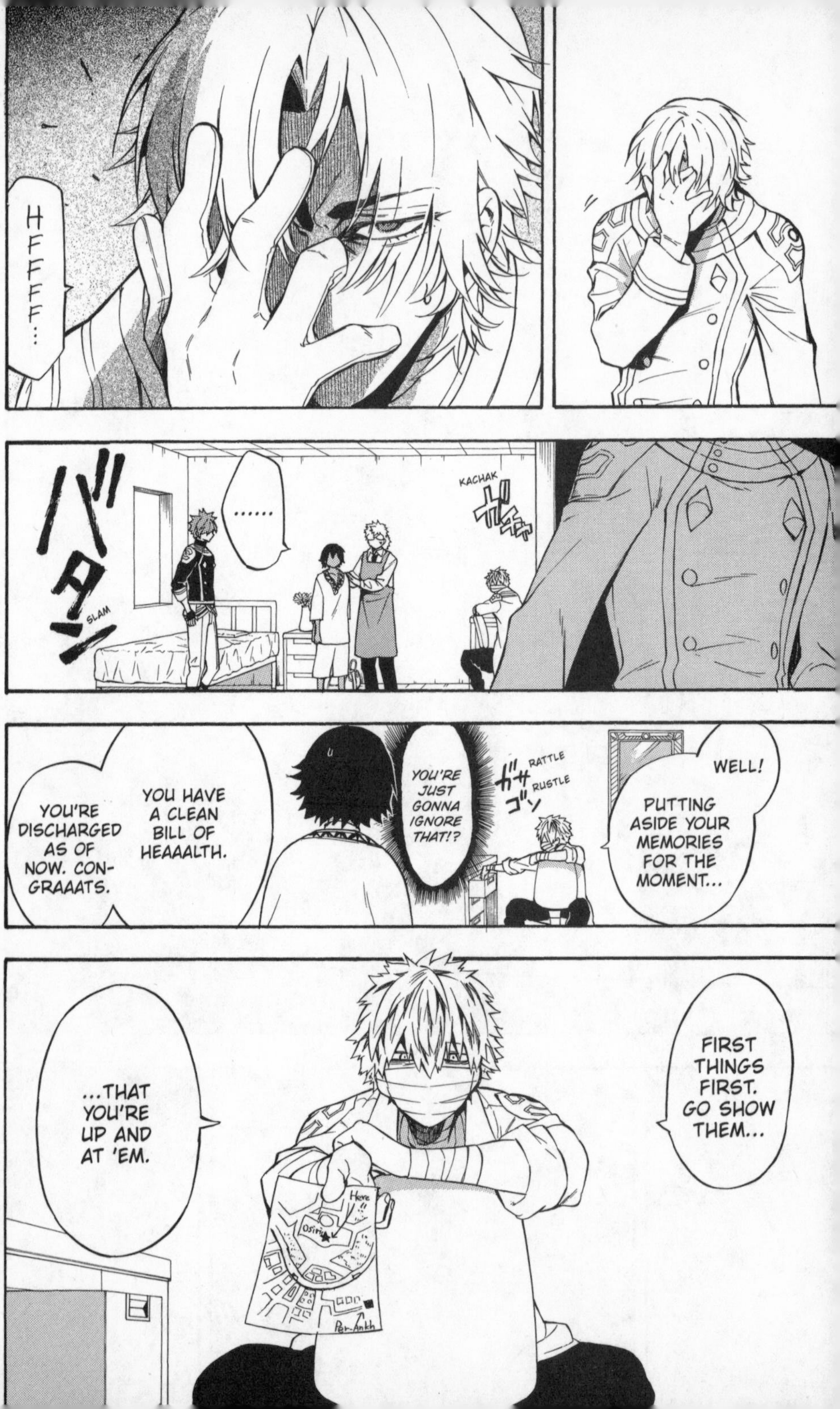
HFFFF...
KACHAK
ガチャ
......
バタン
SLAM
WELL!
PUTTING ASIDE YOUR MEMORIES FOR THE MOMENT...
ガサゴソ
RATTLE RUSTLE
YOU'RE JUST GONNA IGNORE THAT!?
YOU HAVE A CLEAN BILL OF HEAAALTH.
YOU'RE DISCHARGED AS OF NOW. CON-GRAAATS.
FIRST THINGS FIRST. GO SHOW THEM...
...THAT YOU'RE UP AND AT 'EM.
Here!!
Osiris
Per-Ankh

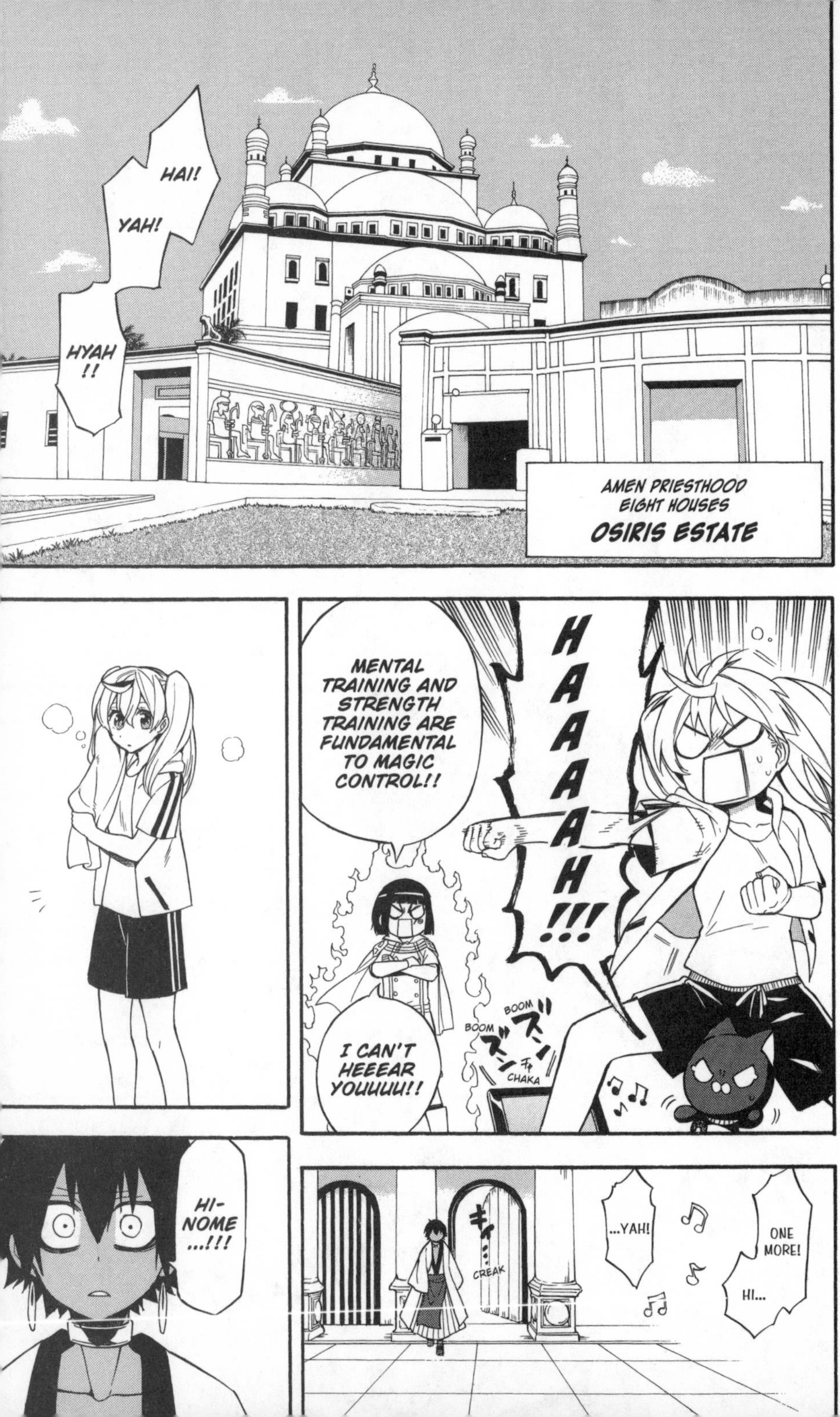
AMEN PRIESTHOOD
EIGHT HOUSES
OSIRIS ESTATE
HAI!
YAH!
HYAH!!
HAAAAAH!!!
MENTAL TRAINING AND STRENGTH TRAINING ARE FUNDAMENTAL TO MAGIC CONTROL!!
BOOM
BOOM
CHAKA
I CAN'T HEEEAR YOUUUU!!
ONE MORE!
HI...
...YAH!
CREAK
HI-NOME...!!!

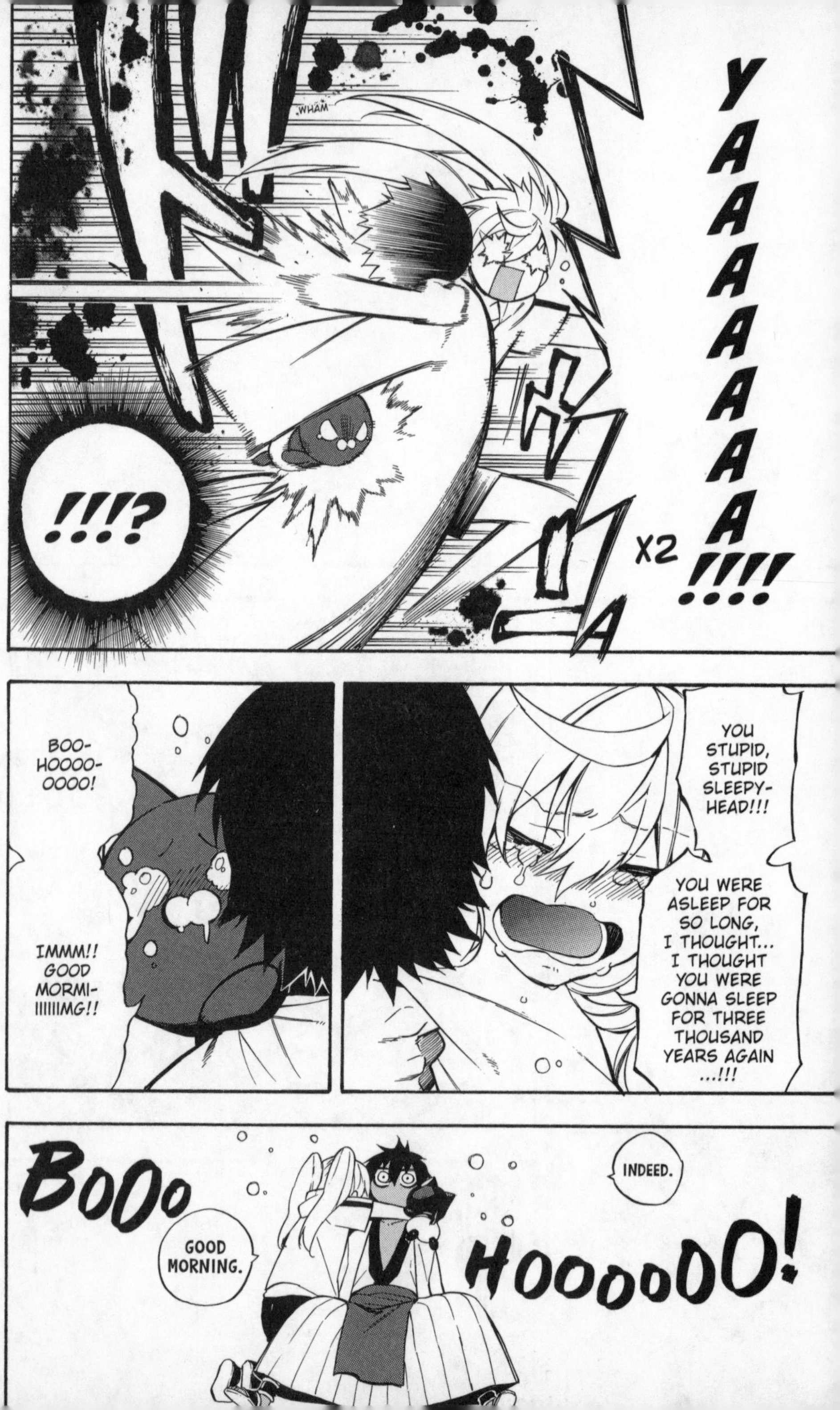
YAAAAAAAA!!!!
X2
WHAM
!!!?
YOU STUPID, STUPID SLEEPY-HEAD!!!
YOU WERE ASLEEP FOR SO LONG, I THOUGHT... I THOUGHT YOU WERE GONNA SLEEP FOR THREE THOUSAND YEARS AGAIN ...!!!
BOO-HOOOO-OOOO!
IMMM!! GOOD MORMI-IIIIIIMG!!
INDEED.
BOOoo HOOOOOOO!
GOOD MORNING.

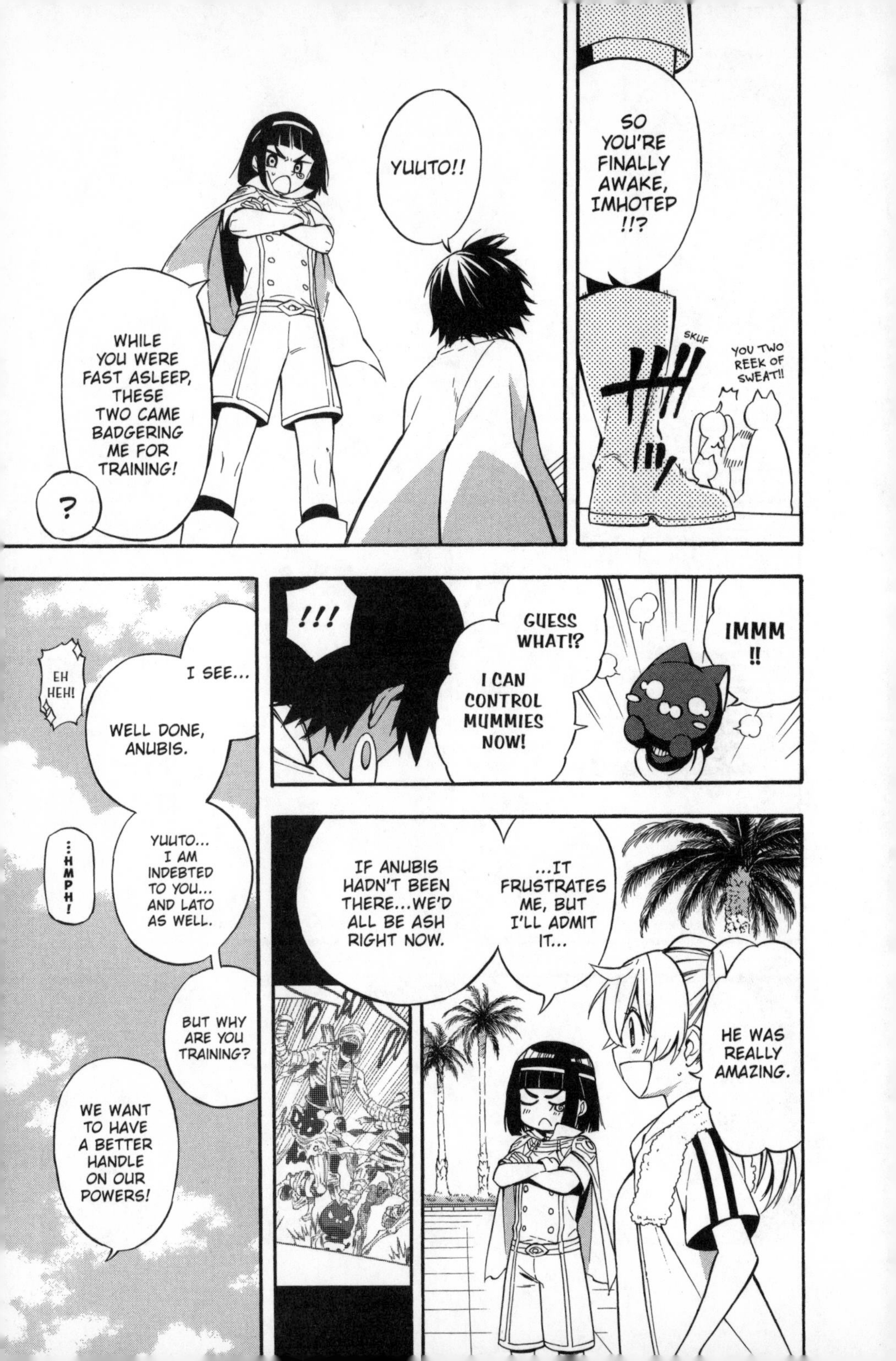
SO YOU'RE FINALLY AWAKE, IMHOTEP!!?
SKUF
YOU TWO REEK OF SWEAT!!
YUUTO!!
WHILE YOU WERE FAST ASLEEP, THESE TWO CAME BADGERING ME FOR TRAINING!
?
IMMM!!
GUESS WHAT!?
I CAN CONTROL MUMMIES NOW!
!!!
HE WAS REALLY AMAZING.
...IT FRUSTRATES ME, BUT I'LL ADMIT IT...
IF ANUBIS HADN'T BEEN THERE...WE'D ALL BE ASH RIGHT NOW.
I SEE...
WELL DONE, ANUBIS.
EH HEH!
YUUTO... I AM INDEBTED TO YOU... AND LATO AS WELL.
...HMPH!
BUT WHY ARE YOU TRAINING?
WE WANT TO HAVE A BETTER HANDLE ON OUR POWERS!

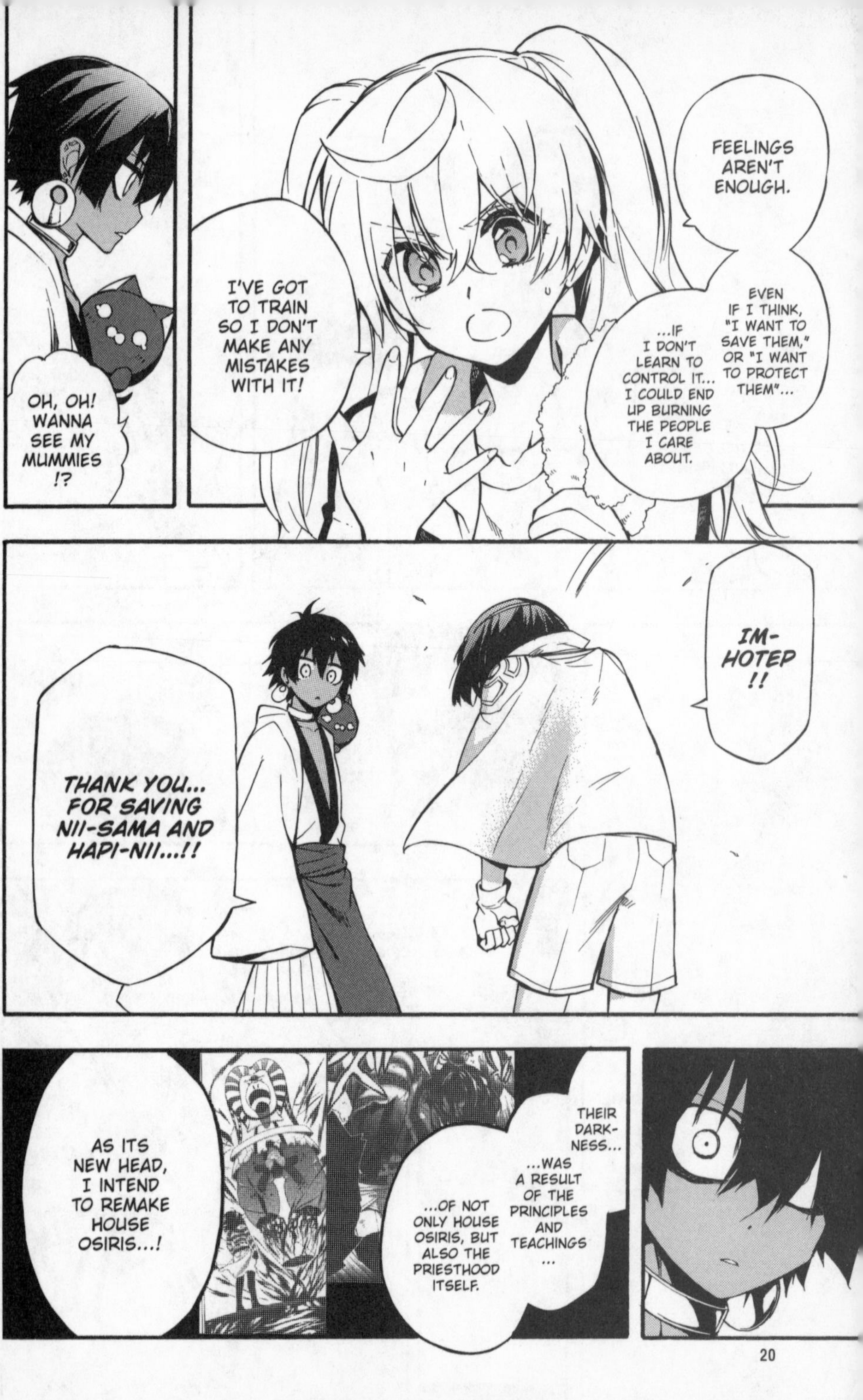
FEELINGS AREN'T ENOUGH.
EVEN IF I THINK, "I WANT TO SAVE THEM," OR "I WANT TO PROTECT THEM"...
...IF I DON'T LEARN TO CONTROL IT... I COULD END UP BURNING THE PEOPLE I CARE ABOUT.
I'VE GOT TO TRAIN SO I DON'T MAKE ANY MISTAKES WITH IT!
OH, OH! WANNA SEE MY MUMMIES!?
IM-HOTEP!!
THANK YOU... FOR SAVING NII-SAMA AND HAPI-NII...!!
THEIR DARKNESS...
...WAS A RESULT OF THE PRINCIPLES AND TEACHINGS...
...OF NOT ONLY HOUSE OSIRIS, BUT ALSO THE PRIESTHOOD ITSELF.
AS ITS NEW HEAD, I INTEND TO REMAKE HOUSE OSIRIS...!

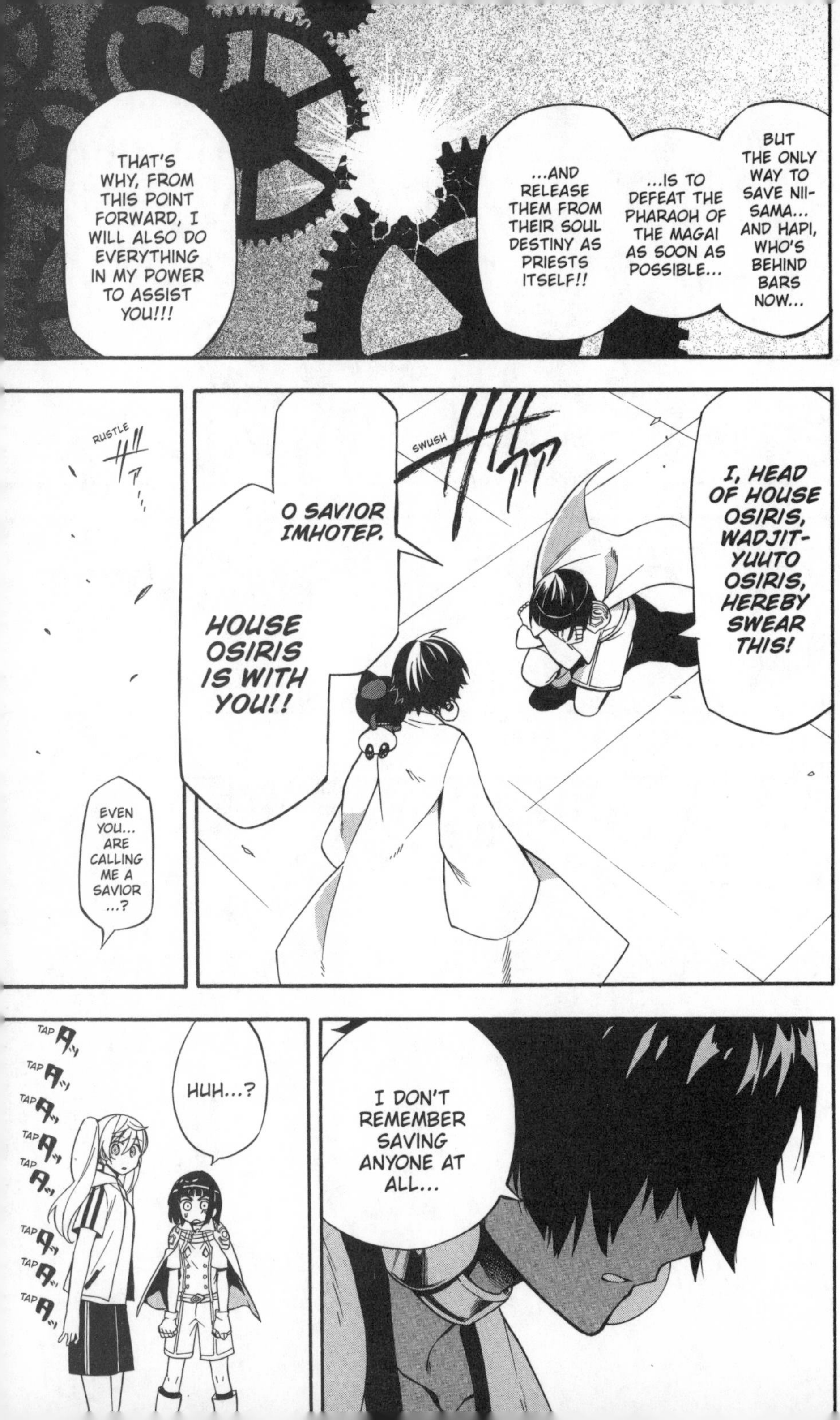

BUT THE ONLY WAY TO SAVE NII-SAMA... AND HAPI, WHO'S BEHIND BARS NOW...
...IS TO DEFEAT THE PHARAOH OF THE MAGAI AS SOON AS POSSIBLE...
...AND RELEASE THEM FROM THEIR SOUL DESTINY AS PRIESTS ITSELF!!
THAT'S WHY, FROM THIS POINT FORWARD, I WILL ALSO DO EVERYTHING IN MY POWER TO ASSIST YOU!!!
I, HEAD OF HOUSE OSIRIS, WADJIT-YUUTO OSIRIS, HEREBY SWEAR THIS!
SWUSH
O SAVIOR IMHOTEP.
HOUSE OSIRIS IS WITH YOU!!
RUSTLE
EVEN YOU... ARE CALLING ME A SAVIOR ...?
I DON'T REMEMBER SAVING ANYONE AT ALL...
HUH...?
TAP
TAP
TAP
TAP
TAP
TAP
TAP
TAP

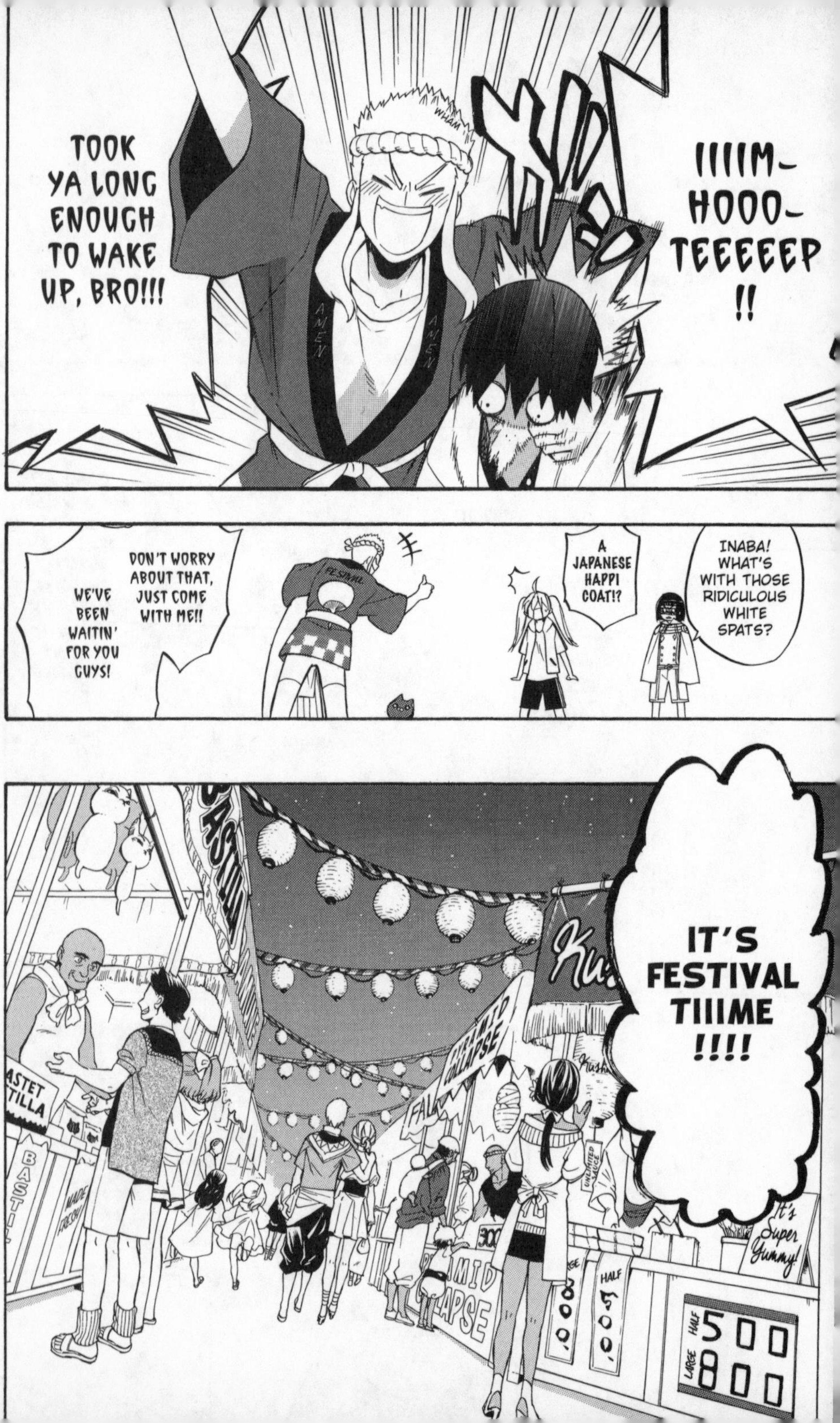
IIIIM-HOOO-TEEEEEP!!
WHAM
TOOK YA LONG ENOUGH TO WAKE UP, BRO!!!
INABA! WHAT'S WITH THOSE RIDICULOUS WHITE SPATS?
A JAPANESE HAPPI COAT!?
DON'T WORRY ABOUT THAT, JUST COME WITH ME!!
WE'VE BEEN WAITIN' FOR YOU GUYS!
IT'S FESTIVAL TIIIME!!!!
It's Super Yummy!
HALF 500
LARGE 800

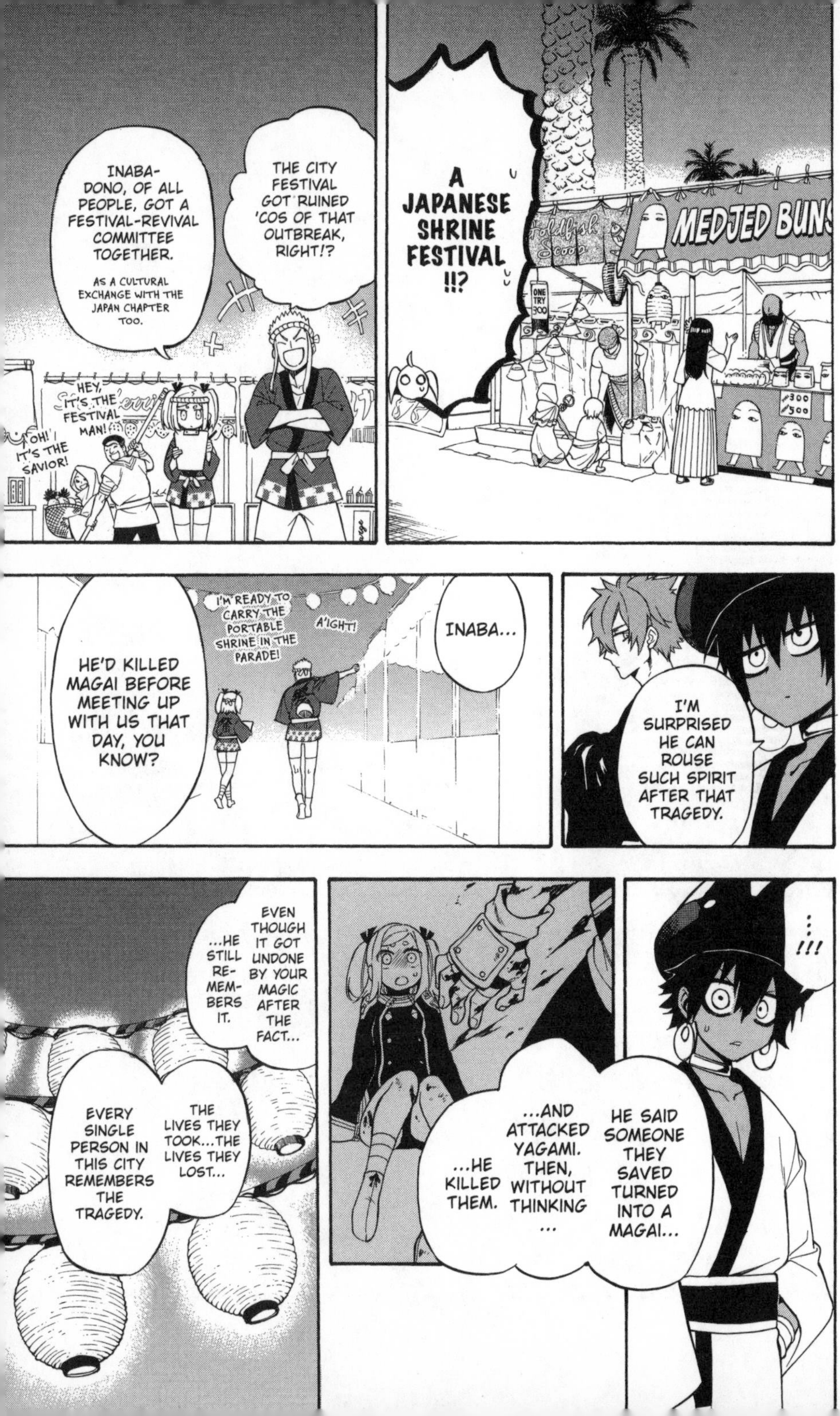
A JAPANESE SHRINE FESTIVAL!!?
MEDJED BUNS
ONE TRY 300
THE CITY FESTIVAL GOT RUINED 'COS OF THAT OUTBREAK, RIGHT!?
INABA-DONO, OF ALL PEOPLE, GOT A FESTIVAL-REVIVAL COMMITTEE TOGETHER.
AS A CULTURAL EXCHANGE WITH THE JAPAN CHAPTER TOO.
HEY, IT'S THE FESTIVAL MAN!
OH! IT'S THE SAVIOR!
I'M SURPRISED HE CAN ROUSE SUCH SPIRIT AFTER THAT TRAGEDY.
INABA...
A'IGHT!
I'M READY TO CARRY THE PORTABLE SHRINE IN THE PARADE!
HE'D KILLED MAGAI BEFORE MEETING UP WITH US THAT DAY, YOU KNOW?
...!!!
HE SAID SOMEONE THEY SAVED TURNED INTO A MAGAI...
...AND ATTACKED YAGAMI. THEN, WITHOUT THINKING...
...HE KILLED THEM.
EVEN THOUGH IT GOT UNDONE BY YOUR MAGIC AFTER THE FACT...
...HE STILL RE-MEM-BERS IT.
THE LIVES THEY TOOK...THE LIVES THEY LOST...
EVERY SINGLE PERSON IN THIS CITY REMEMBERS THE TRAGEDY.

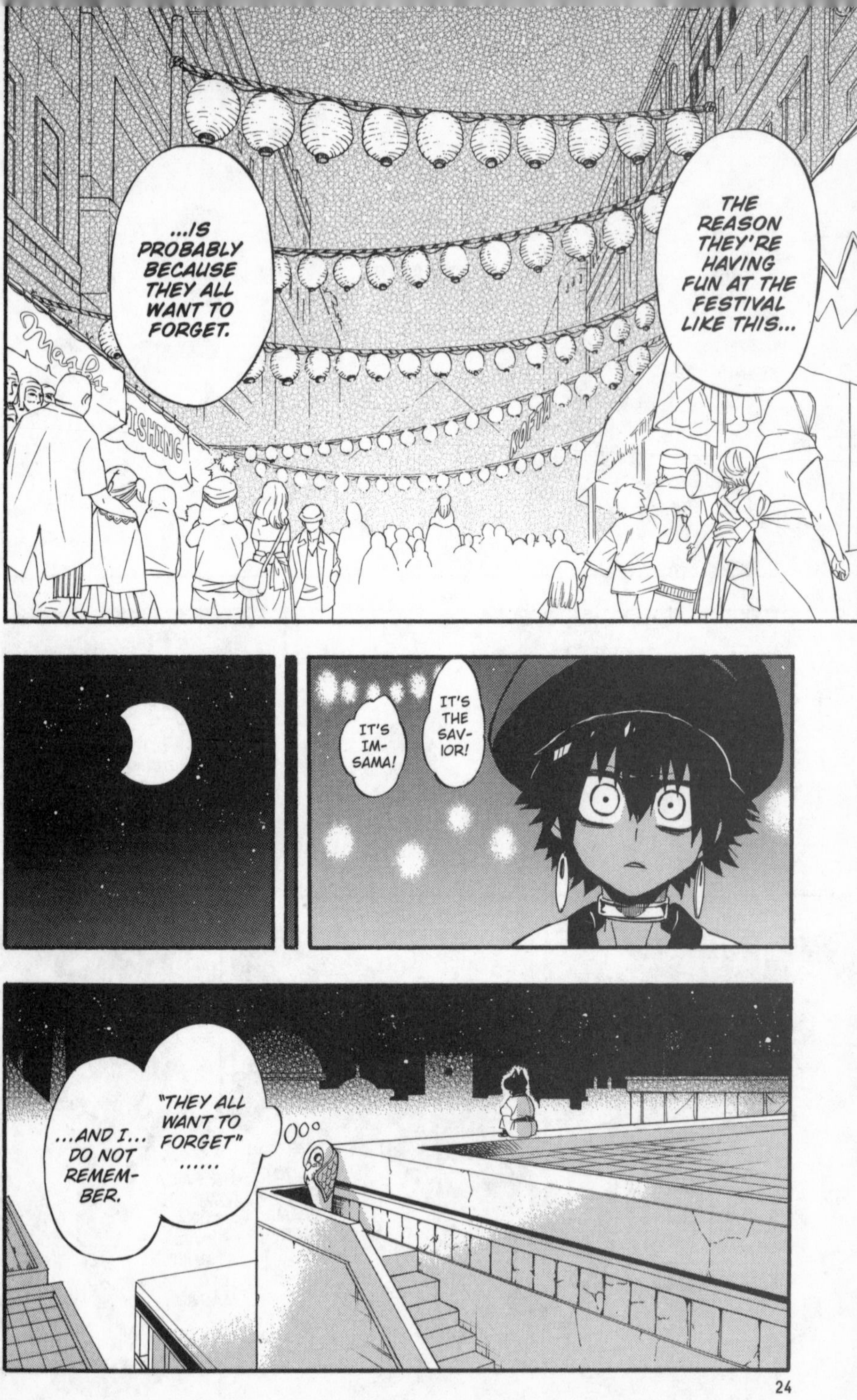
THE REASON THEY'RE HAVING FUN AT THE FESTIVAL LIKE THIS...
...IS PROBABLY BECAUSE THEY ALL WANT TO FORGET.
KOFTA
ISHING
IT'S THE SAV-IOR!
IT'S IM-SAMA!
"THEY ALL WANT TO FORGET" ......
...AND I... DO NOT REMEM-BER.

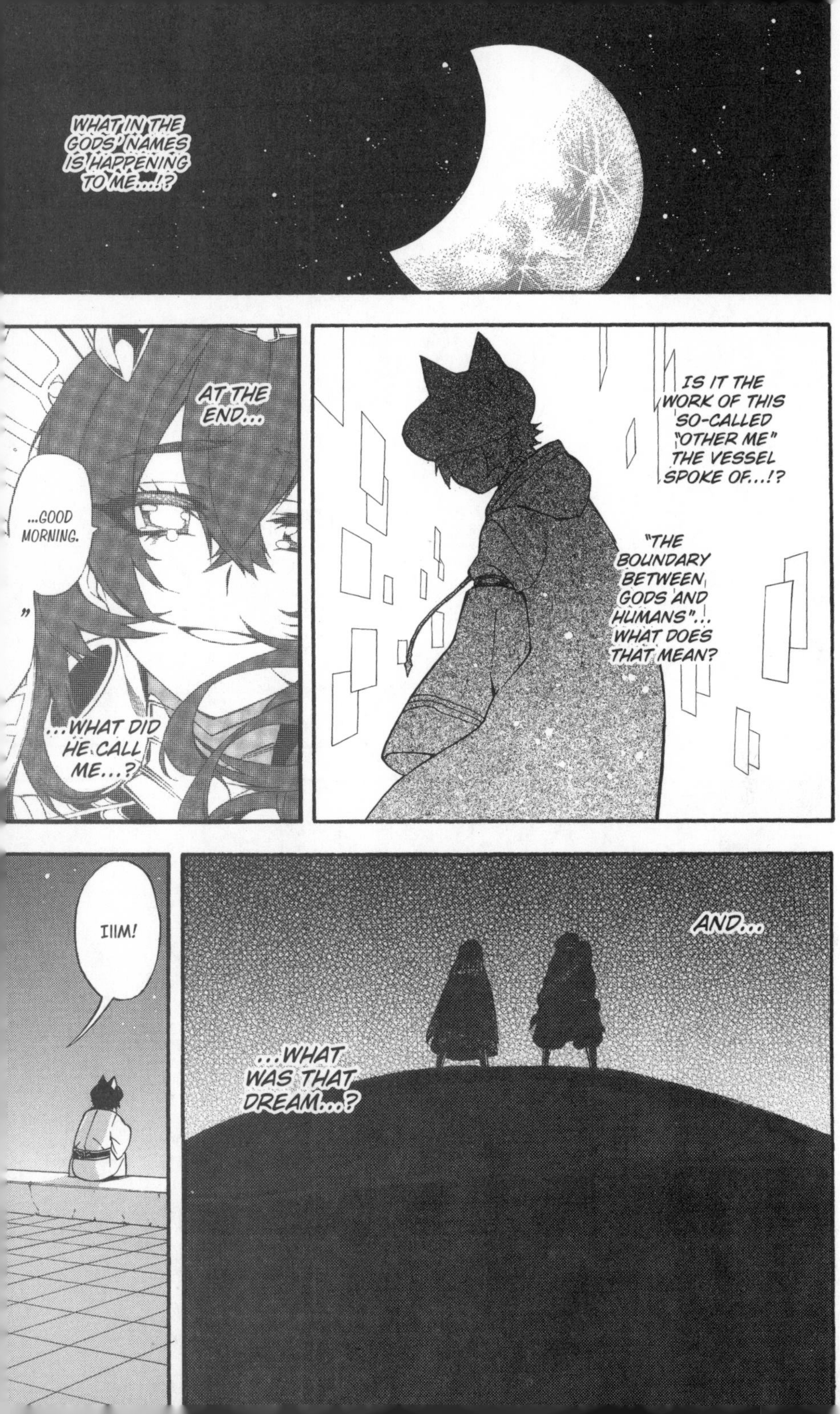
WHAT IN THE GODS' NAMES IS HAPPENING TO ME...!?
IS IT THE WORK OF THIS SO-CALLED "OTHER ME" THE VESSEL SPOKE OF...!?
"THE BOUNDARY BETWEEN GODS AND HUMANS"... WHAT DOES THAT MEAN?
AT THE END...
...GOOD MORNING.
...WHAT DID HE CALL ME...?
AND...
...WHAT WAS THAT DREAM...?
IIIM!

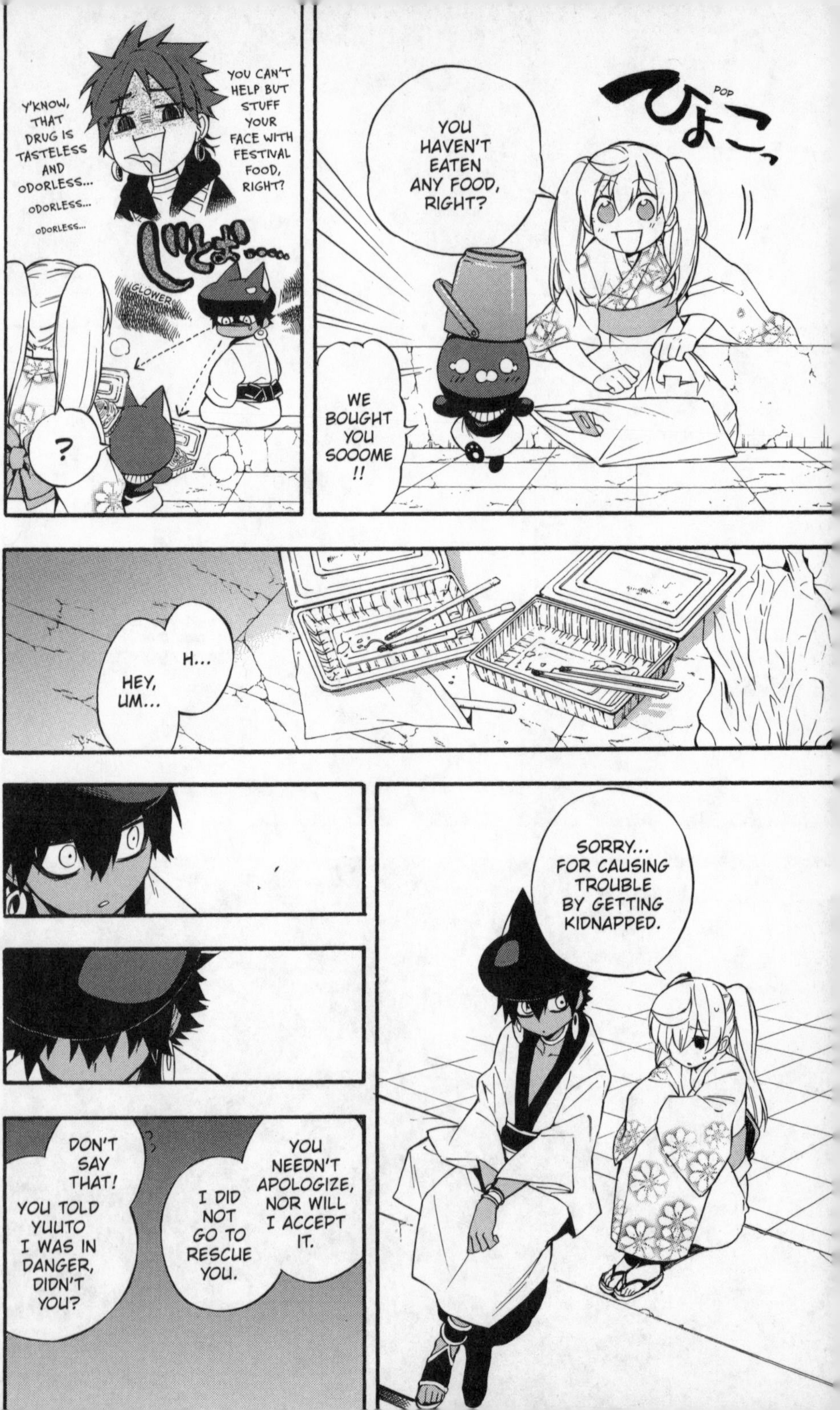
ひょこっ
POP
YOU HAVEN'T EATEN ANY FOOD, RIGHT?
WE BOUGHT YOU SOOOME !!
YOU CAN'T HELP BUT STUFF YOUR FACE WITH FESTIVAL FOOD, RIGHT?
Y'KNOW, THAT DRUG IS TASTELESS AND ODORLESS...
ODORLESS...
ODORLESS...
GLOWER
?
H...
HEY, UM...
SORRY... FOR CAUSING TROUBLE BY GETTING KIDNAPPED.
YOU NEEDN'T APOLOGIZE, NOR WILL I ACCEPT IT.
I DID NOT GO TO RESCUE YOU.
DON'T SAY THAT! YOU TOLD YUUTO I WAS IN DANGER, DIDN'T YOU?

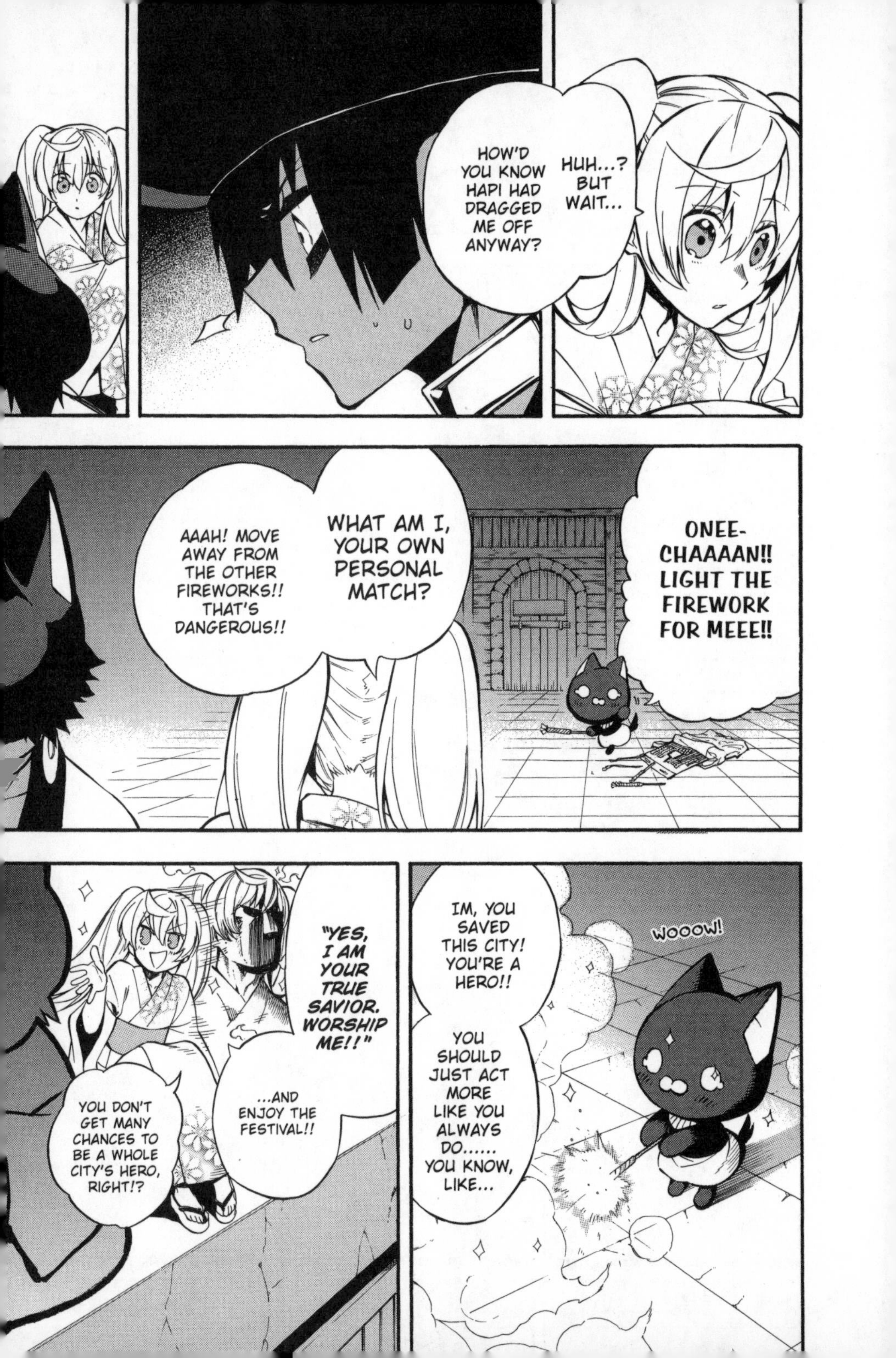
HUH...? BUT WAIT...
HOW'D YOU KNOW HAPI HAD DRAGGED ME OFF ANYWAY?
ONEE-CHAAAAN!! LIGHT THE FIREWORK FOR MEEE!!
WHAT AM I, YOUR OWN PERSONAL MATCH?
AAAH! MOVE AWAY FROM THE OTHER FIREWORKS!! THAT'S DANGEROUS!!
WOOOW!
IM, YOU SAVED THIS CITY! YOU'RE A HERO!!
YOU SHOULD JUST ACT MORE LIKE YOU ALWAYS DO...... YOU KNOW, LIKE...
"YES, I AM YOUR TRUE SAVIOR. WORSHIP ME!!"
...AND ENJOY THE FESTIVAL!!
YOU DON'T GET MANY CHANCES TO BE A WHOLE CITY'S HERO, RIGHT!?

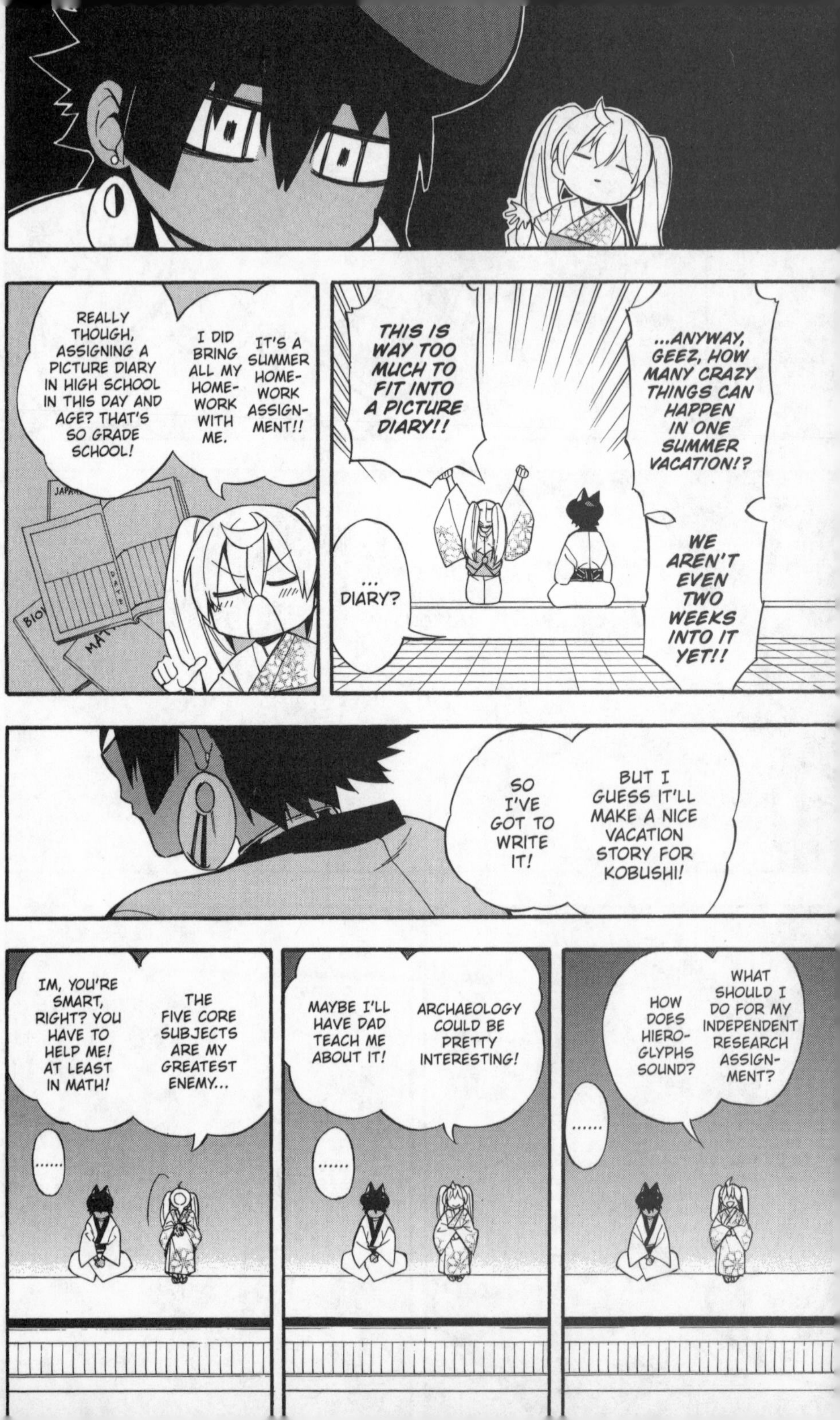

...ANYWAY, GEEZ, HOW MANY CRAZY THINGS CAN HAPPEN IN ONE SUMMER VACATION!?
WE AREN'T EVEN TWO WEEKS INTO IT YET!!
THIS IS WAY TOO MUCH TO FIT INTO A PICTURE DIARY!!
... DIARY?
IT'S A SUMMER HOMEWORK ASSIGNMENT!!
I DID BRING ALL MY HOMEWORK WITH ME.
REALLY THOUGH, ASSIGNING A PICTURE DIARY IN HIGH SCHOOL IN THIS DAY AND AGE? THAT'S SO GRADE SCHOOL!
DATE
BUT I GUESS IT'LL MAKE A NICE VACATION STORY FOR KOBUSHI!
SO I'VE GOT TO WRITE IT!
WHAT SHOULD I DO FOR MY INDEPENDENT RESEARCH ASSIGNMENT?
HOW DOES HIEROGLYPHS SOUND?
......
ARCHAEOLOGY COULD BE PRETTY INTERESTING!
MAYBE I'LL HAVE DAD TEACH ME ABOUT IT!
......
THE FIVE CORE SUBJECTS ARE MY GREATEST ENEMY...
IM, YOU'RE SMART, RIGHT? YOU HAVE TO HELP ME! AT LEAST IN MATH!
......

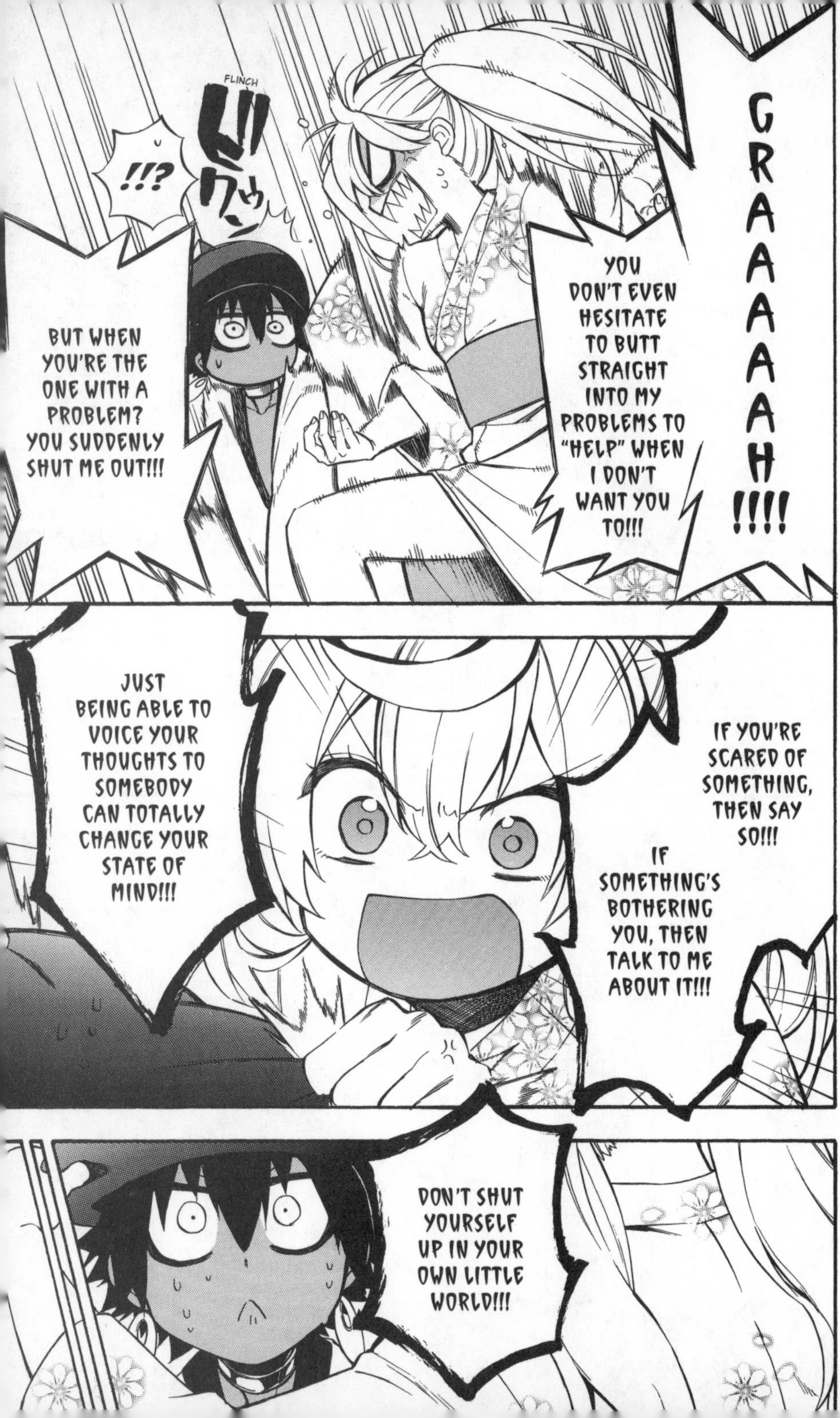
GRAAAAAAH!!!!
YOU DON'T EVEN HESITATE TO BUTT STRAIGHT INTO MY PROBLEMS TO "HELP" WHEN I DON'T WANT YOU TO!!!
FLINCH
!!?
BUT WHEN YOU'RE THE ONE WITH A PROBLEM? YOU SUDDENLY SHUT ME OUT!!!
IF YOU'RE SCARED OF SOMETHING, THEN SAY SO!!!
IF SOMETHING'S BOTHERING YOU, THEN TALK TO ME ABOUT IT!!!
JUST BEING ABLE TO VOICE YOUR THOUGHTS TO SOMEBODY CAN TOTALLY CHANGE YOUR STATE OF MIND!!!
DON'T SHUT YOURSELF UP IN YOUR OWN LITTLE WORLD!!!

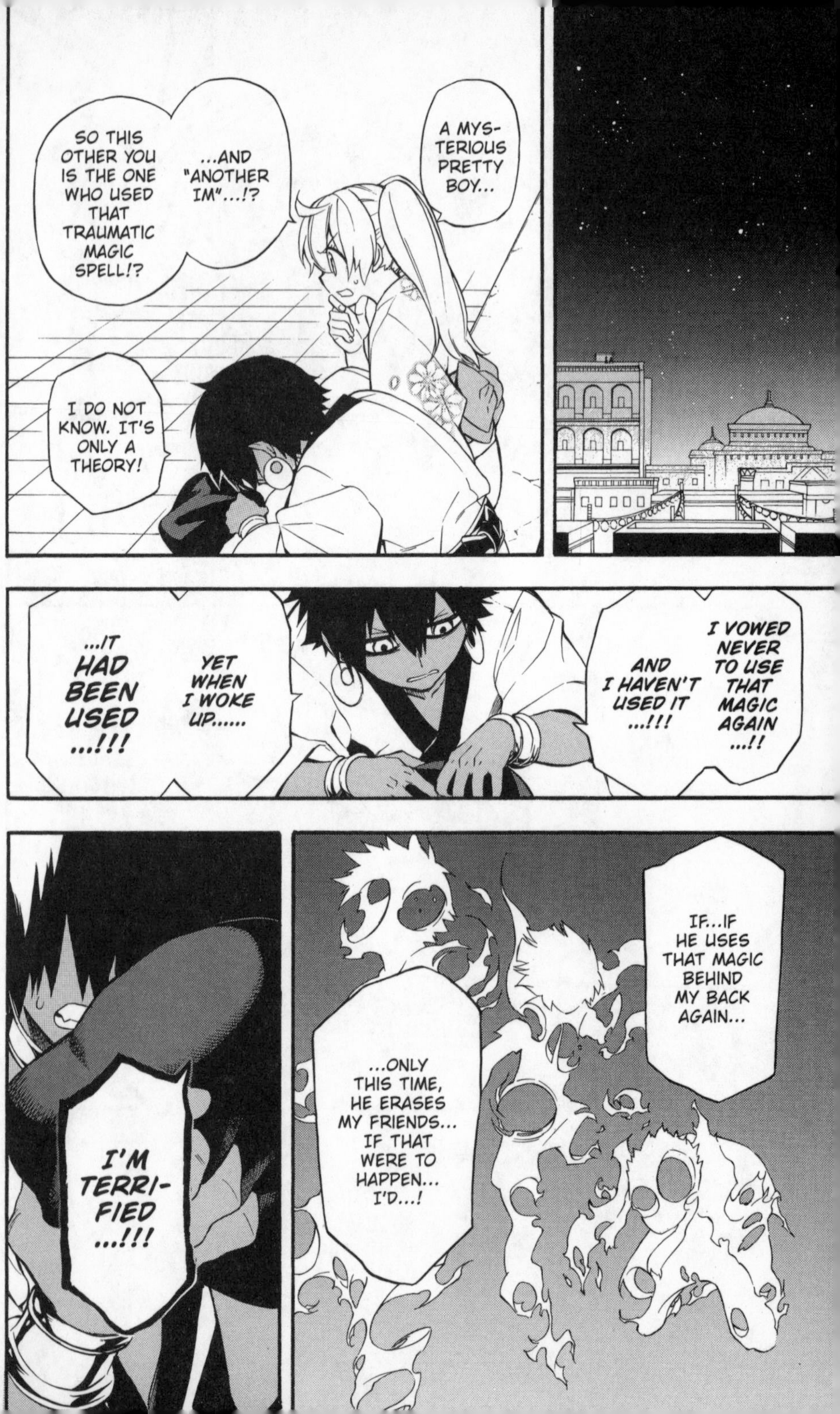
A MYSTERIOUS PRETTY BOY...
...AND "ANOTHER IM"...!?
SO THIS OTHER YOU IS THE ONE WHO USED THAT TRAUMATIC MAGIC SPELL!?
I DO NOT KNOW. IT'S ONLY A THEORY!
I VOWED NEVER TO USE THAT MAGIC AGAIN ...!!
AND I HAVEN'T USED IT ...!!!
YET WHEN I WOKE UP......
...IT HAD BEEN USED ...!!!
IF...IF HE USES THAT MAGIC BEHIND MY BACK AGAIN...
...ONLY THIS TIME, HE ERASES MY FRIENDS... IF THAT WERE TO HAPPEN... I'D...!
I'M TERRIFIED ...!!!

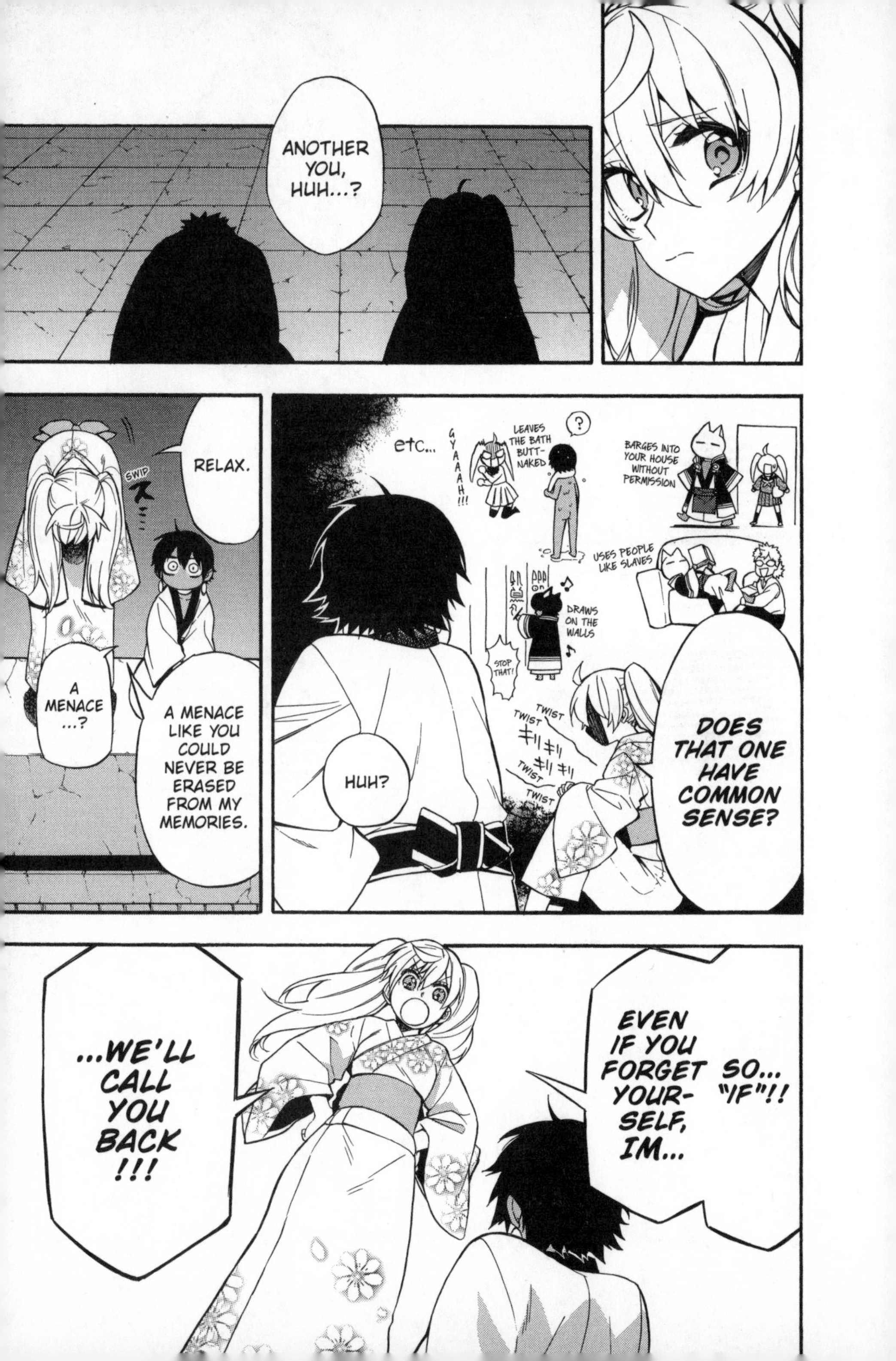
ANOTHER YOU, HUH...?
BARGES INTO YOUR HOUSE WITHOUT PERMISSION
?
LEAVES THE BATH BUTT-NAKED
GYAAAAH!!!
etc...
USES PEOPLE LIKE SLAVES
DRAWS ON THE WALLS
STOP THAT!
DOES THAT ONE HAVE COMMON SENSE?
TWIST TWIST
TWIST TWIST
HUH?
RELAX.
SWIP
A MENACE LIKE YOU COULD NEVER BE ERASED FROM MY MEMORIES.
A MENACE ...?
EVEN IF YOU FORGET YOURSELF, IM...
SO... "IF"!!
...WE'LL CALL YOU BACK!!!

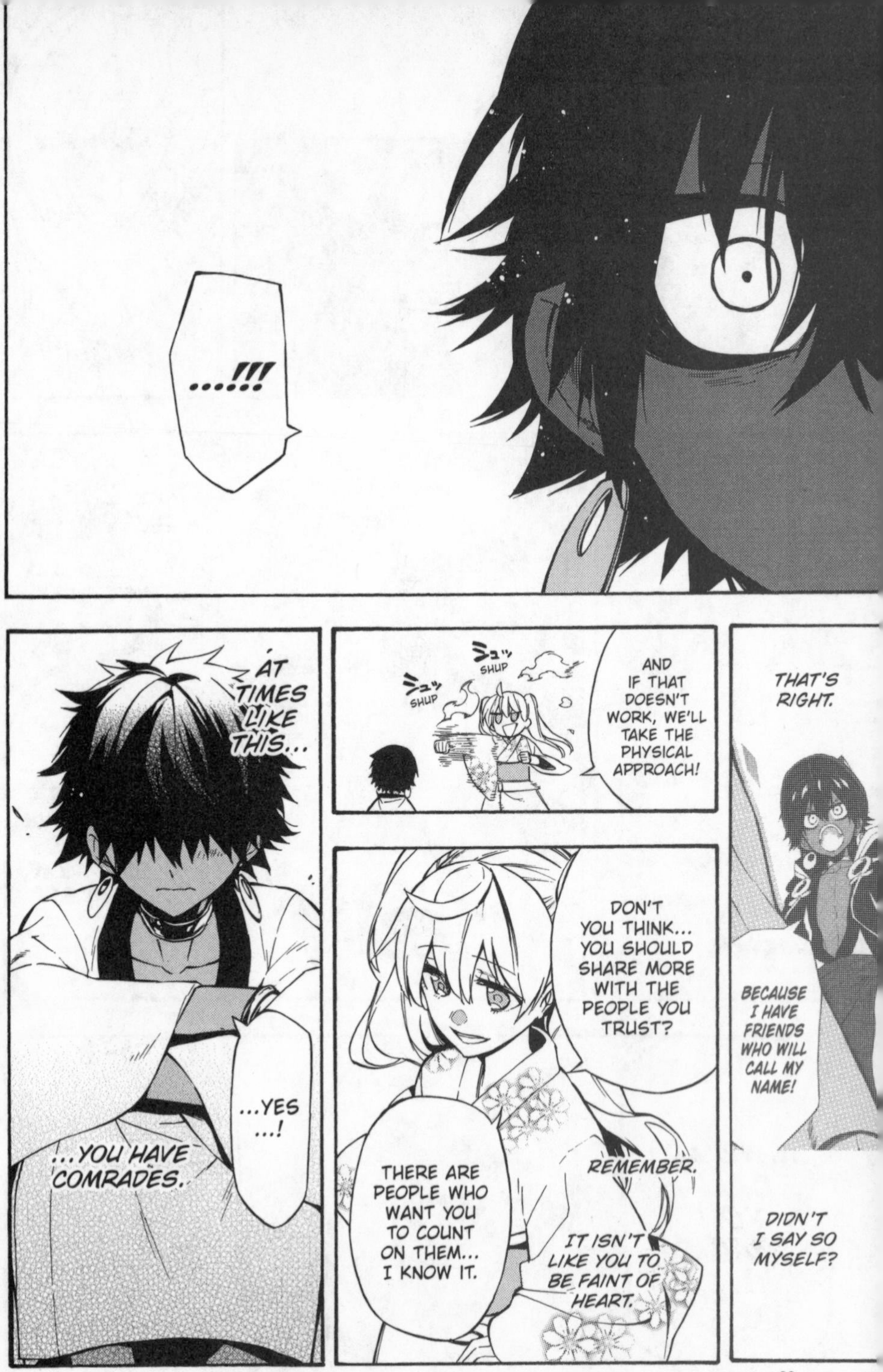
...!!!
THAT'S RIGHT.
BECAUSE I HAVE FRIENDS WHO WILL CALL MY NAME!
DIDN'T I SAY SO MYSELF?
AND IF THAT DOESN'T WORK, WE'LL TAKE THE PHYSICAL APPROACH!
シュッ SHUP
シュッ SHUP
DON'T YOU THINK... YOU SHOULD SHARE MORE WITH THE PEOPLE YOU TRUST?
REMEMBER.
IT ISN'T LIKE YOU TO BE FAINT OF HEART.
THERE ARE PEOPLE WHO WANT YOU TO COUNT ON THEM... I KNOW IT.
AT TIMES LIKE THIS...
...YES ...!
...YOU HAVE COMRADES.

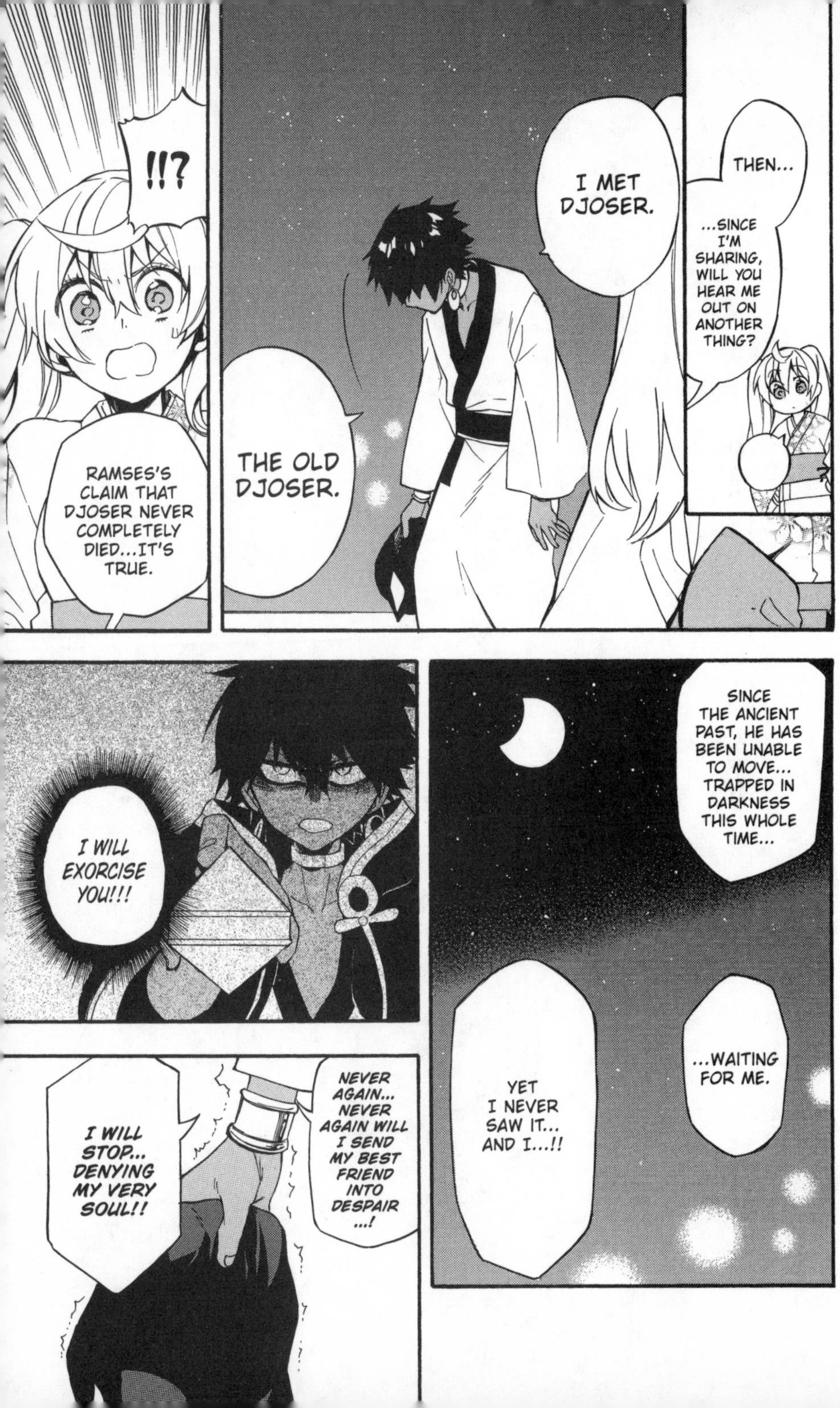

THEN...
...SINCE I'M SHARING, WILL YOU HEAR ME OUT ON ANOTHER THING?
I MET DJOSER.
THE OLD DJOSER.
!!?
RAMSES'S CLAIM THAT DJOSER NEVER COMPLETELY DIED...IT'S TRUE.
SINCE THE ANCIENT PAST, HE HAS BEEN UNABLE TO MOVE... TRAPPED IN DARKNESS THIS WHOLE TIME...
...WAITING FOR ME.
YET I NEVER SAW IT... AND I...!!
I WILL EXORCISE YOU!!!
NEVER AGAIN... NEVER AGAIN WILL I SEND MY BEST FRIEND INTO DESPAIR ...!
I WILL STOP... DENYING MY VERY SOUL!!

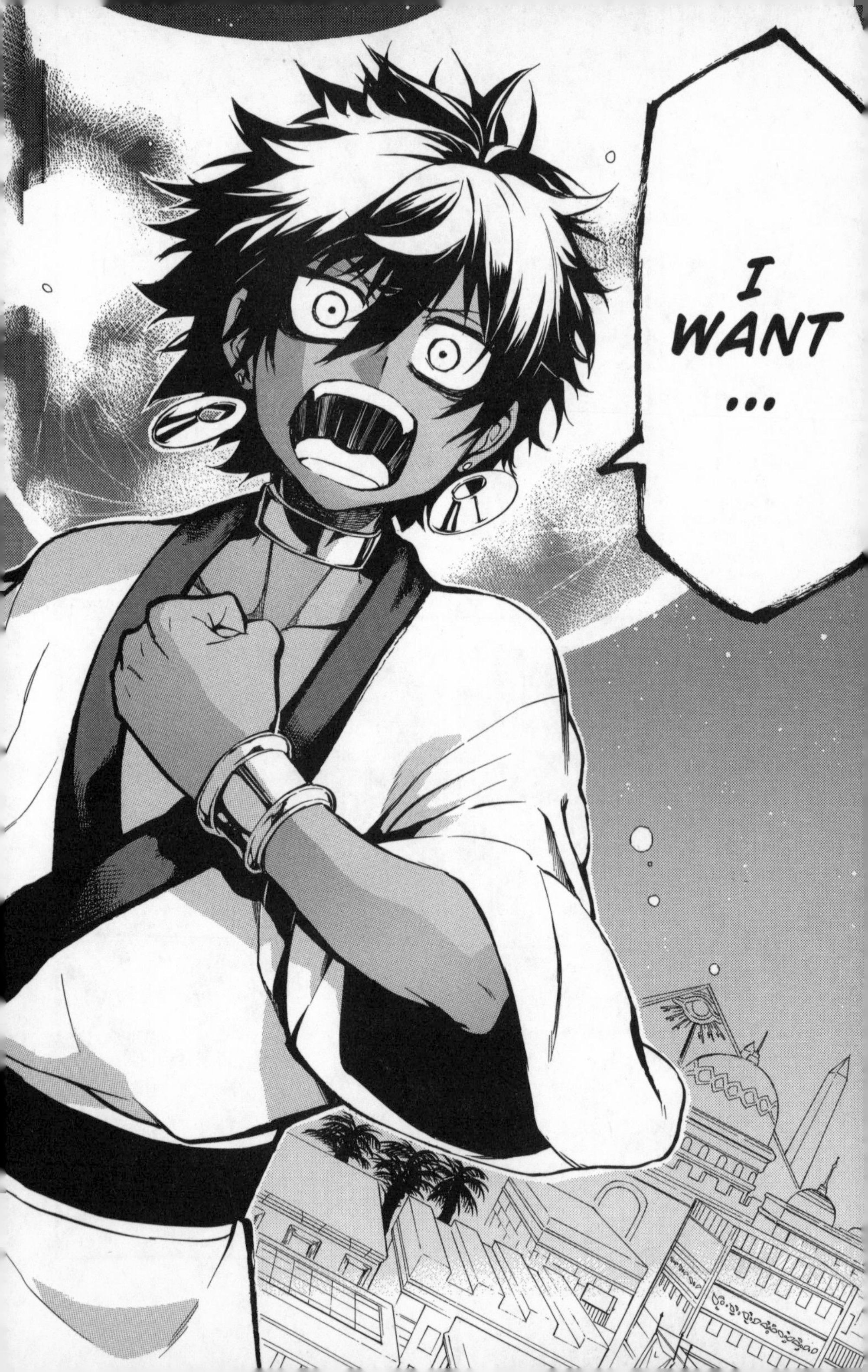
I WANT...

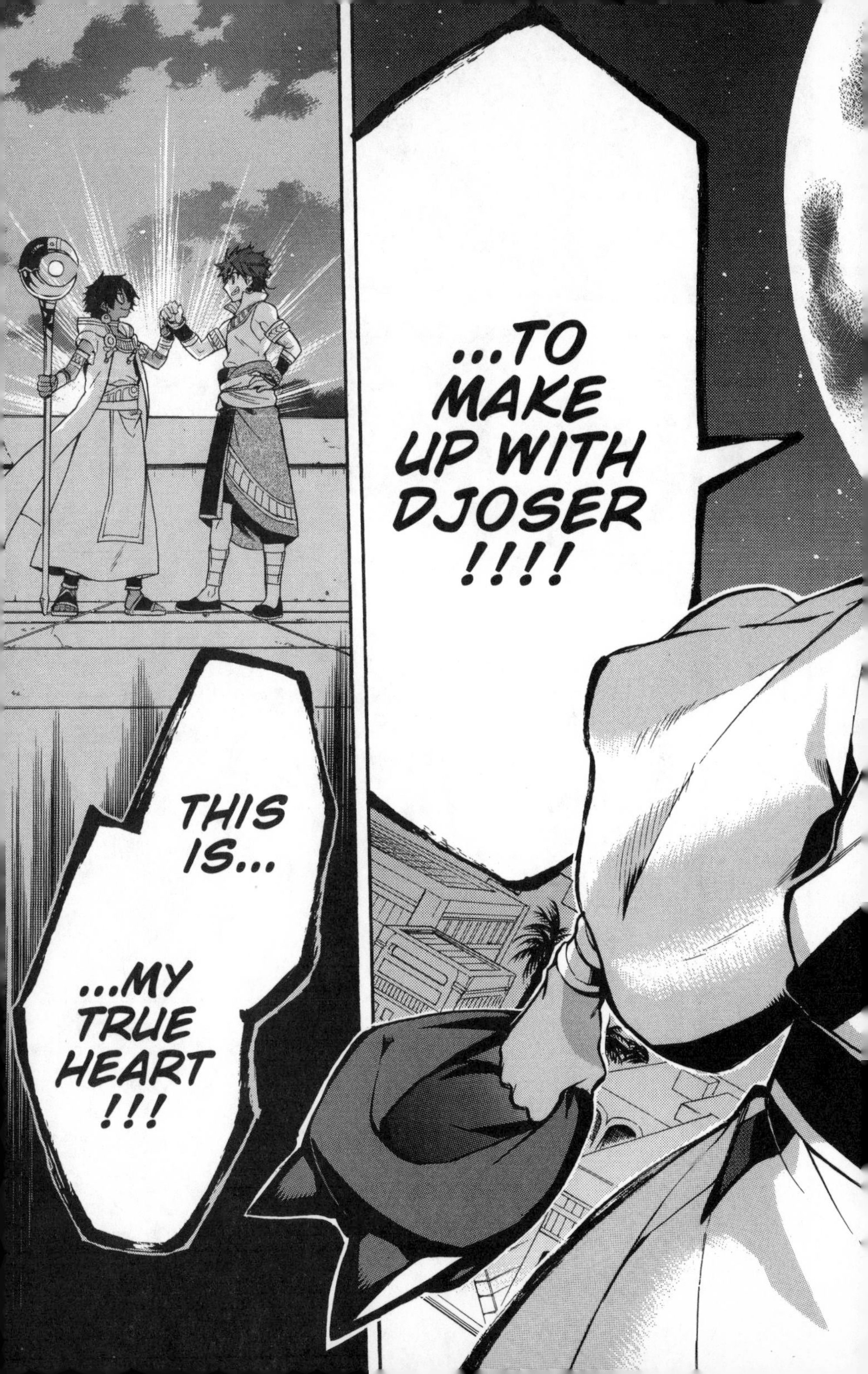
...TO MAKE UP WITH DJOSER!!!!
THIS IS...
...MY TRUE HEART!!!

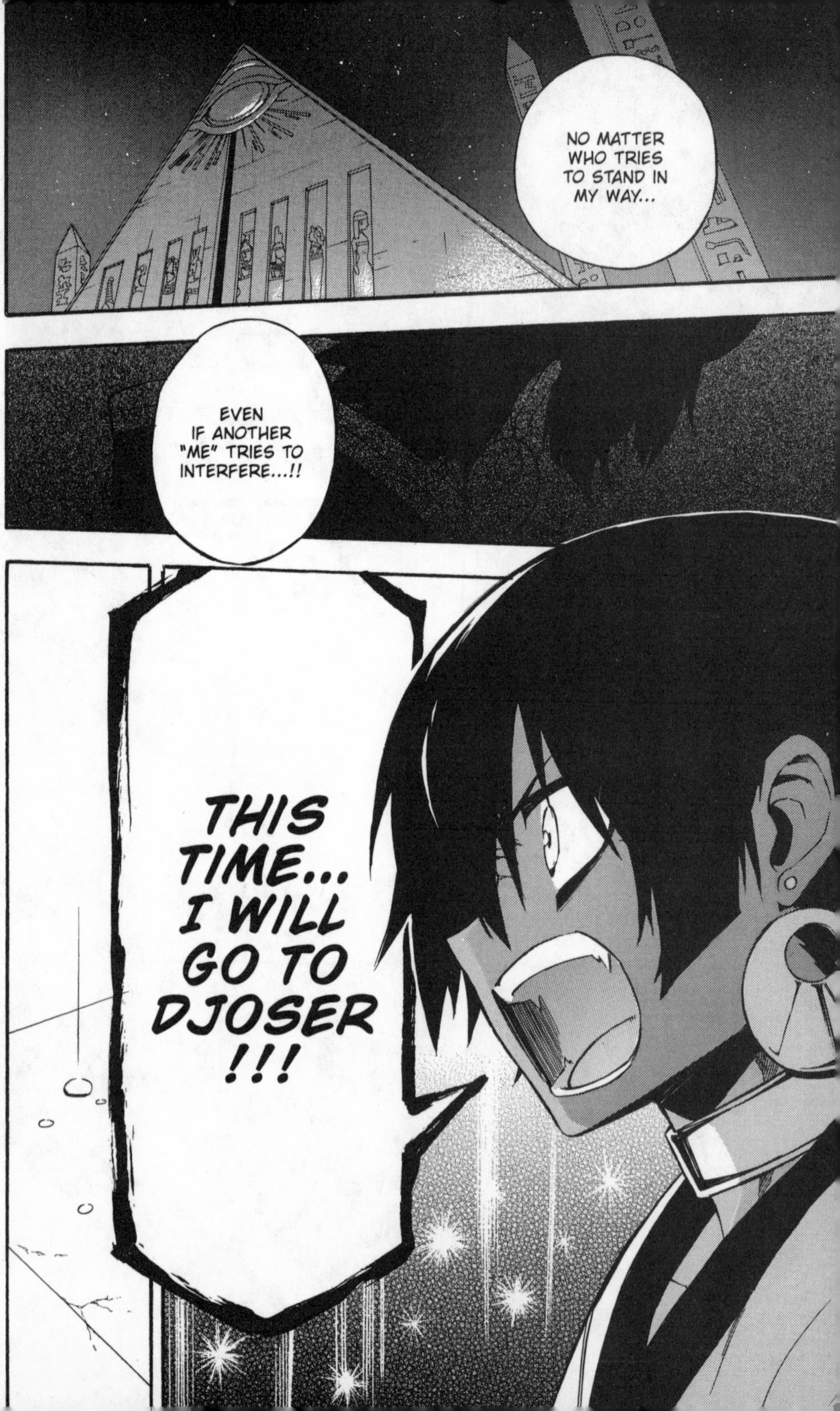
NO MATTER WHO TRIES TO STAND IN MY WAY...
EVEN IF ANOTHER "ME" TRIES TO INTERFERE...!!
THIS TIME... I WILL GO TO DJOSER !!!

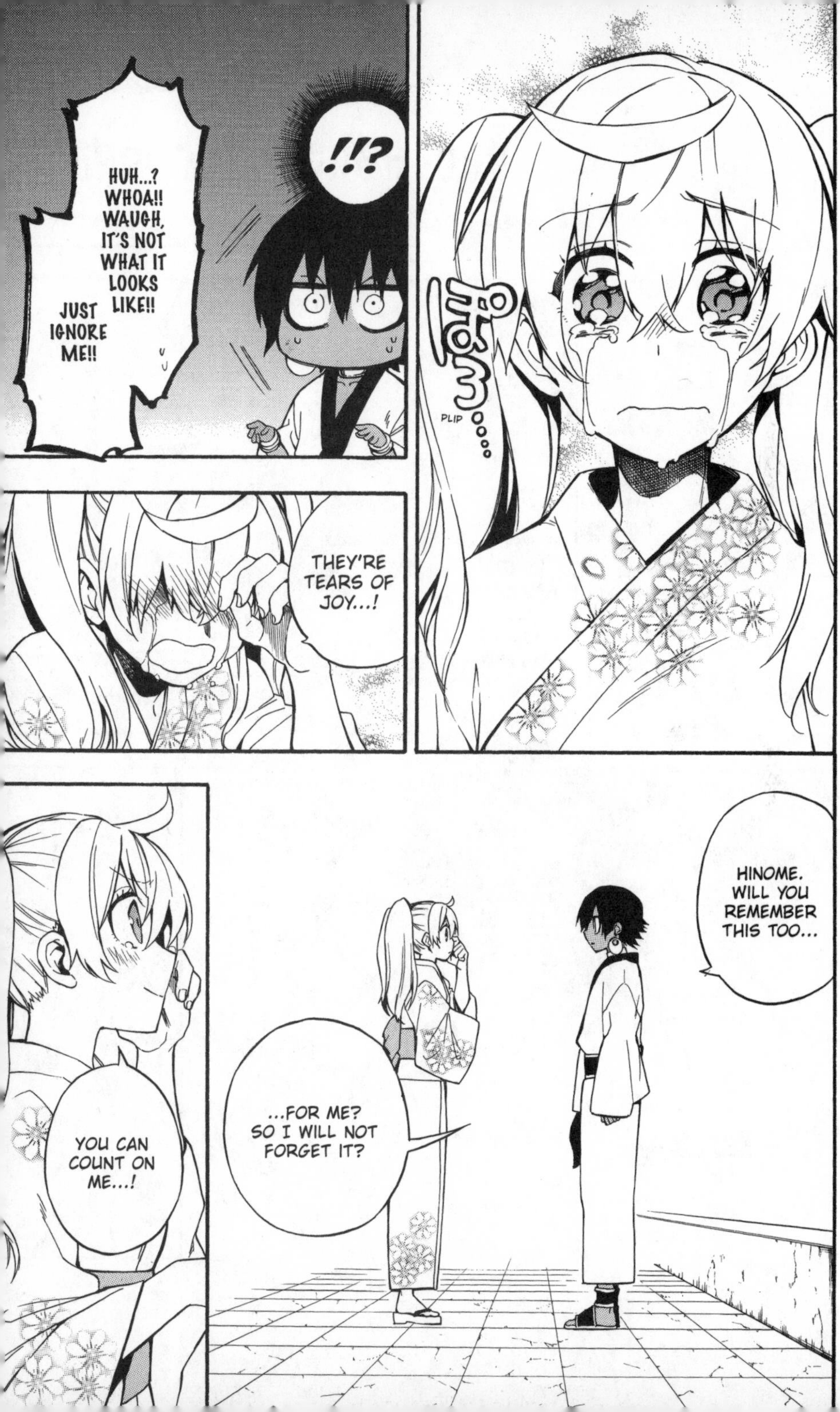
PLIP
!!?
HUH...? WHOA!! WAUGH, IT'S NOT WHAT IT LOOKS LIKE!!
JUST IGNORE ME!!
THEY'RE TEARS OF JOY...!
HINOME. WILL YOU REMEMBER THIS TOO...
...FOR ME? SO I WILL NOT FORGET IT?
YOU CAN COUNT ON ME...!

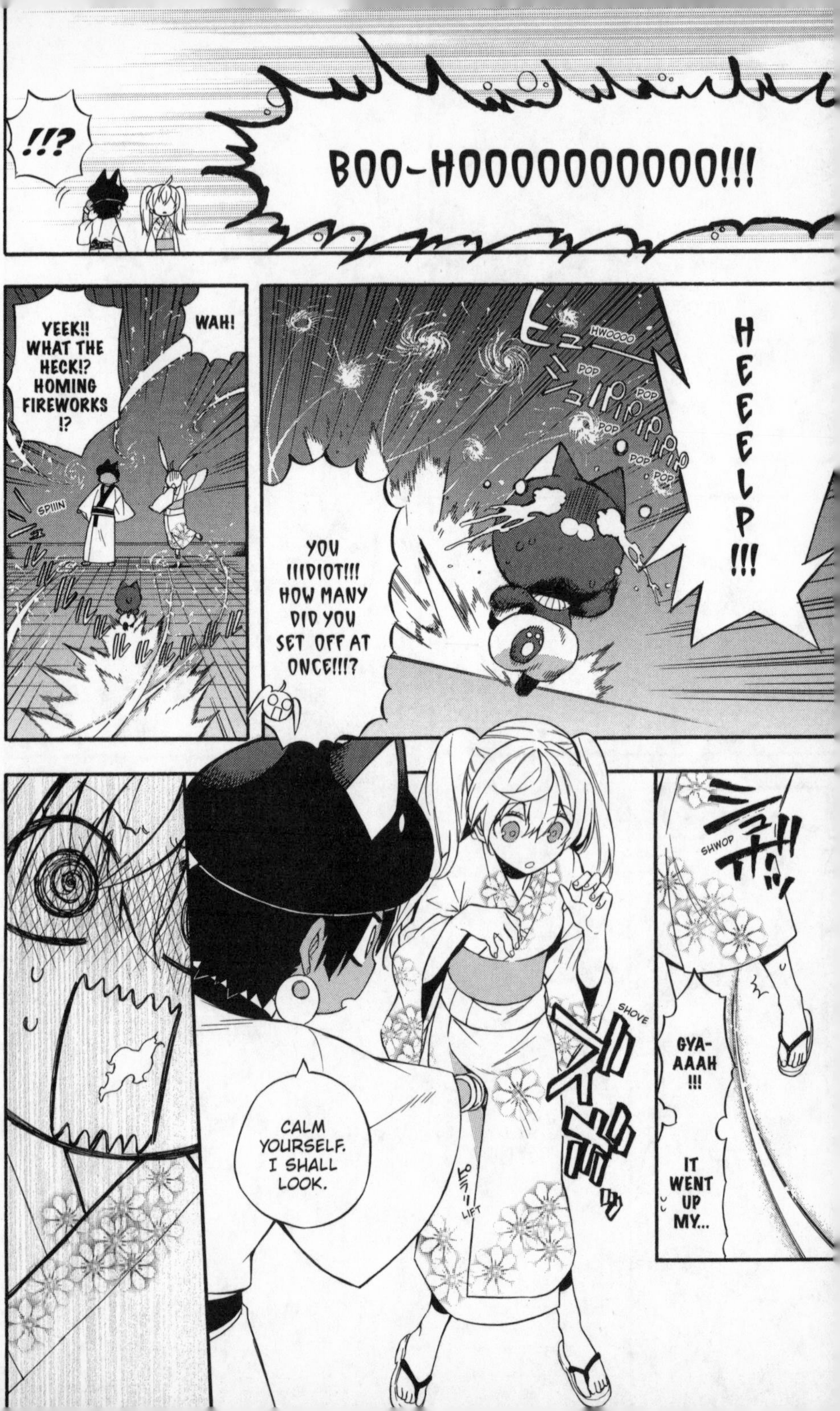
BOO-HOOOOOOOOOO!!!
!!?
HEEEELP!!!
HWOOOO
POP
POP
POP
POP
POP
YOU IIIDIOT!!! HOW MANY DID YOU SET OFF AT ONCE!!!?
WAH!
YEEK!! WHAT THE HECK!? HOMING FIREWORKS!?
SPIIIN
SHWOP
GYA-AAAH!!!
IT WENT UP MY...
SHOVE
LIFT
CALM YOURSELF. I SHALL LOOK.

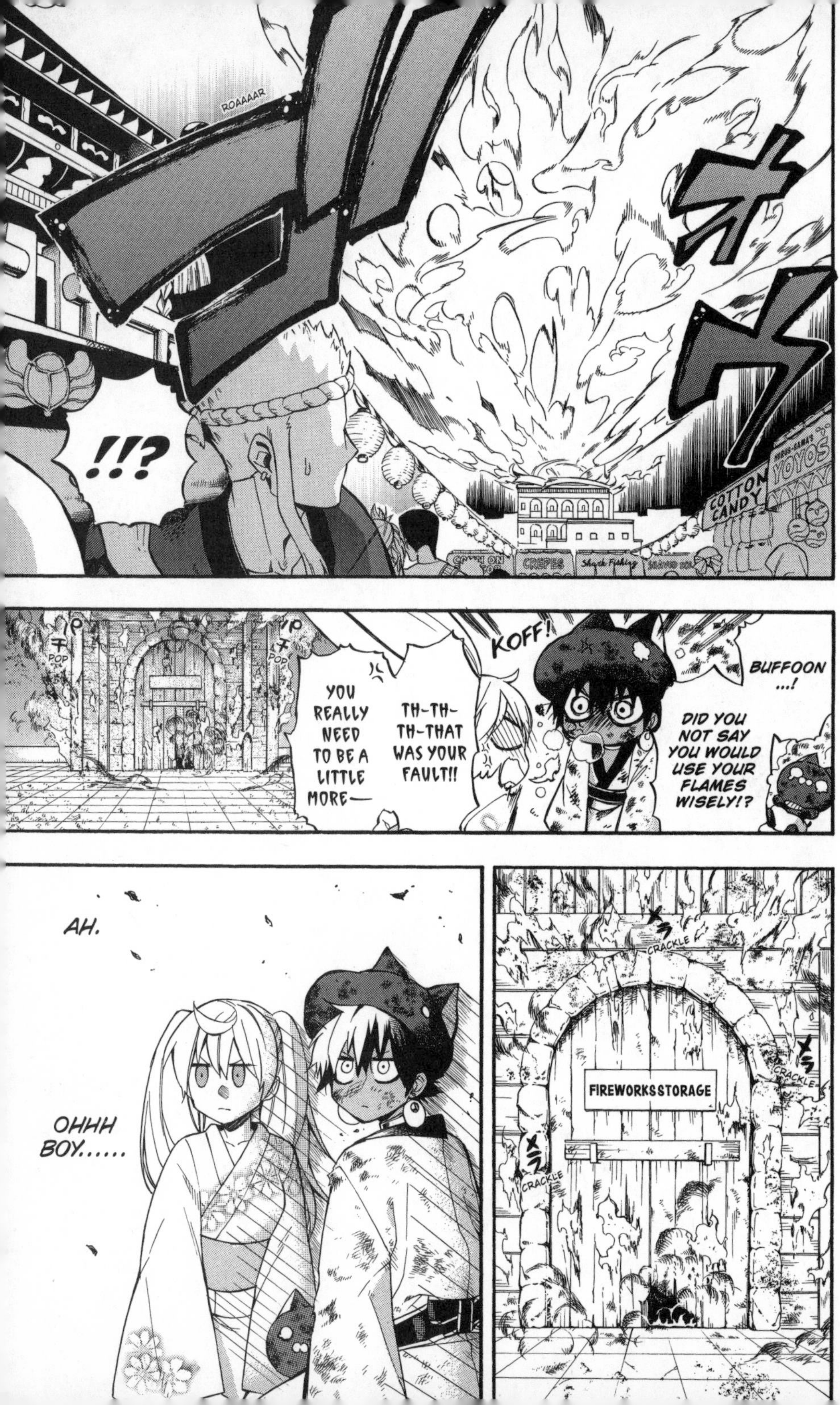
ROAAAAR
!!?
COTTON CANDY
YOYOS
CREPES
Shark Fishing
BUFFOON ...!
DID YOU NOT SAY YOU WOULD USE YOUR FLAMES WISELY!?
KOFF!
TH-TH-TH-THAT WAS YOUR FAULT!!
YOU REALLY NEED TO BE A LITTLE MORE—
POP
POP
CRACKLE
FIREWORKSSTORAGE
CRACKLE
CRACKLE
AH.
OHHH BOY......

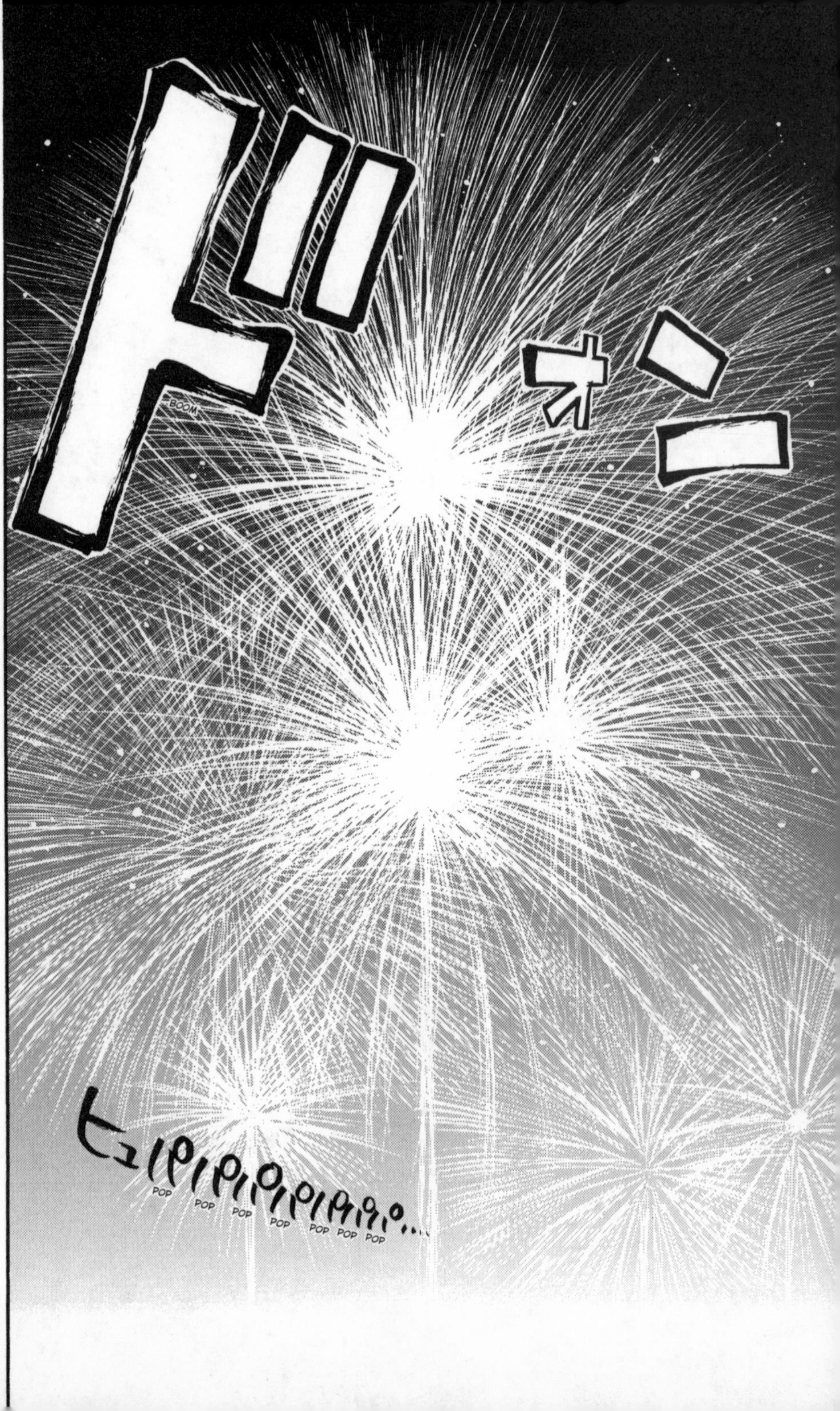
BOOM
POP POP POP POP POP POP POP

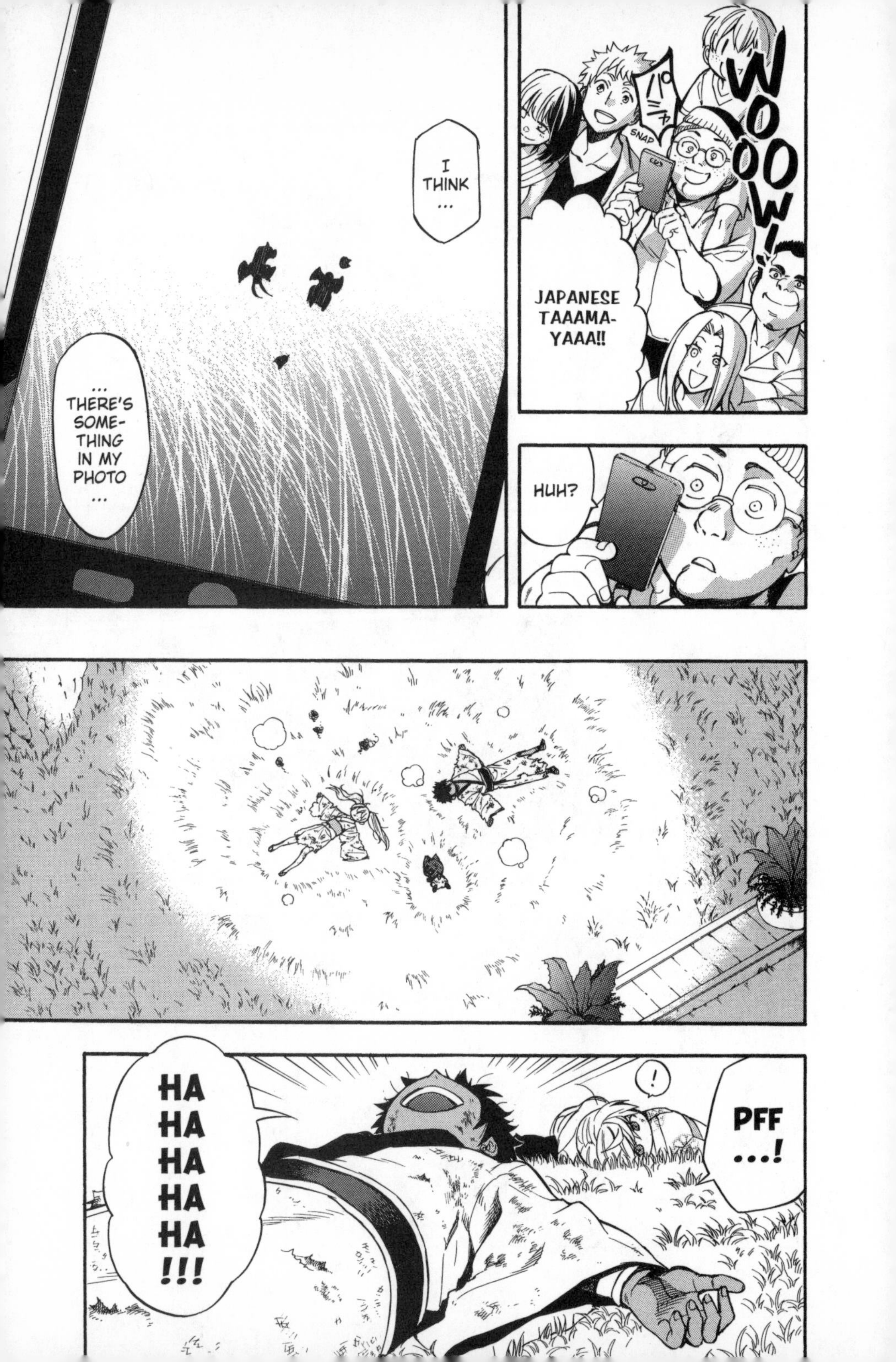
WOOOOW!!
SNAP
JAPANESE TAAAMA-YAAA!!
HUH?
I THINK...
...THERE'S SOMETHING IN MY PHOTO...
PFF...!
!
HA HA HA HA HA!!!

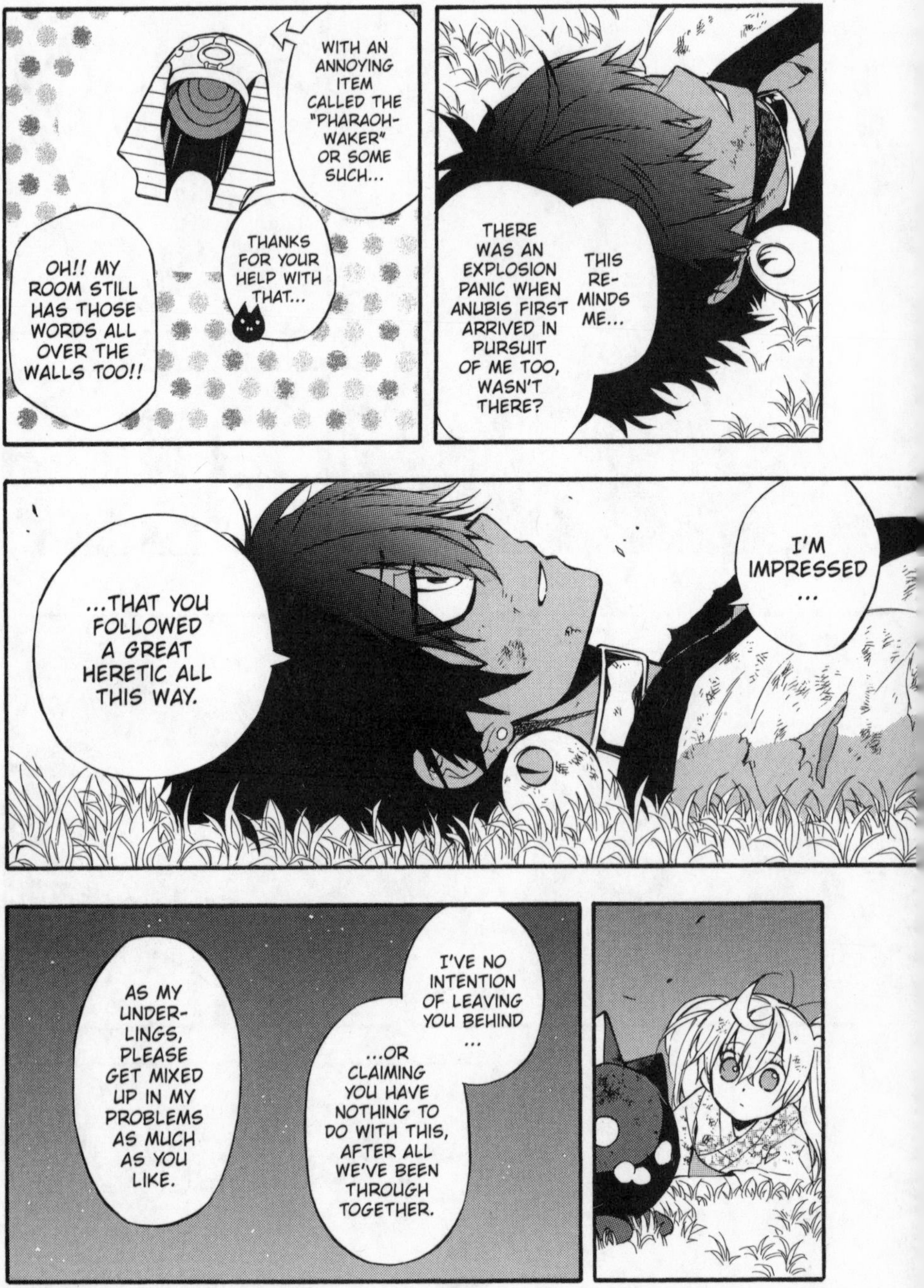
THIS RE-MINDS ME...
THERE WAS AN EXPLOSION PANIC WHEN ANUBIS FIRST ARRIVED IN PURSUIT OF ME TOO, WASN'T THERE?
WITH AN ANNOYING ITEM CALLED THE "PHARAOH-WAKER" OR SOME SUCH...
THANKS FOR YOUR HELP WITH THAT...
OH!! MY ROOM STILL HAS THOSE WORDS ALL OVER THE WALLS TOO!!
I'M IMPRESSED...
...THAT YOU FOLLOWED A GREAT HERETIC ALL THIS WAY.
I'VE NO INTENTION OF LEAVING YOU BEHIND...
...OR CLAIMING YOU HAVE NOTHING TO DO WITH THIS, AFTER ALL WE'VE BEEN THROUGH TOGETHER.
AS MY UNDER-LINGS, PLEASE GET MIXED UP IN MY PROBLEMS AS MUCH AS YOU LIKE.

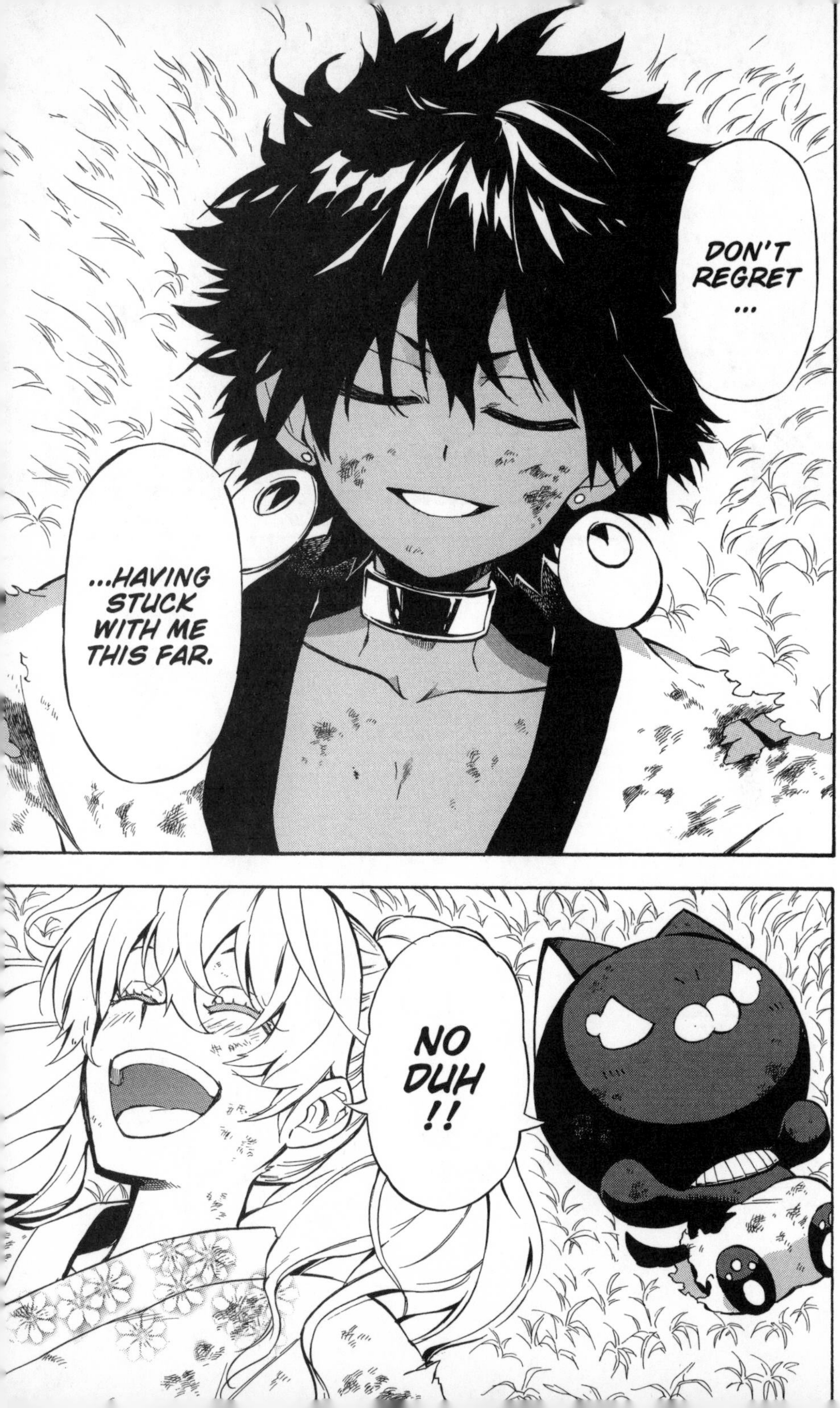
DON'T REGRET ...
...HAVING STUCK WITH ME THIS FAR.
NO DUH !!

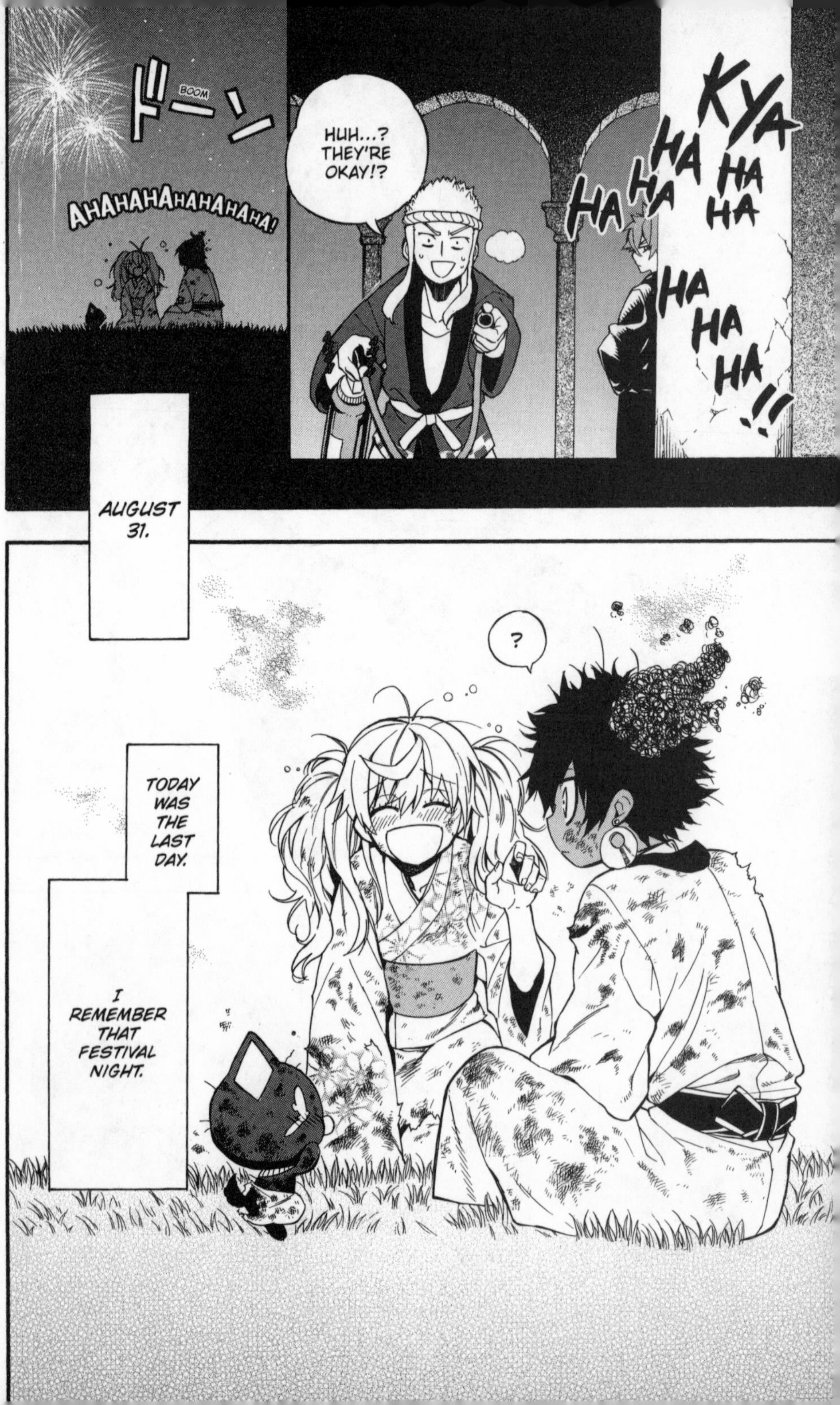

KYAHAHAHAHAHAHAHAHAHAHA!!
HUH...? THEY'RE OKAY!?
ドーン
BOOM
AHAHAHAHAHAHAHAHA!
AUGUST 31.
?
TODAY WAS THE LAST DAY.
I REMEMBER THAT FESTIVAL NIGHT.

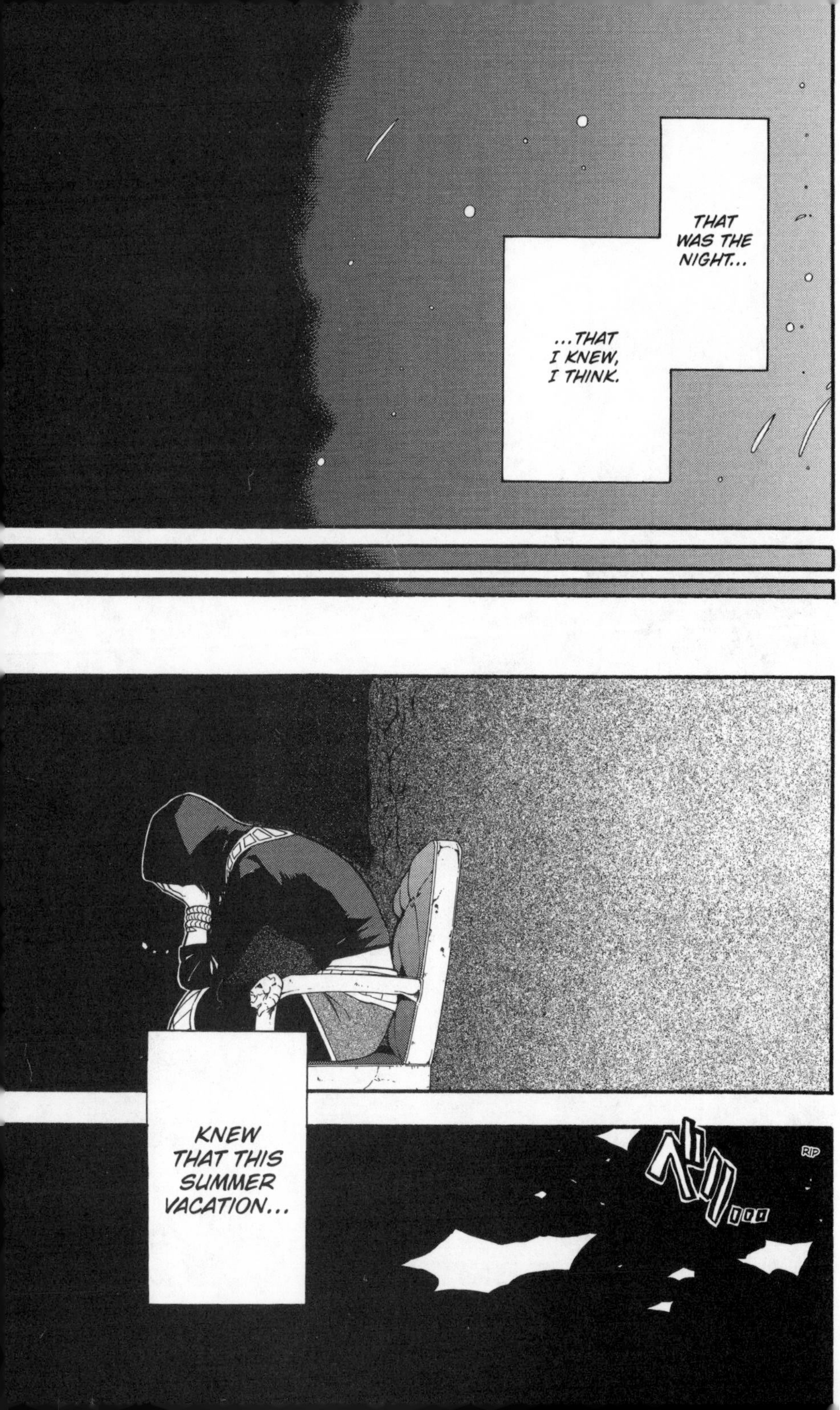
THAT WAS THE NIGHT...
...THAT I KNEW, I THINK.
KNEW THAT THIS SUMMER VACATION...
RIP

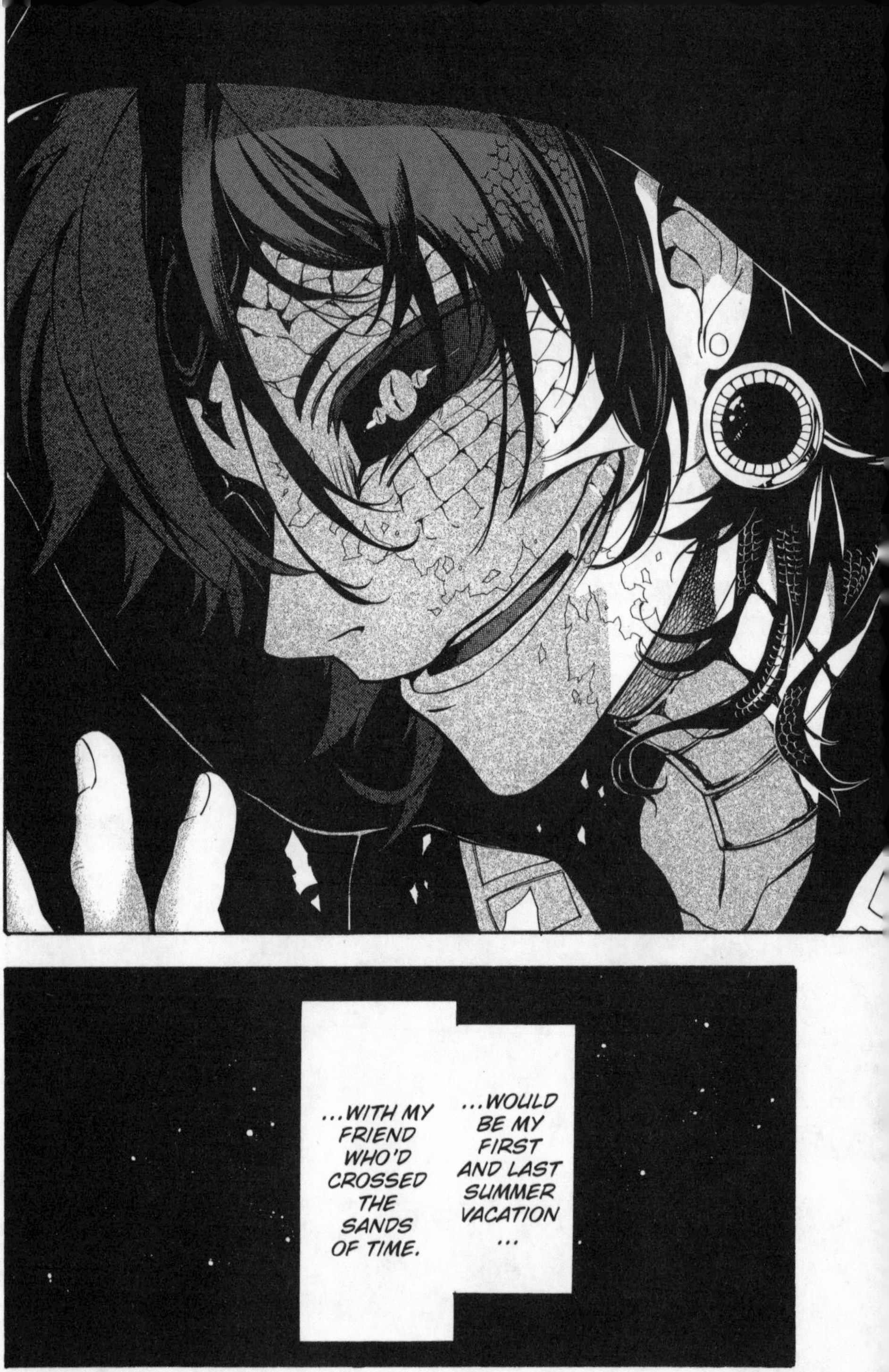
...WOULD BE MY FIRST AND LAST SUMMER VACATION...
...WITH MY FRIEND WHO'D CROSSED THE SANDS OF TIME.

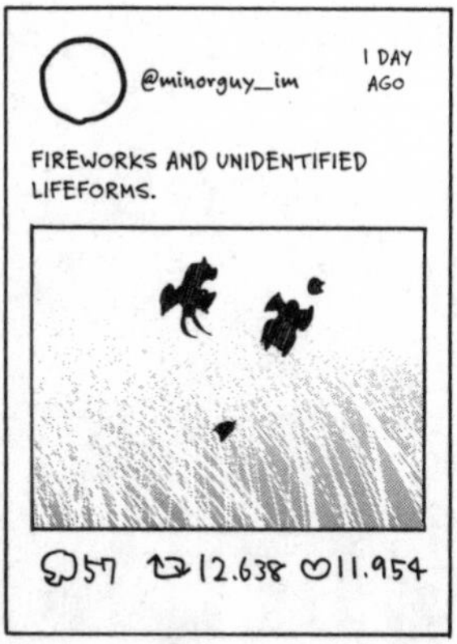
@minorguy_im
1 DAY AGO
FIREWORKS AND UNIDENTIFIED LIFEFORMS.
57
12.638
11.954

THEY TRENDED.

Great Priest Imhotep

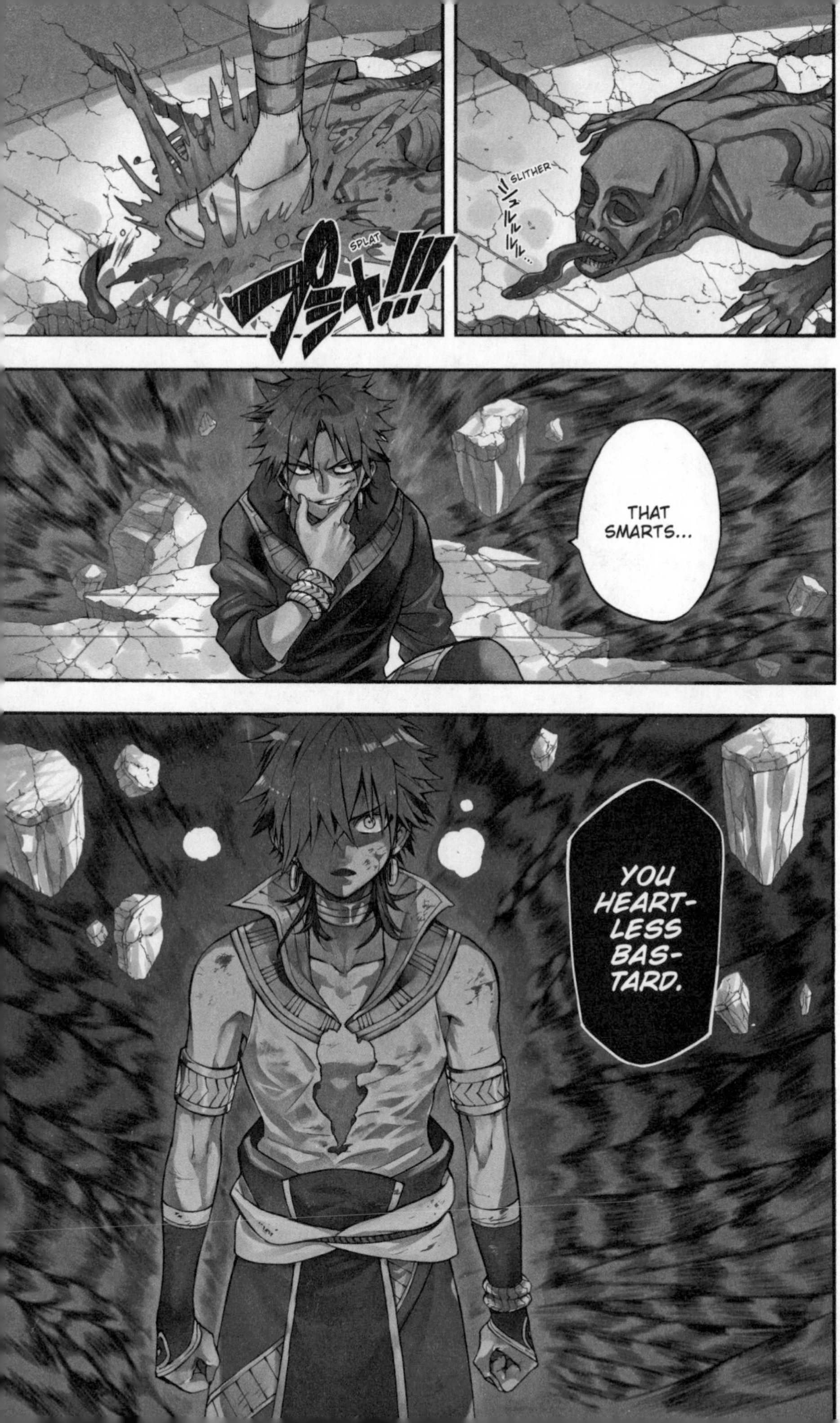
SLITHER
SPLAT
プシャ!!!
THAT SMARTS...
YOU HEART-LESS BAS-TARD.

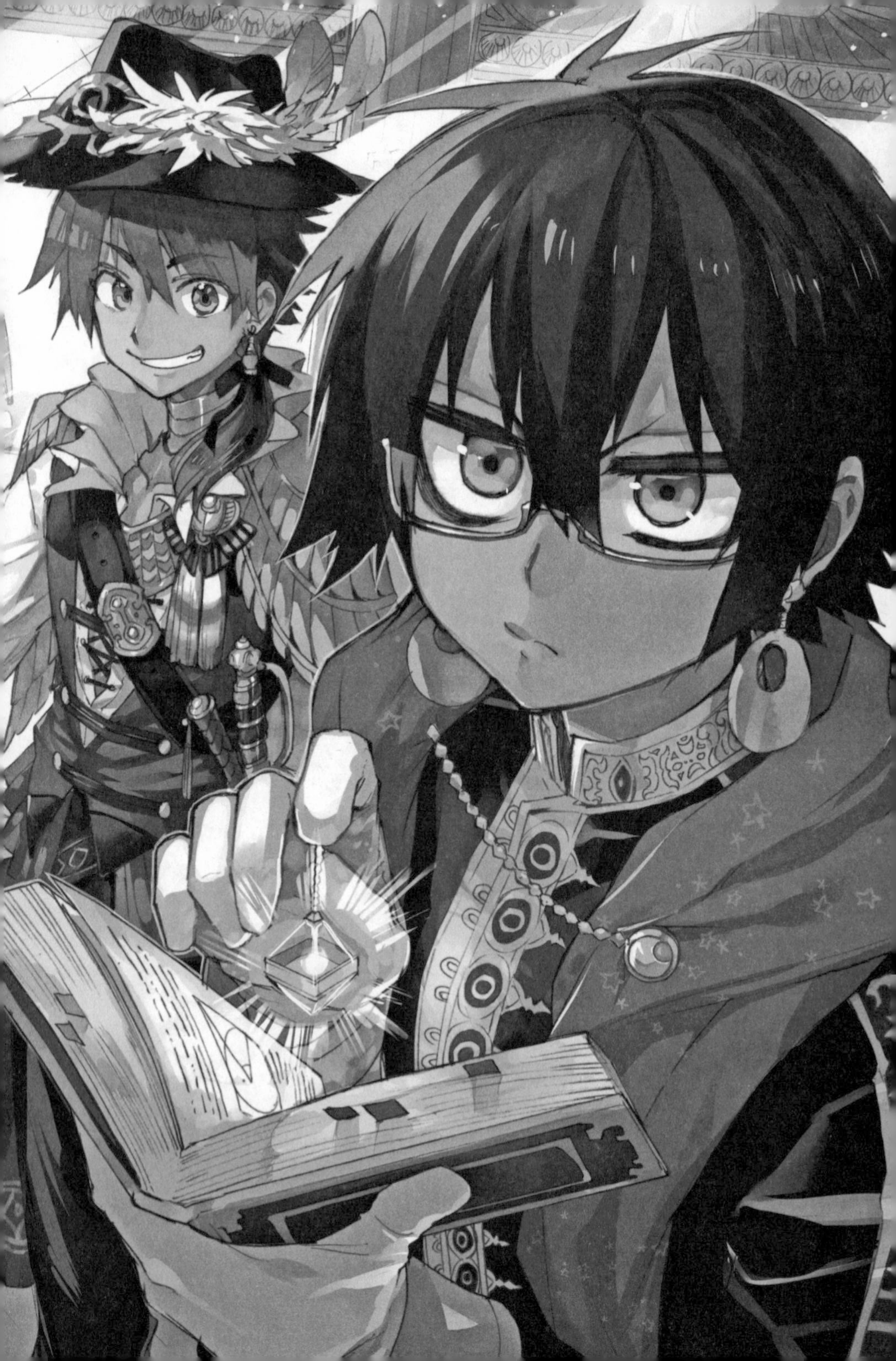

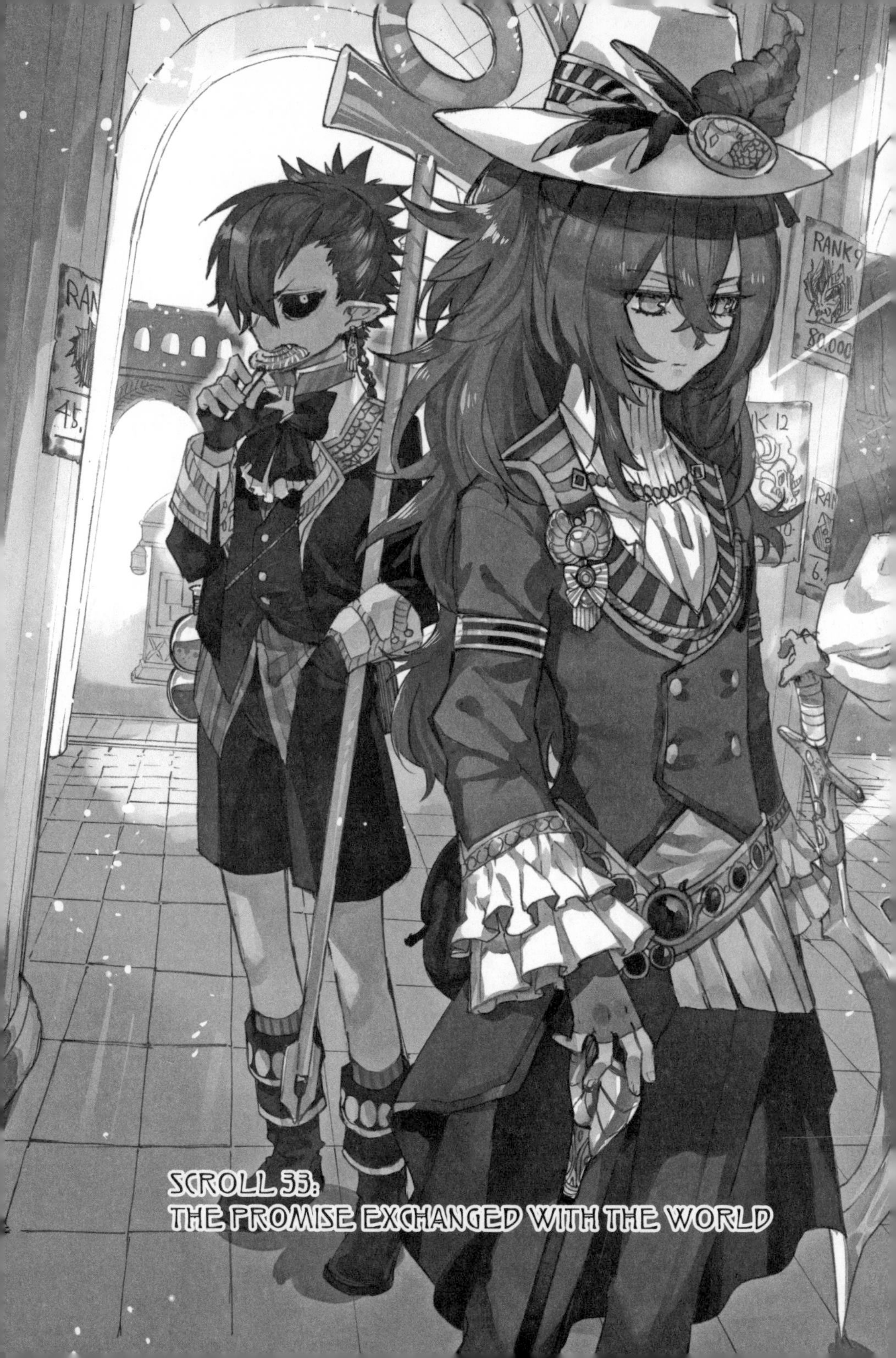
RANK9

SCROLL 33:
THE PROMISE EXCHANGED WITH THE WORLD

Im
Great Priest Imhotep

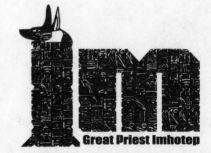

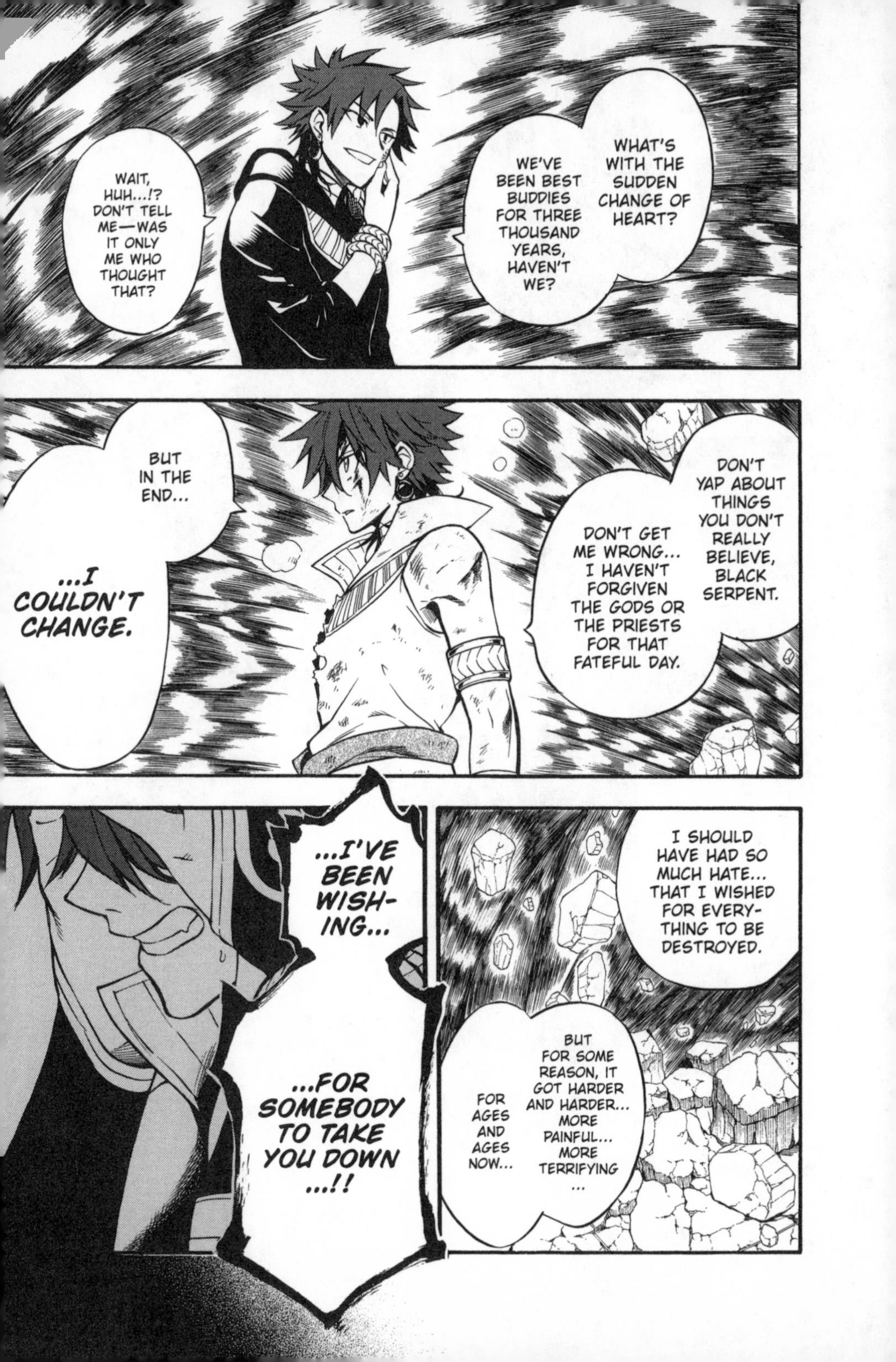
WHAT'S WITH THE SUDDEN CHANGE OF HEART?
WE'VE BEEN BEST BUDDIES FOR THREE THOUSAND YEARS, HAVEN'T WE?
WAIT, HUH...!? DON'T TELL ME—WAS IT ONLY ME WHO THOUGHT THAT?
DON'T YAP ABOUT THINGS YOU DON'T REALLY BELIEVE, BLACK SERPENT.
DON'T GET ME WRONG... I HAVEN'T FORGIVEN THE GODS OR THE PRIESTS FOR THAT FATEFUL DAY.
BUT IN THE END...
...I COULDN'T CHANGE.
I SHOULD HAVE HAD SO MUCH HATE... THAT I WISHED FOR EVERY-THING TO BE DESTROYED.
BUT FOR SOME REASON, IT GOT HARDER AND HARDER... MORE PAINFUL... MORE TERRIFYING...
FOR AGES AND AGES NOW...
...I'VE BEEN WISH-ING...
...FOR SOMEBODY TO TAKE YOU DOWN...!!

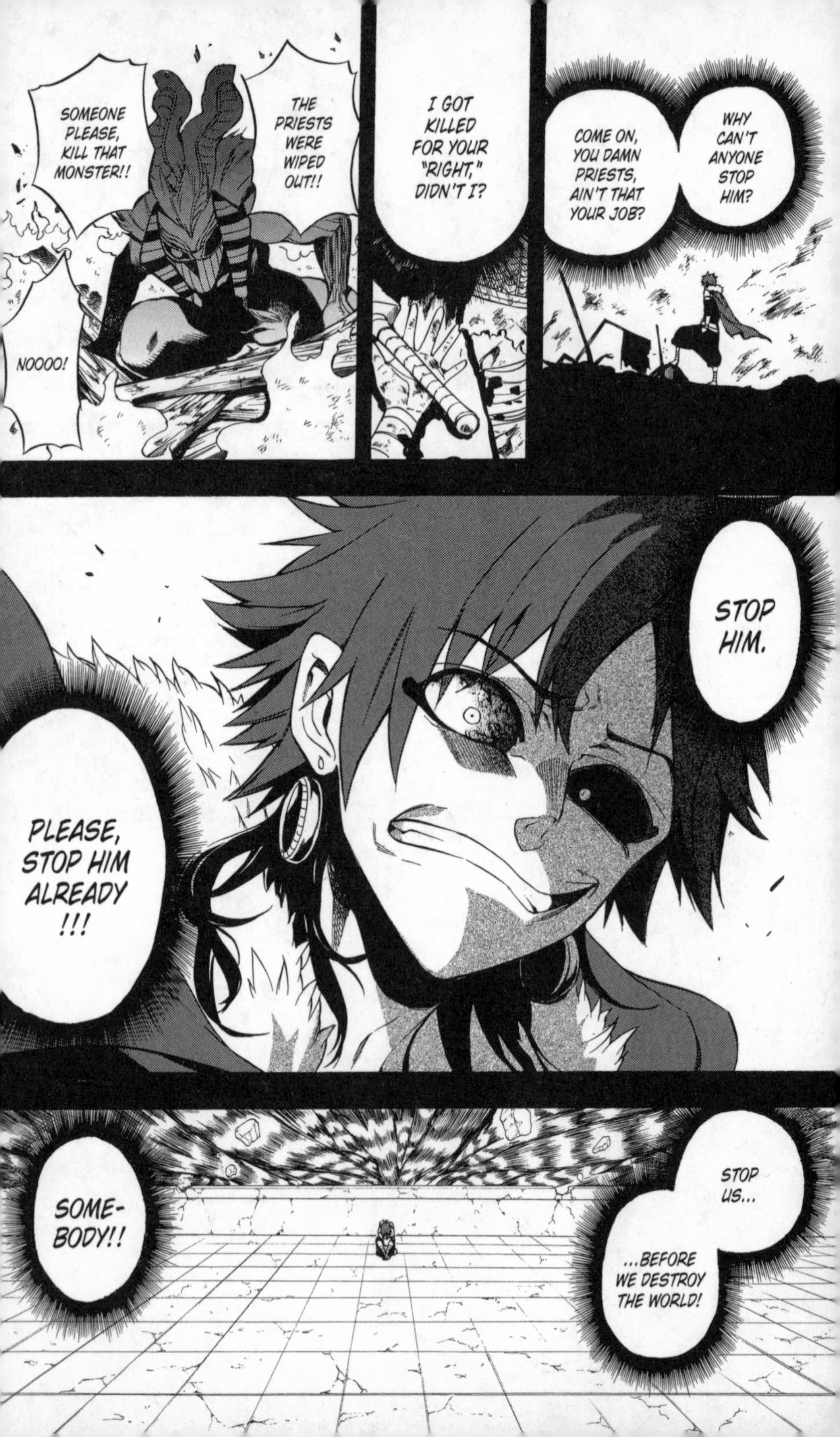
WHY CAN'T ANYONE STOP HIM?
COME ON, YOU DAMN PRIESTS, AIN'T THAT YOUR JOB?
I GOT KILLED FOR YOUR "RIGHT," DIDN'T I?
THE PRIESTS WERE WIPED OUT!!
SOMEONE PLEASE, KILL THAT MONSTER!!
NOOOO!
STOP HIM.
PLEASE, STOP HIM ALREADY !!!
STOP US...
...BEFORE WE DESTROY THE WORLD!
SOME-BODY!!

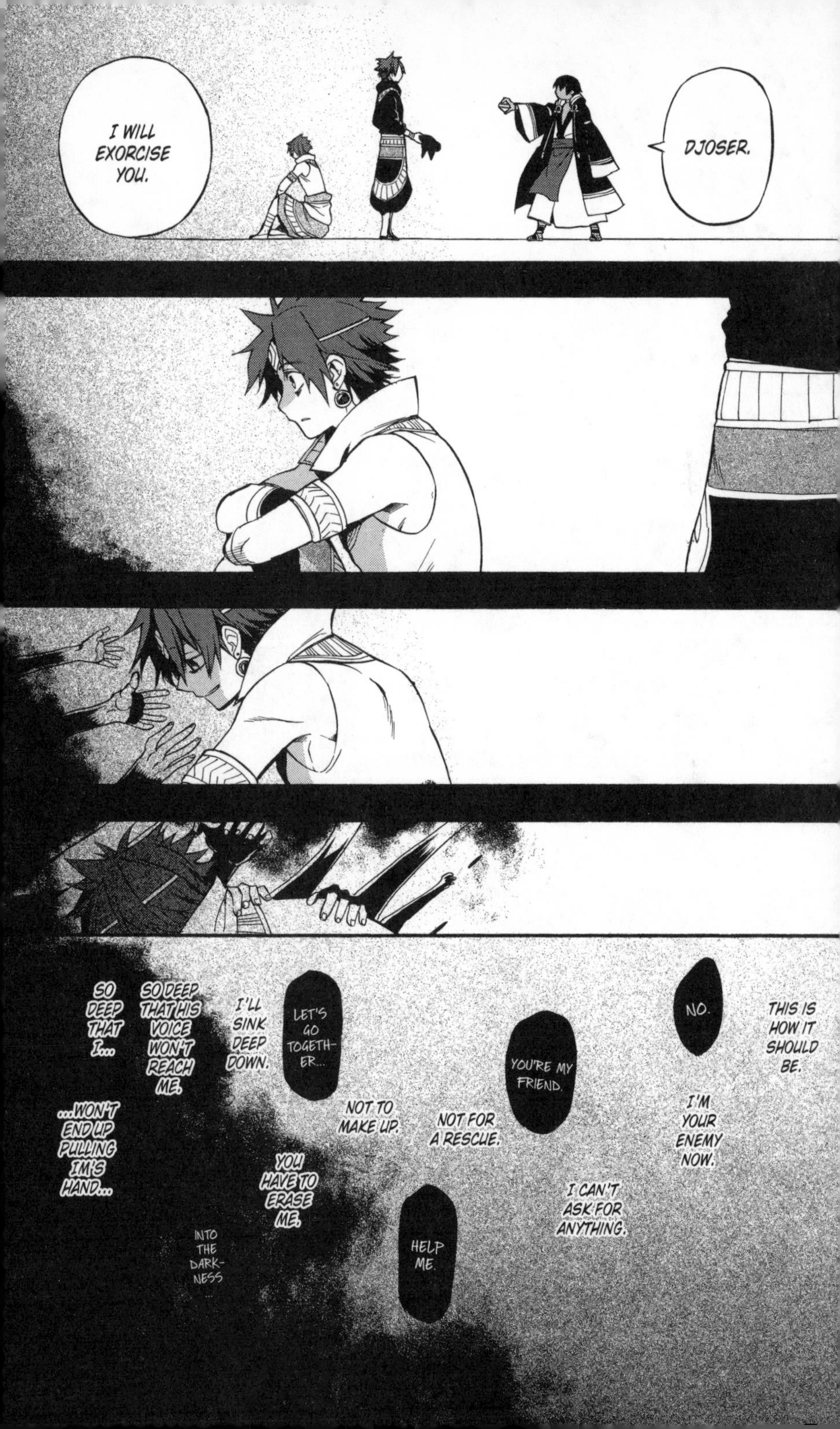
DJOSER.
I WILL EXORCISE YOU.
THIS IS HOW IT SHOULD BE.
NO.
I'M YOUR ENEMY NOW.
YOU'RE MY FRIEND.
I CAN'T ASK FOR ANYTHING.
NOT FOR A RESCUE.
NOT TO MAKE UP.
LET'S GO TOGETHER...
HELP ME.
I'LL SINK DEEP DOWN.
YOU HAVE TO ERASE ME.
INTO THE DARKNESS...
SO DEEP THAT HIS VOICE WON'T REACH ME.
SO DEEP THAT I...
...WON'T END UP PULLING IM'S HAND...

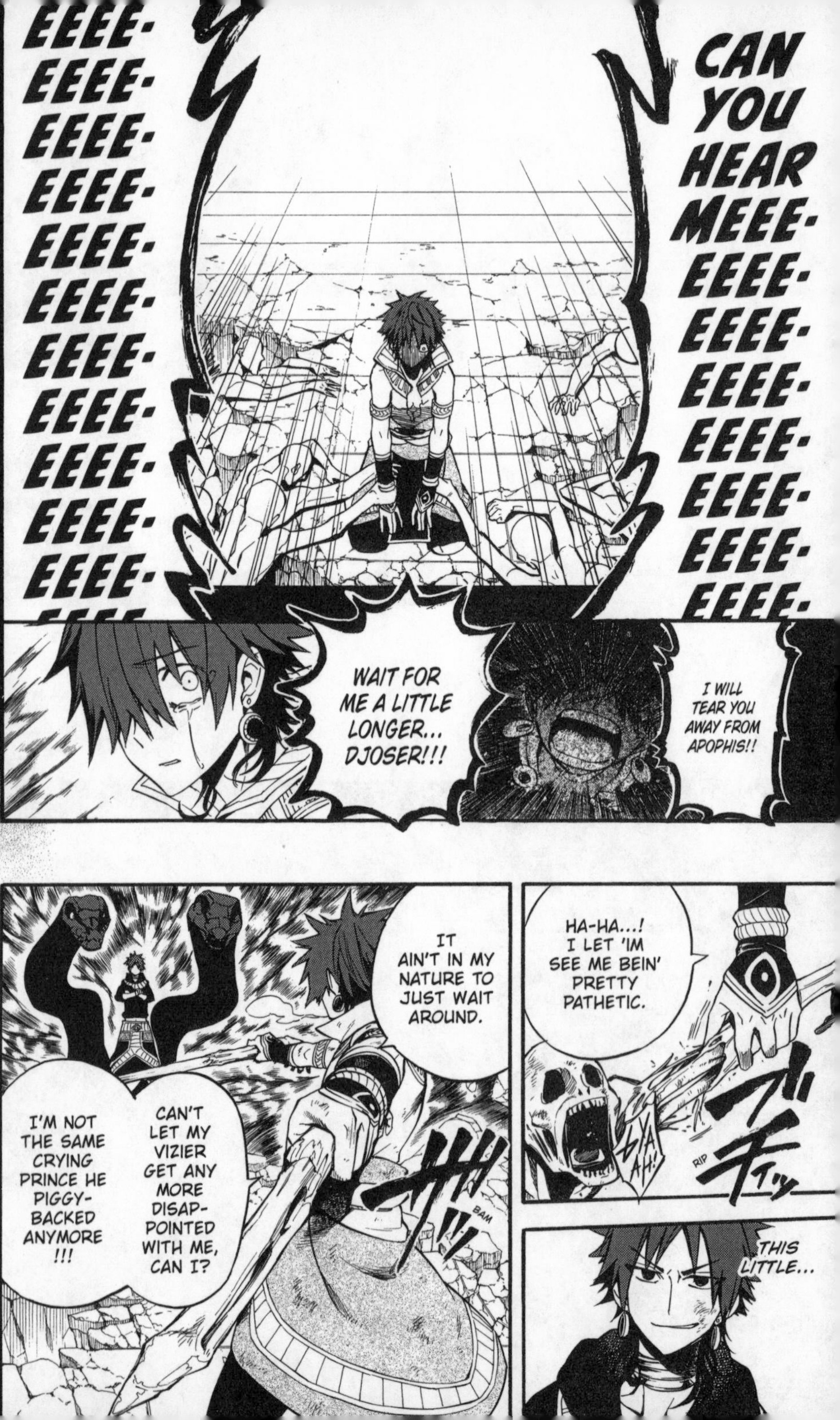
CAN YOU HEAR MEEE-EEEE-EEEE-EEEE-EEEE-EEEE-EEEE-EEEE-EEEE-
EEEE-EEEE-EEEE-EEEE-EEEE-EEEE-EEEE-EEEE-EEEE-EEEE-EEEE-EEEE-EEEE-
I WILL TEAR YOU AWAY FROM APOPHIS!!
WAIT FOR ME A LITTLE LONGER... DJOSER!!!
HA-HA...! I LET 'IM SEE ME BEIN' PRETTY PATHETIC.
RIP
THIS LITTLE...
IT AIN'T IN MY NATURE TO JUST WAIT AROUND.
CAN'T LET MY VIZIER GET ANY MORE DISAP-POINTED WITH ME, CAN I?
I'M NOT THE SAME CRYING PRINCE HE PIGGY-BACKED ANYMORE!!!
BAM

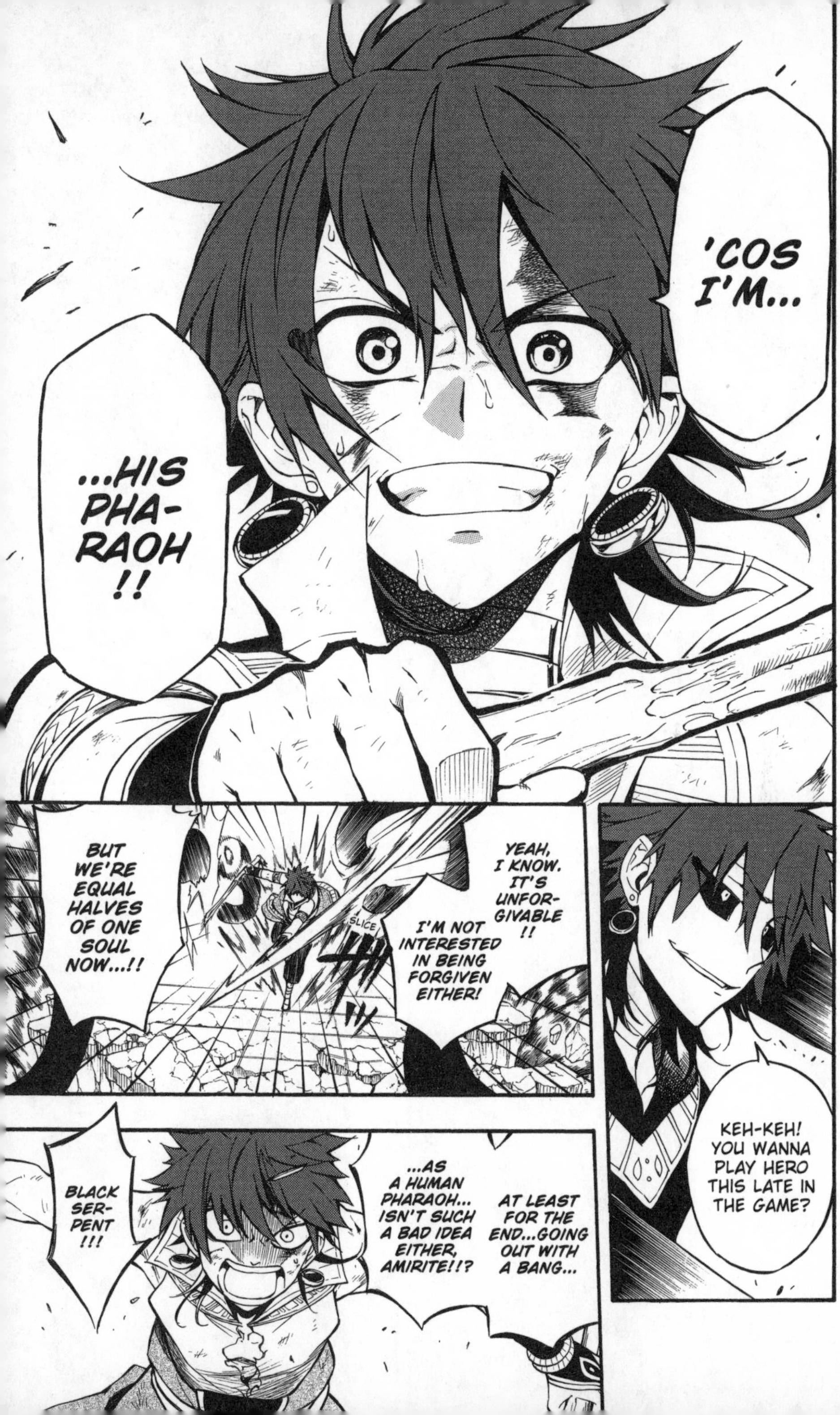
'COS I'M...
...HIS PHARAOH!!
KEH-KEH! YOU WANNA PLAY HERO THIS LATE IN THE GAME?
YEAH, I KNOW. IT'S UNFORGIVABLE!!
I'M NOT INTERESTED IN BEING FORGIVEN EITHER!
SLICE
BUT WE'RE EQUAL HALVES OF ONE SOUL NOW...!!
AT LEAST FOR THE END...GOING OUT WITH A BANG...
...AS A HUMAN PHARAOH... ISN'T SUCH A BAD IDEA EITHER, AMIRITE!!?
BLACK SERPENT!!!

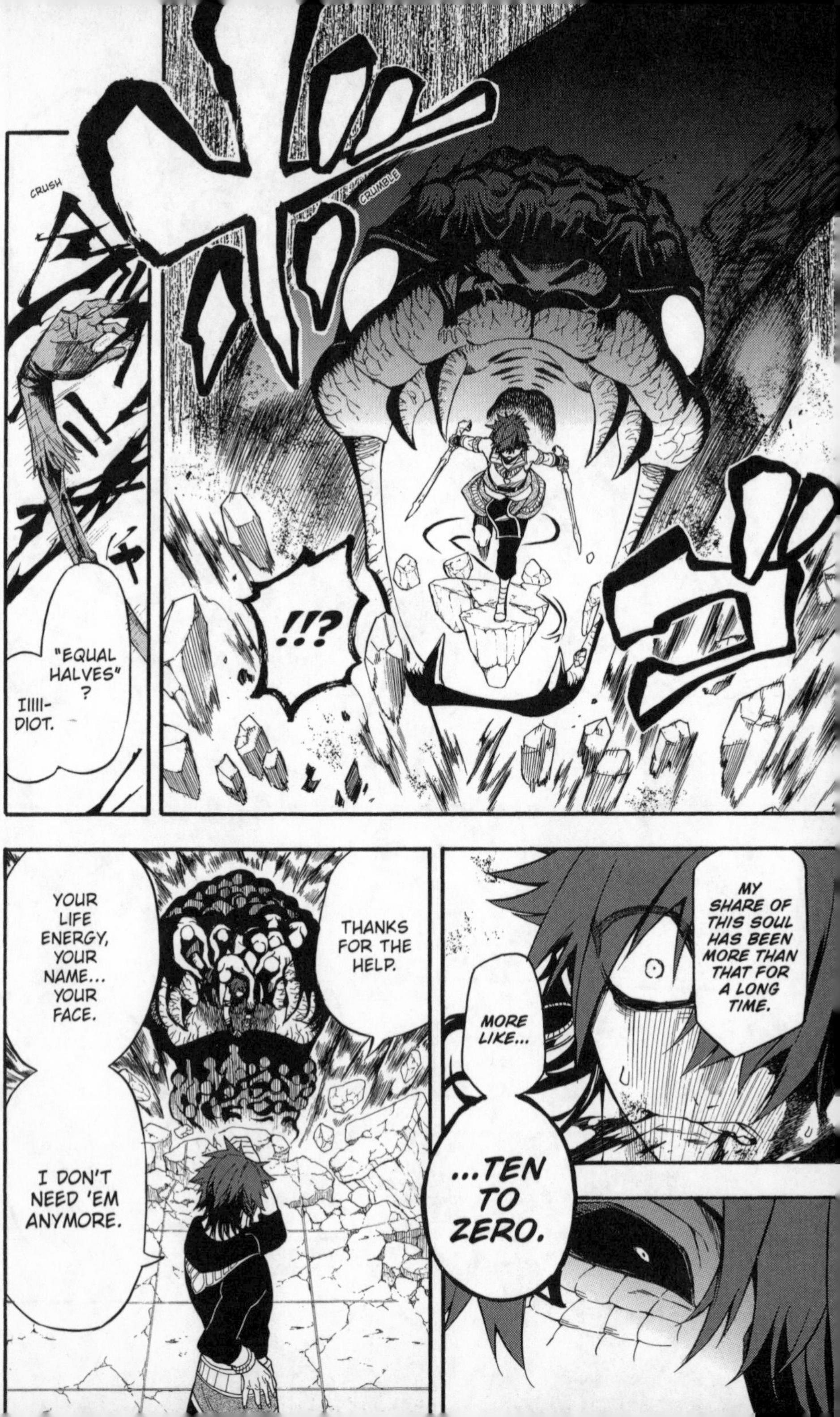
CRUMBLE
!!?
CRUSH
"EQUAL HALVES"?
IIIII-DIOT.
MY SHARE OF THIS SOUL HAS BEEN MORE THAN THAT FOR A LONG TIME.
MORE LIKE...
...TEN TO ZERO.
THANKS FOR THE HELP.
YOUR LIFE ENERGY, YOUR NAME... YOUR FACE.
I DON'T NEED 'EM ANYMORE.

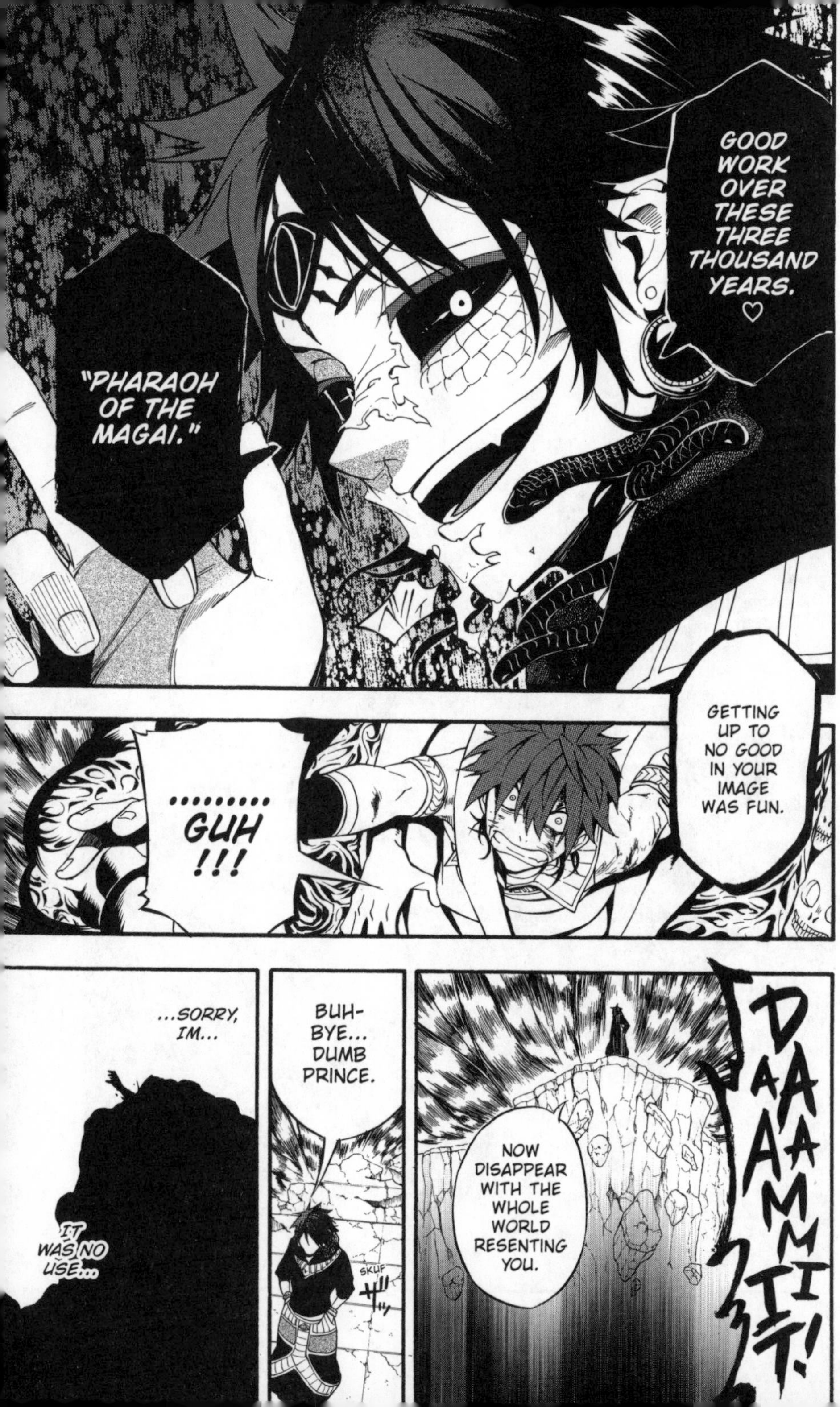
GOOD WORK OVER THESE THREE THOUSAND YEARS. ♡
"PHARAOH OF THE MAGAI."
GETTING UP TO NO GOOD IN YOUR IMAGE WAS FUN.
..........GUH!!!
DAAAMMIT!
NOW DISAPPEAR WITH THE WHOLE WORLD RESENTING YOU.
BUH-BYE... DUMB PRINCE.
SKUF
...SORRY, IM...
IT WAS NO USE...

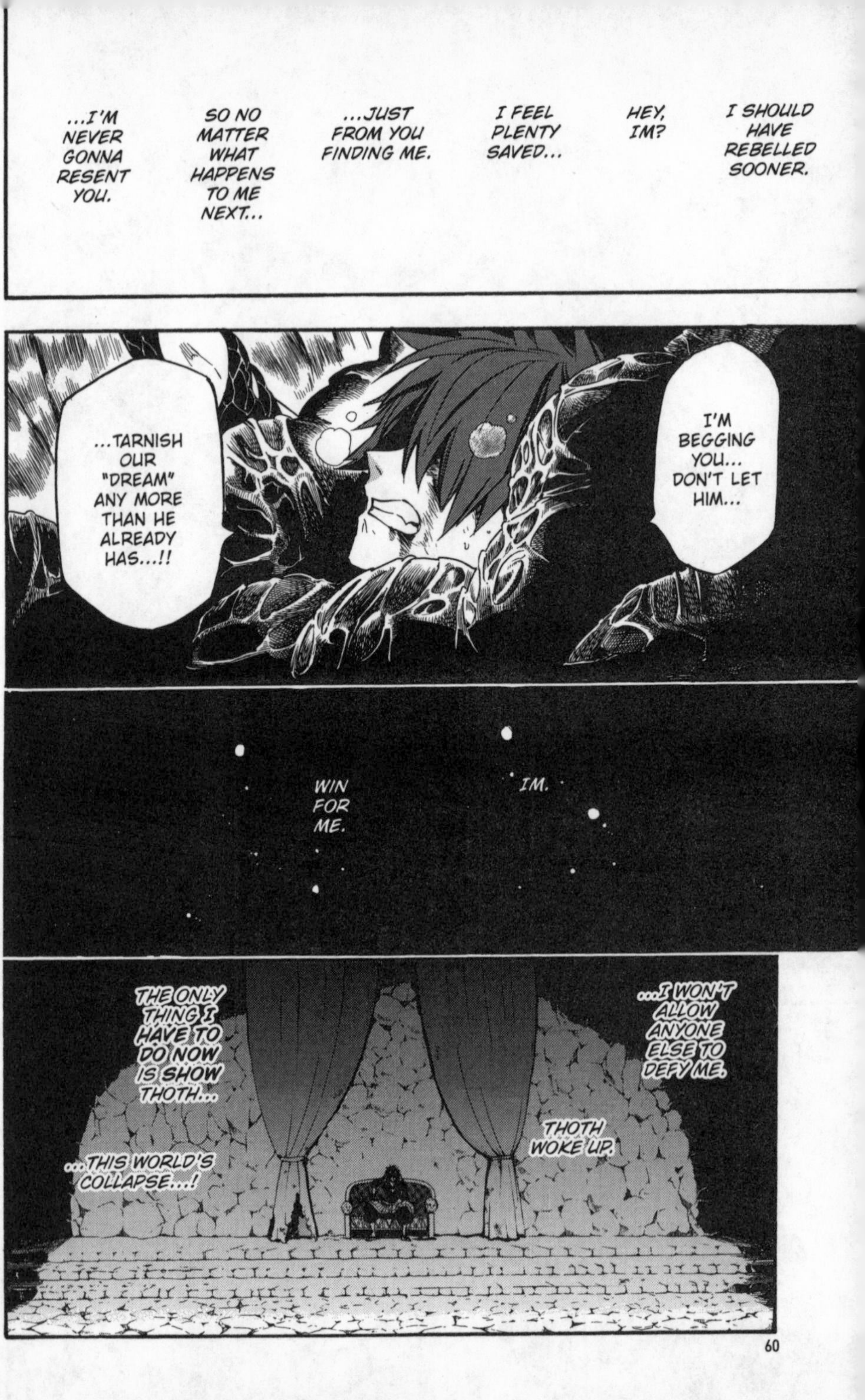
I SHOULD HAVE REBELLED SOONER.
HEY, IM?
I FEEL PLENTY SAVED...
...JUST FROM YOU FINDING ME.
SO NO MATTER WHAT HAPPENS TO ME NEXT...
...I'M NEVER GONNA RESENT YOU.
I'M BEGGING YOU... DON'T LET HIM...
...TARNISH OUR "DREAM" ANY MORE THAN HE ALREADY HAS...!!
IM.
WIN FOR ME.
...I WON'T ALLOW ANYONE ELSE TO DEFY ME.
THOTH WOKE UP.
THE ONLY THING I HAVE TO DO NOW IS SHOW THOTH...
...THIS WORLD'S COLLAPSE...!

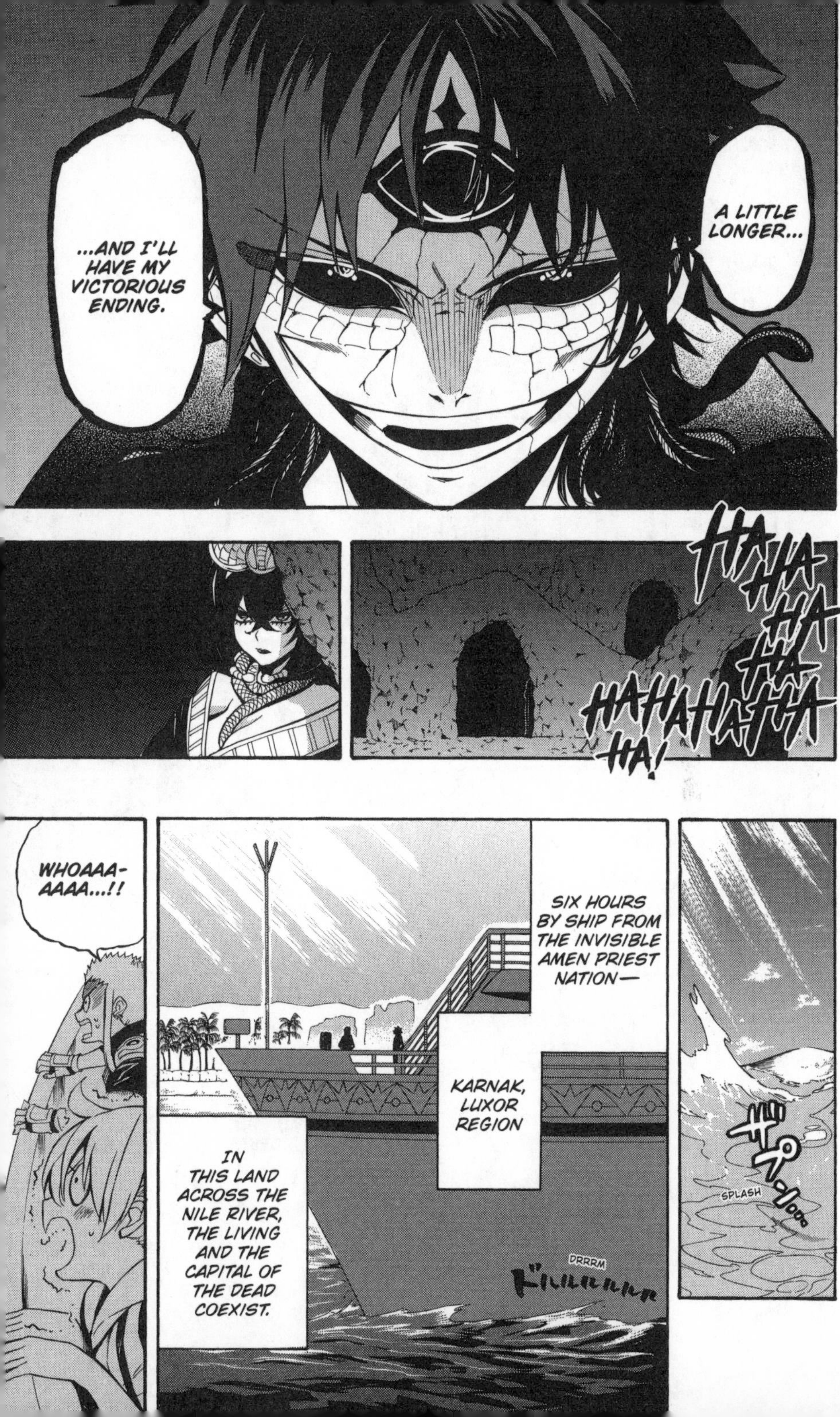
A LITTLE LONGER...
...AND I'LL HAVE MY VICTORIOUS ENDING.
HA HA HA HA HA
HAHAHAHAHA
HA!
SPLASH
SIX HOURS BY SHIP FROM THE INVISIBLE AMEN PRIEST NATION—
KARNAK, LUXOR REGION
IN THIS LAND ACROSS THE NILE RIVER, THE LIVING AND THE CAPITAL OF THE DEAD COEXIST.
DRRRM
WHOAAA-AAAA...!!

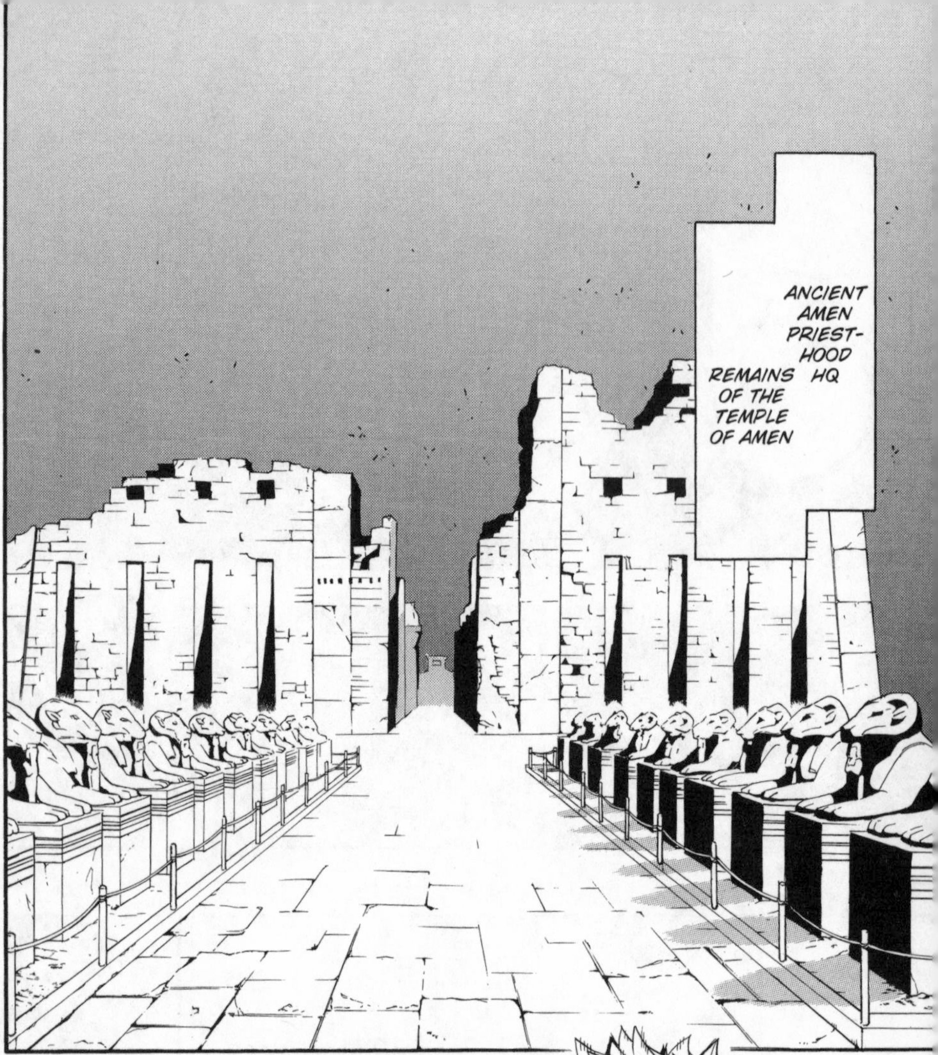
ANCIENT AMEN PRIEST-HOOD HQ
REMAINS OF THE TEMPLE OF AMEN

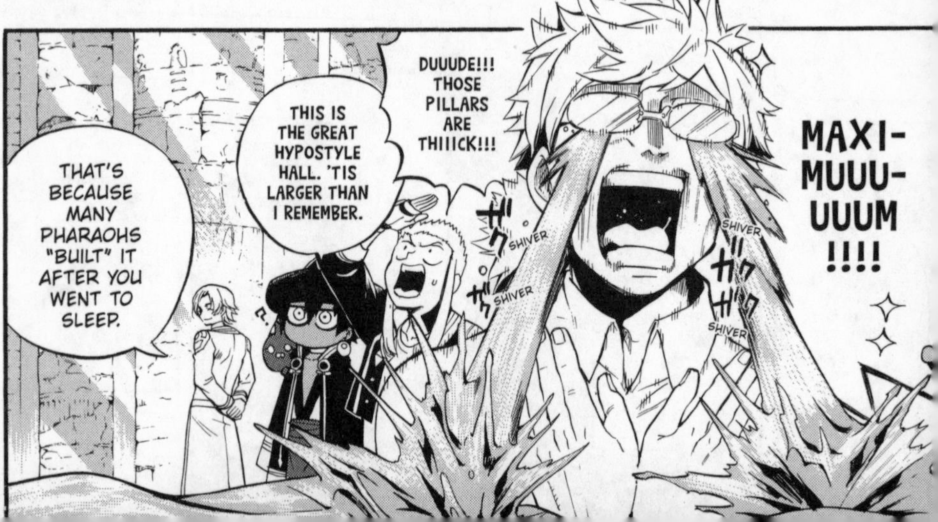
MAXI-MUUU-UUUM!!!!
SHIVER
SHIVER
SHIVER
SHIVER
DUUUDE!!! THOSE PILLARS ARE THIIICK!!!
THIS IS THE GREAT HYPOSTYLE HALL. 'TIS LARGER THAN I REMEMBER.
THAT'S BECAUSE MANY PHARAOHS "BUILT" IT AFTER YOU WENT TO SLEEP.

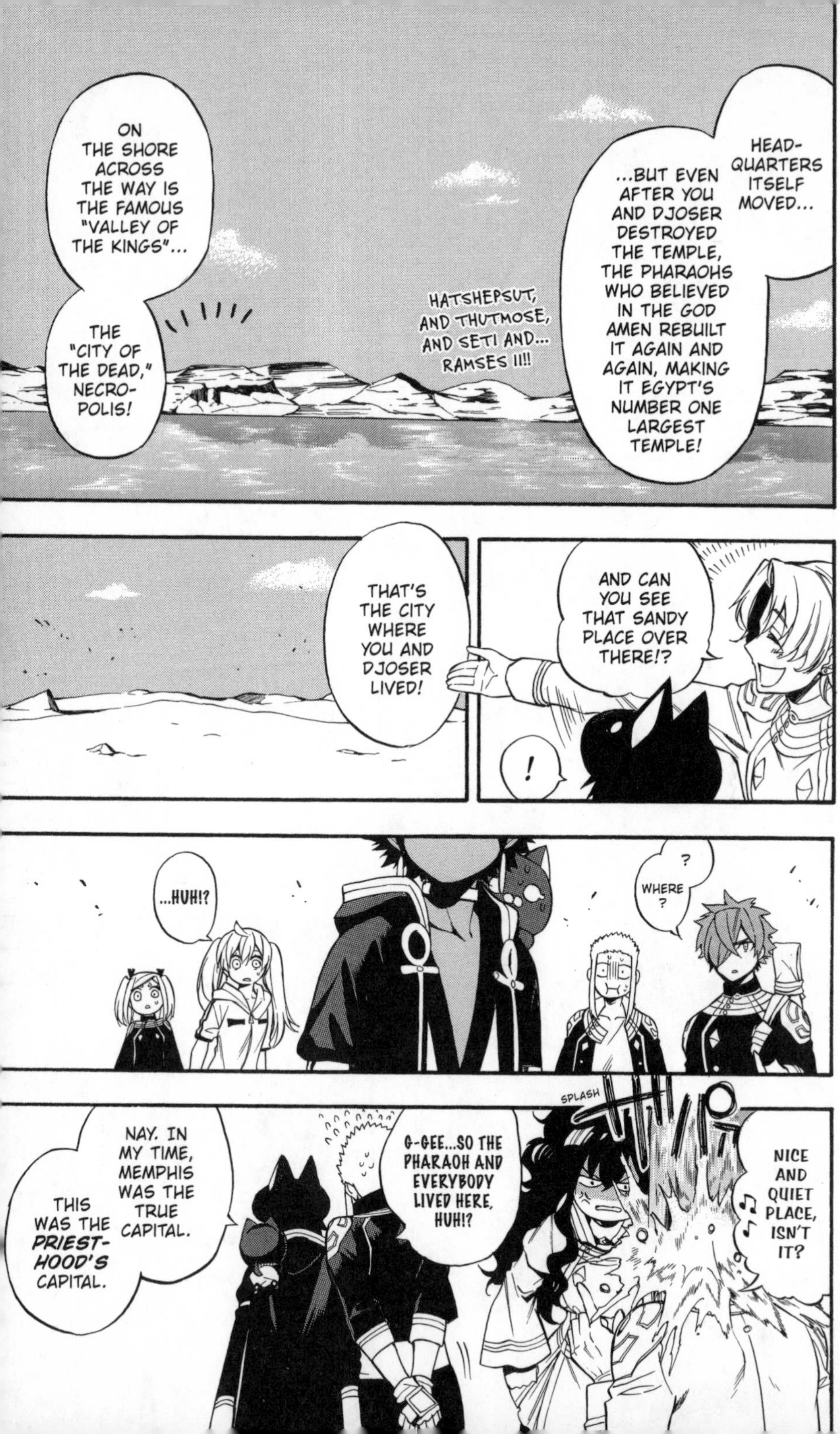
HEAD-QUARTERS ITSELF MOVED...
...BUT EVEN AFTER YOU AND DJOSER DESTROYED THE TEMPLE, THE PHARAOHS WHO BELIEVED IN THE GOD AMEN REBUILT IT AGAIN AND AGAIN, MAKING IT EGYPT'S NUMBER ONE LARGEST TEMPLE!
HATSHEPSUT, AND THUTMOSE, AND SETI AND... RAMSES II!!
ON THE SHORE ACROSS THE WAY IS THE FAMOUS "VALLEY OF THE KINGS"...
THE "CITY OF THE DEAD," NECRO-POLIS!
AND CAN YOU SEE THAT SANDY PLACE OVER THERE!?
!
THAT'S THE CITY WHERE YOU AND DJOSER LIVED!
? WHERE ?
...HUH!?
NICE AND QUIET PLACE, ISN'T IT?
SPLASH
G-GEE...SO THE PHARAOH AND EVERYBODY LIVED HERE, HUH!?
NAY. IN MY TIME, MEMPHIS WAS THE TRUE CAPITAL.
THIS WAS THE *PRIEST-HOOD'S* CAPITAL.

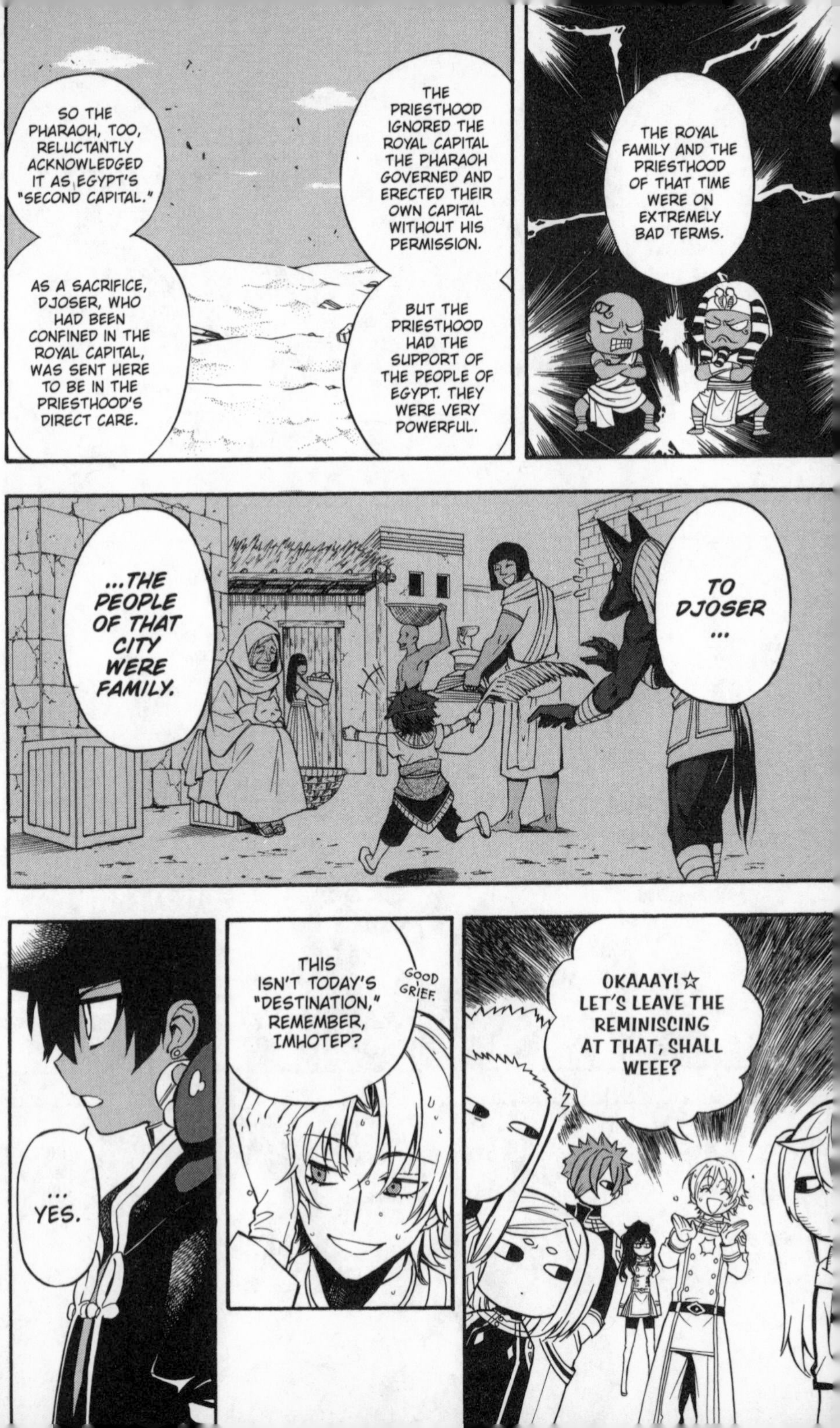
THE ROYAL FAMILY AND THE PRIESTHOOD OF THAT TIME WERE ON EXTREMELY BAD TERMS.
THE PRIESTHOOD IGNORED THE ROYAL CAPITAL THE PHARAOH GOVERNED AND ERECTED THEIR OWN CAPITAL WITHOUT HIS PERMISSION.
BUT THE PRIESTHOOD HAD THE SUPPORT OF THE PEOPLE OF EGYPT. THEY WERE VERY POWERFUL.
SO THE PHARAOH, TOO, RELUCTANTLY ACKNOWLEDGED IT AS EGYPT'S "SECOND CAPITAL."
AS A SACRIFICE, DJOSER, WHO HAD BEEN CONFINED IN THE ROYAL CAPITAL, WAS SENT HERE TO BE IN THE PRIESTHOOD'S DIRECT CARE.
TO DJOSER ...
...THE PEOPLE OF THAT CITY WERE FAMILY.
OKAAAY!☆ LET'S LEAVE THE REMINISCING AT THAT, SHALL WEEE?
THIS ISN'T TODAY'S "DESTINATION," REMEMBER, IMHOTEP?
GOOD GRIEF.
... YES.

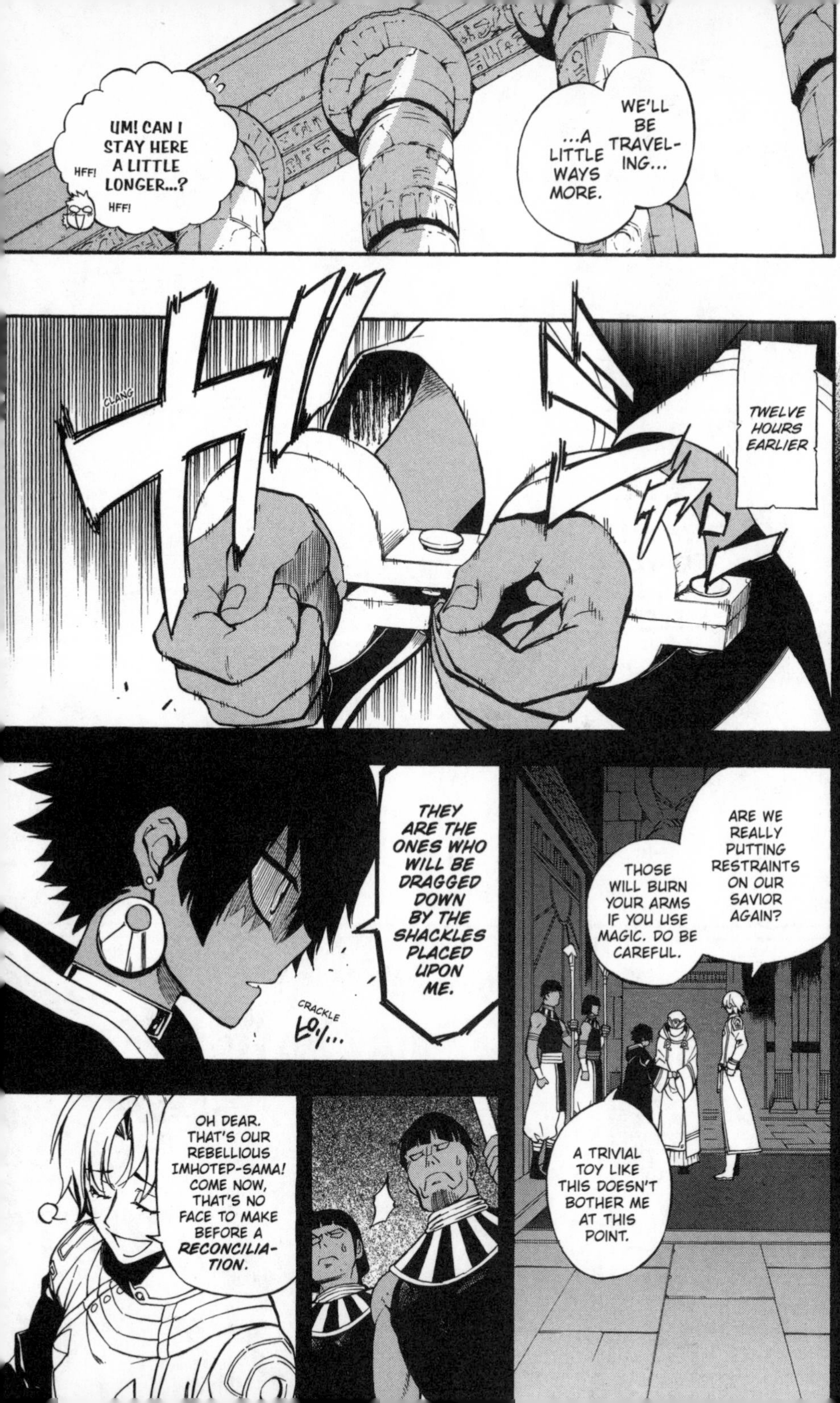
WE'LL BE TRAVELING...
...A LITTLE WAYS MORE.
UM! CAN I STAY HERE A LITTLE LONGER...?
HFF!
HFF!
TWELVE HOURS EARLIER
CLANG
ARE WE REALLY PUTTING RESTRAINTS ON OUR SAVIOR AGAIN?
THOSE WILL BURN YOUR ARMS IF YOU USE MAGIC. DO BE CAREFUL.
A TRIVIAL TOY LIKE THIS DOESN'T BOTHER ME AT THIS POINT.
THEY ARE THE ONES WHO WILL BE DRAGGED DOWN BY THE SHACKLES PLACED UPON ME.
CRACKLE
OH DEAR. THAT'S OUR REBELLIOUS IMHOTEP-SAMA! COME NOW, THAT'S NO FACE TO MAKE BEFORE A RECONCILIATION.

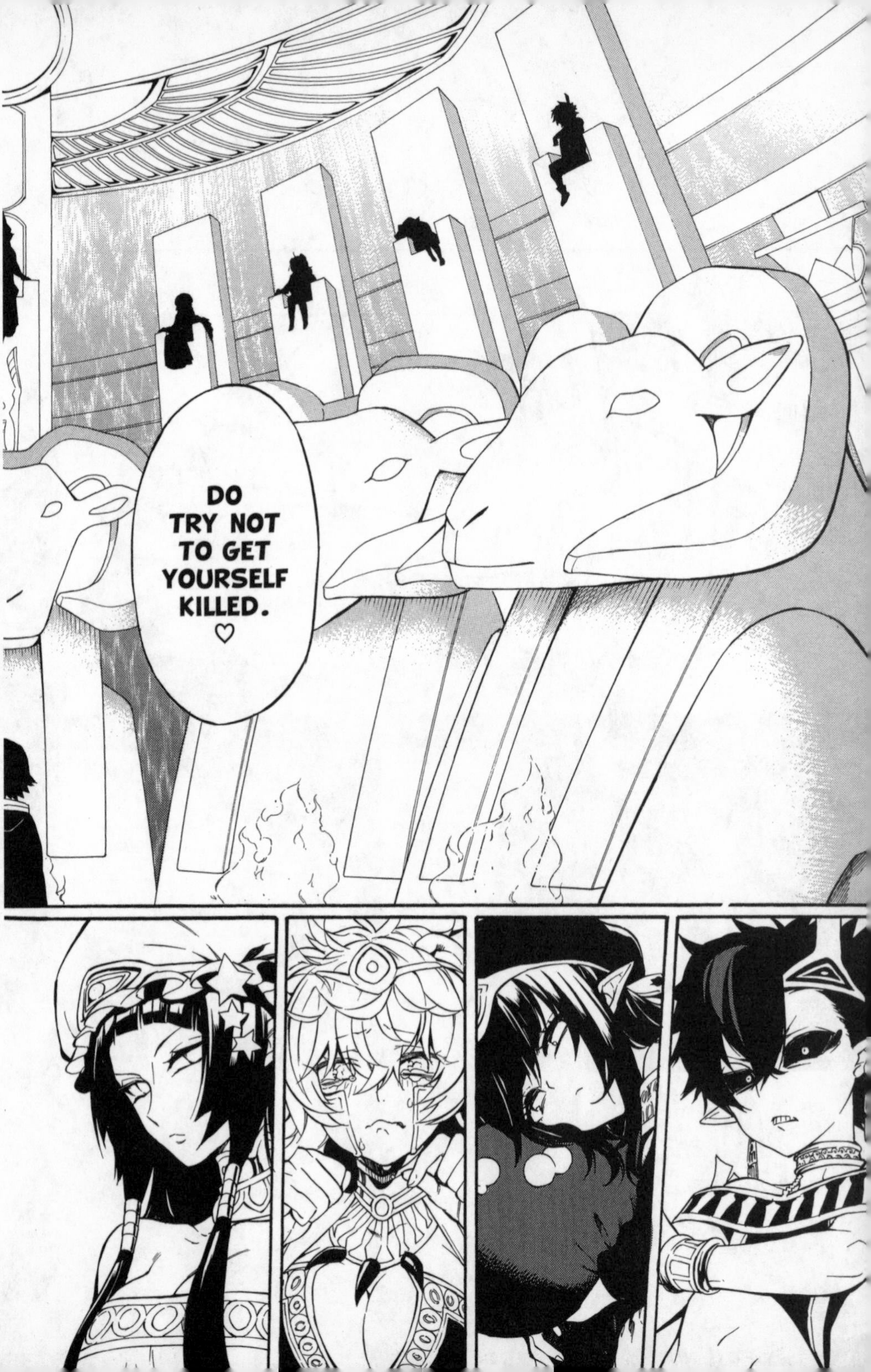
DO TRY NOT TO GET YOURSELF KILLED. ♡

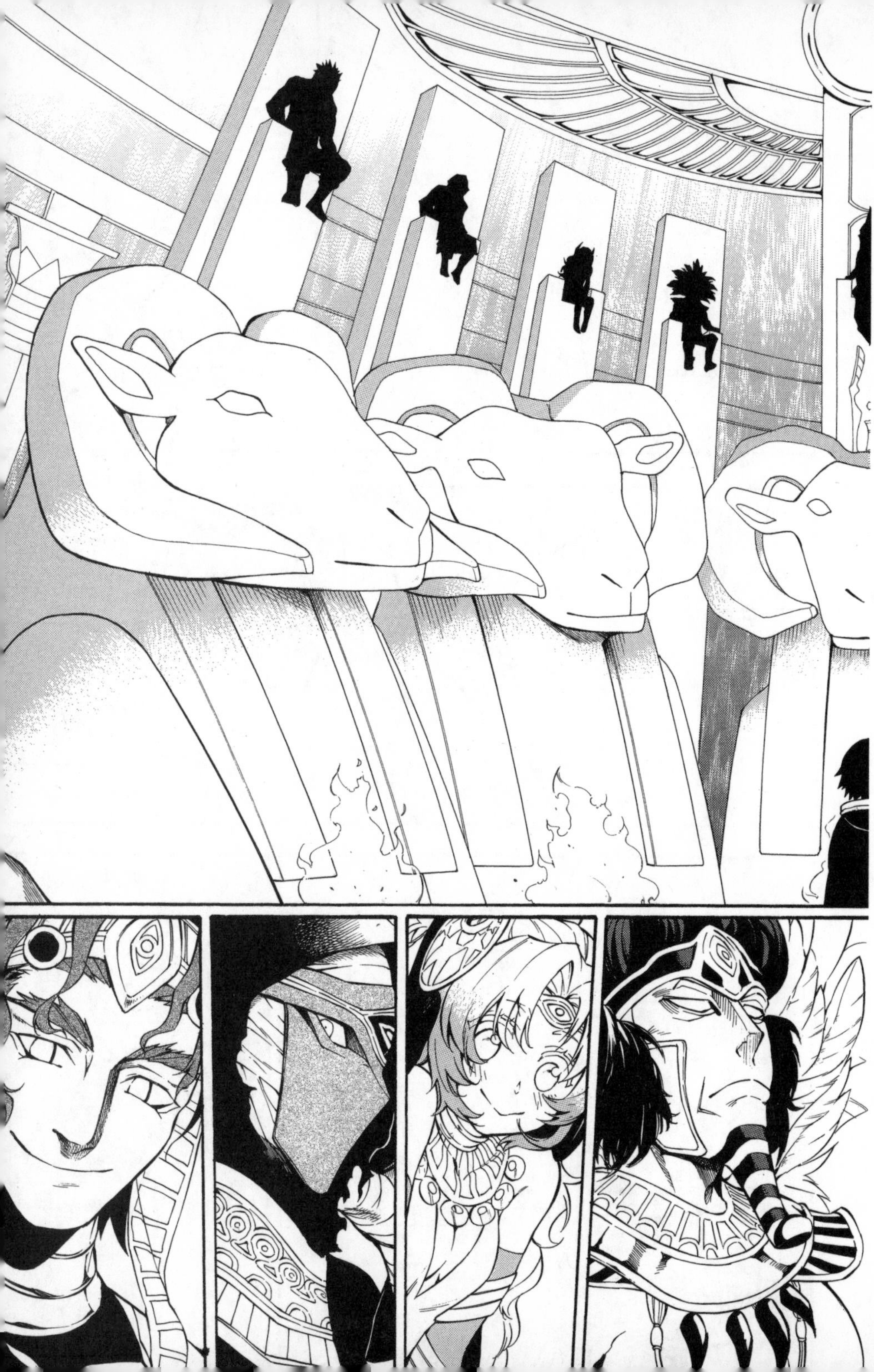

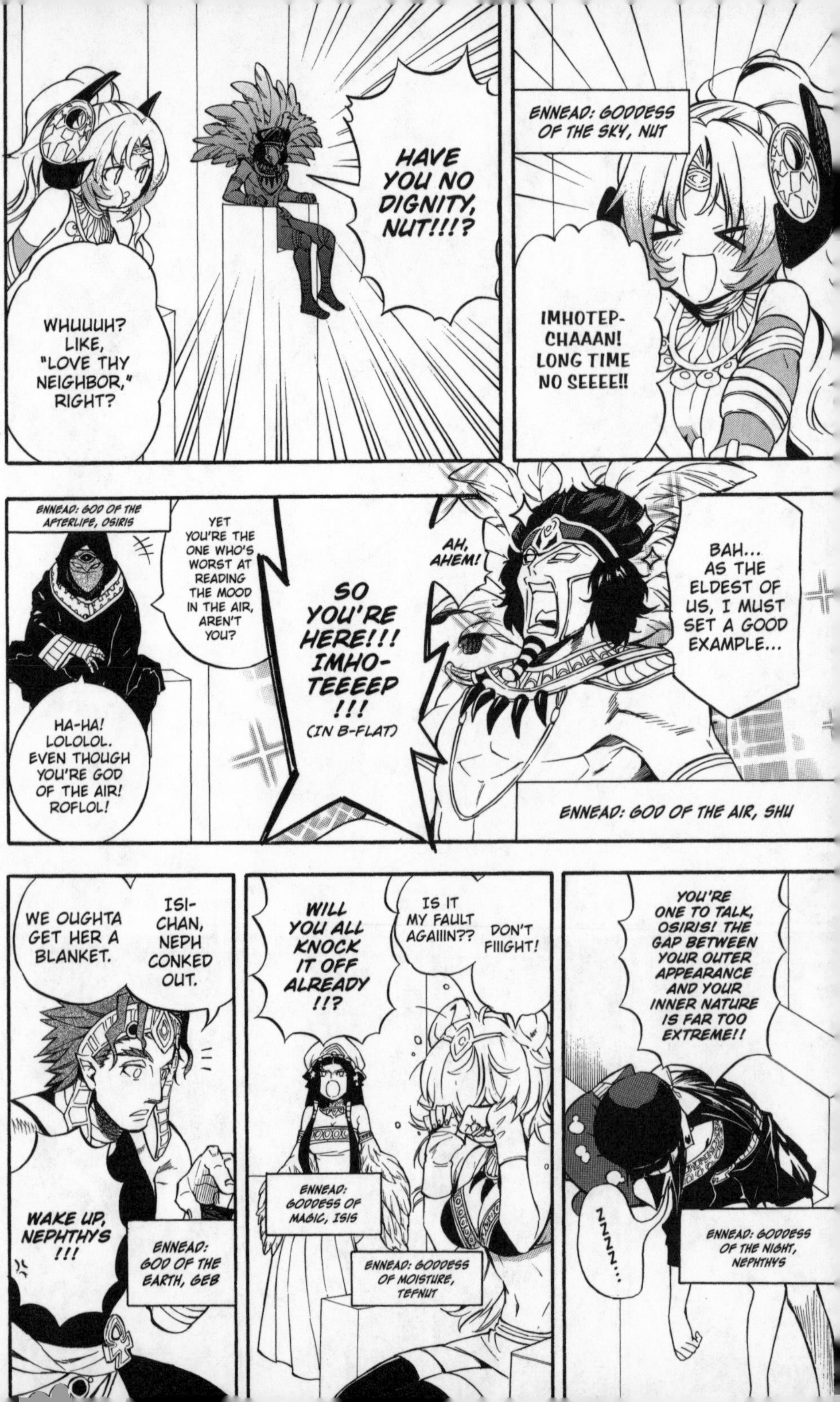
ENNEAD: GODDESS OF THE SKY, NUT
IMHOTEP-CHAAAN! LONG TIME NO SEEEE!!
HAVE YOU NO DIGNITY, NUT!!!?
WHUUUH? LIKE, "LOVE THY NEIGHBOR," RIGHT?
BAH... AS THE ELDEST OF US, I MUST SET A GOOD EXAMPLE...
AH, AHEM!
SO YOU'RE HERE!!! IMHO-TEEEEP!!!
(IN B-FLAT)
ENNEAD: GOD OF THE AIR, SHU
ENNEAD: GOD OF THE AFTERLIFE, OSIRIS
YET YOU'RE THE ONE WHO'S WORST AT READING THE MOOD IN THE AIR, AREN'T YOU?
HA-HA! LOLOLOL. EVEN THOUGH YOU'RE GOD OF THE AIR! ROFLOL!
YOU'RE ONE TO TALK, OSIRIS! THE GAP BETWEEN YOUR OUTER APPEARANCE AND YOUR INNER NATURE IS FAR TOO EXTREME!!
ZZZZ...
ENNEAD: GODDESS OF THE NIGHT, NEPHTHYS
IS IT MY FAULT AGAIIIN??
DON'T FIIIGHT!
WILL YOU ALL KNOCK IT OFF ALREADY!!?
ENNEAD: GODDESS OF MAGIC, ISIS
ENNEAD: GODDESS OF MOISTURE, TEFNUT
ISI-CHAN, NEPH CONKED OUT.
WE OUGHTA GET HER A BLANKET.
WAKE UP, NEPHTHYS!!!
ENNEAD: GOD OF THE EARTH, GEB

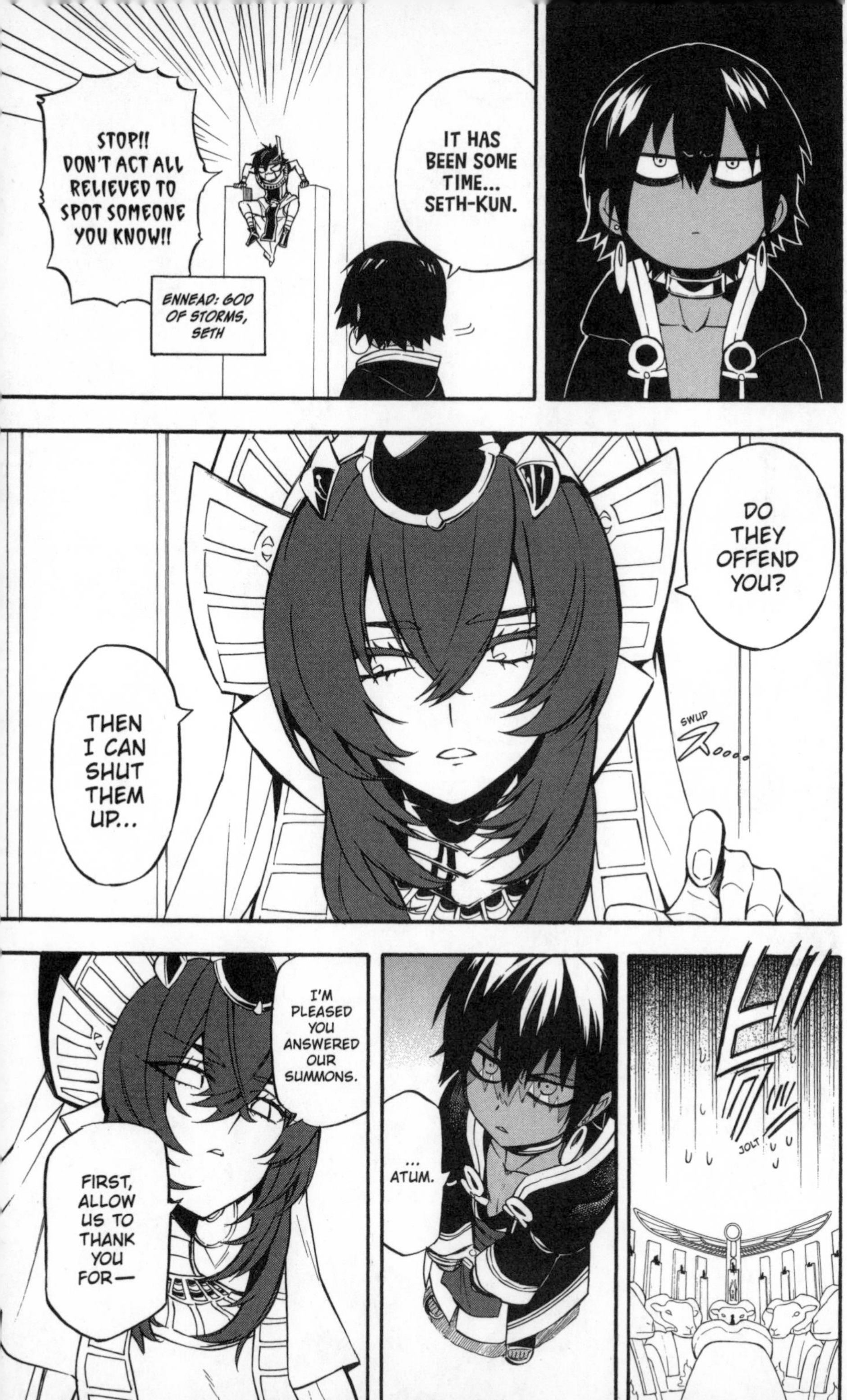
IT HAS BEEN SOME TIME... SETH-KUN.
STOP!! DON'T ACT ALL RELIEVED TO SPOT SOMEONE YOU KNOW!!
ENNEAD: GOD OF STORMS, SETH
DO THEY OFFEND YOU?
SWUP
THEN I CAN SHUT THEM UP...
JOLT
... ATUM.
I'M PLEASED YOU ANSWERED OUR SUMMONS.
FIRST, ALLOW US TO THANK YOU FOR—

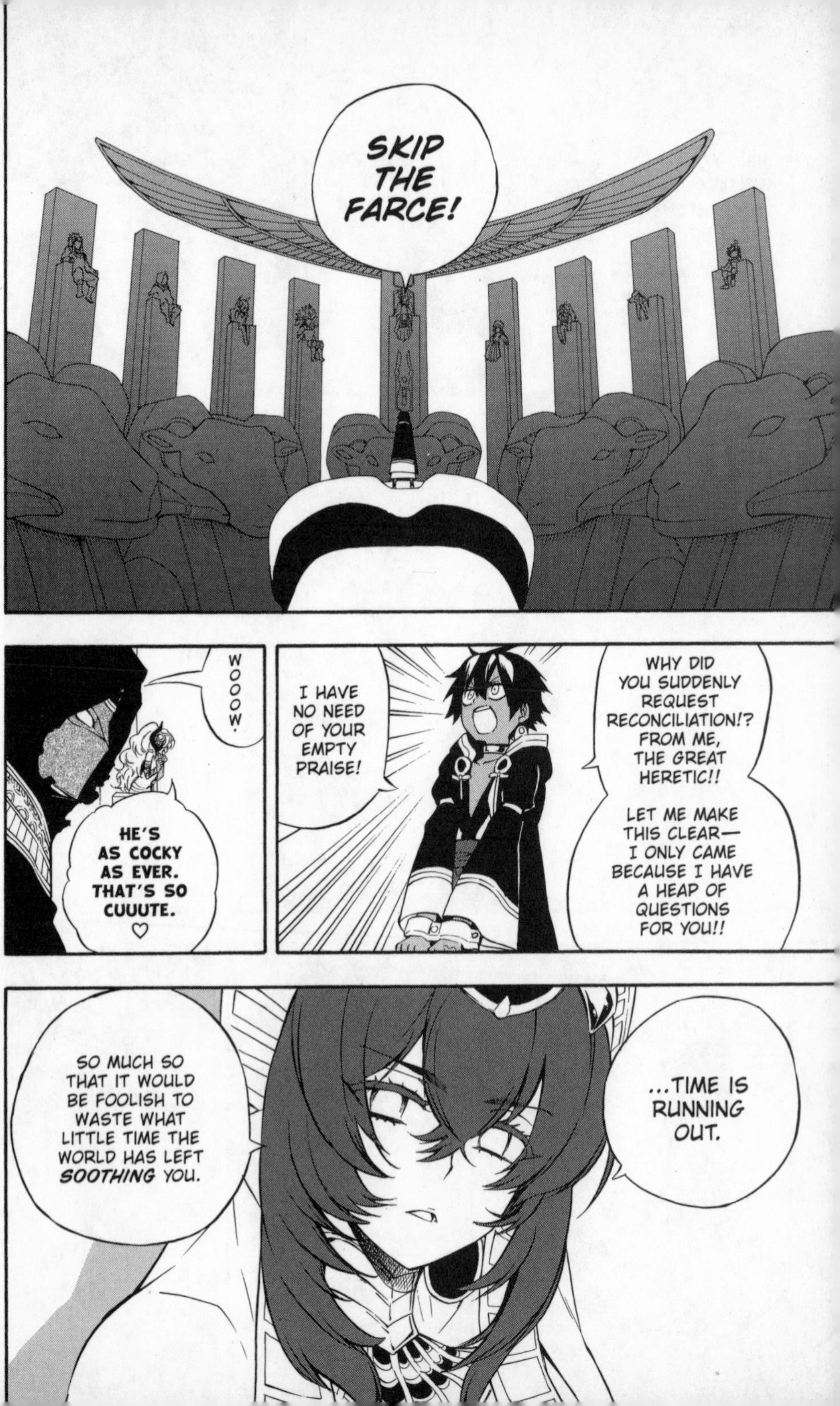
SKIP THE FARCE!
WHY DID YOU SUDDENLY REQUEST RECONCILIATION!? FROM ME, THE GREAT HERETIC!!
LET ME MAKE THIS CLEAR— I ONLY CAME BECAUSE I HAVE A HEAP OF QUESTIONS FOR YOU!!
I HAVE NO NEED OF YOUR EMPTY PRAISE!
WOOOOW.
HE'S AS COCKY AS EVER. THAT'S SO CUUUTE. ♡
...TIME IS RUNNING OUT.
SO MUCH SO THAT IT WOULD BE FOOLISH TO WASTE WHAT LITTLE TIME THE WORLD HAS LEFT *SOOTHING* YOU.

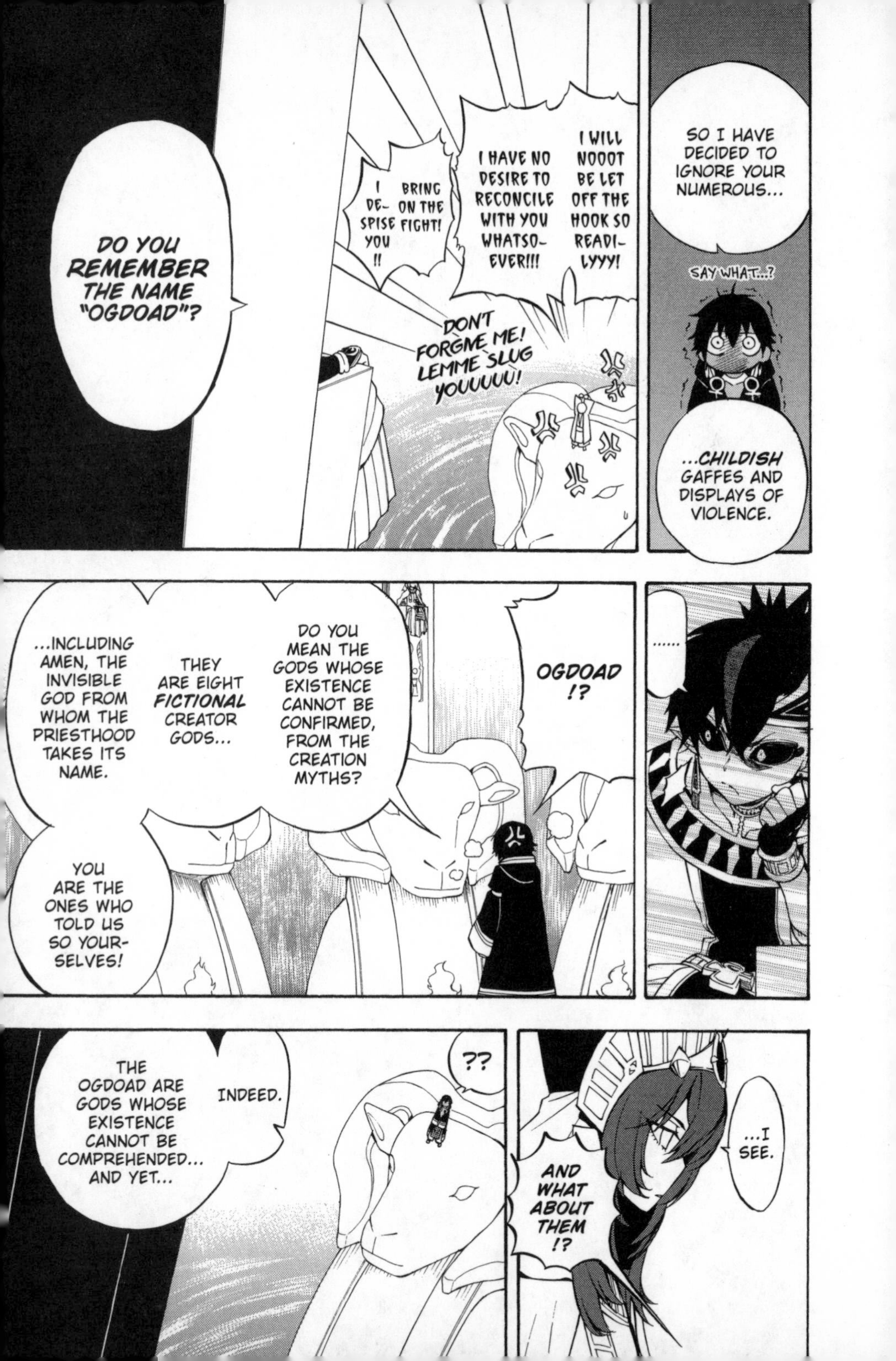
SO I HAVE DECIDED TO IGNORE YOUR NUMEROUS...
SAY WHAT...?
...CHILDISH GAFFES AND DISPLAYS OF VIOLENCE.
I WILL NOOOT BE LET OFF THE HOOK SO READI-LYYY!
I HAVE NO DESIRE TO RECONCILE WITH YOU WHATSO-EVER!!!
BRING ON THE FIGHT!
I DE-SPISE YOU !!
DON'T FORGIVE ME! LEMME SLUG YOUUUUU!
DO YOU REMEMBER THE NAME "OGDOAD"?
......
OGDOAD !?
DO YOU MEAN THE GODS WHOSE EXISTENCE CANNOT BE CONFIRMED, FROM THE CREATION MYTHS?
THEY ARE EIGHT FICTIONAL CREATOR GODS...
...INCLUDING AMEN, THE INVISIBLE GOD FROM WHOM THE PRIESTHOOD TAKES ITS NAME.
YOU ARE THE ONES WHO TOLD US SO YOUR-SELVES!
...I SEE.
AND WHAT ABOUT THEM !?
??
INDEED.
THE OGDOAD ARE GODS WHOSE EXISTENCE CANNOT BE COMPREHENDED... AND YET...

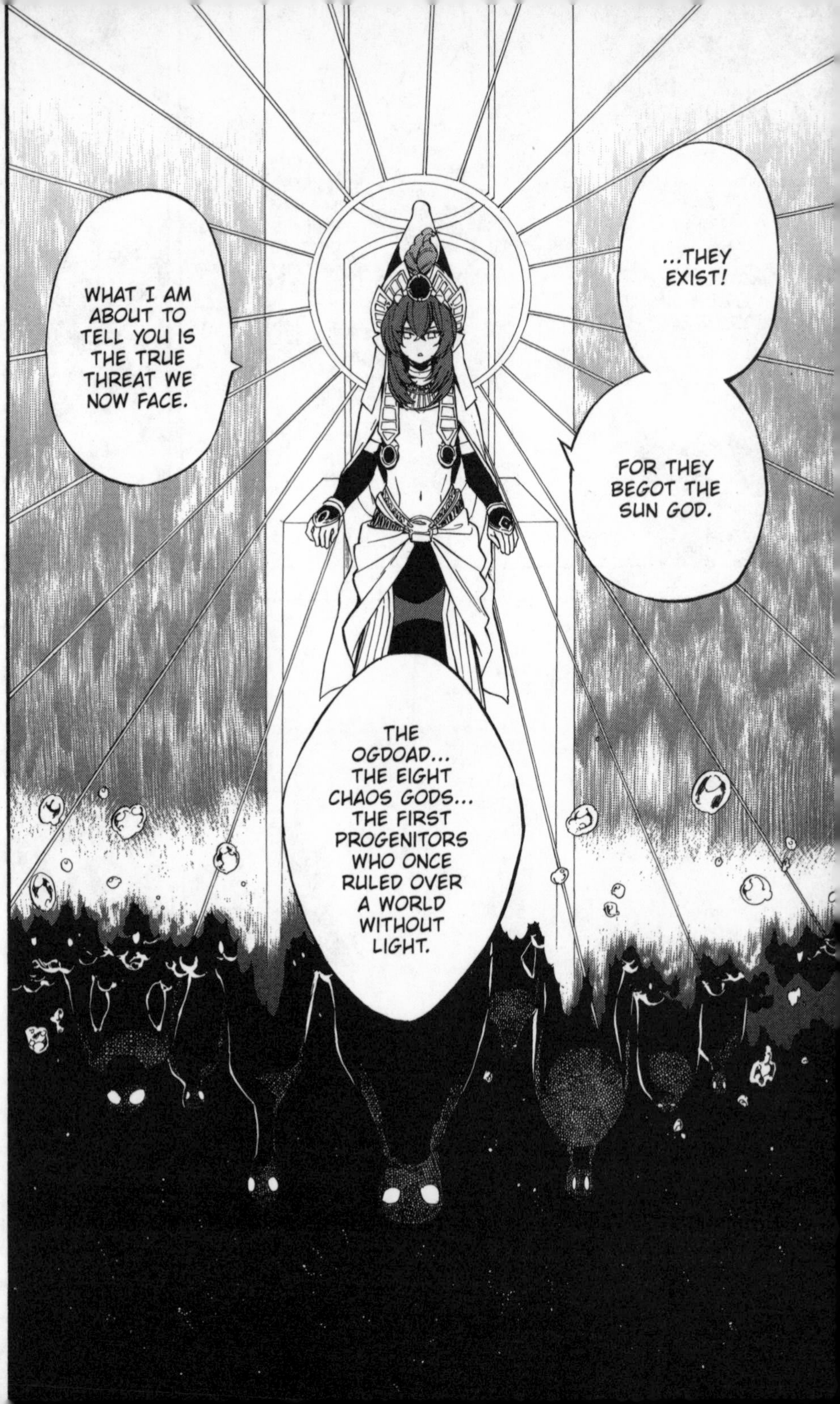

...THEY EXIST!
FOR THEY BEGOT THE SUN GOD.
WHAT I AM ABOUT TO TELL YOU IS THE TRUE THREAT WE NOW FACE.
THE OGDOAD... THE EIGHT CHAOS GODS... THE FIRST PROGENITORS WHO ONCE RULED OVER A WORLD WITHOUT LIGHT.

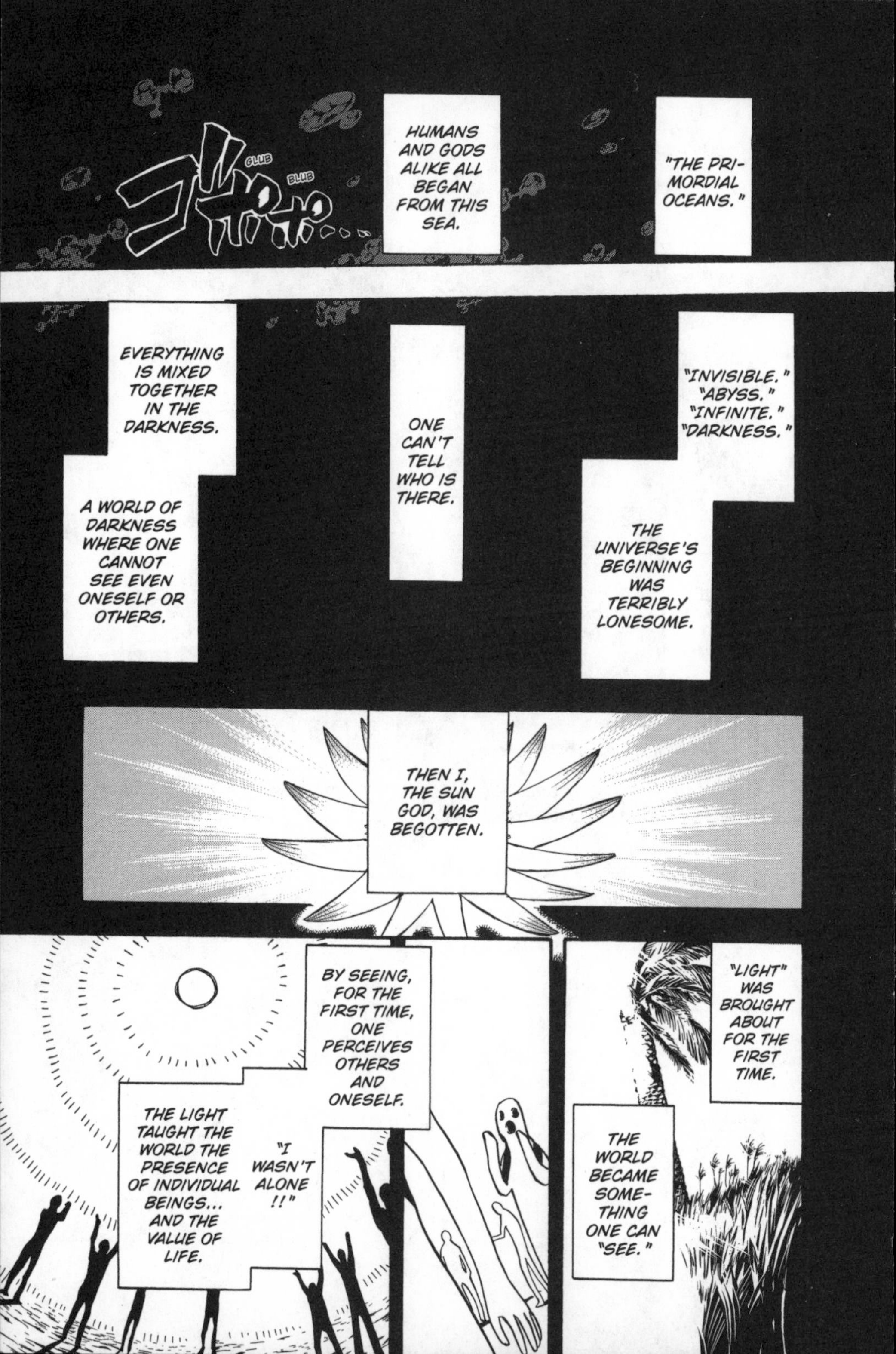
"THE PRIMORDIAL OCEANS."
HUMANS AND GODS ALIKE ALL BEGAN FROM THIS SEA.
GLUB
BLUB
"INVISIBLE." "ABYSS." "INFINITE." "DARKNESS."
THE UNIVERSE'S BEGINNING WAS TERRIBLY LONESOME.
ONE CAN'T TELL WHO IS THERE.
EVERYTHING IS MIXED TOGETHER IN THE DARKNESS.
A WORLD OF DARKNESS WHERE ONE CANNOT SEE EVEN ONESELF OR OTHERS.
THEN I, THE SUN GOD, WAS BEGOTTEN.
"LIGHT" WAS BROUGHT ABOUT FOR THE FIRST TIME.
THE WORLD BECAME SOMETHING ONE CAN "SEE."
BY SEEING, FOR THE FIRST TIME, ONE PERCEIVES OTHERS AND ONESELF.
THE LIGHT TAUGHT THE WORLD THE PRESENCE OF INDIVIDUAL BEINGS... AND THE VALUE OF LIFE.
"I WASN'T ALONE!!"

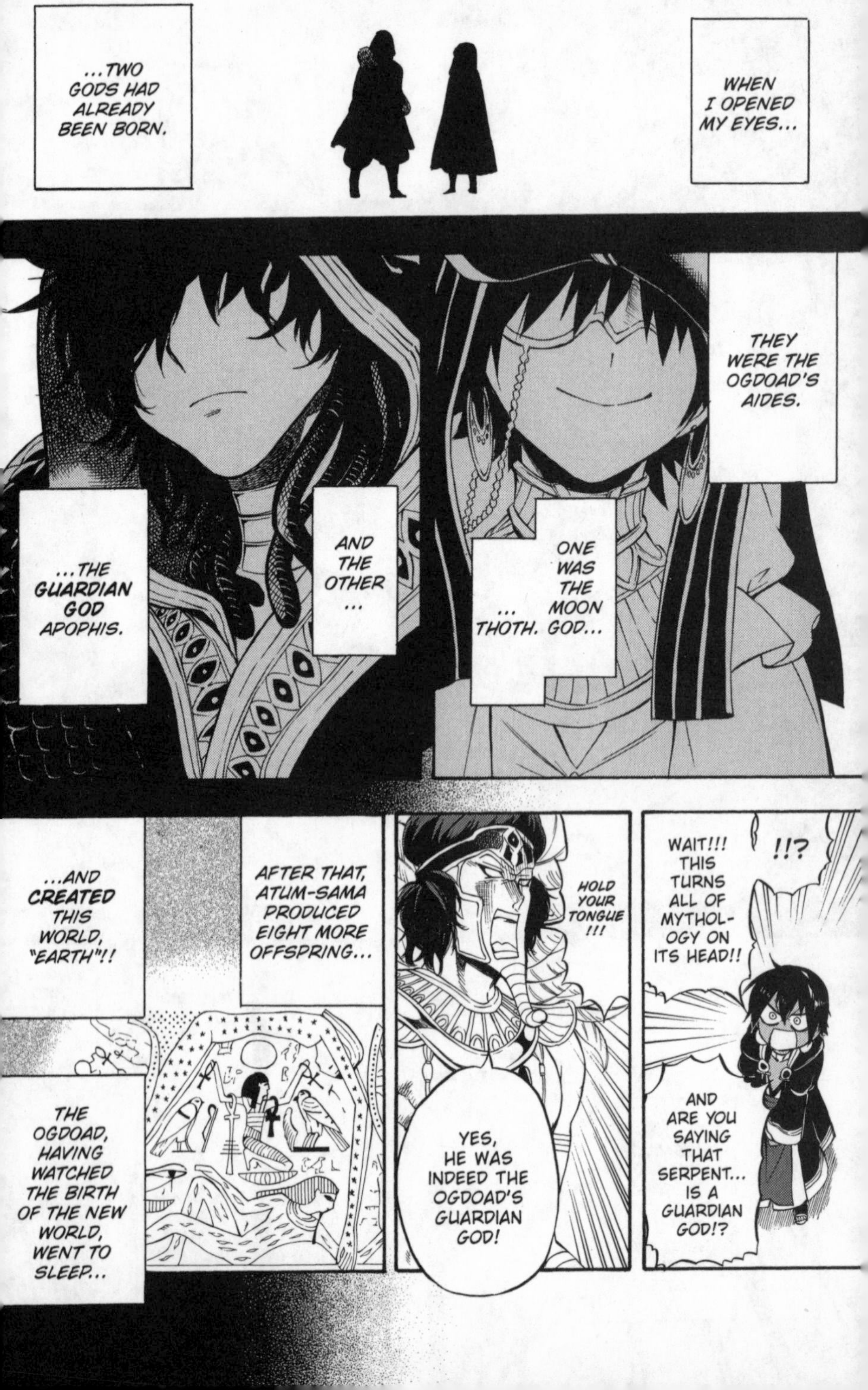
WHEN I OPENED MY EYES...
...TWO GODS HAD ALREADY BEEN BORN.
THEY WERE THE OGDOAD'S AIDES.
ONE WAS THE MOON GOD...
...THOTH.
AND THE OTHER...
...THE GUARDIAN GOD APOPHIS.
!!?
WAIT!!! THIS TURNS ALL OF MYTHOLOGY ON ITS HEAD!!
AND ARE YOU SAYING THAT SERPENT... IS A GUARDIAN GOD!?
HOLD YOUR TONGUE!!!
YES, HE WAS INDEED THE OGDOAD'S GUARDIAN GOD!
AFTER THAT, ATUM-SAMA PRODUCED EIGHT MORE OFFSPRING...
...AND CREATED THIS WORLD, "EARTH"!!
THE OGDOAD, HAVING WATCHED THE BIRTH OF THE NEW WORLD, WENT TO SLEEP...

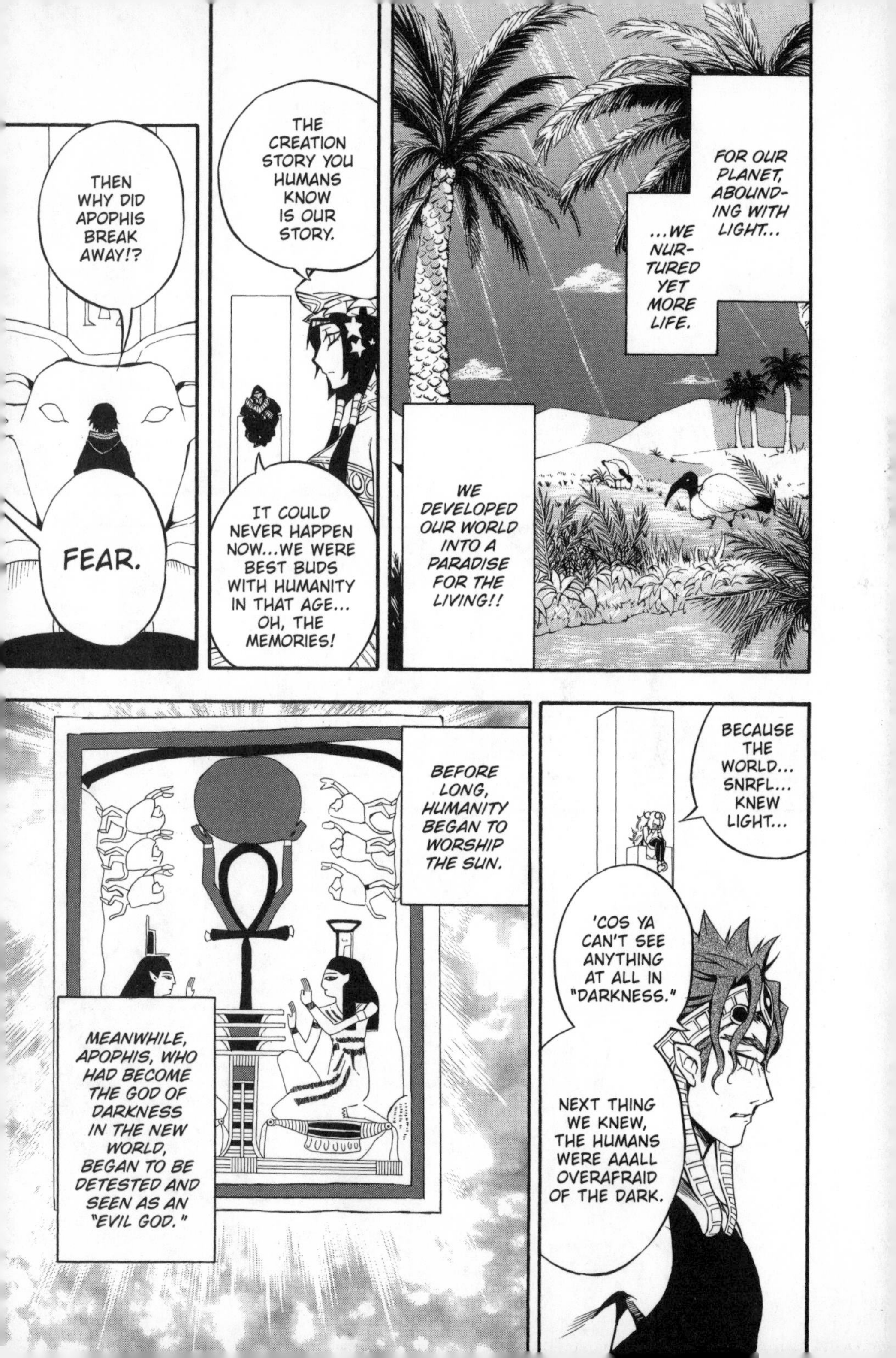

FOR OUR PLANET, ABOUNDING WITH LIGHT...
...WE NURTURED YET MORE LIFE.
WE DEVELOPED OUR WORLD INTO A PARADISE FOR THE LIVING!!
THE CREATION STORY YOU HUMANS KNOW IS OUR STORY.
IT COULD NEVER HAPPEN NOW...WE WERE BEST BUDS WITH HUMANITY IN THAT AGE... OH, THE MEMORIES!
THEN WHY DID APOPHIS BREAK AWAY!?
FEAR.
BECAUSE THE WORLD... SNRFL... KNEW LIGHT...
'COS YA CAN'T SEE ANYTHING AT ALL IN "DARKNESS."
NEXT THING WE KNEW, THE HUMANS WERE AAALL OVERAFRAID OF THE DARK.
BEFORE LONG, HUMANITY BEGAN TO WORSHIP THE SUN.
MEANWHILE, APOPHIS, WHO HAD BECOME THE GOD OF DARKNESS IN THE NEW WORLD, BEGAN TO BE DETESTED AND SEEN AS AN "EVIL GOD."

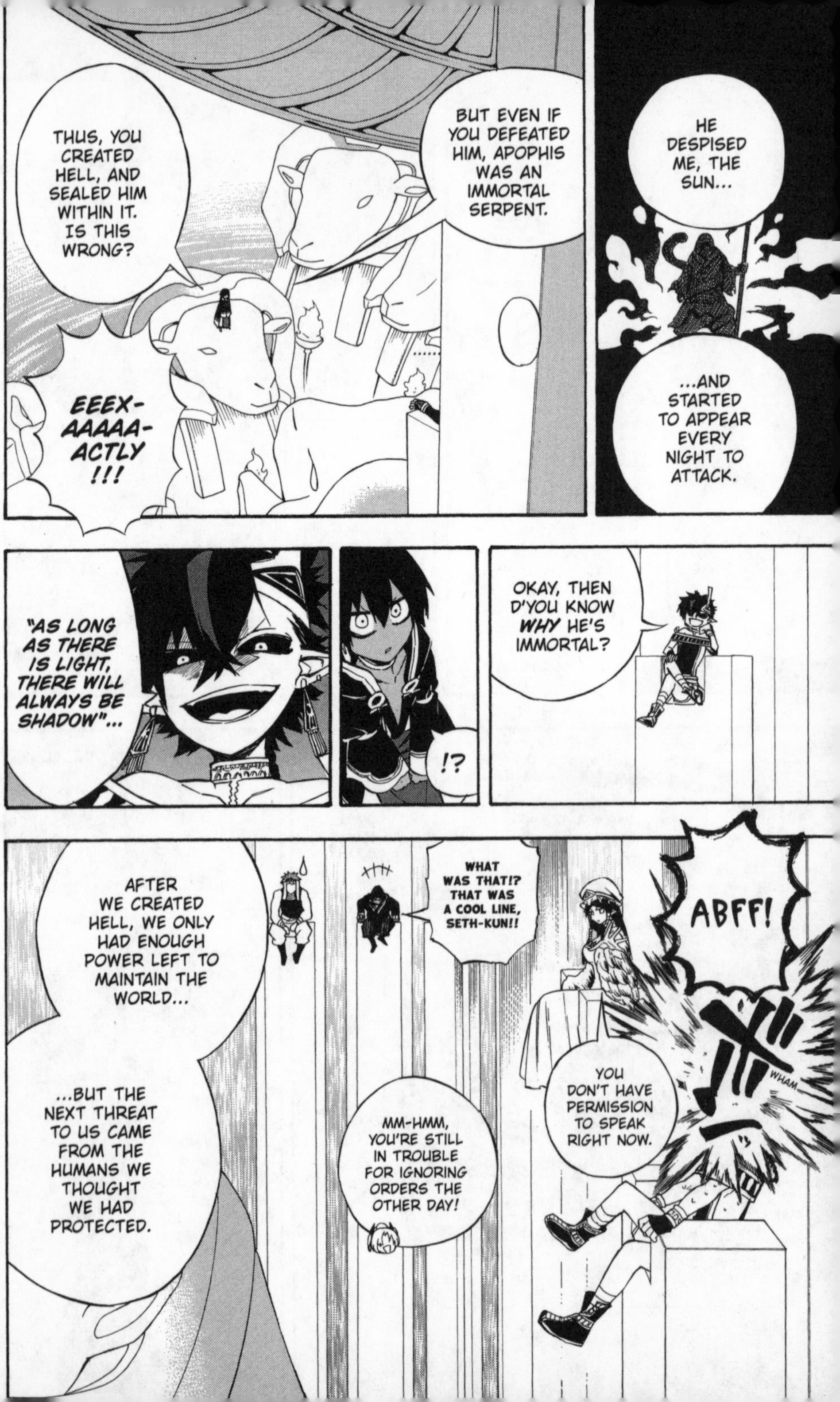
HE DESPISED ME, THE SUN...
...AND STARTED TO APPEAR EVERY NIGHT TO ATTACK.
BUT EVEN IF YOU DEFEATED HIM, APOPHIS WAS AN IMMORTAL SERPENT.
THUS, YOU CREATED HELL, AND SEALED HIM WITHIN IT. IS THIS WRONG?
EEEX-AAAAA-ACTLY!!!
OKAY, THEN D'YOU KNOW WHY HE'S IMMORTAL?
!?
"AS LONG AS THERE IS LIGHT, THERE WILL ALWAYS BE SHADOW"...
WHAT WAS THAT!? THAT WAS A COOL LINE, SETH-KUN!!
ABFF!
WHAM
YOU DON'T HAVE PERMISSION TO SPEAK RIGHT NOW.
MM-HMM, YOU'RE STILL IN TROUBLE FOR IGNORING ORDERS THE OTHER DAY!
AFTER WE CREATED HELL, WE ONLY HAD ENOUGH POWER LEFT TO MAINTAIN THE WORLD...
...BUT THE NEXT THREAT TO US CAME FROM THE HUMANS WE THOUGHT WE HAD PROTECTED.

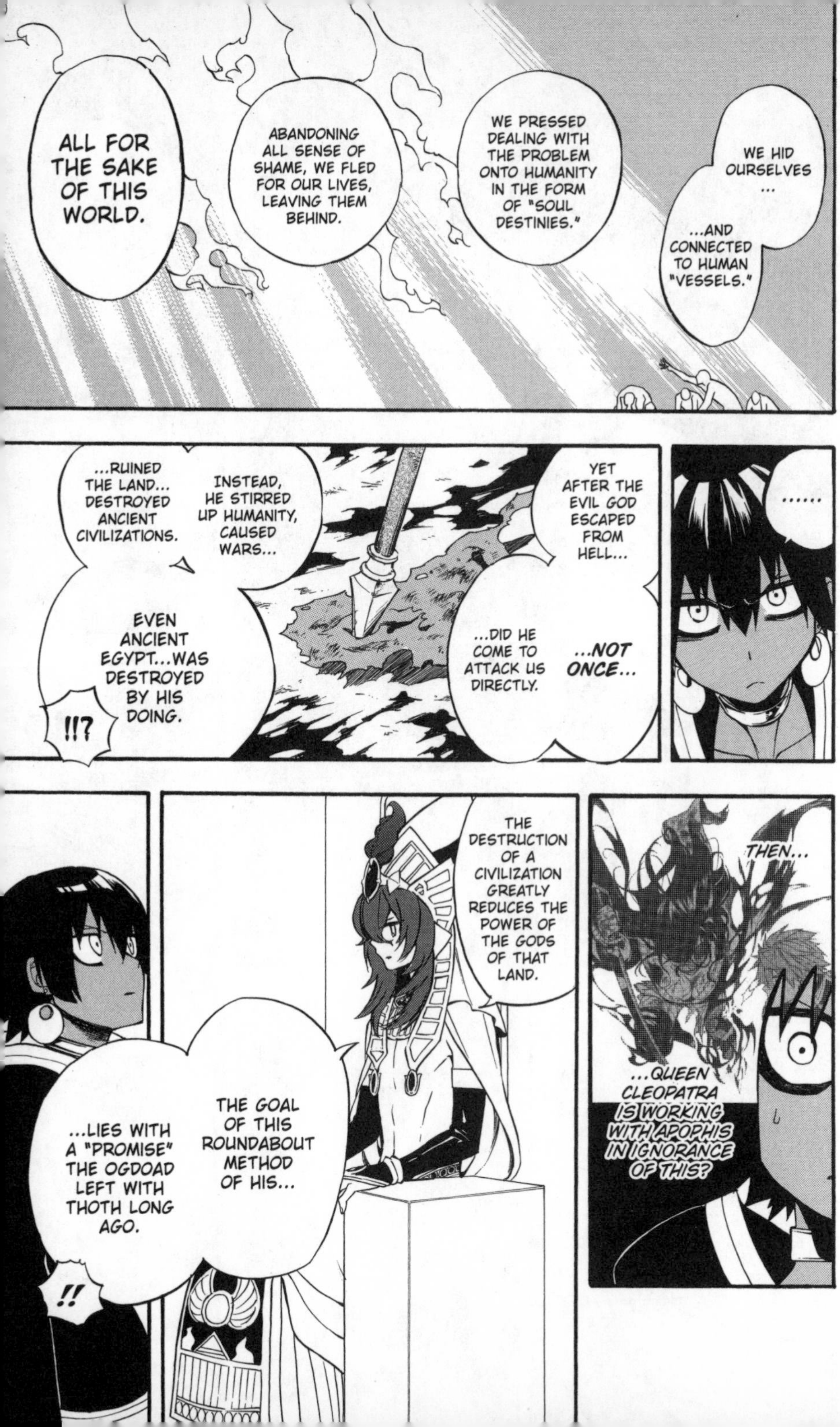
WE HID OURSELVES ...
...AND CONNECTED TO HUMAN "VESSELS."
WE PRESSED DEALING WITH THE PROBLEM ONTO HUMANITY IN THE FORM OF "SOUL DESTINIES."
ABANDONING ALL SENSE OF SHAME, WE FLED FOR OUR LIVES, LEAVING THEM BEHIND.
ALL FOR THE SAKE OF THIS WORLD.
......
YET AFTER THE EVIL GOD ESCAPED FROM HELL...
...NOT ONCE...
...DID HE COME TO ATTACK US DIRECTLY.
INSTEAD, HE STIRRED UP HUMANITY, CAUSED WARS...
...RUINED THE LAND... DESTROYED ANCIENT CIVILIZATIONS.
EVEN ANCIENT EGYPT...WAS DESTROYED BY HIS DOING.
!!?
THEN...
...QUEEN CLEOPATRA IS WORKING WITH APOPHIS IN IGNORANCE OF THIS?
THE DESTRUCTION OF A CIVILIZATION GREATLY REDUCES THE POWER OF THE GODS OF THAT LAND.
THE GOAL OF THIS ROUNDABOUT METHOD OF HIS...
...LIES WITH A "PROMISE" THE OGDOAD LEFT WITH THOTH LONG AGO.
!!

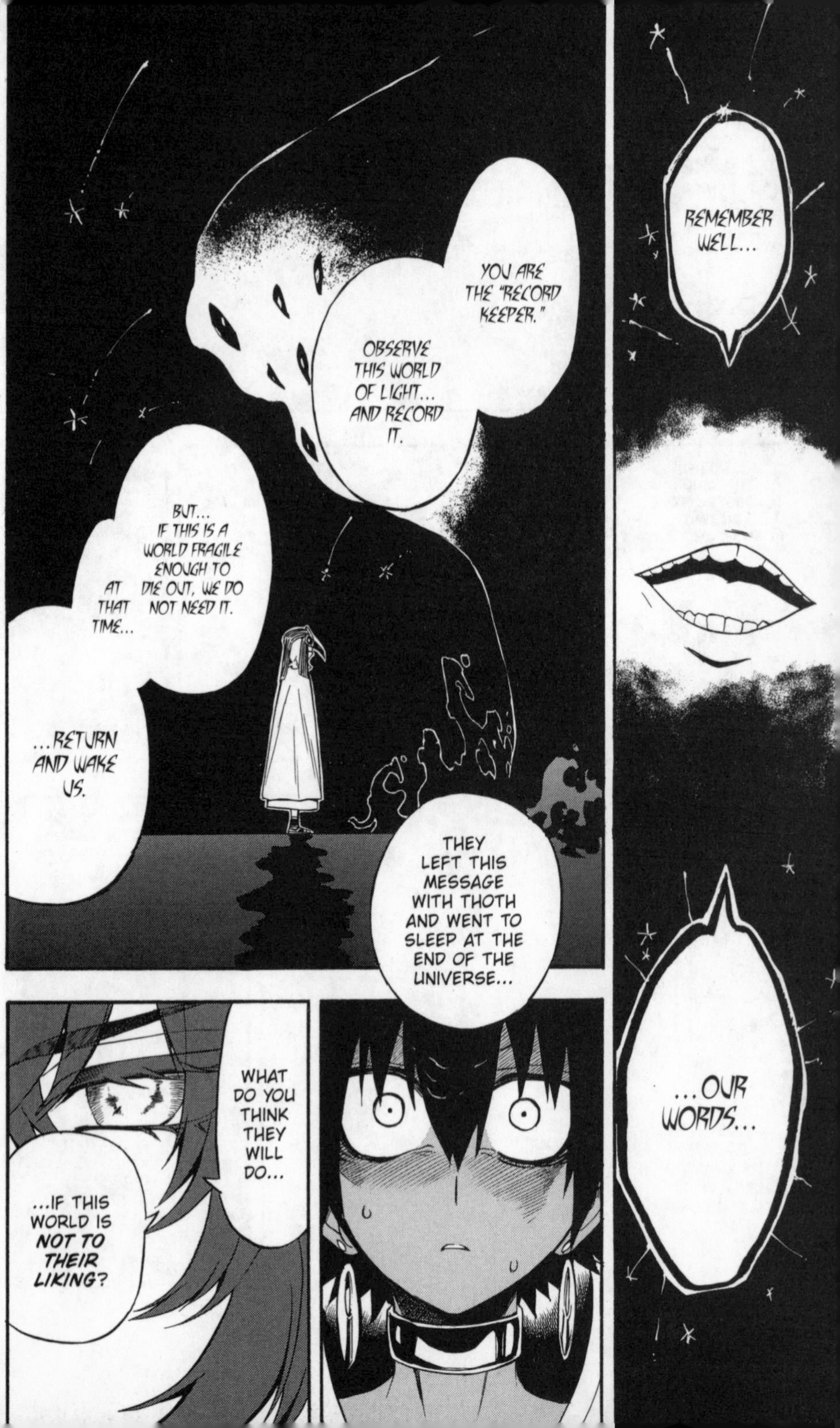
REMEMBER WELL...
...OUR WORDS...
YOU ARE THE "RECORD KEEPER."
OBSERVE THIS WORLD OF LIGHT... AND RECORD IT.
BUT... IF THIS IS A WORLD FRAGILE ENOUGH TO DIE OUT, WE DO NOT NEED IT.
AT THAT TIME...
...RETURN AND WAKE US.
THEY LEFT THIS MESSAGE WITH THOTH AND WENT TO SLEEP AT THE END OF THE UNIVERSE...
WHAT DO YOU THINK THEY WILL DO...
...IF THIS WORLD IS ***NOT TO THEIR LIKING***?

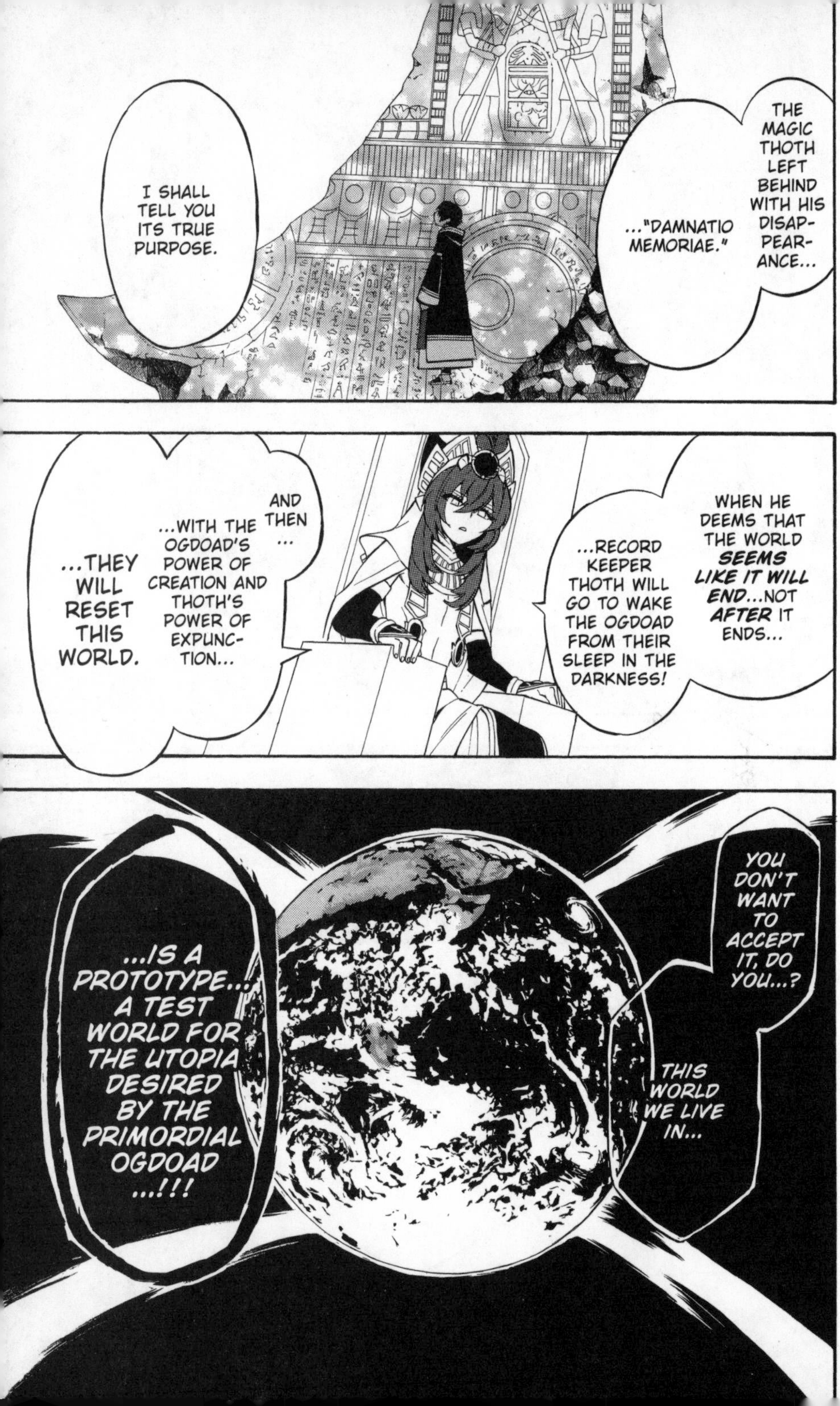
THE MAGIC THOTH LEFT BEHIND WITH HIS DISAPPEARANCE...
..."DAMNATIO MEMORIAE."
I SHALL TELL YOU ITS TRUE PURPOSE.
WHEN HE DEEMS THAT THE WORLD *SEEMS LIKE IT WILL END*...NOT *AFTER* IT ENDS...
...RECORD KEEPER THOTH WILL GO TO WAKE THE OGDOAD FROM THEIR SLEEP IN THE DARKNESS!
AND THEN...
...WITH THE OGDOAD'S POWER OF CREATION AND THOTH'S POWER OF EXPUNCTION...
...THEY WILL RESET THIS WORLD.
YOU DON'T WANT TO ACCEPT IT, DO YOU...?
THIS WORLD WE LIVE IN...
...IS A PROTOTYPE... A TEST WORLD FOR THE UTOPIA DESIRED BY THE PRIMORDIAL OGDOAD...!!!

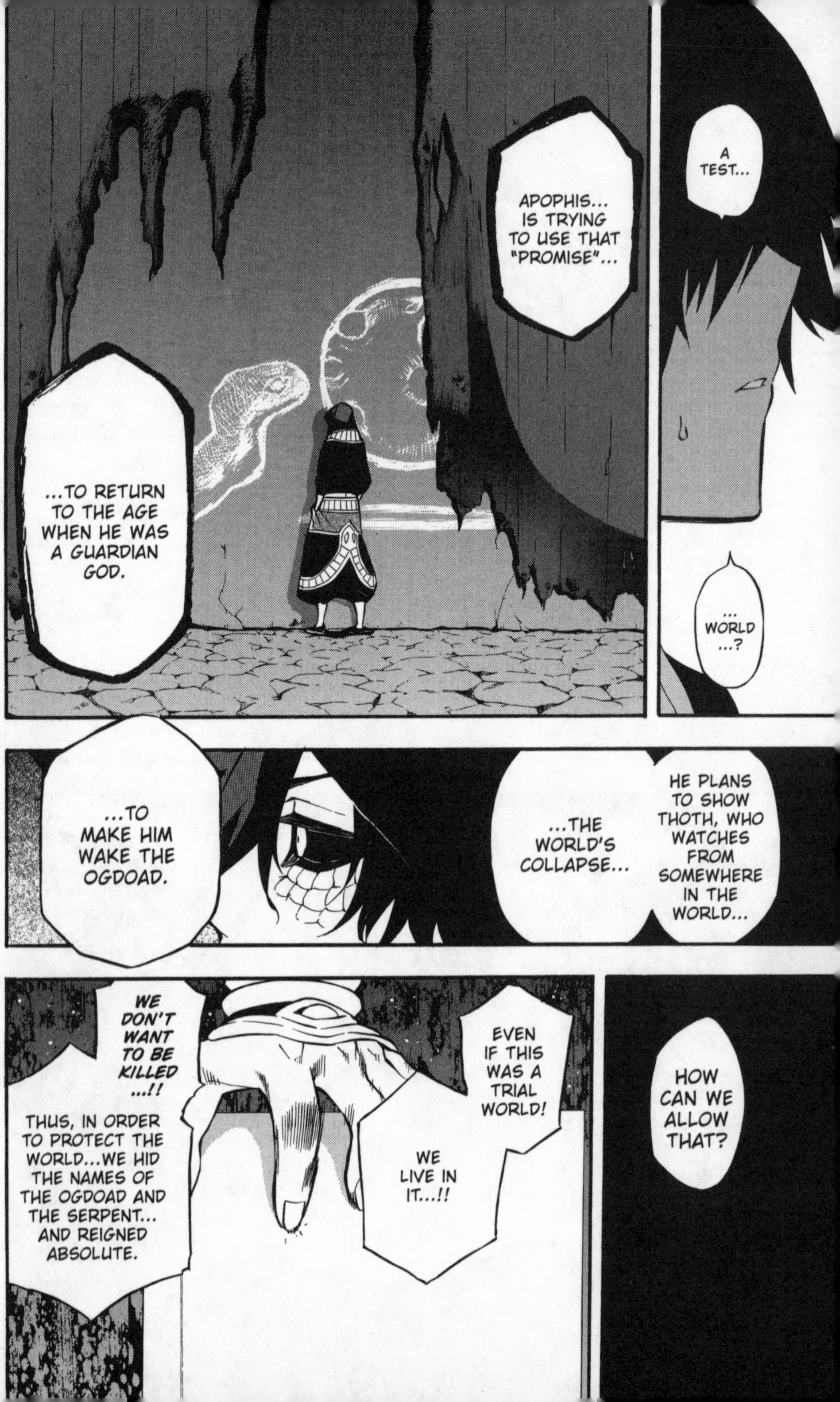
A TEST...
...WORLD...?
APOPHIS... IS TRYING TO USE THAT "PROMISE"...
...TO RETURN TO THE AGE WHEN HE WAS A GUARDIAN GOD.
HE PLANS TO SHOW THOTH, WHO WATCHES FROM SOMEWHERE IN THE WORLD...
...THE WORLD'S COLLAPSE...
...TO MAKE HIM WAKE THE OGDOAD.
HOW CAN WE ALLOW THAT?
EVEN IF THIS WAS A TRIAL WORLD!
WE LIVE IN IT...!!
WE DON'T WANT TO BE KILLED...!!
THUS, IN ORDER TO PROTECT THE WORLD...WE HID THE NAMES OF THE OGDOAD AND THE SERPENT... AND REIGNED ABSOLUTE.

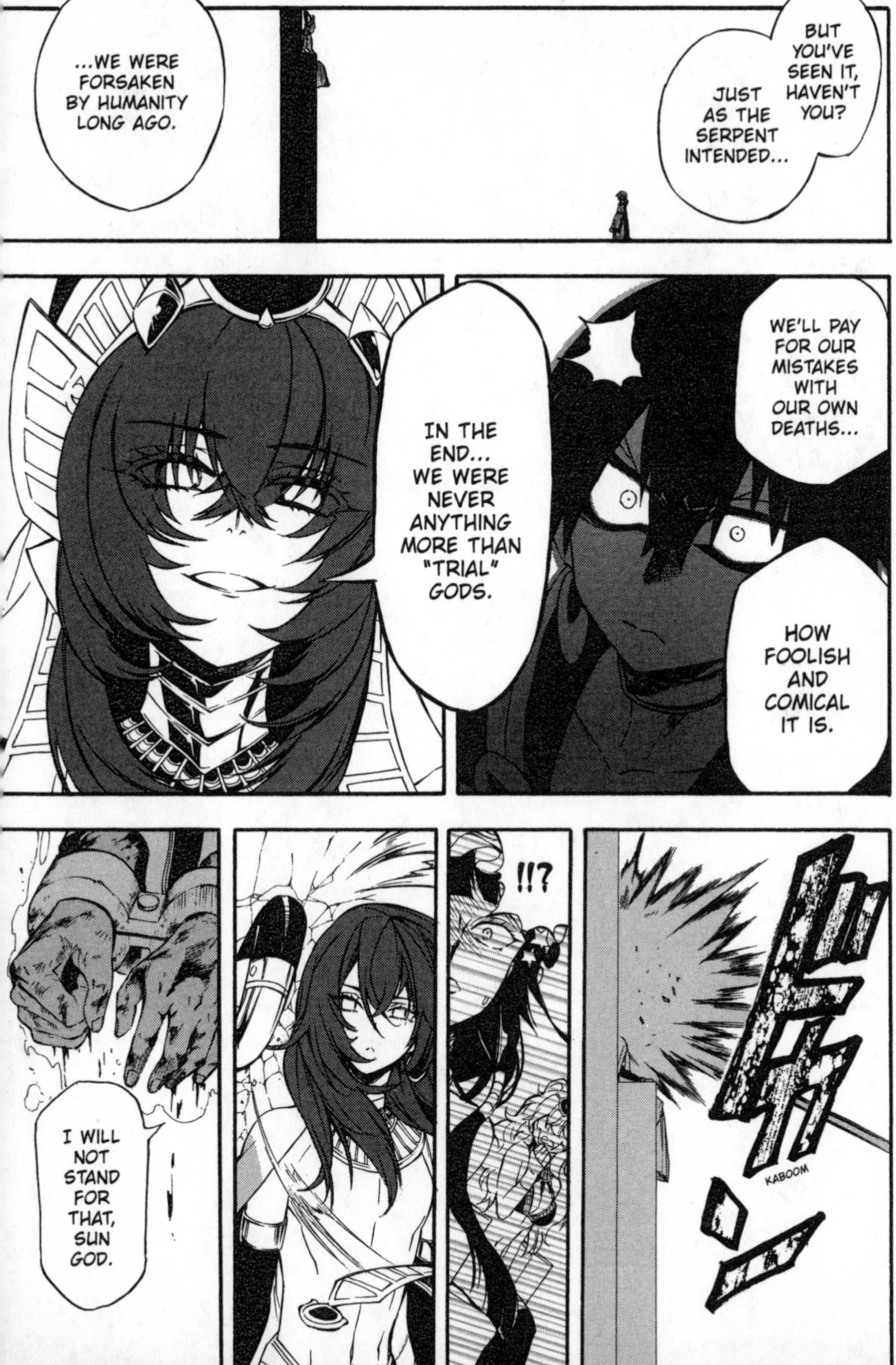
BUT YOU'VE SEEN IT, HAVEN'T YOU?
JUST AS THE SERPENT INTENDED...
...WE WERE FORSAKEN BY HUMANITY LONG AGO.
WE'LL PAY FOR OUR MISTAKES WITH OUR OWN DEATHS...
HOW FOOLISH AND COMICAL IT IS.
IN THE END... WE WERE NEVER ANYTHING MORE THAN "TRIAL" GODS.
KABOOM
!!?
I WILL NOT STAND FOR THAT, SUN GOD.

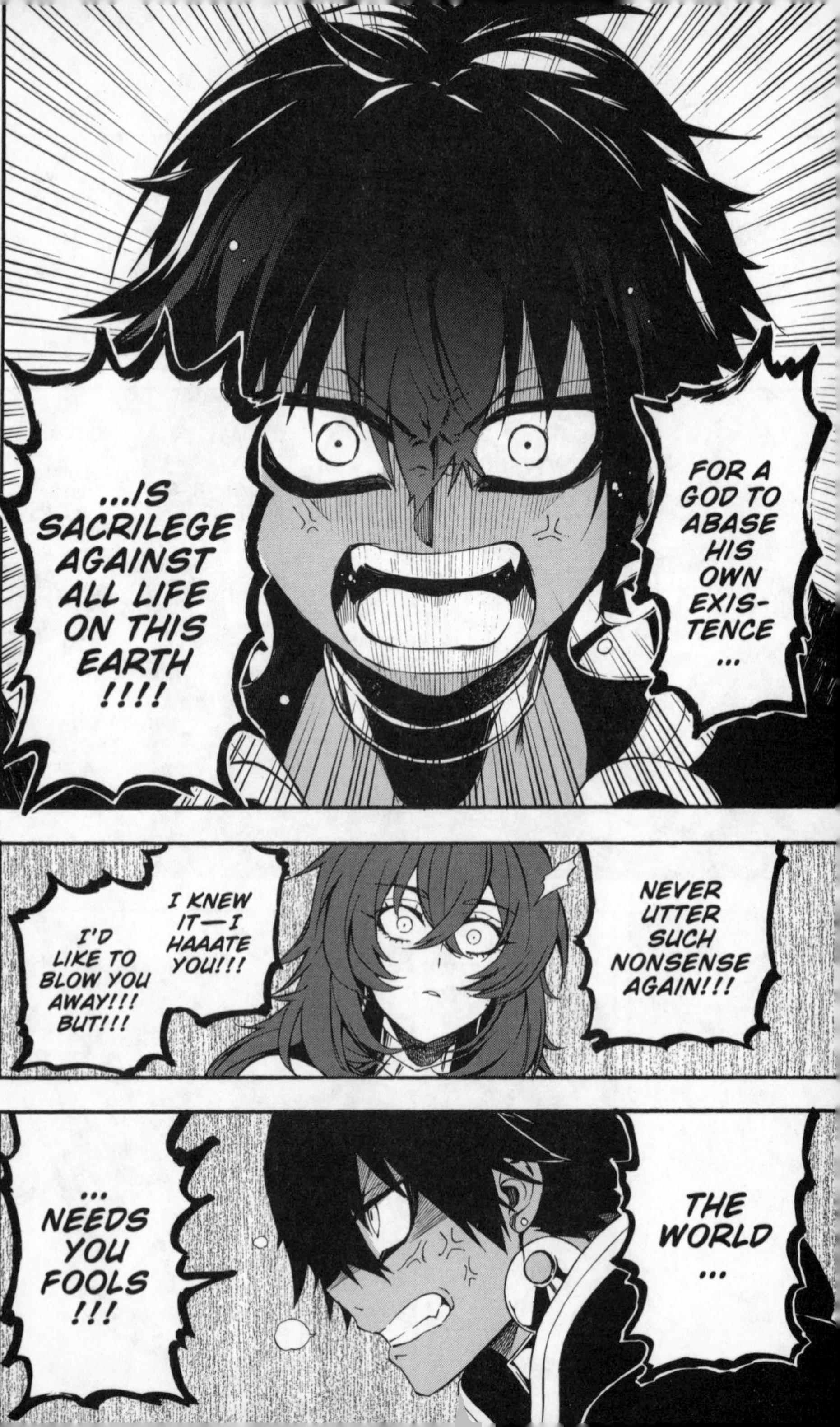
FOR A GOD TO ABASE HIS OWN EXISTENCE...
...IS SACRILEGE AGAINST ALL LIFE ON THIS EARTH!!!!
NEVER UTTER SUCH NONSENSE AGAIN!!!
I KNEW IT—I HAAATE YOU!!!
I'D LIKE TO BLOW YOU AWAY!!! BUT!!!
THE WORLD...
...NEEDS YOU FOOLS!!!

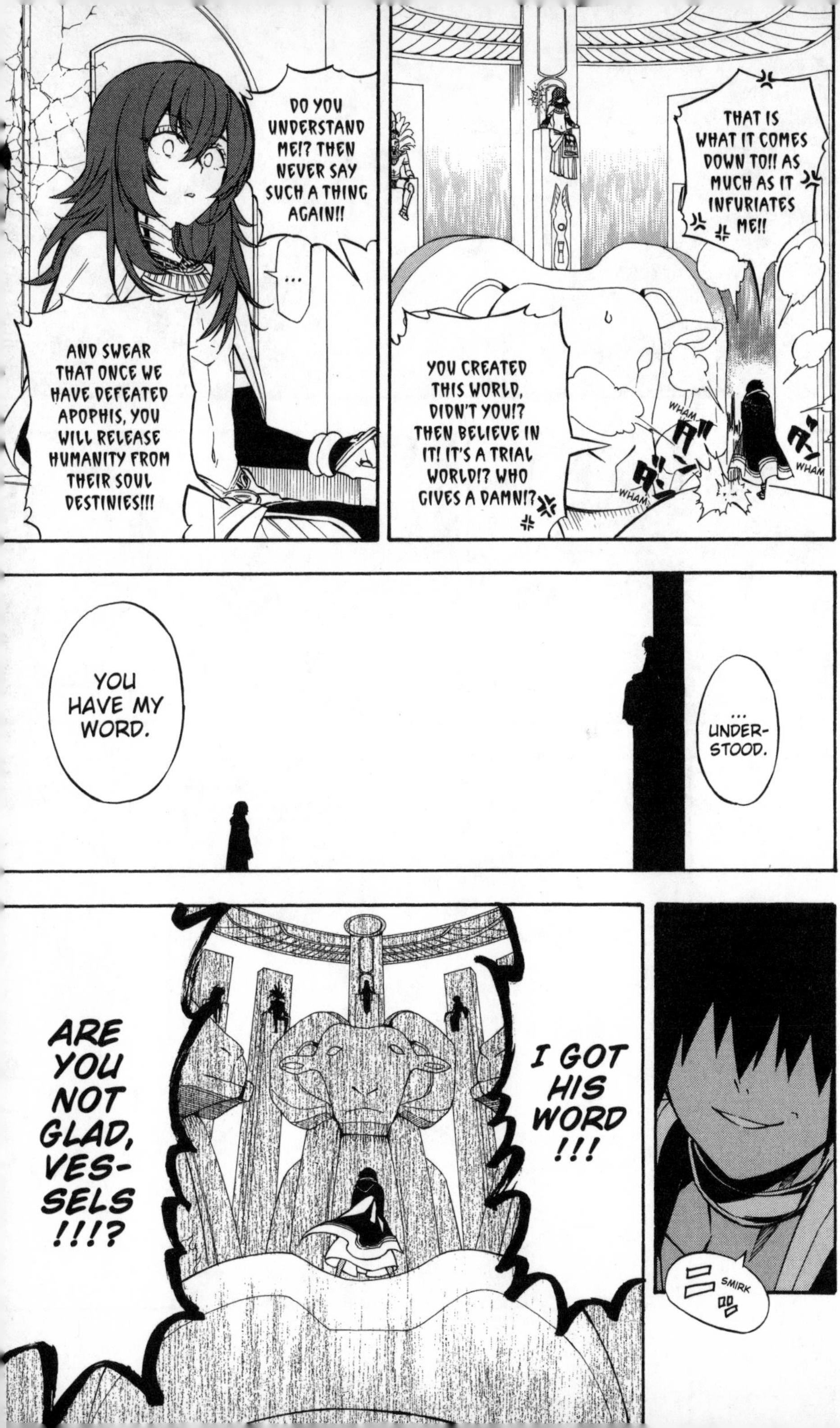
THAT IS WHAT IT COMES DOWN TO!! AS MUCH AS IT INFURIATES ME!!
YOU CREATED THIS WORLD, DIDN'T YOU!? THEN BELIEVE IN IT! IT'S A TRIAL WORLD!? WHO GIVES A DAMN!?
WHAM
WHAM
WHAM
DO YOU UNDERSTAND ME!? THEN NEVER SAY SUCH A THING AGAIN!!
...
AND SWEAR THAT ONCE WE HAVE DEFEATED APOPHIS, YOU WILL RELEASE HUMANITY FROM THEIR SOUL DESTINIES!!!
... UNDER-STOOD.
YOU HAVE MY WORD.
SMIRK
I GOT HIS WORD !!!
ARE YOU NOT GLAD, VES-SELS !!!?

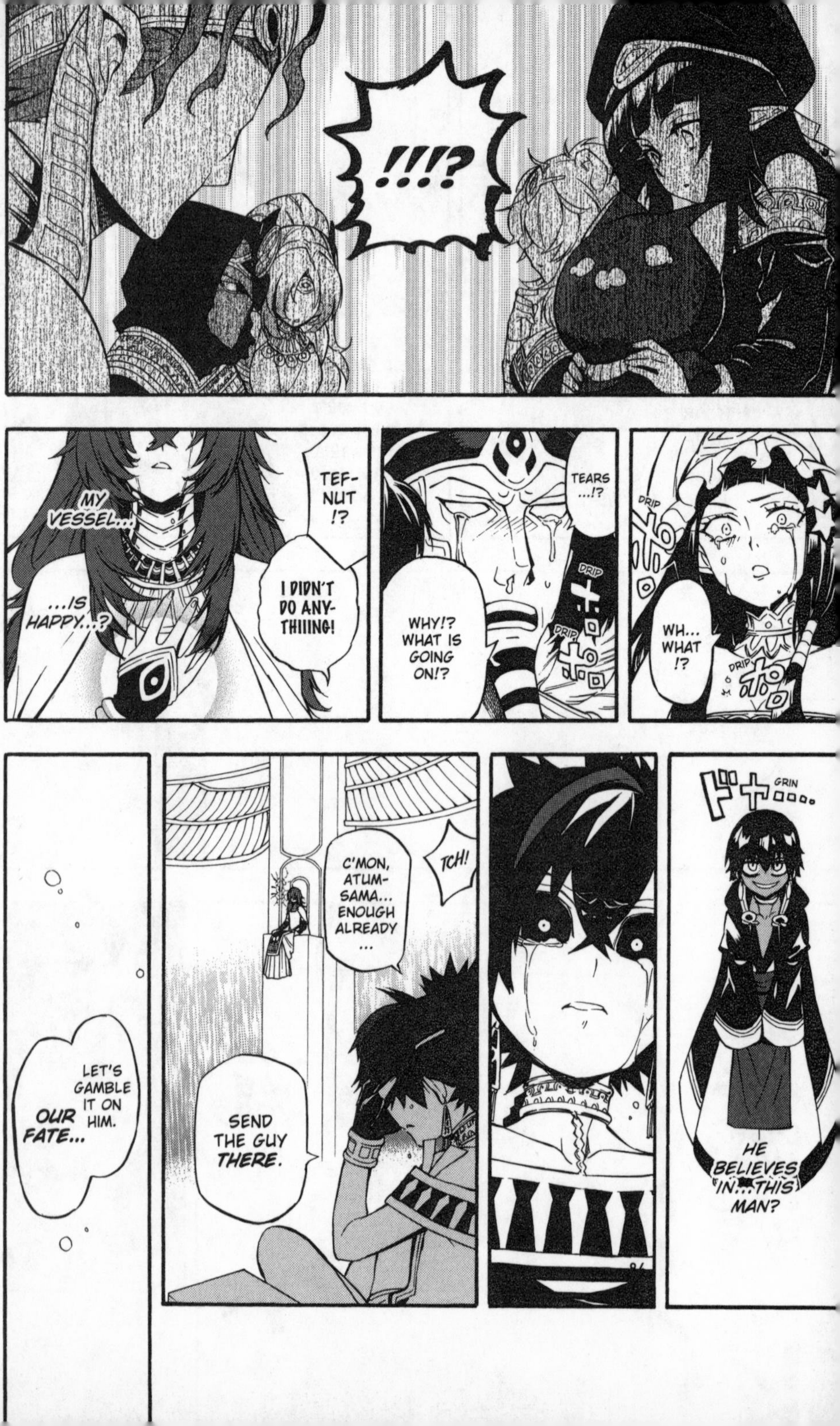
!!!?
DRIP
WH... WHAT !?
DRIP
TEARS ...!?
DRIP
DRIP
WHY!? WHAT IS GOING ON!?
TEF-NUT !?
MY VESSEL...
I DIDN'T DO ANY-THIIING!
...IS HAPPY...?
GRIN
HE BELIEVES IN... THIS MAN?
TCH!
C'MON, ATUM-SAMA... ENOUGH ALREADY...
SEND THE GUY THERE.
LET'S GAMBLE IT ON HIM.
OUR FATE...

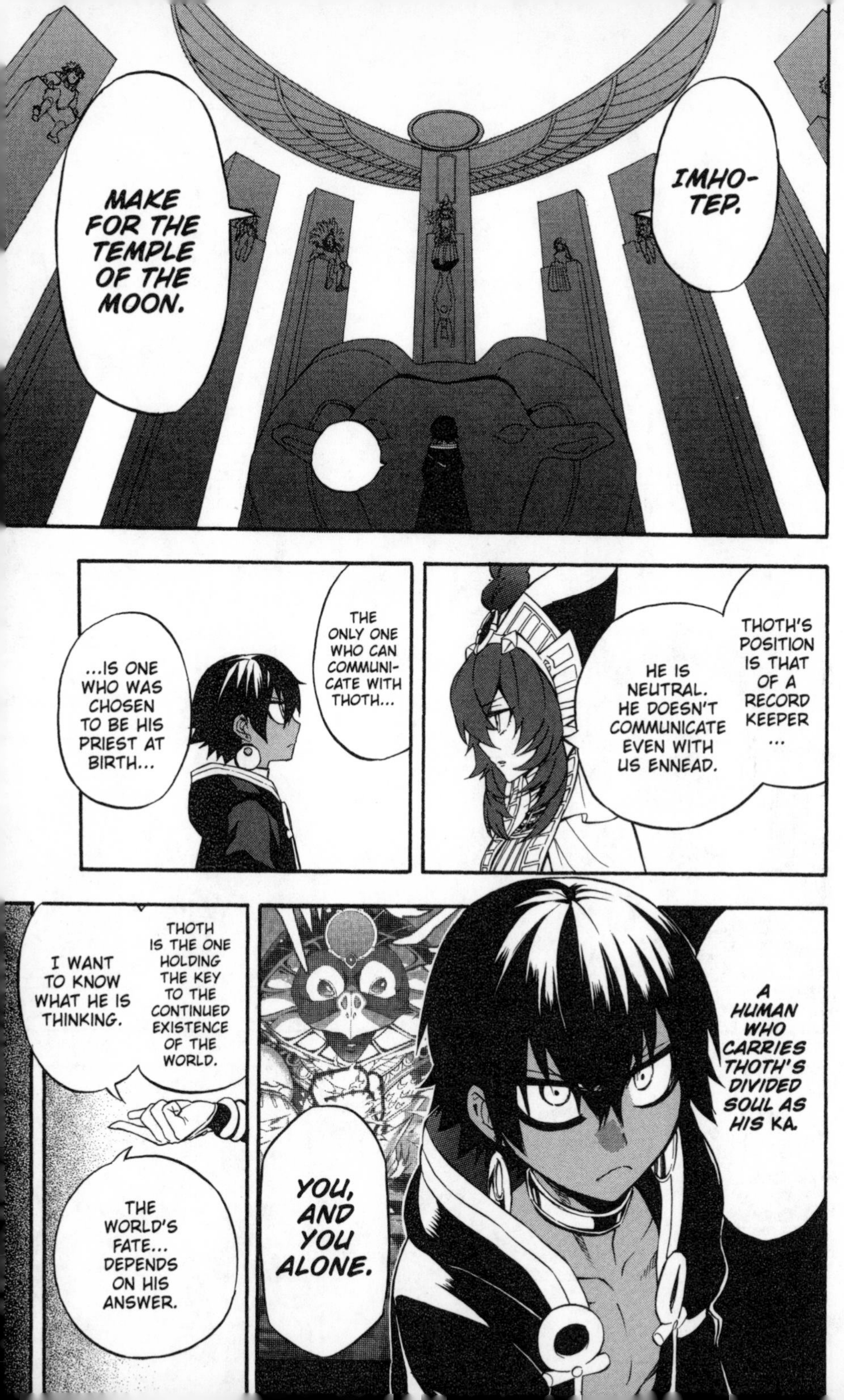
IMHO-TEP.
MAKE FOR THE TEMPLE OF THE MOON.
THOTH'S POSITION IS THAT OF A RECORD KEEPER ...
HE IS NEUTRAL. HE DOESN'T COMMUNICATE EVEN WITH US ENNEAD.
THE ONLY ONE WHO CAN COMMUNICATE WITH THOTH...
...IS ONE WHO WAS CHOSEN TO BE HIS PRIEST AT BIRTH...
A HUMAN WHO CARRIES THOTH'S DIVIDED SOUL AS HIS KA.
YOU, AND YOU ALONE.
THOTH IS THE ONE HOLDING THE KEY TO THE CONTINUED EXISTENCE OF THE WORLD.
I WANT TO KNOW WHAT HE IS THINKING.
THE WORLD'S FATE... DEPENDS ON HIS ANSWER.

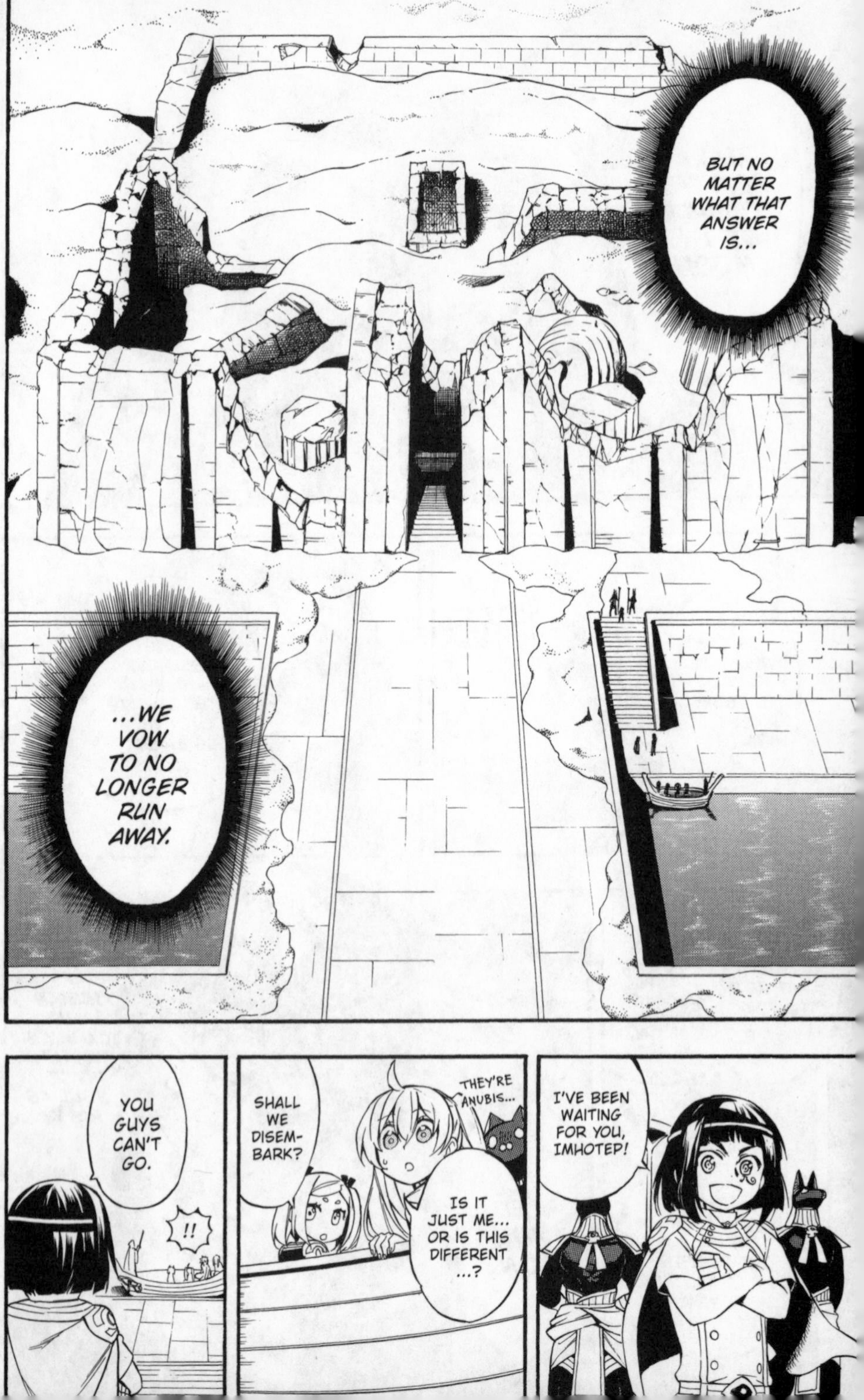
BUT NO MATTER WHAT THAT ANSWER IS...
...WE VOW TO NO LONGER RUN AWAY.
I'VE BEEN WAITING FOR YOU, IMHOTEP!
THEY'RE ANUBIS...
SHALL WE DISEMBARK?
IS IT JUST ME... OR IS THIS DIFFERENT ...?
YOU GUYS CAN'T GO.
!!

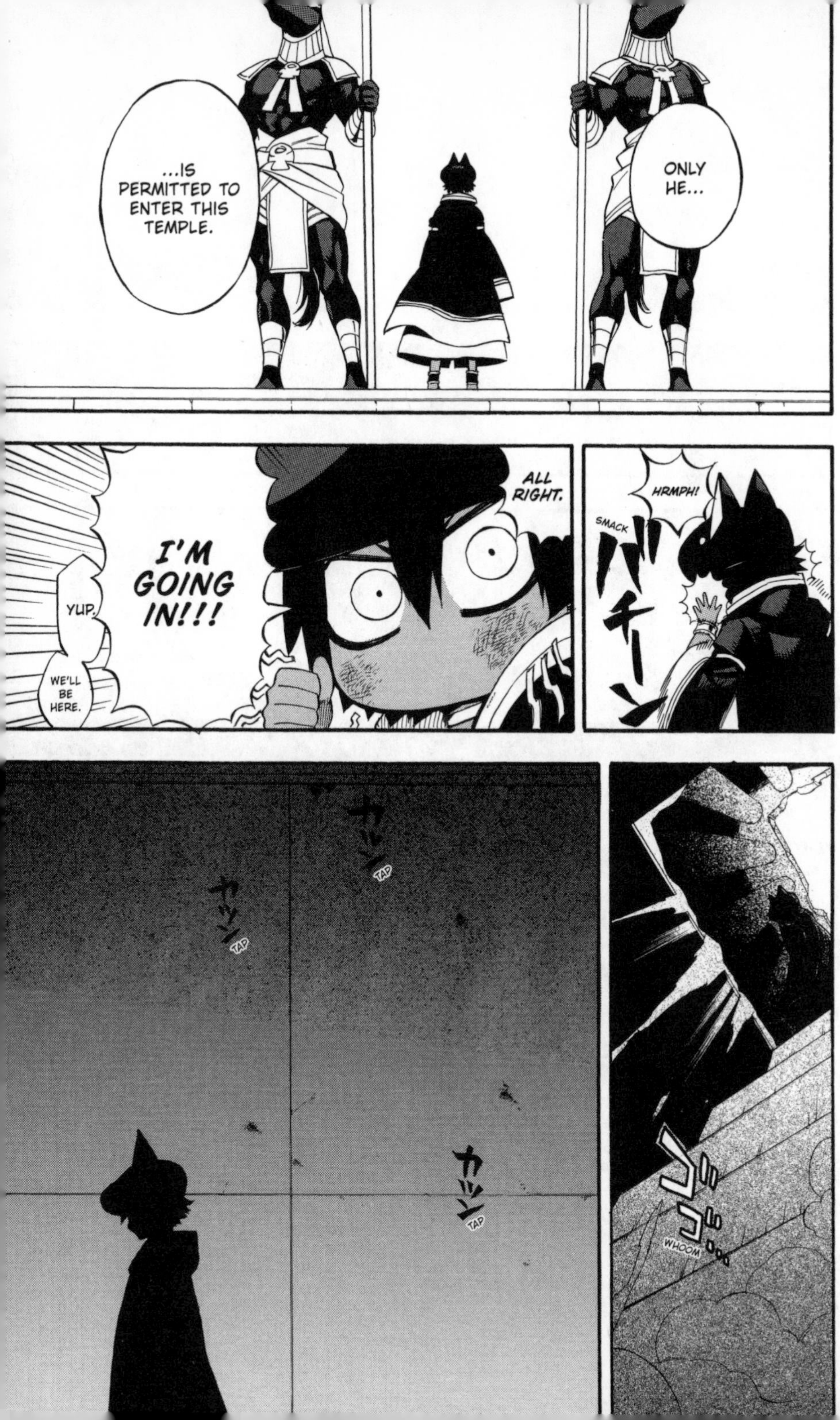
ONLY HE...
...IS PERMITTED TO ENTER THIS TEMPLE.
HRMPH!
SMACK
ALL RIGHT.
I'M GOING IN!!!
YUP.
WE'LL BE HERE.
WHOOM
TAP
TAP
TAP

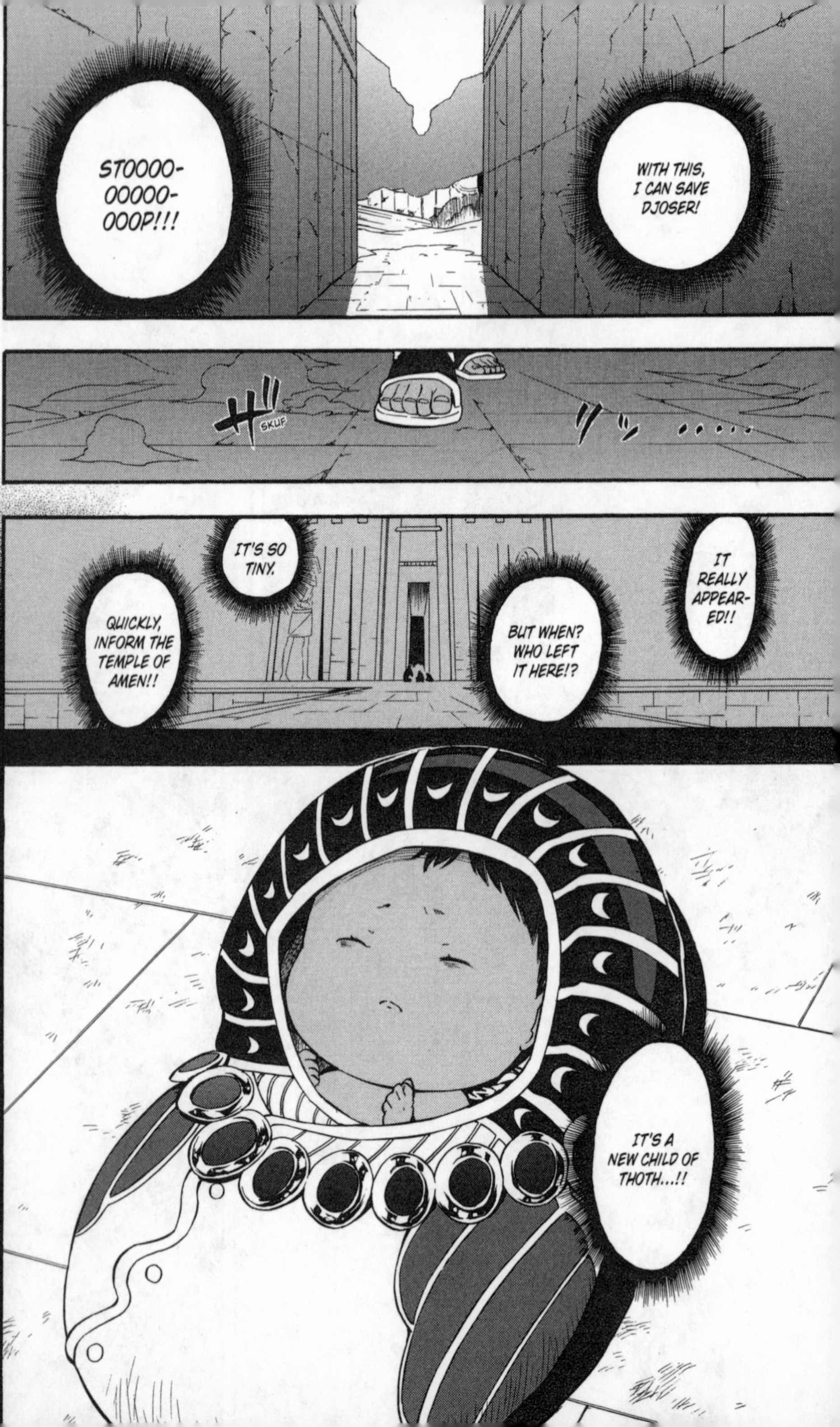
WITH THIS, I CAN SAVE DJOSER!
STOOOO-OOOOO-OOOP!!!
SKUF
IT REALLY APPEARED!!
BUT WHEN? WHO LEFT IT HERE!?
IT'S SO TINY.
QUICKLY, INFORM THE TEMPLE OF AMEN!!
IT'S A NEW CHILD OF THOTH...!!

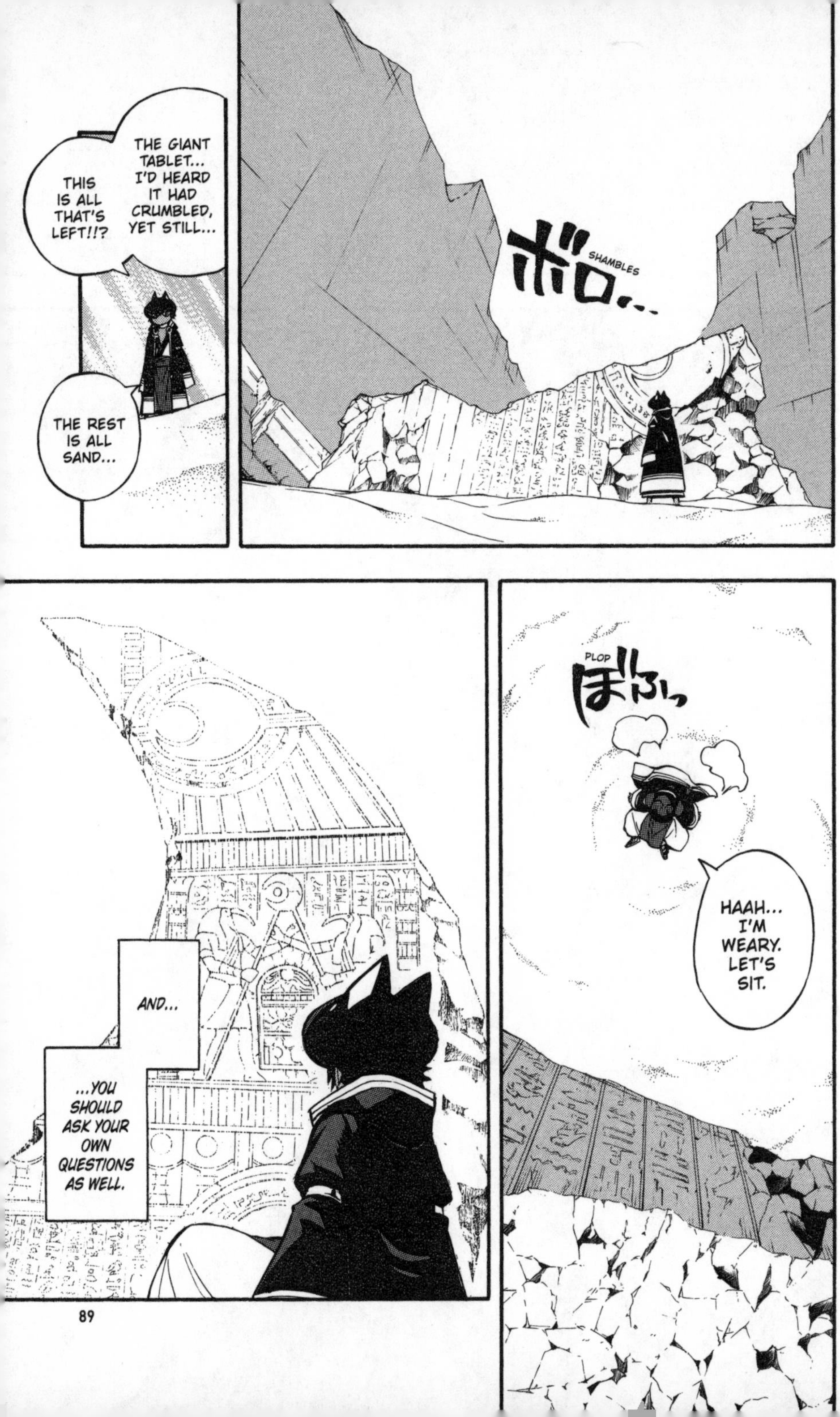
ボロ…
SHAMBLES
THE GIANT TABLET... I'D HEARD IT HAD CRUMBLED, YET STILL...
THIS IS ALL THAT'S LEFT!!?
THE REST IS ALL SAND...
PLOP
ぼふっ
HAAH... I'M WEARY. LET'S SIT.
AND...
...YOU SHOULD ASK YOUR OWN QUESTIONS AS WELL.

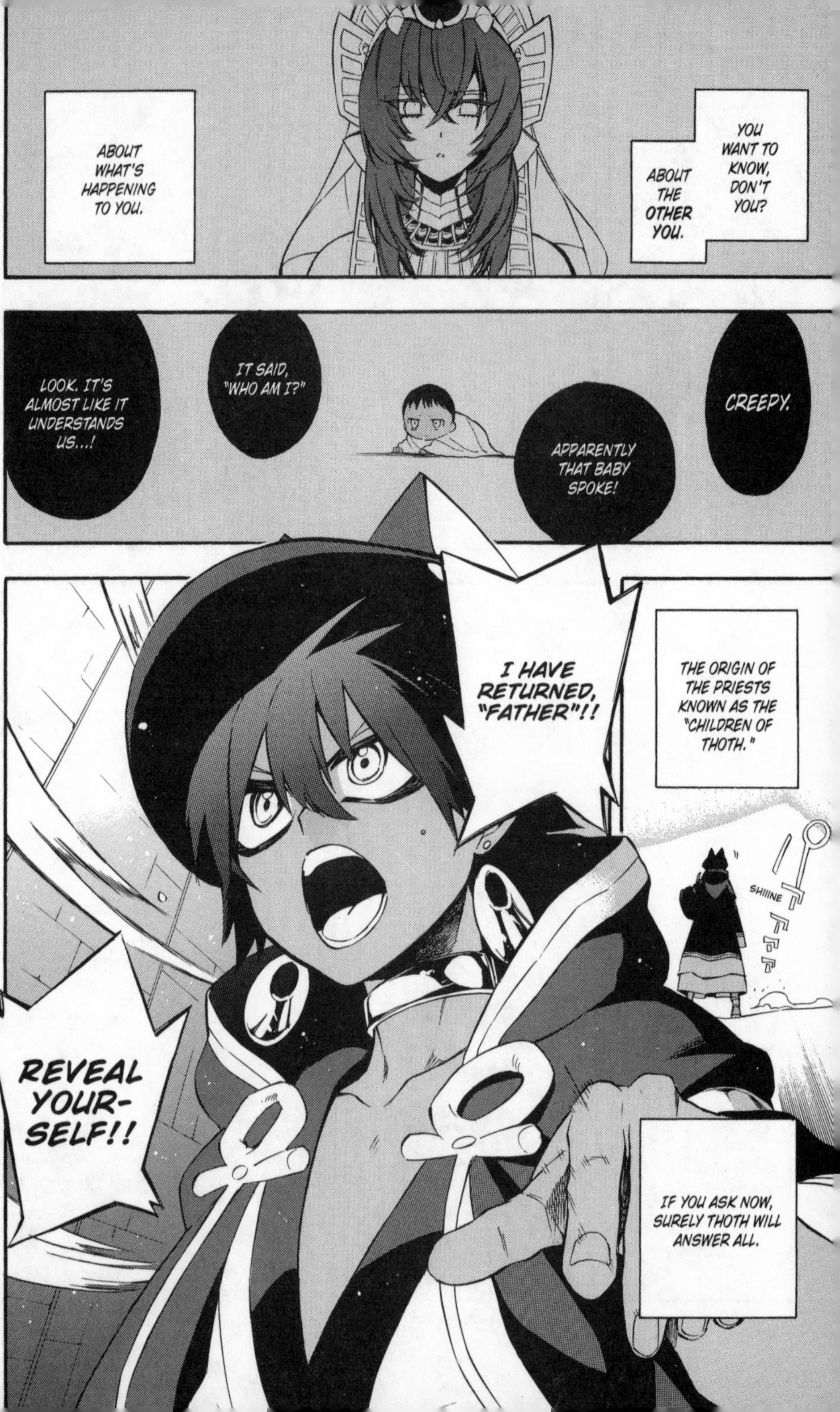
YOU WANT TO KNOW, DON'T YOU?
ABOUT THE OTHER YOU.
ABOUT WHAT'S HAPPENING TO YOU.
CREEPY.
APPARENTLY THAT BABY SPOKE!
IT SAID, "WHO AM I?"
LOOK. IT'S ALMOST LIKE IT UNDERSTANDS US...!
THE ORIGIN OF THE PRIESTS KNOWN AS THE "CHILDREN OF THOTH."
SHIIINE
I HAVE RETURNED, "FATHER"!!
IF YOU ASK NOW, SURELY THOTH WILL ANSWER ALL.
REVEAL YOUR-SELF!!

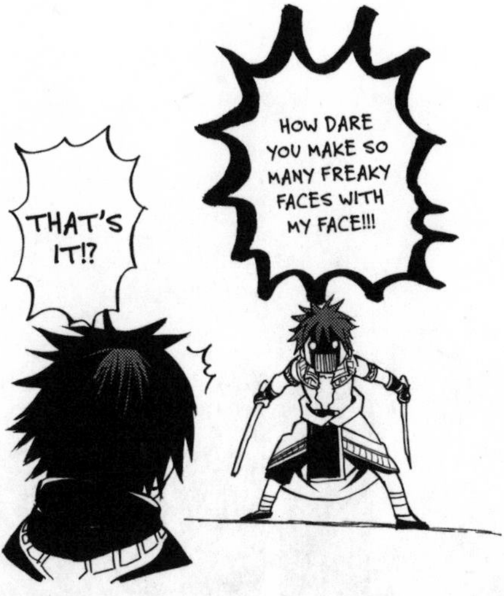
HOW DARE YOU MAKE SO MANY FREAKY FACES WITH MY FACE!!!
THAT'S IT!?

Great Priest Imhotep

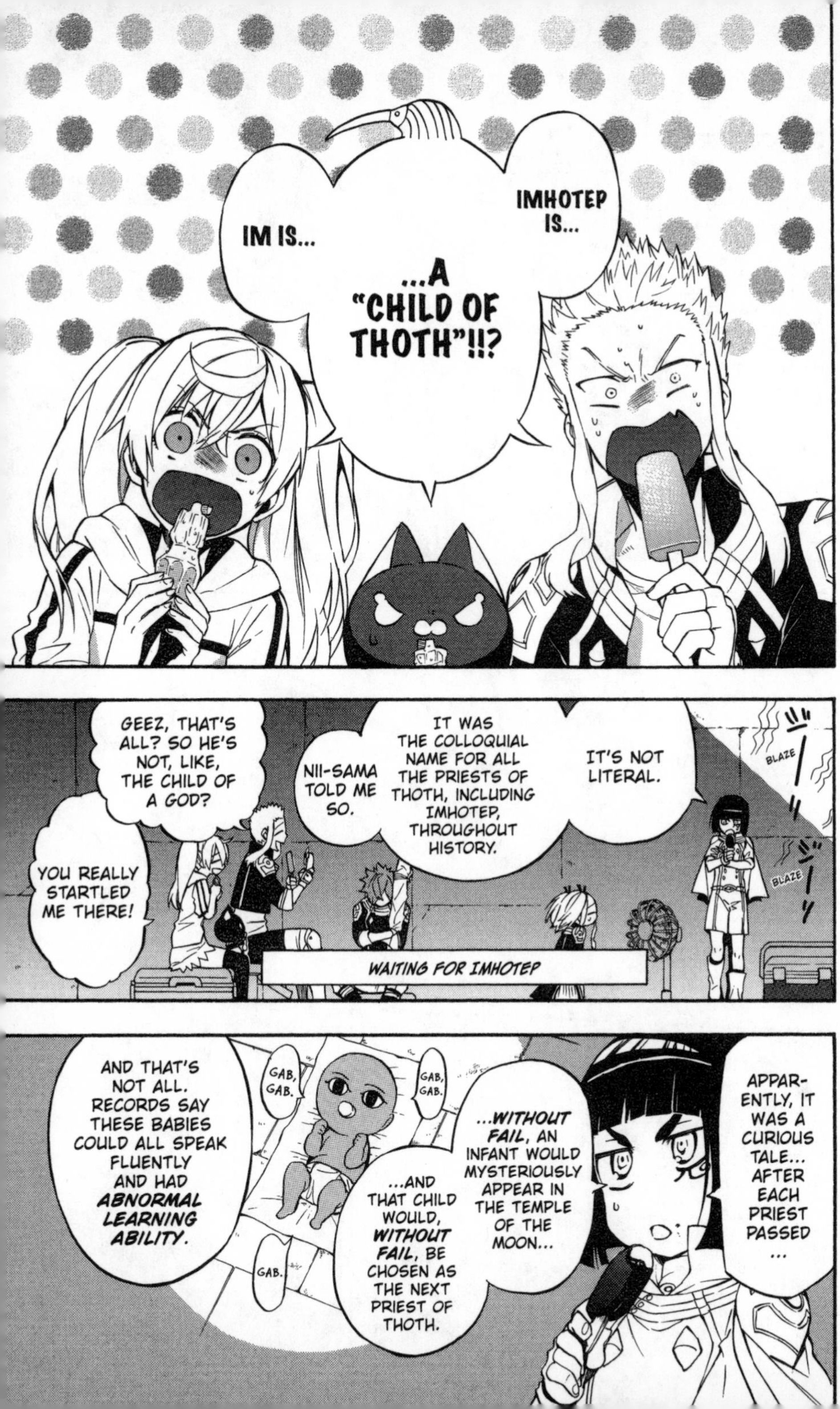
IMHOTEP IS...
IM IS...
...A "CHILD OF THOTH"!!?
BLAZE
BLAZE
IT'S NOT LITERAL.
IT WAS THE COLLOQUIAL NAME FOR ALL THE PRIESTS OF THOTH, INCLUDING IMHOTEP, THROUGHOUT HISTORY.
NII-SAMA TOLD ME SO.
GEEZ, THAT'S ALL? SO HE'S NOT, LIKE, THE CHILD OF A GOD?
YOU REALLY STARTLED ME THERE!
WAITING FOR IMHOTEP
APPARENTLY, IT WAS A CURIOUS TALE... AFTER EACH PRIEST PASSED...
...WITHOUT FAIL, AN INFANT WOULD MYSTERIOUSLY APPEAR IN THE TEMPLE OF THE MOON...
...AND THAT CHILD WOULD, WITHOUT FAIL, BE CHOSEN AS THE NEXT PRIEST OF THOTH.
GAB, GAB.
GAB, GAB.
GAB.
AND THAT'S NOT ALL. RECORDS SAY THESE BABIES COULD ALL SPEAK FLUENTLY AND HAD ABNORMAL LEARNING ABILITY.

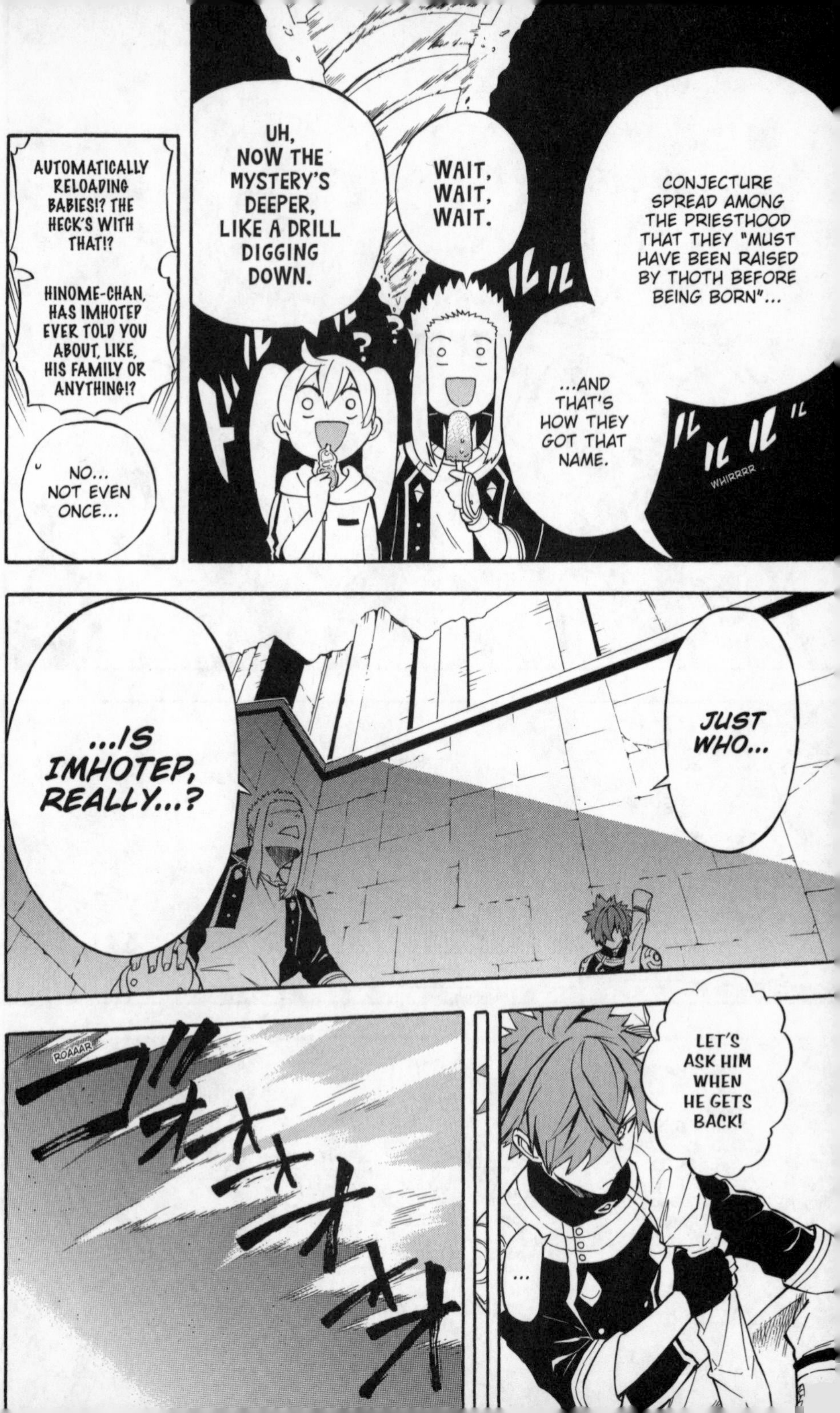
CONJECTURE SPREAD AMONG THE PRIESTHOOD THAT THEY "MUST HAVE BEEN RAISED BY THOTH BEFORE BEING BORN"...
...AND THAT'S HOW THEY GOT THAT NAME.
WHIRRRR
WAIT, WAIT, WAIT.
UH, NOW THE MYSTERY'S DEEPER, LIKE A DRILL DIGGING DOWN.
AUTOMATICALLY RELOADING BABIES!? THE HECK'S WITH THAT!?
HINOME-CHAN, HAS IMHOTEP EVER TOLD YOU ABOUT, LIKE, HIS FAMILY OR ANYTHING!?
NO... NOT EVEN ONCE...
JUST WHO...
...IS IMHOTEP, REALLY...?
LET'S ASK HIM WHEN HE GETS BACK!
...
ROAAAR

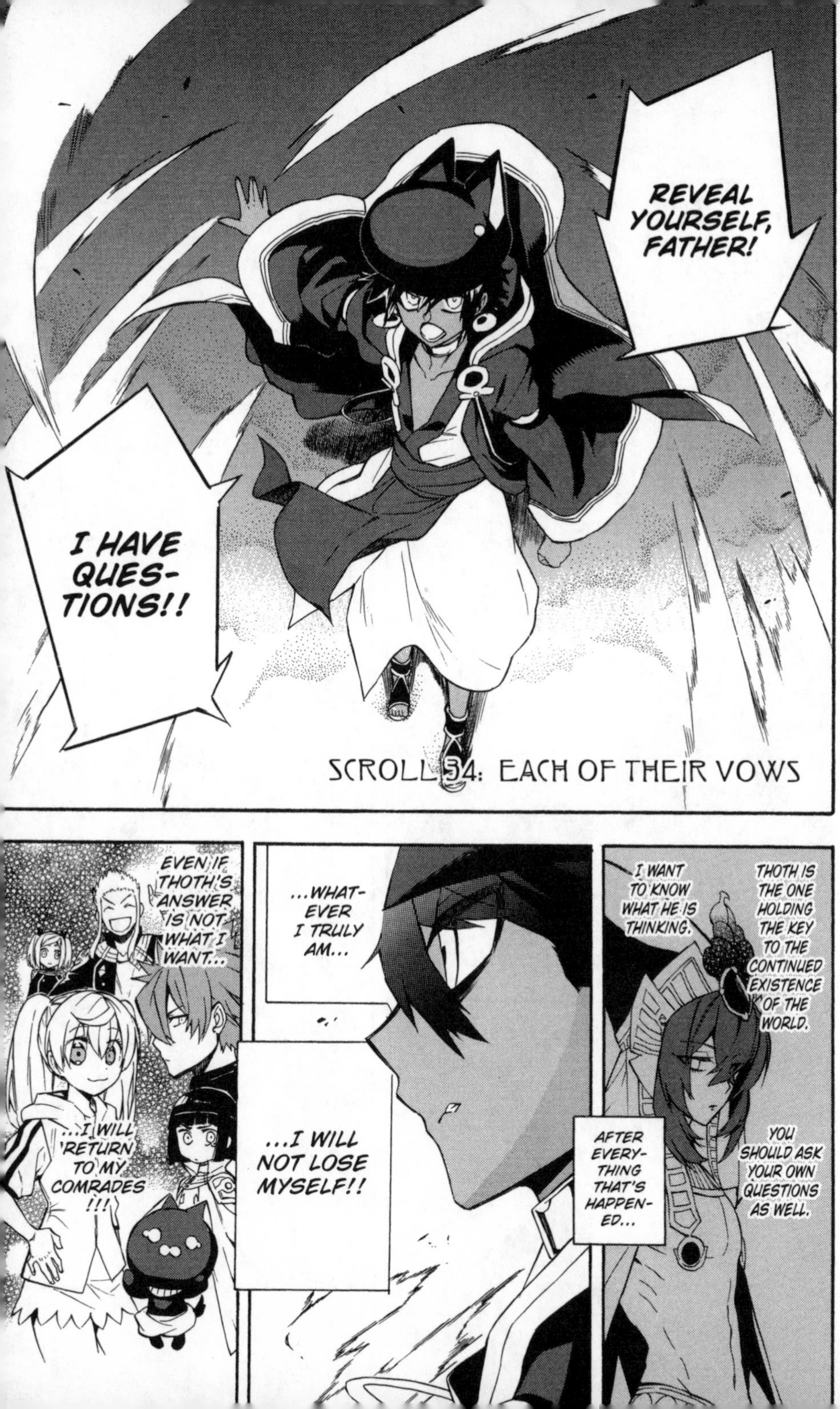
REVEAL YOURSELF, FATHER!
I HAVE QUES-TIONS!!
SCROLL 34: EACH OF THEIR VOWS
THOTH IS THE ONE HOLDING THE KEY TO THE CONTINUED EXISTENCE OF THE WORLD.
I WANT TO KNOW WHAT HE IS THINKING.
YOU SHOULD ASK YOUR OWN QUESTIONS AS WELL.
AFTER EVERY-THING THAT'S HAPPEN-ED...
...WHAT-EVER I TRULY AM...
...I WILL NOT LOSE MYSELF!!
EVEN IF THOTH'S ANSWER IS NOT WHAT I WANT...
...I WILL RETURN TO MY COMRADES!!!

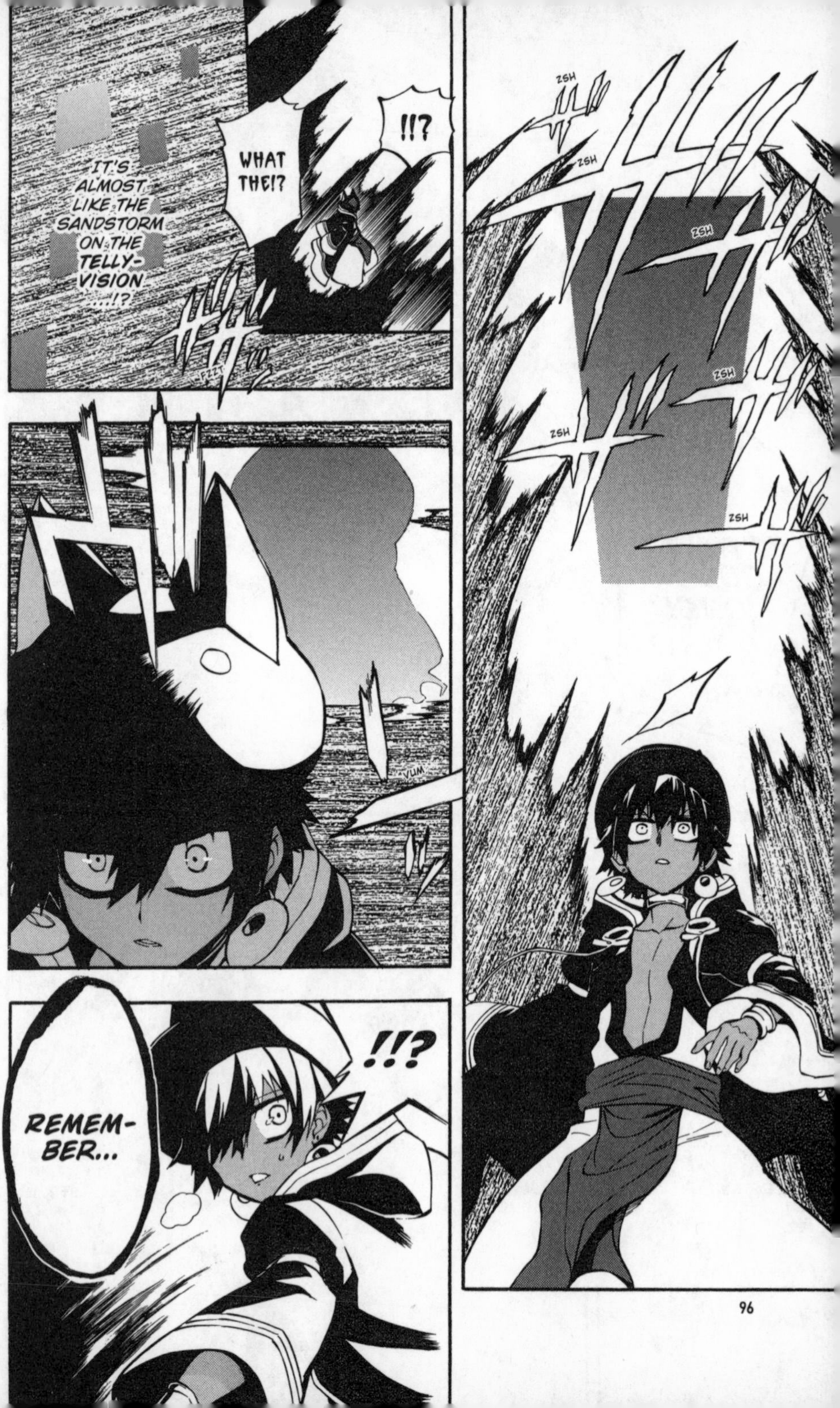
ZSH
ZSH
ZSH
ZSH
ZSH
ZSH
!!?
WHAT THE!?
IT'S ALMOST LIKE THE SANDSTORM ON THE TELLY-VISION ...!?
FZZT
VUM
!!?
REMEM-BER...

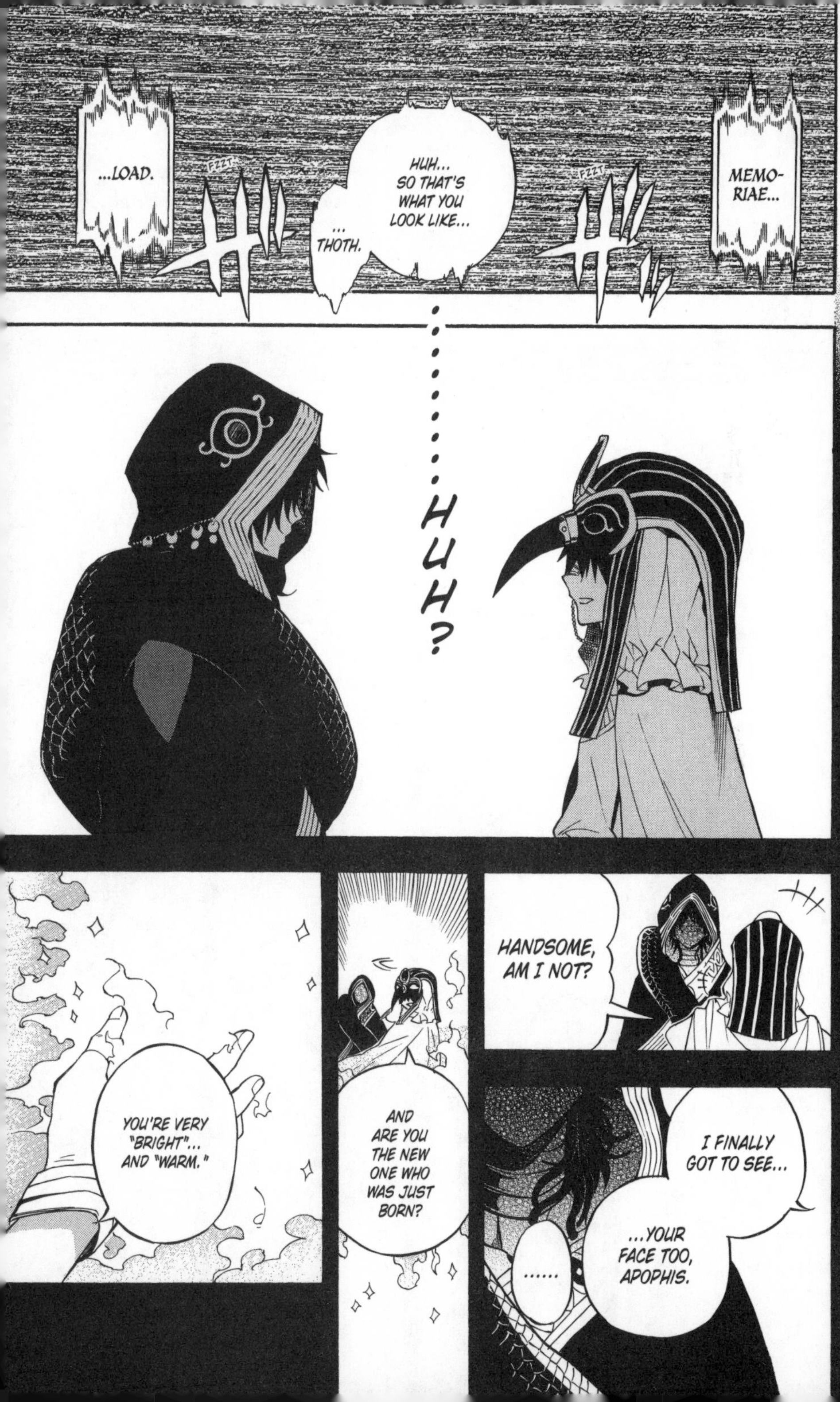
MEMO-RIAE...
FZZT
HUH... SO THAT'S WHAT YOU LOOK LIKE...
... THOTH.
FZZT
...LOAD.
........HUH?
HANDSOME, AM I NOT?
I FINALLY GOT TO SEE...
...YOUR FACE TOO, APOPHIS.
......
AND ARE YOU THE NEW ONE WHO WAS JUST BORN?
YOU'RE VERY "BRIGHT"... AND "WARM."

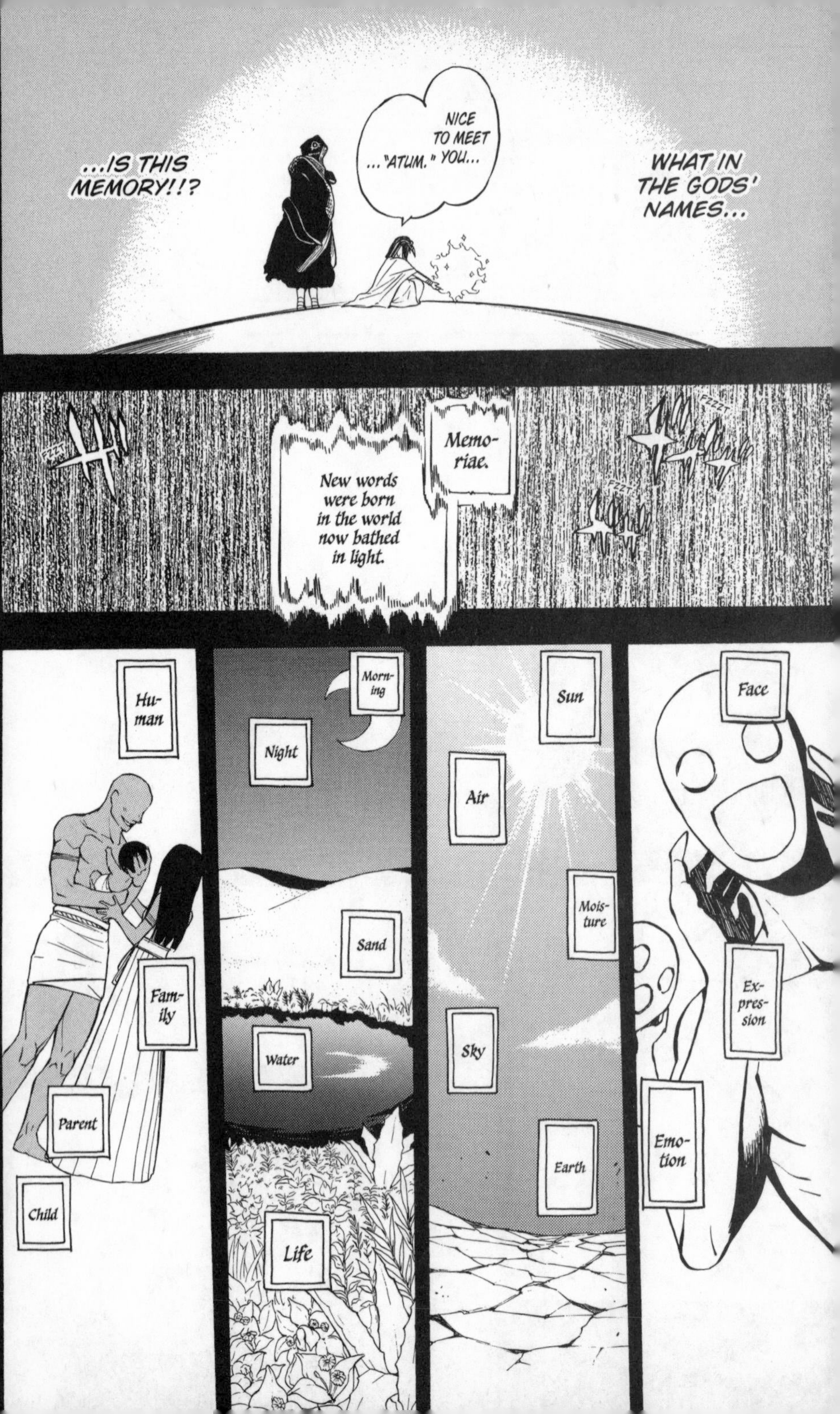

WHAT IN THE GODS' NAMES...
NICE TO MEET YOU... ..."ATUM."
...IS THIS MEMORY!!?
FZZZT
FZZZT
Memoriae.
New words were born in the world now bathed in light.
FZZZT
Face
Expression
Emotion
Sun
Air
Moisture
Sky
Earth
Morning
Night
Sand
Water
Life
Human
Family
Parent
Child

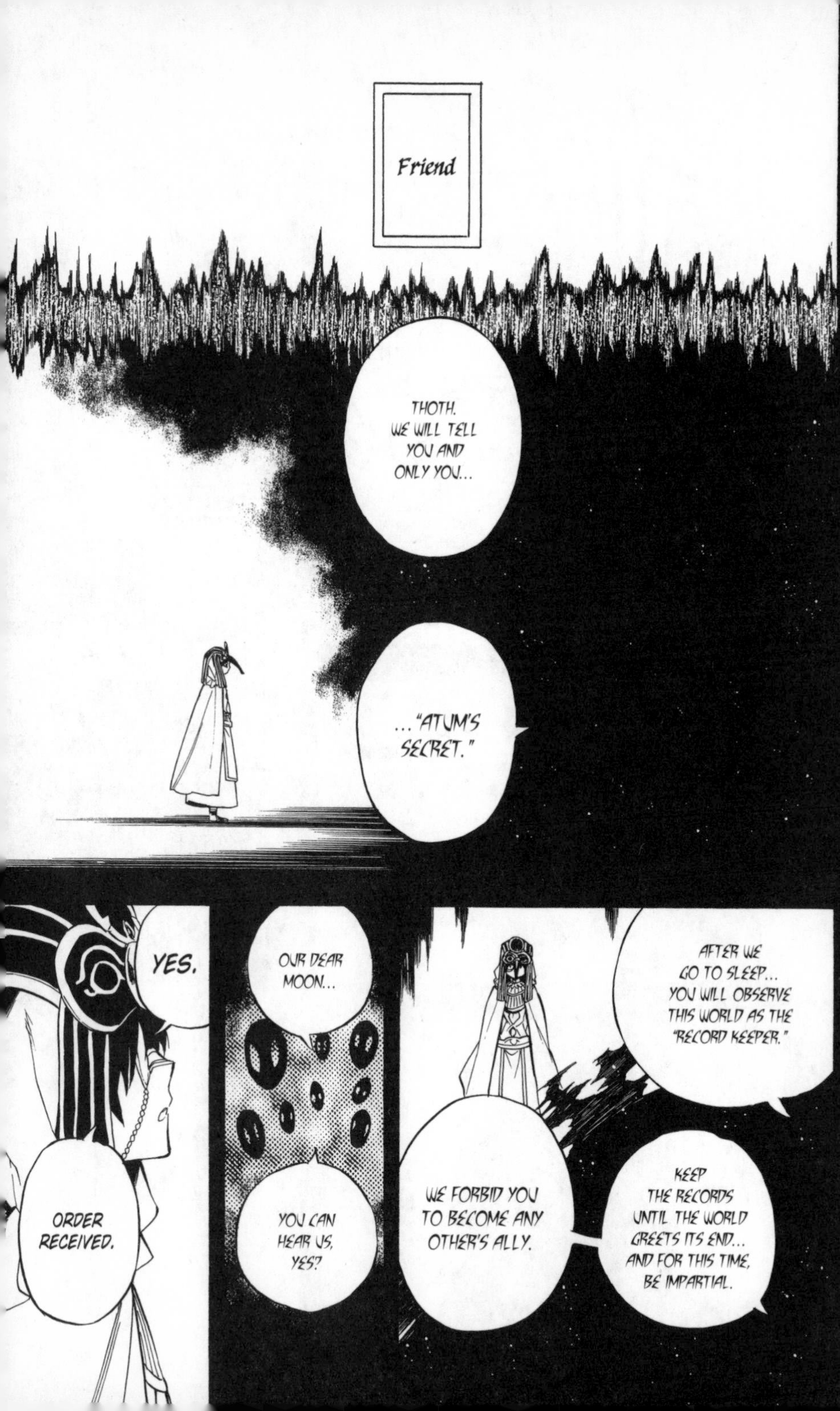

Friend
THOTH. WE WILL TELL YOU AND ONLY YOU...
..."ATUM'S SECRET."
AFTER WE GO TO SLEEP... YOU WILL OBSERVE THIS WORLD AS THE "RECORD KEEPER."
WE FORBID YOU TO BECOME ANY OTHER'S ALLY.
KEEP THE RECORDS UNTIL THE WORLD GREETS ITS END... AND FOR THIS TIME, BE IMPARTIAL.
OUR DEAR MOON...
YOU CAN HEAR US, YES?
YES.
ORDER RECEIVED.

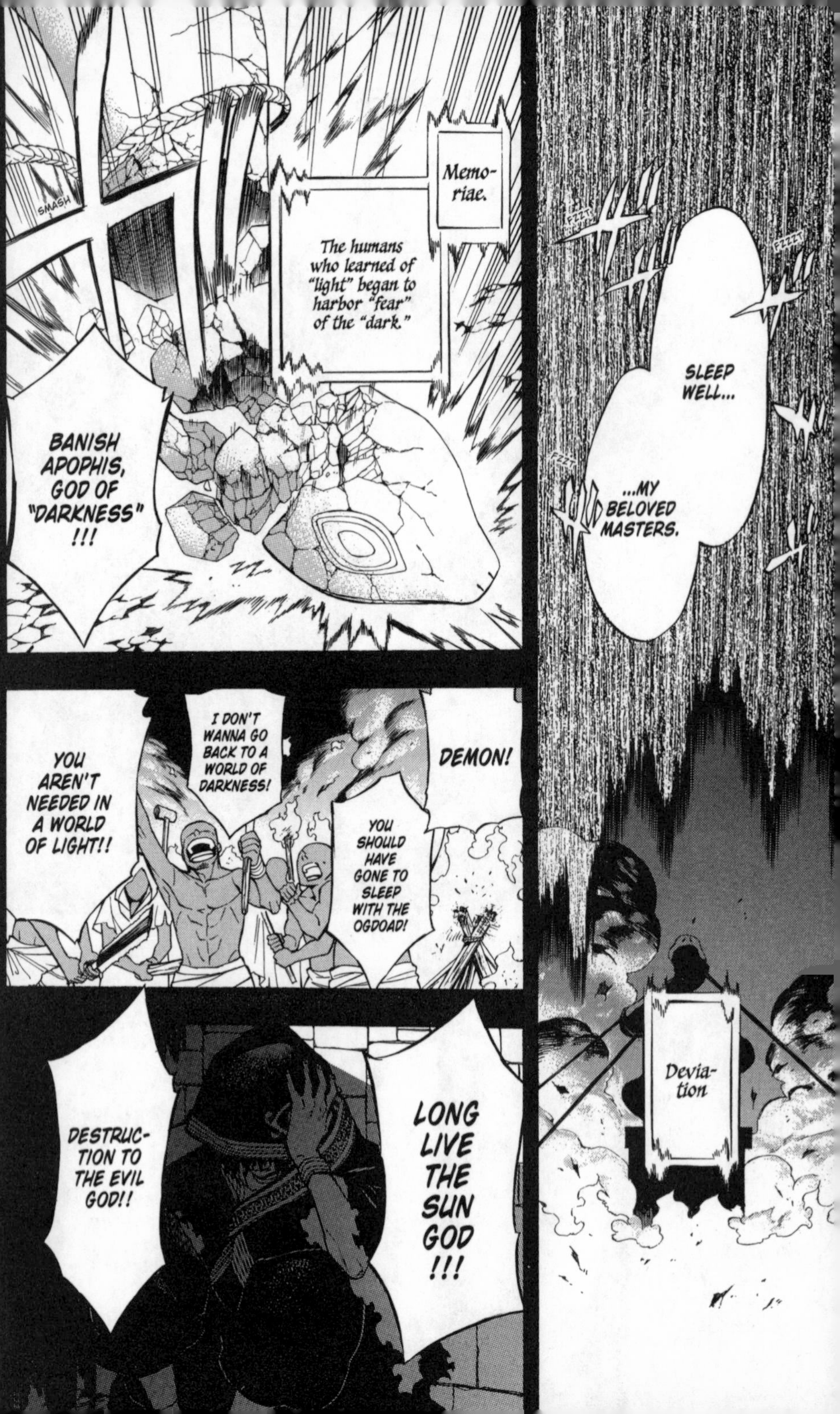
FZZT
FZZZT
SLEEP WELL...
FZZT
...MY BELOVED MASTERS.
Deviation
Memoriae.
The humans who learned of "light" began to harbor "fear" of the "dark."
SMASH
BANISH APOPHIS, GOD OF "DARKNESS"!!!
DEMON!
I DON'T WANNA GO BACK TO A WORLD OF DARKNESS!
YOU SHOULD HAVE GONE TO SLEEP WITH THE OGDOAD!
YOU AREN'T NEEDED IN A WORLD OF LIGHT!!
LONG LIVE THE SUN GOD!!!
DESTRUCTION TO THE EVIL GOD!!

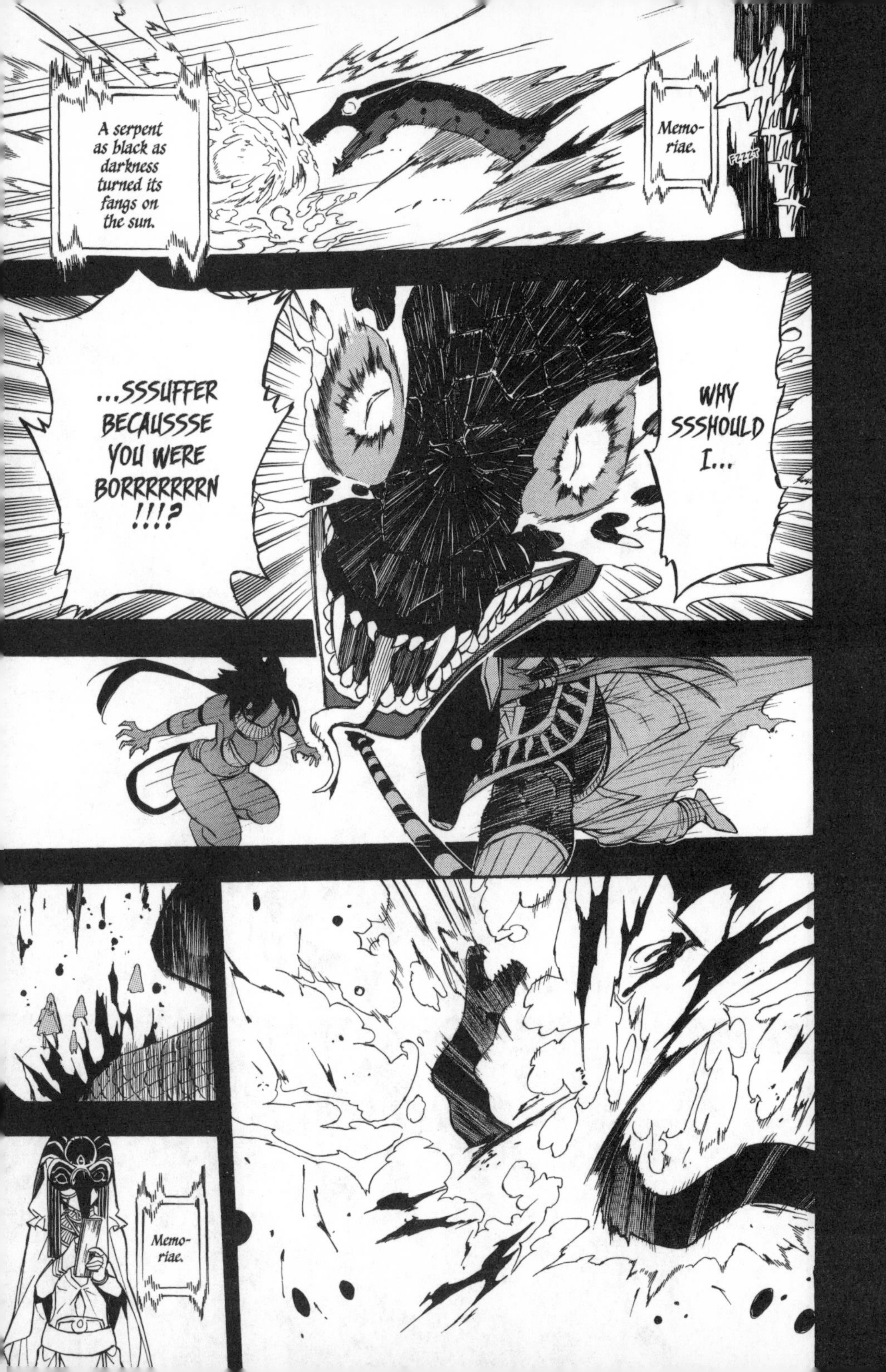
Memoriae.
FZZZT
A serpent as black as darkness turned its fangs on the sun.
WHY SSSHOULD I...
...SSSUFFER BECAUSSSE YOU WERE BORRRRRRRN!!!?
Memoriae.

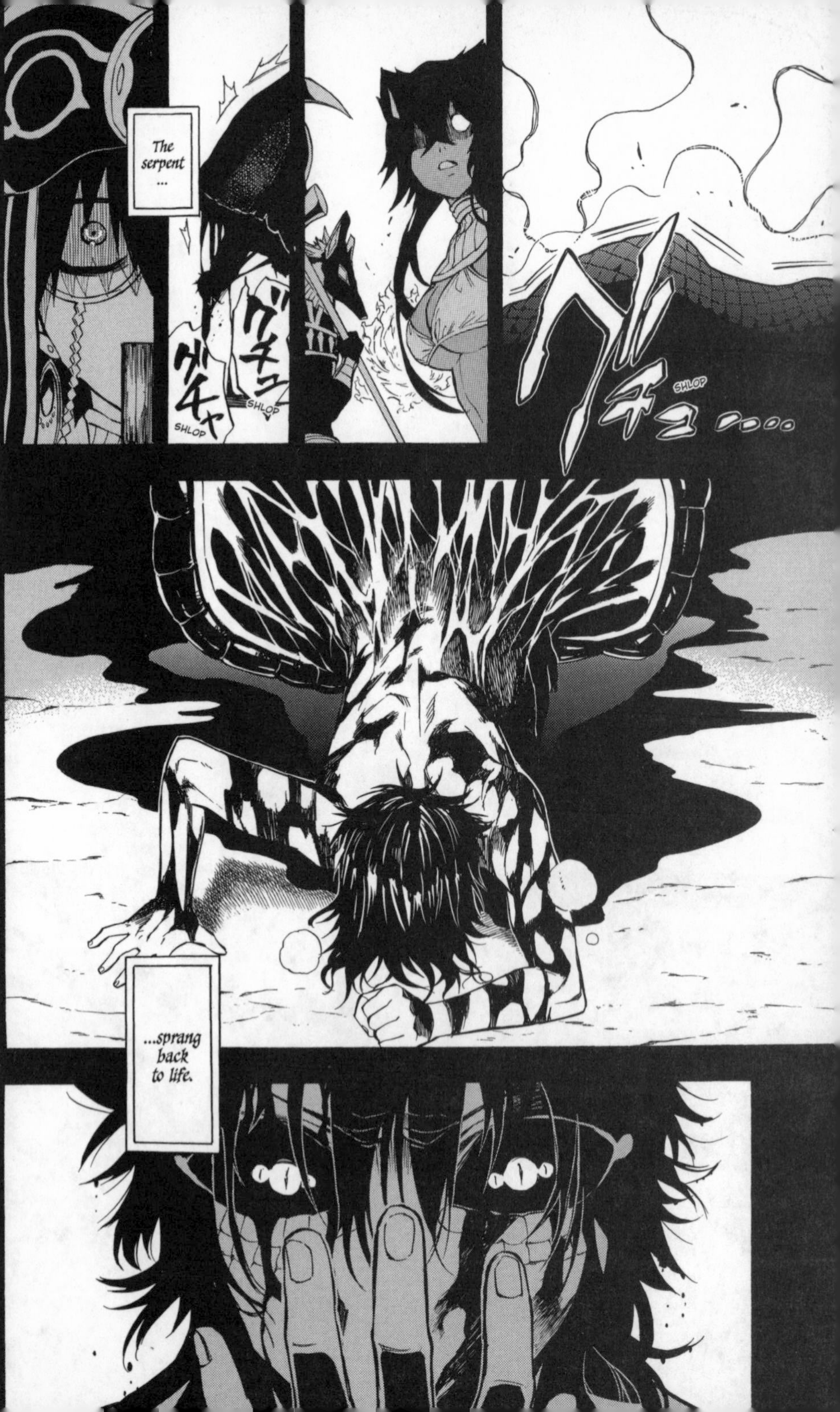
SHLOP
SHLOP
SHLOP
The serpent ...
...sprang back to life.

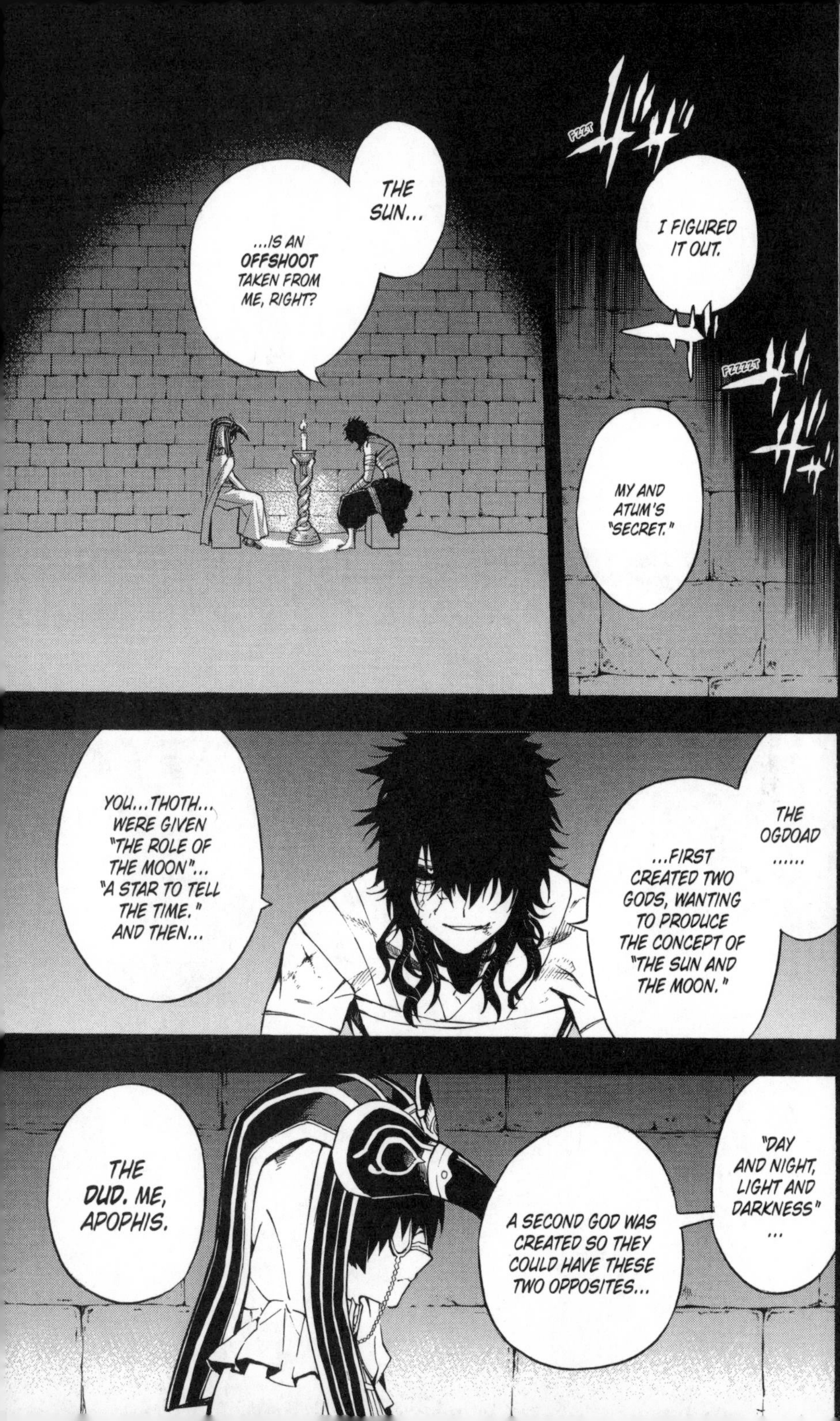
FZZT
I FIGURED IT OUT.
FZZZZT
MY AND ATUM'S "SECRET."
THE SUN...
...IS AN OFFSHOOT TAKEN FROM ME, RIGHT?
THE OGDOAD ......
...FIRST CREATED TWO GODS, WANTING TO PRODUCE THE CONCEPT OF "THE SUN AND THE MOON."
YOU...THOTH... WERE GIVEN "THE ROLE OF THE MOON"... "A STAR TO TELL THE TIME." AND THEN...
"DAY AND NIGHT, LIGHT AND DARKNESS" ...
A SECOND GOD WAS CREATED SO THEY COULD HAVE THESE TWO OPPOSITES...
THE DUD. ME, APOPHIS.

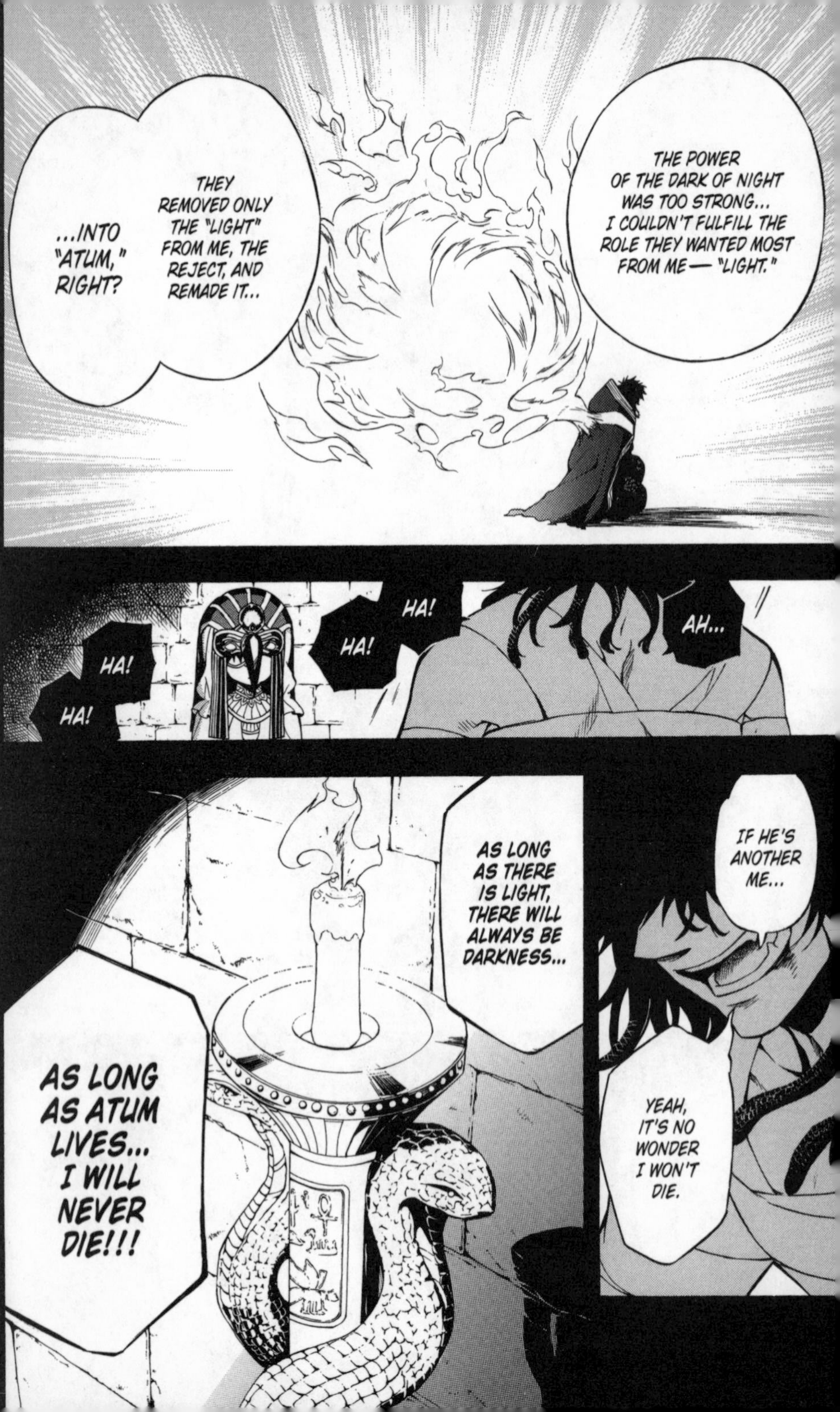
THE POWER OF THE DARK OF NIGHT WAS TOO STRONG... I COULDN'T FULFILL THE ROLE THEY WANTED MOST FROM ME— "LIGHT."
THEY REMOVED ONLY THE "LIGHT" FROM ME, THE REJECT, AND REMADE IT...
...INTO "ATUM," RIGHT?
AH...
HA!
HA!
HA!
HA!
IF HE'S ANOTHER ME...
YEAH, IT'S NO WONDER I WON'T DIE.
AS LONG AS THERE IS LIGHT, THERE WILL ALWAYS BE DARKNESS...
AS LONG AS ATUM LIVES... I WILL NEVER DIE!!!

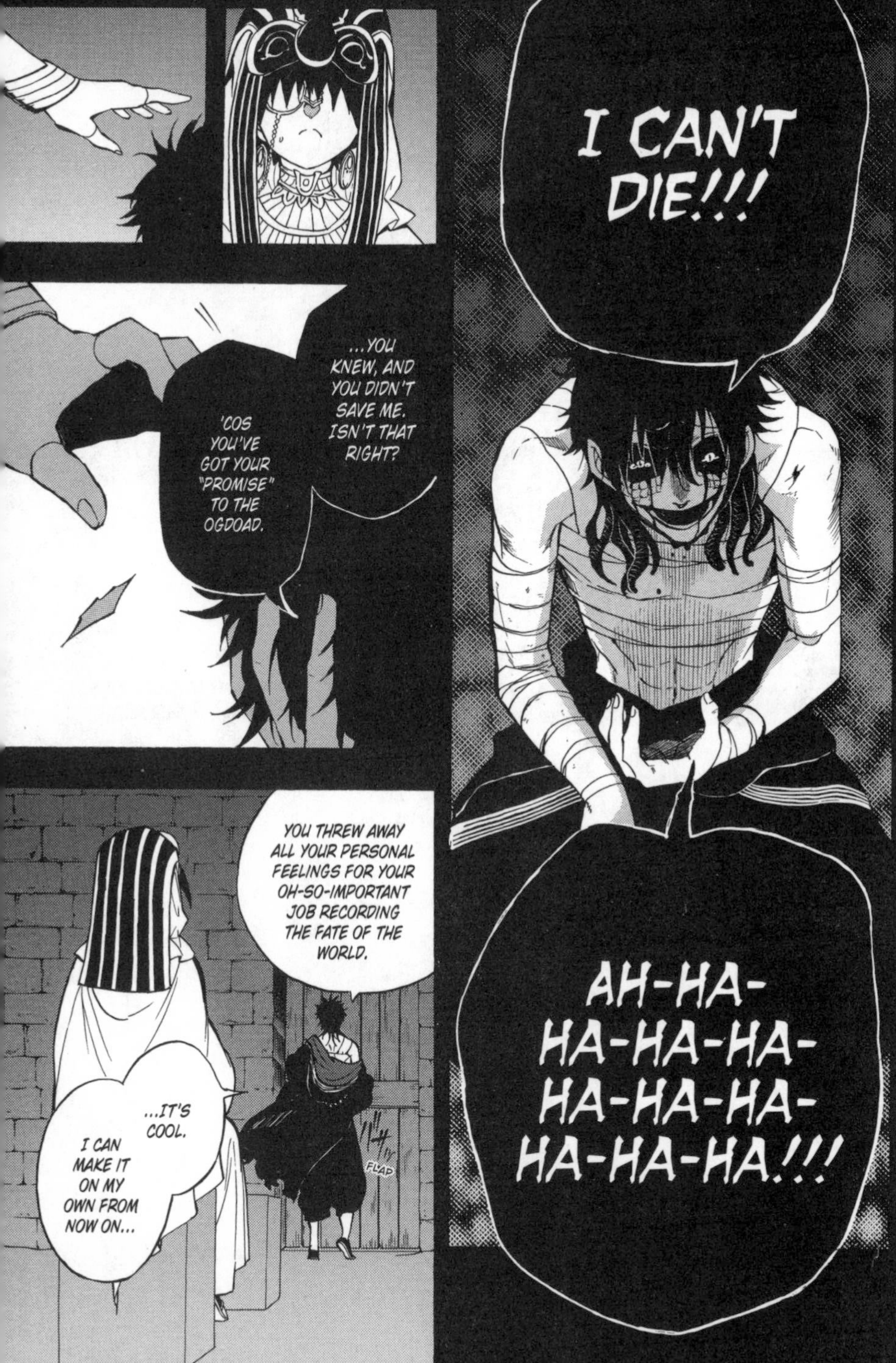
I CAN'T DIE!!!
AH-HA-HA-HA-HA-HA-HA-HA-HA-HA-HA-HA!!!
...YOU KNEW, AND YOU DIDN'T SAVE ME. ISN'T THAT RIGHT?
'COS YOU'VE GOT YOUR "PROMISE" TO THE OGDOAD.
YOU THREW AWAY ALL YOUR PERSONAL FEELINGS FOR YOUR OH-SO-IMPORTANT JOB RECORDING THE FATE OF THE WORLD.
...IT'S COOL.
I CAN MAKE IT ON MY OWN FROM NOW ON...
FLAP

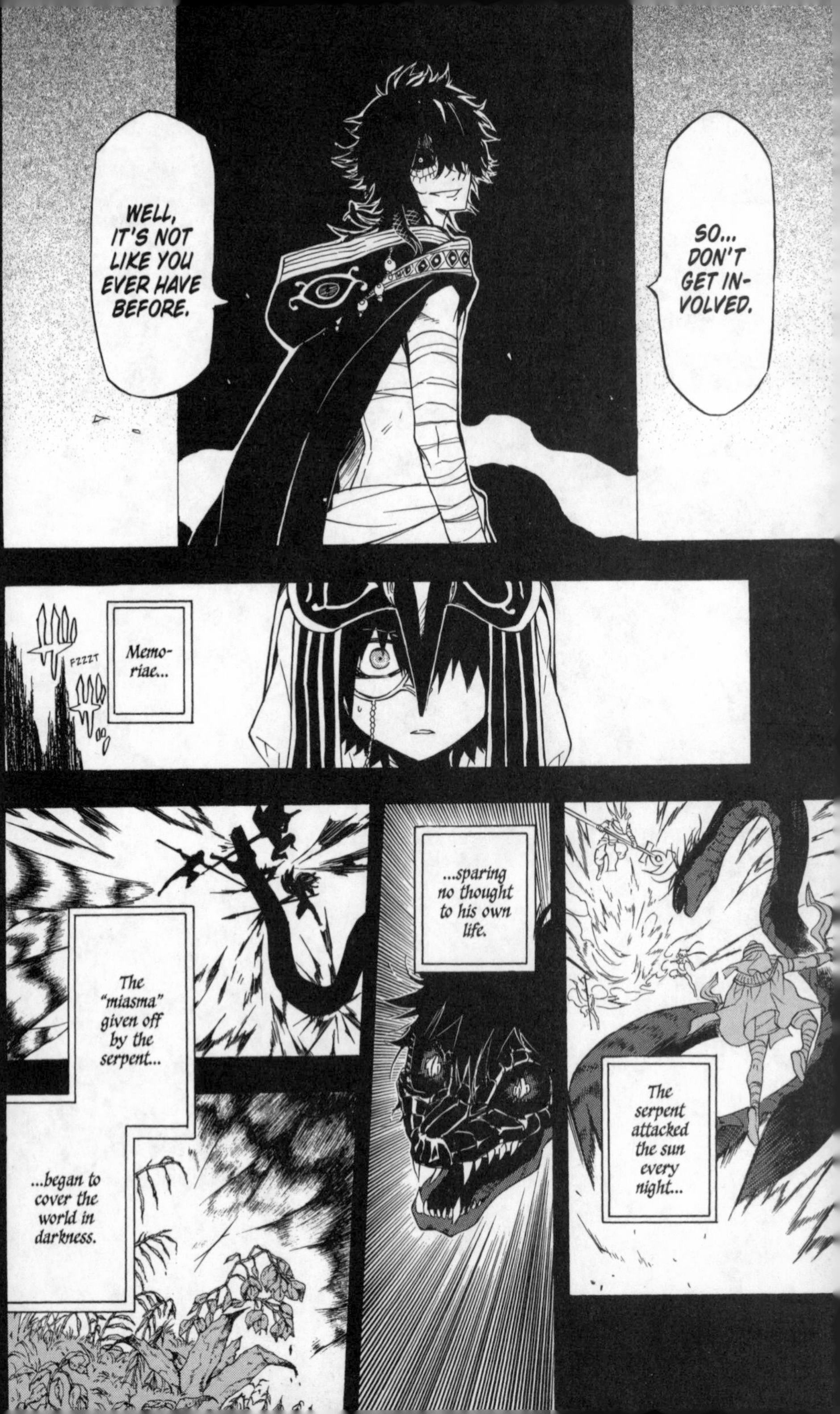
SO... DON'T GET IN-VOLVED.
WELL, IT'S NOT LIKE YOU EVER HAVE BEFORE.
FZZZT
Memoriae...
The serpent attacked the sun every night...
...sparing no thought to his own life.
The "miasma" given off by the serpent...
...began to cover the world in darkness.

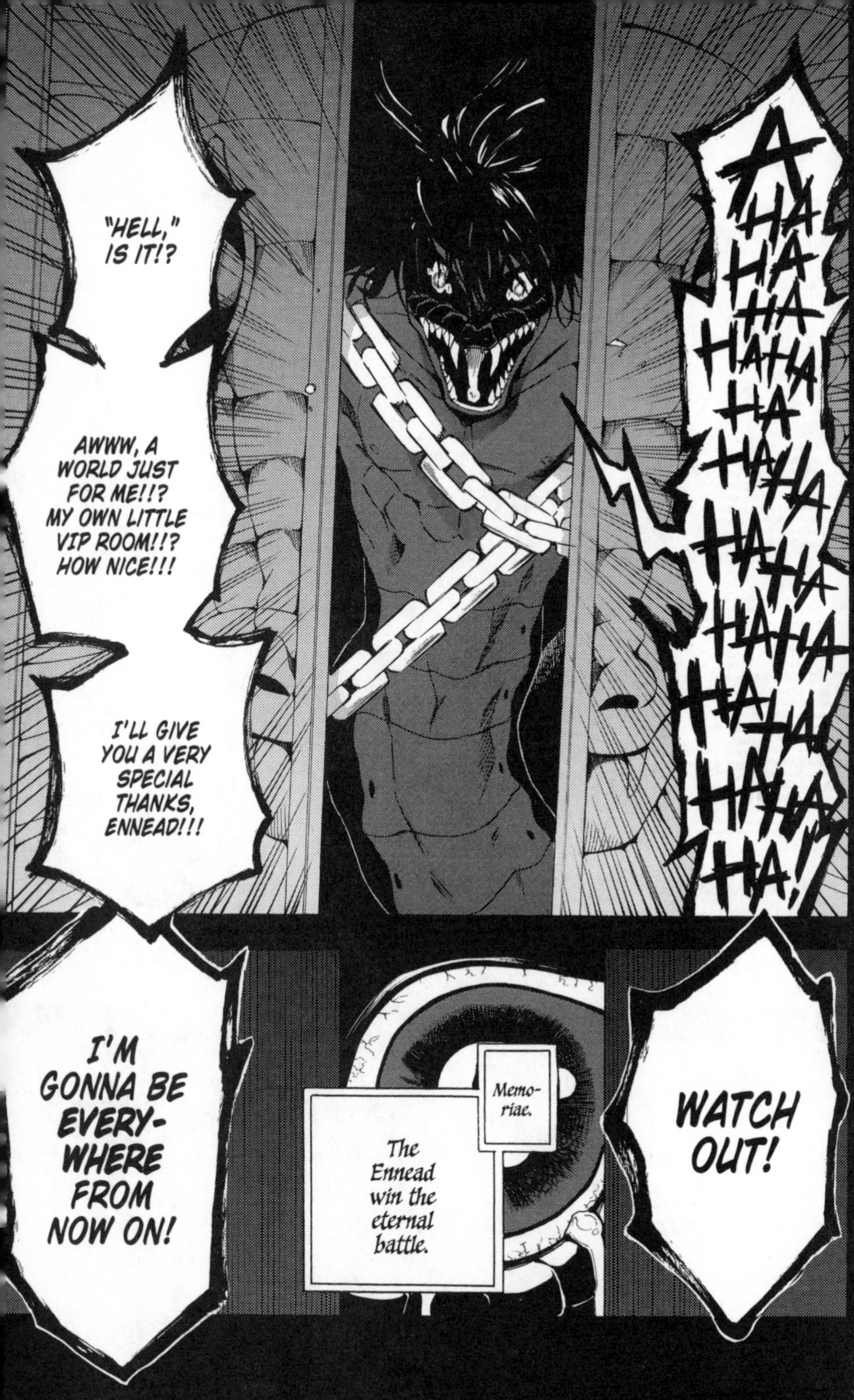
AHAHAHAHAHAHAHAHAHAHAHAHAHAHAHAHAHAHA!
"HELL," IS IT!?
AWWW, A WORLD JUST FOR ME!!? MY OWN LITTLE VIP ROOM!!? HOW NICE!!!
I'LL GIVE YOU A VERY SPECIAL THANKS, ENNEAD!!!
WATCH OUT!
Memoriae.
The Ennead win the eternal battle.
I'M GONNA BE EVERYWHERE FROM NOW ON!

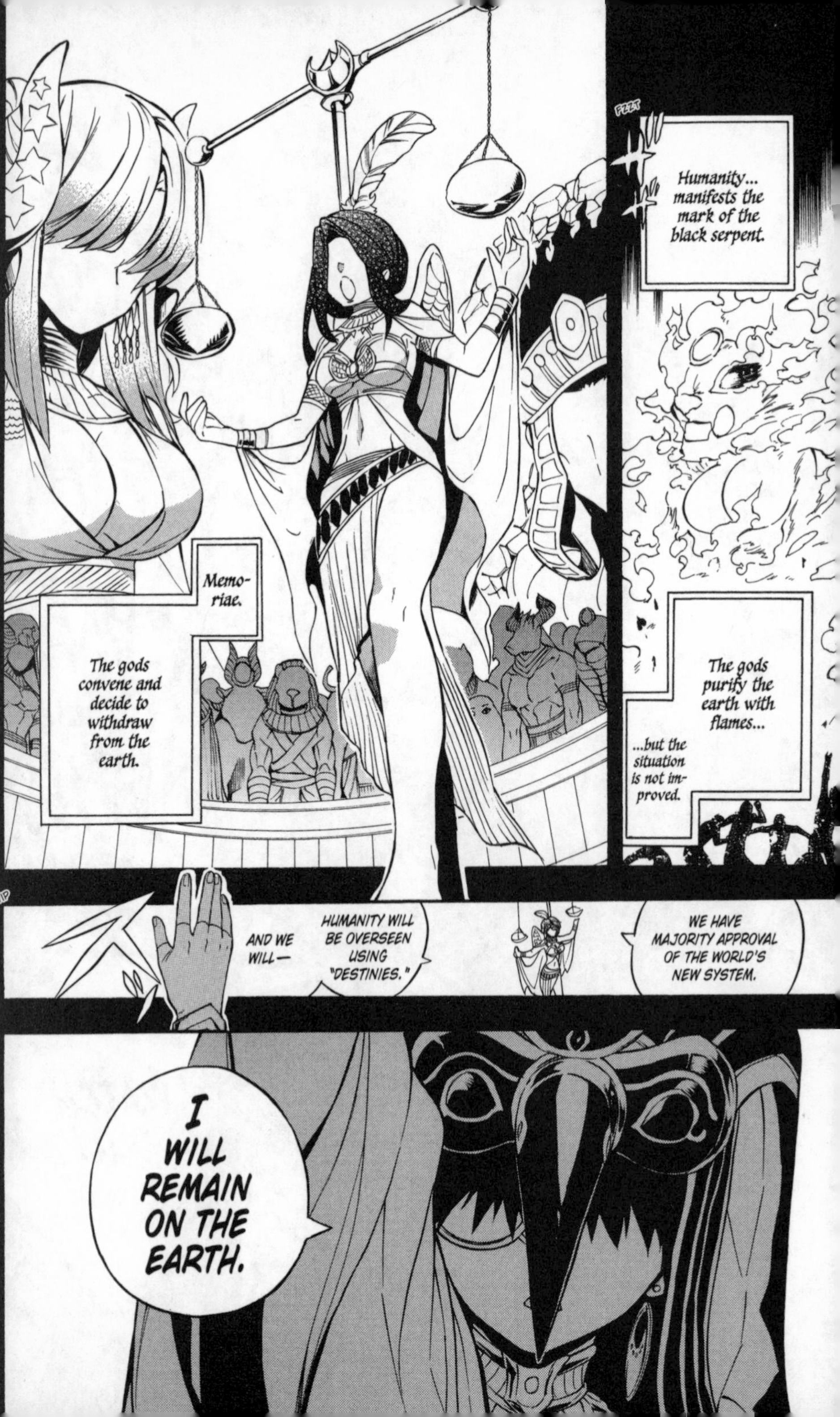
FZZT
Humanity... manifests the mark of the black serpent.
The gods purify the earth with flames...
...but the situation is not improved.
Memoriae.
The gods convene and decide to withdraw from the earth.
WE HAVE MAJORITY APPROVAL OF THE WORLD'S NEW SYSTEM.
HUMANITY WILL BE OVERSEEN USING "DESTINIES."
AND WE WILL—
SWIP
I WILL REMAIN ON THE EARTH.

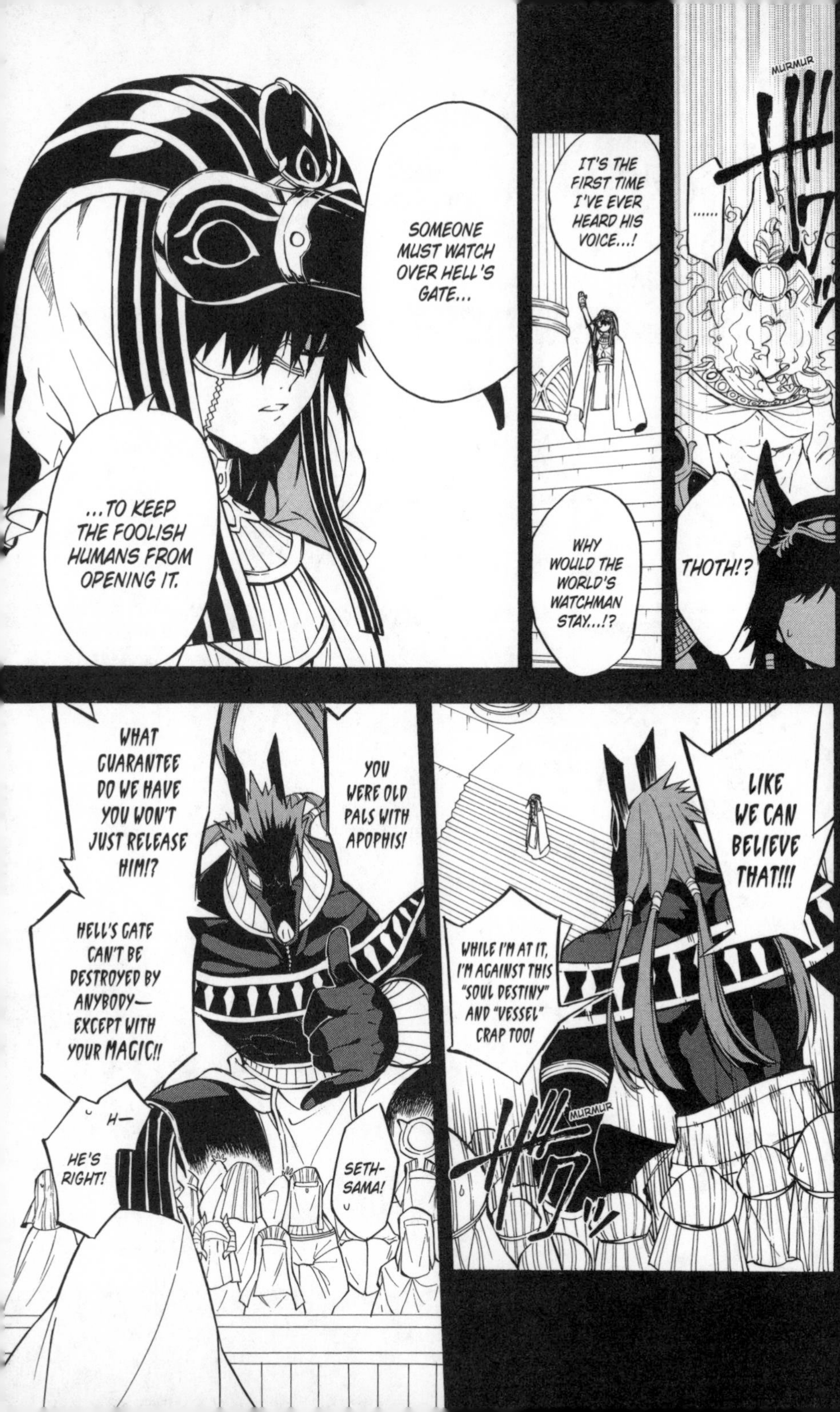
MURMUR
......
THOTH!?
IT'S THE FIRST TIME I'VE EVER HEARD HIS VOICE...!
WHY WOULD THE WORLD'S WATCHMAN STAY...!?
SOMEONE MUST WATCH OVER HELL'S GATE...
...TO KEEP THE FOOLISH HUMANS FROM OPENING IT.
LIKE WE CAN BELIEVE THAT!!!
WHILE I'M AT IT, I'M AGAINST THIS "SOUL DESTINY" AND "VESSEL" CRAP TOO!
MURMUR
YOU WERE OLD PALS WITH APOPHIS!
WHAT GUARANTEE DO WE HAVE YOU WON'T JUST RELEASE HIM!?
HELL'S GATE CAN'T BE DESTROYED BY ANYBODY— EXCEPT WITH YOUR MAGIC!!
SETH-SAMA!
H— HE'S RIGHT!

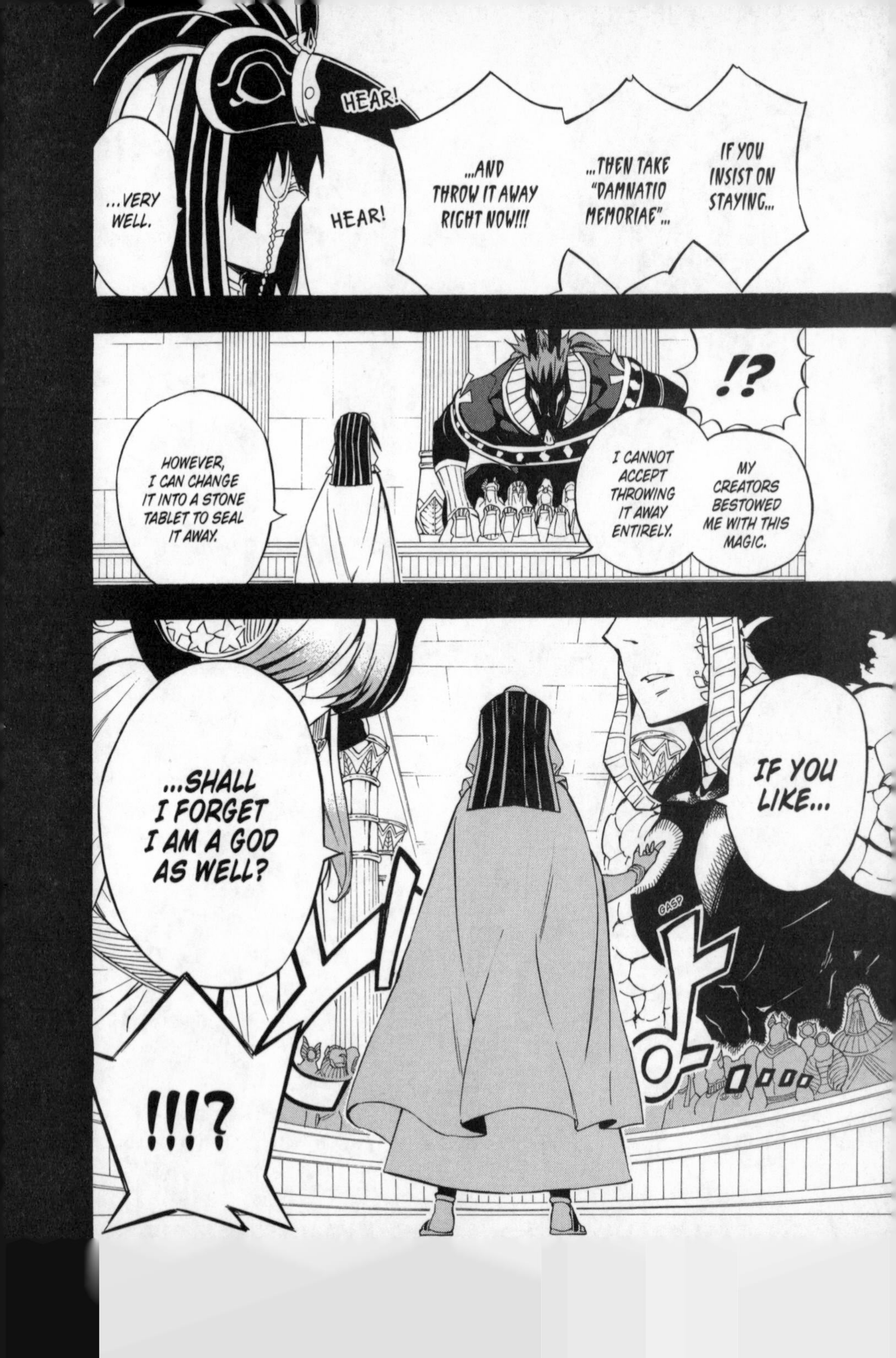
IF YOU INSIST ON STAYING...
...THEN TAKE "DAMNATIO MEMORIAE"...
...AND THROW IT AWAY RIGHT NOW!!!
HEAR!
HEAR!
...VERY WELL.
!?
MY CREATORS BESTOWED ME WITH THIS MAGIC.
I CANNOT ACCEPT THROWING IT AWAY ENTIRELY.
HOWEVER, I CAN CHANGE IT INTO A STONE TABLET TO SEAL IT AWAY.
IF YOU LIKE...
GASP
...SHALL I FORGET I AM A GOD AS WELL?
!!!?

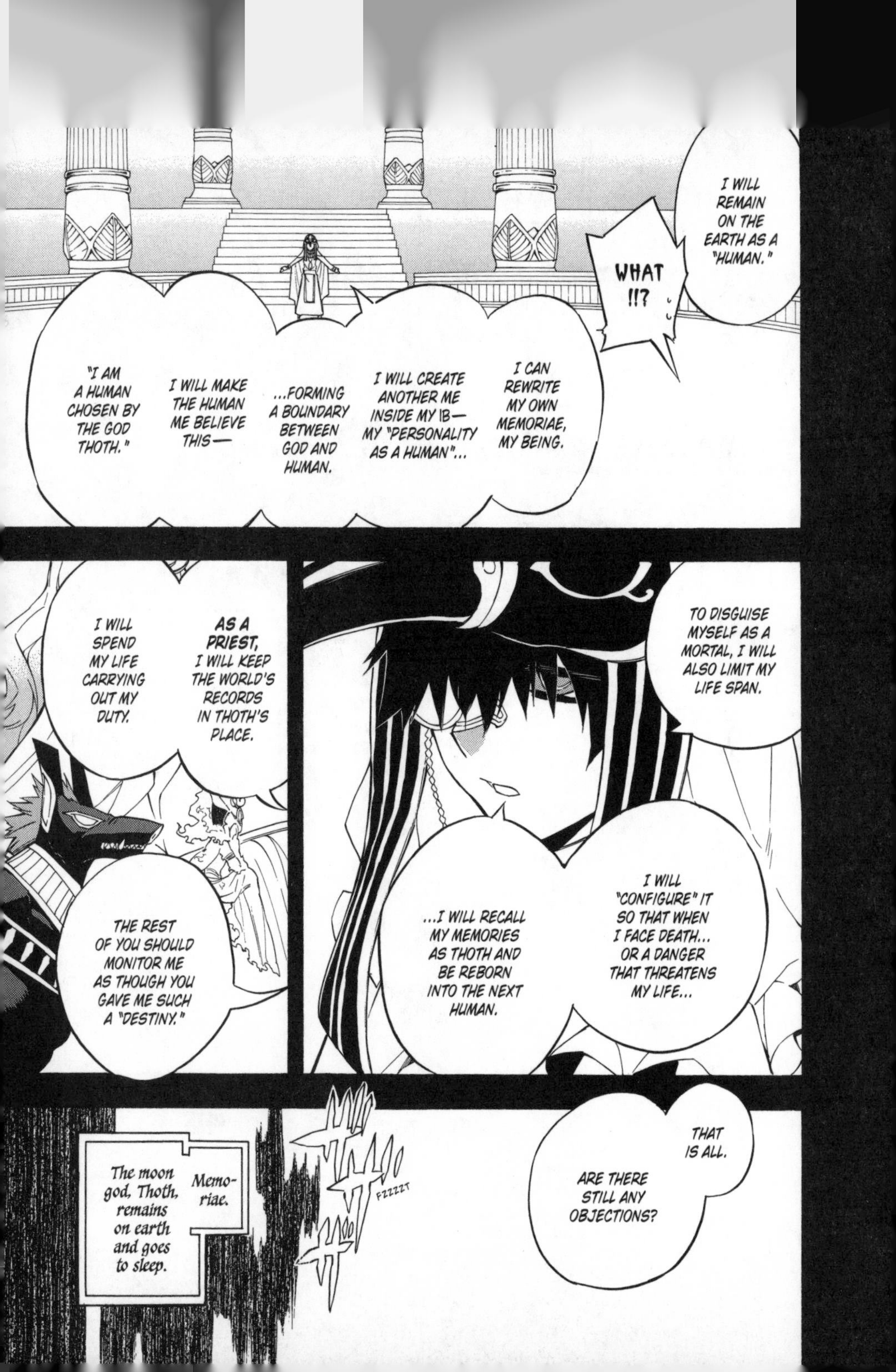
I WILL REMAIN ON THE EARTH AS A "HUMAN."
WHAT!!?
I CAN REWRITE MY OWN MEMORIAE, MY BEING.
I WILL CREATE ANOTHER ME INSIDE MY IB— MY "PERSONALITY AS A HUMAN"...
...FORMING A BOUNDARY BETWEEN GOD AND HUMAN.
I WILL MAKE THE HUMAN ME BELIEVE THIS—
"I AM A HUMAN CHOSEN BY THE GOD THOTH."
TO DISGUISE MYSELF AS A MORTAL, I WILL ALSO LIMIT MY LIFE SPAN.
I WILL "CONFIGURE" IT SO THAT WHEN I FACE DEATH... OR A DANGER THAT THREATENS MY LIFE...
...I WILL RECALL MY MEMORIES AS THOTH AND BE REBORN INTO THE NEXT HUMAN.
AS A PRIEST, I WILL KEEP THE WORLD'S RECORDS IN THOTH'S PLACE.
I WILL SPEND MY LIFE CARRYING OUT MY DUTY.
THE REST OF YOU SHOULD MONITOR ME AS THOUGH YOU GAVE ME SUCH A "DESTINY."
THAT IS ALL.
ARE THERE STILL ANY OBJECTIONS?
FZZZZT
Memoriae.
The moon god, Thoth, remains on earth and goes to sleep.

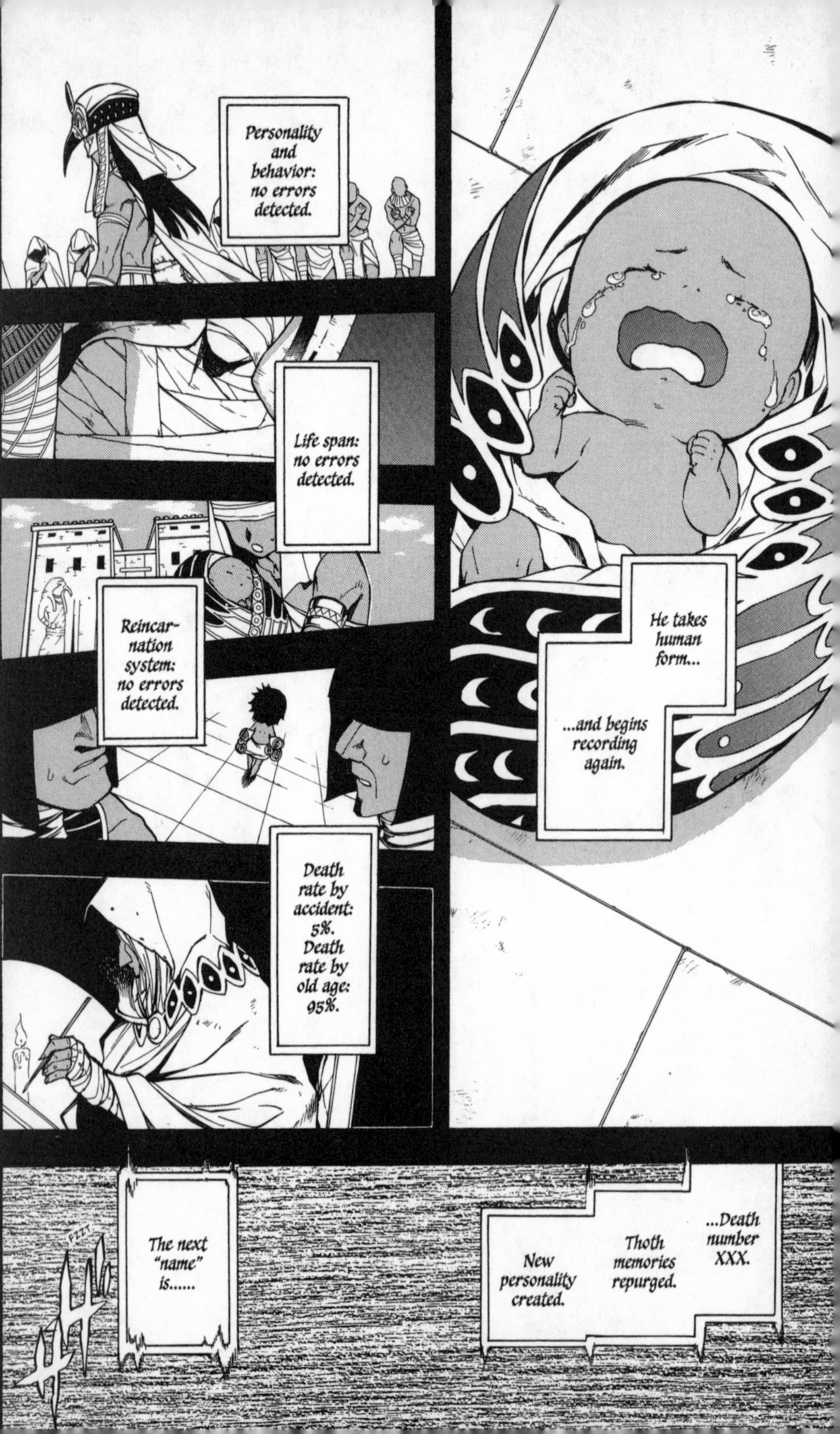
He takes human form...
...and begins recording again.
Personality and behavior: no errors detected.
Life span: no errors detected.
Reincarnation system: no errors detected.
Death rate by accident: 5%. Death rate by old age: 95%.
...Death number XXX.
Thoth memories repurged.
New personality created.
The next "name" is......
FZZT

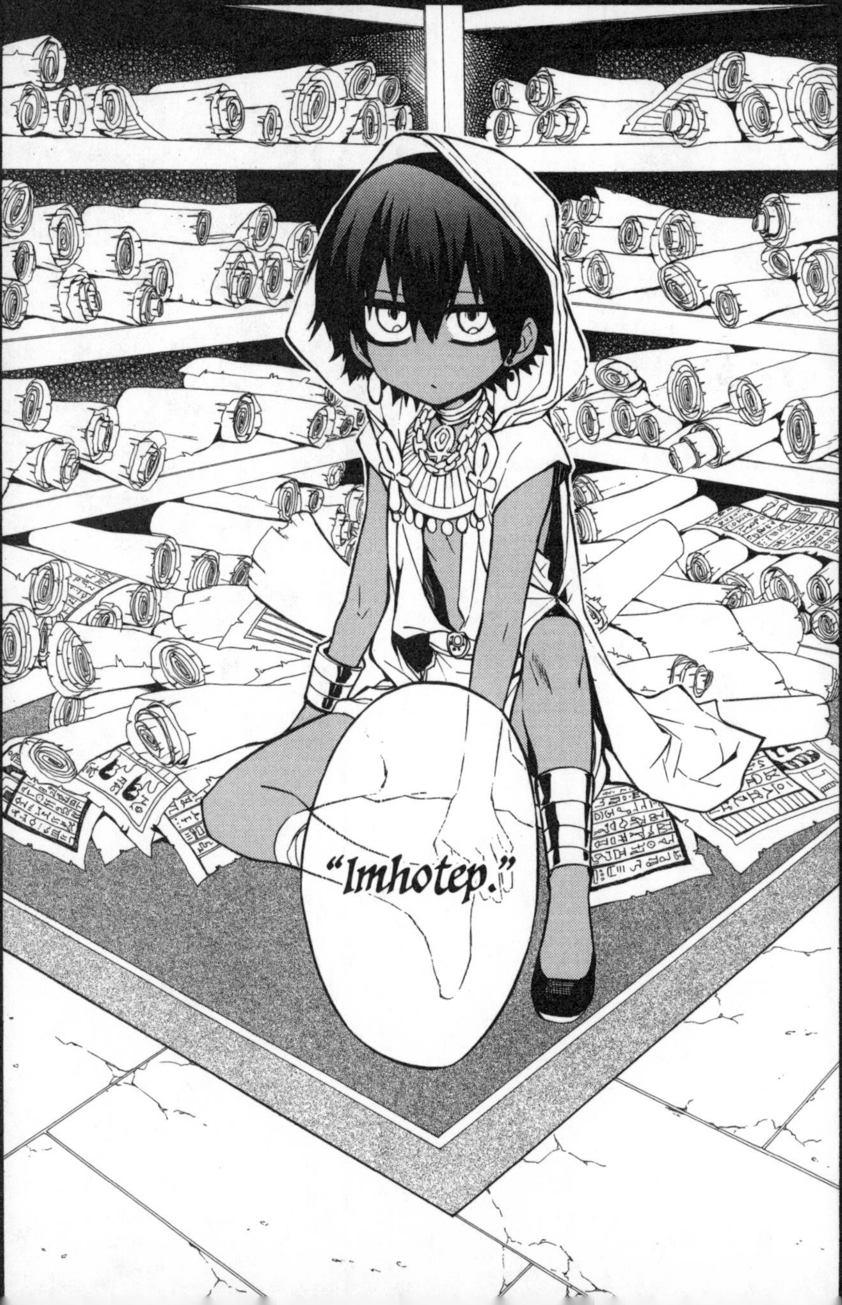
"Imhotep."

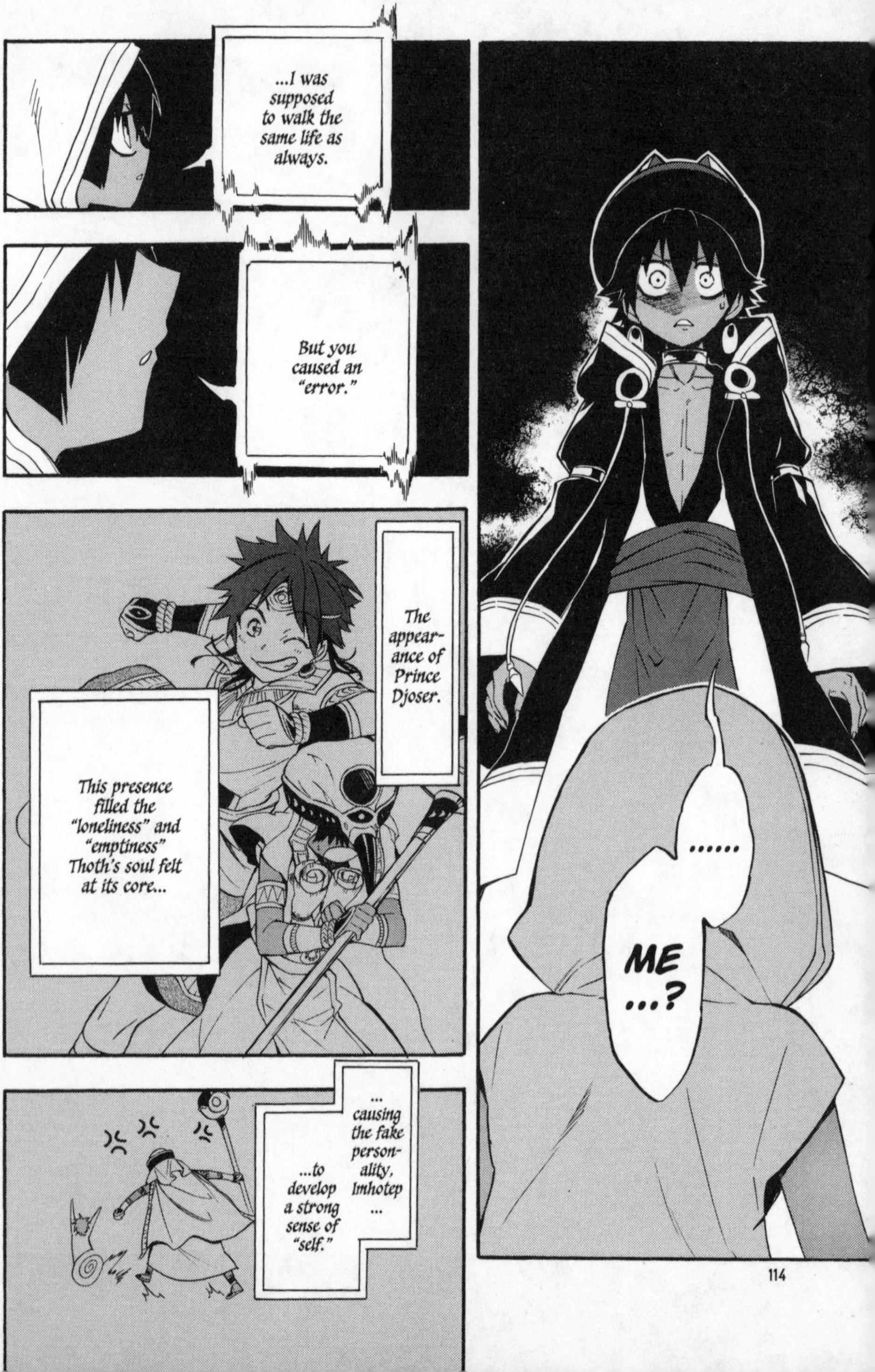
......
ME ...?
...I was supposed to walk the same life as always.
But you caused an "error."
The appear-ance of Prince Djoser.
This presence filled the "loneliness" and "emptiness" Thoth's soul felt at its core...
... causing the fake person-ality, Imhotep ...
...to develop a strong sense of "self."

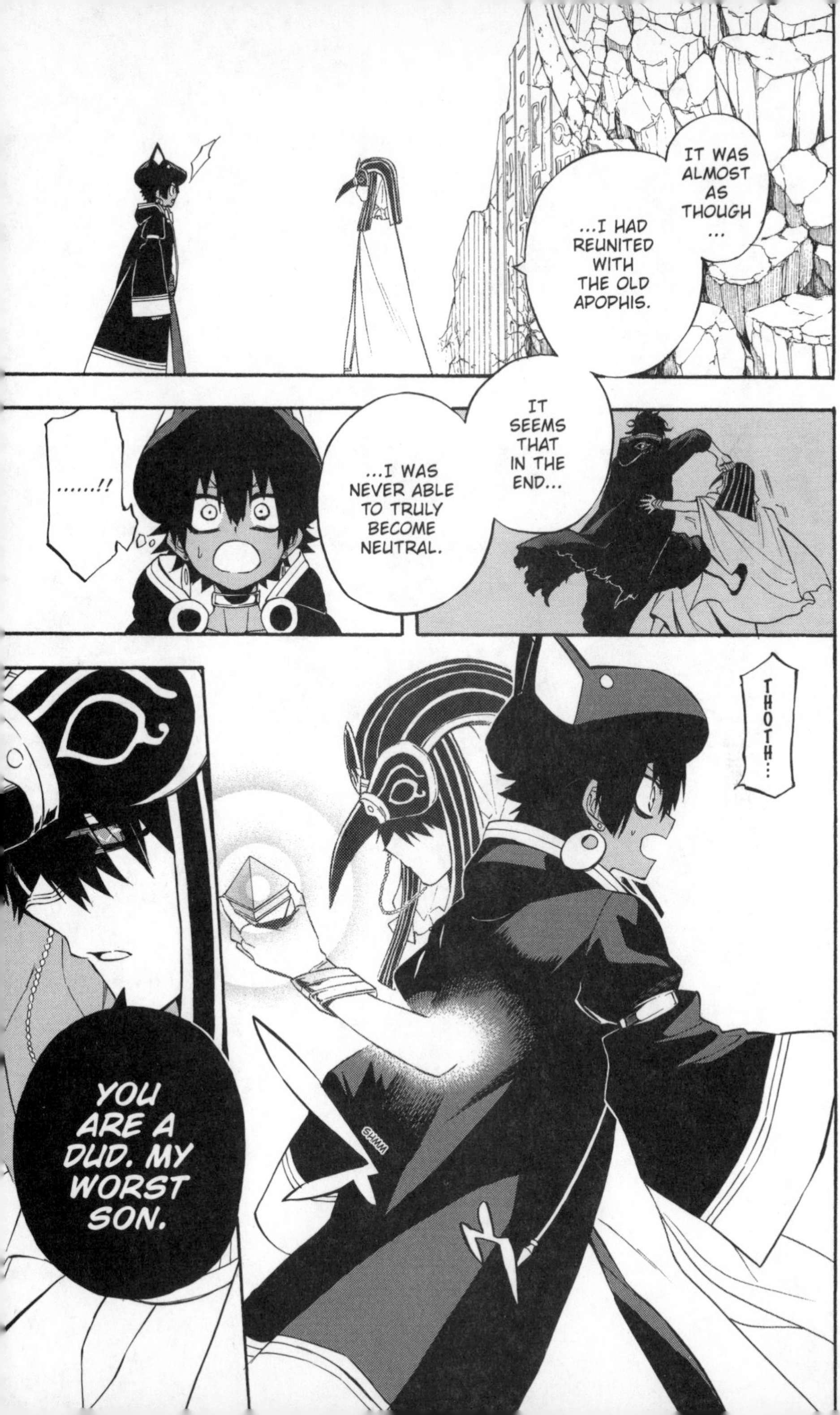
IT WAS ALMOST AS THOUGH...
...I HAD REUNITED WITH THE OLD APOPHIS.
IT SEEMS THAT IN THE END...
...I WAS NEVER ABLE TO TRULY BECOME NEUTRAL.
......!!
THOTH...
YOU ARE A DUD. MY WORST SON.

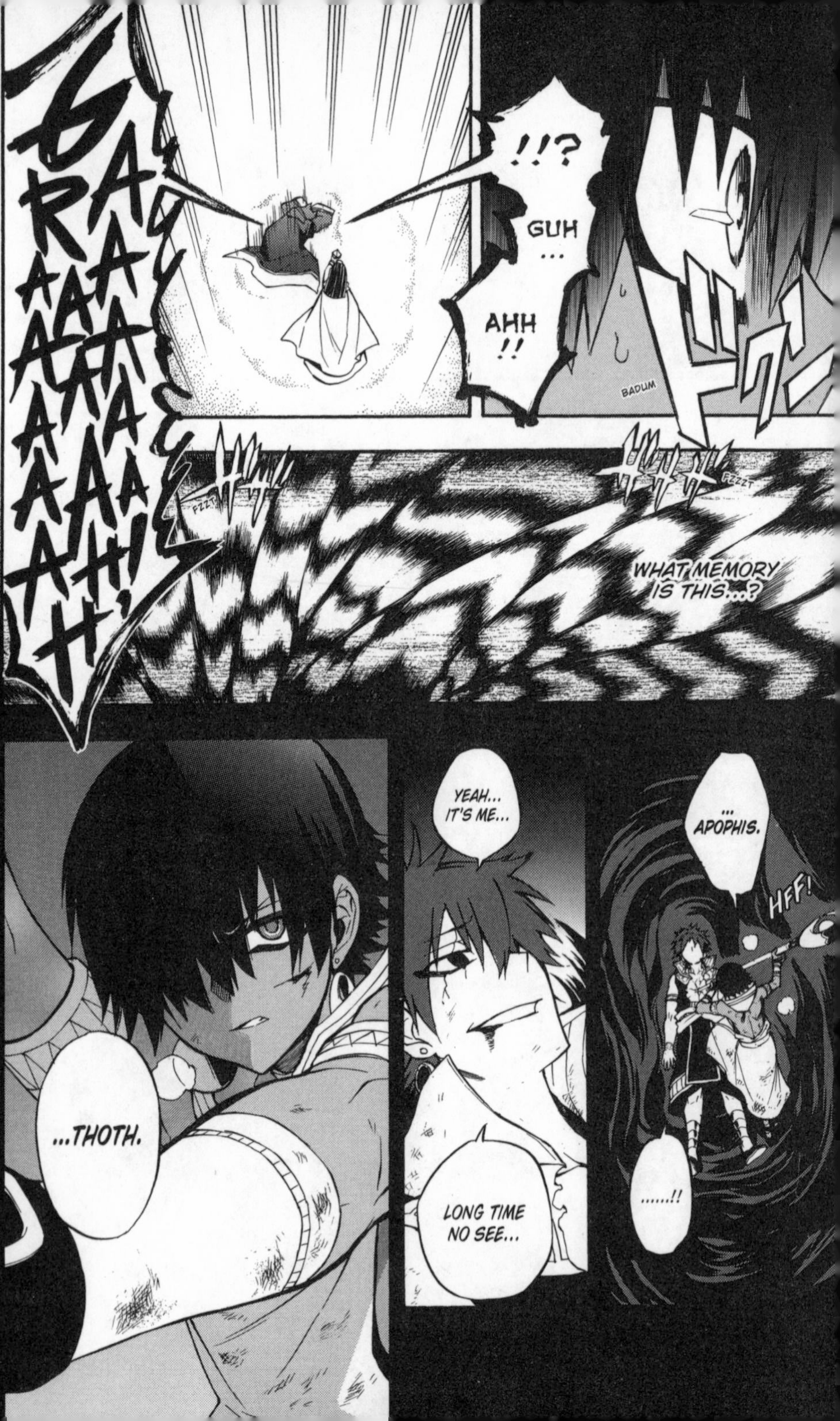
!!?
GUH...
AHH!!
BADUM
SARAAAAAAAAAAAAAAAH!!
FZZZT
FZZZT
WHAT MEMORY IS THIS...?
... APOPHIS.
HFF!
......!!
YEAH... IT'S ME...
LONG TIME NO SEE...
...THOTH.

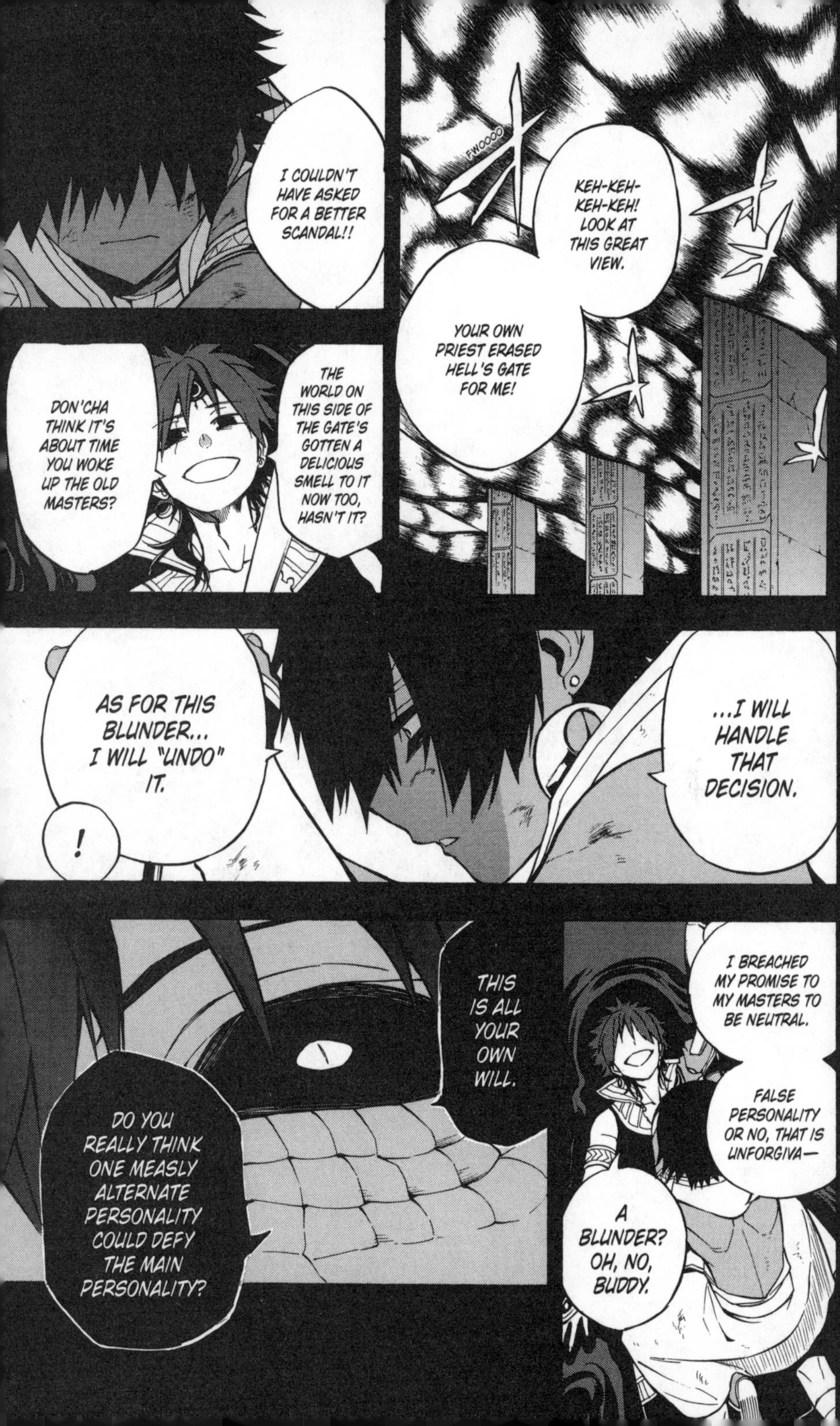
FWOOOO
KEH-KEH-KEH-KEH! LOOK AT THIS GREAT VIEW.
YOUR OWN PRIEST ERASED HELL'S GATE FOR ME!
I COULDN'T HAVE ASKED FOR A BETTER SCANDAL!!
THE WORLD ON THIS SIDE OF THE GATE'S GOTTEN A DELICIOUS SMELL TO IT NOW TOO, HASN'T IT?
DON'CHA THINK IT'S ABOUT TIME YOU WOKE UP THE OLD MASTERS?
...I WILL HANDLE THAT DECISION.
AS FOR THIS BLUNDER... I WILL "UNDO" IT.
!
I BREACHED MY PROMISE TO MY MASTERS TO BE NEUTRAL.
FALSE PERSONALITY OR NO, THAT IS UNFORGIVA—
A BLUNDER? OH, NO, BUDDY.
THIS IS ALL YOUR OWN WILL.
DO YOU REALLY THINK ONE MEASLY ALTERNATE PERSONALITY COULD DEFY THE MAIN PERSONALITY?

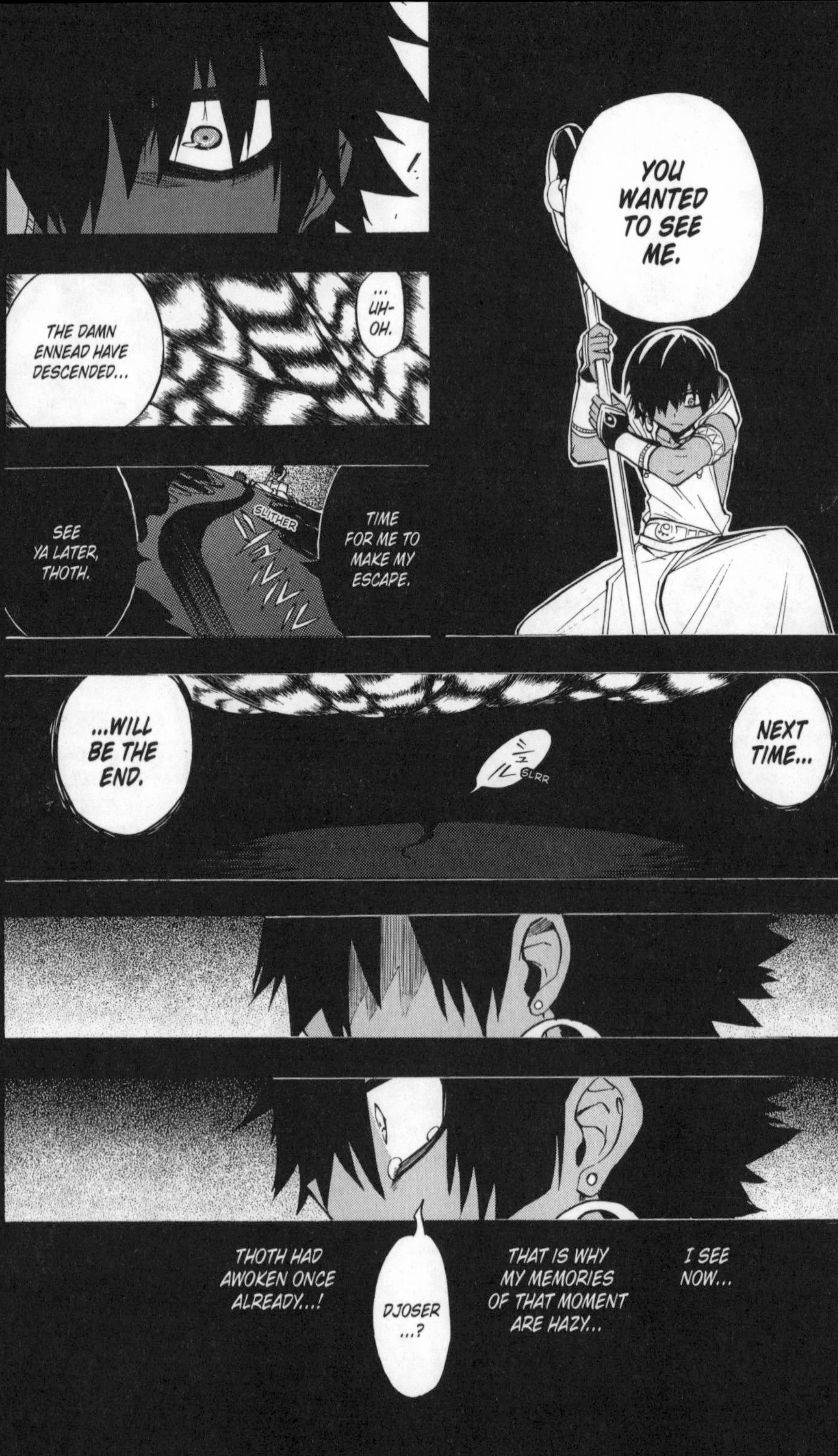
YOU WANTED TO SEE ME.
!
...UH-OH.
THE DAMN ENNEAD HAVE DESCENDED...
TIME FOR ME TO MAKE MY ESCAPE.
SLITHER
SEE YA LATER, THOTH.
NEXT TIME...
SLRR
...WILL BE THE END.
I SEE NOW...
THAT IS WHY MY MEMORIES OF THAT MOMENT ARE HAZY...
DJOSER ...?
THOTH HAD AWOKEN ONCE ALREADY...!

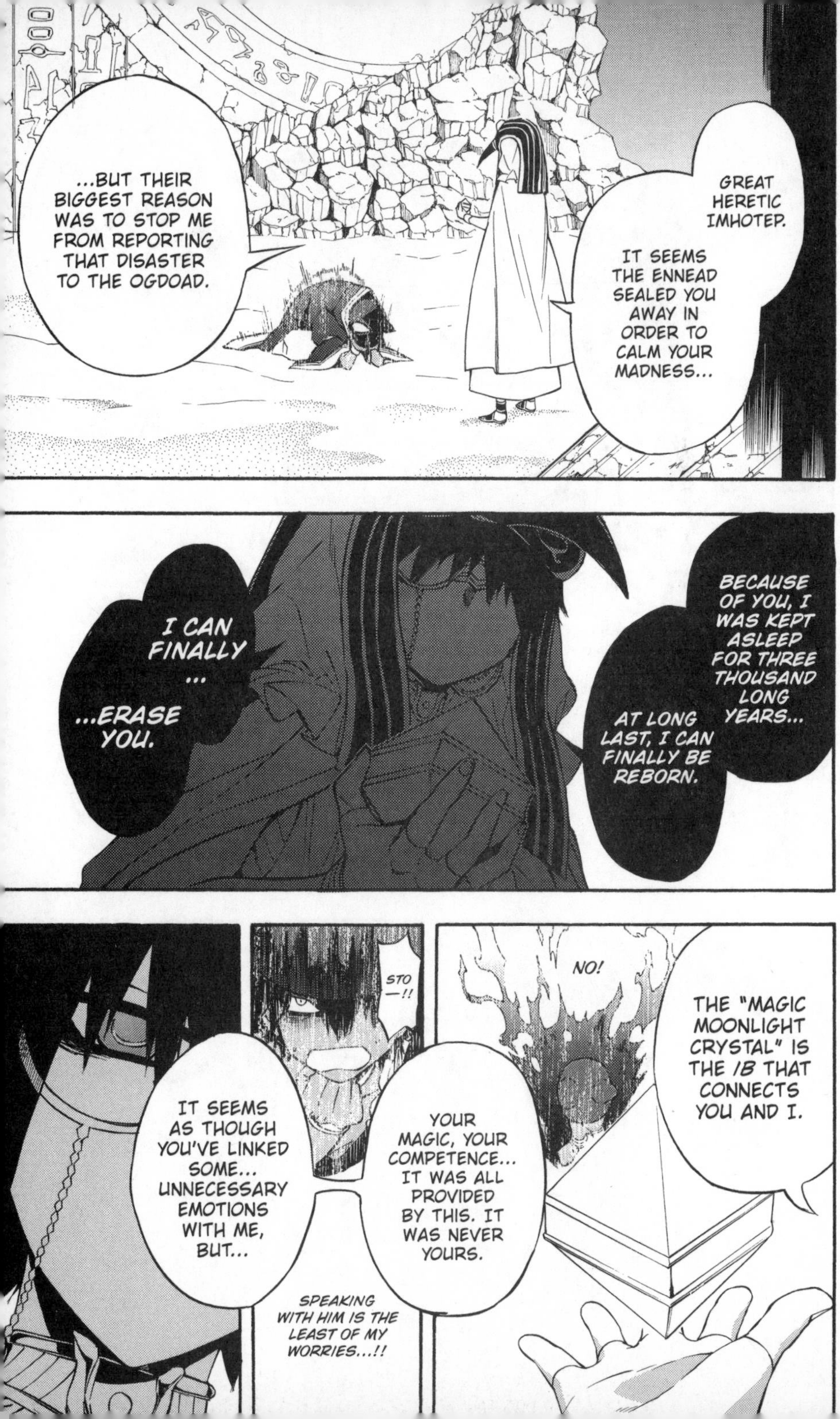
GREAT HERETIC IMHOTEP.
IT SEEMS THE ENNEAD SEALED YOU AWAY IN ORDER TO CALM YOUR MADNESS...
...BUT THEIR BIGGEST REASON WAS TO STOP ME FROM REPORTING THAT DISASTER TO THE OGDOAD.
BECAUSE OF YOU, I WAS KEPT ASLEEP FOR THREE THOUSAND LONG YEARS...
AT LONG LAST, I CAN FINALLY BE REBORN.
I CAN FINALLY ...
...ERASE YOU.
NO!
THE "MAGIC MOONLIGHT CRYSTAL" IS THE *IB* THAT CONNECTS YOU AND I.
YOUR MAGIC, YOUR COMPETENCE... IT WAS ALL PROVIDED BY THIS. IT WAS NEVER YOURS.
STO—!!
IT SEEMS AS THOUGH YOU'VE LINKED SOME... UNNECESSARY EMOTIONS WITH ME, BUT...
SPEAKING WITH HIM IS THE LEAST OF MY WORRIES...!!

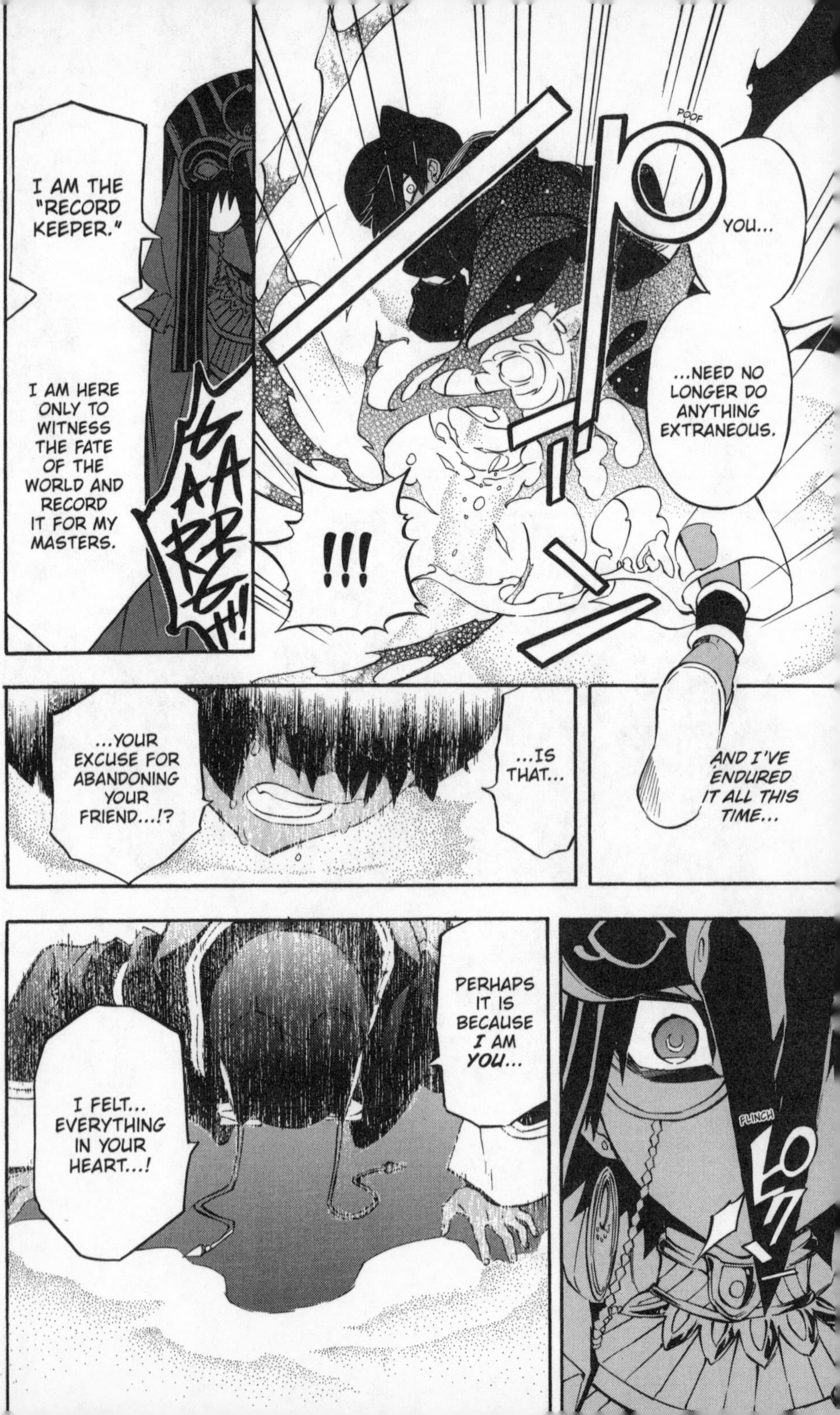
POOF
YOU...
...NEED NO LONGER DO ANYTHING EXTRANEOUS.
!!!
I AM THE "RECORD KEEPER."
I AM HERE ONLY TO WITNESS THE FATE OF THE WORLD AND RECORD IT FOR MY MASTERS.
AND I'VE ENDURED IT ALL THIS TIME...
...IS THAT...
...YOUR EXCUSE FOR ABANDONING YOUR FRIEND...!?
FLINCH
PERHAPS IT IS BECAUSE *I AM YOU*...
I FELT... EVERYTHING IN YOUR HEART...!

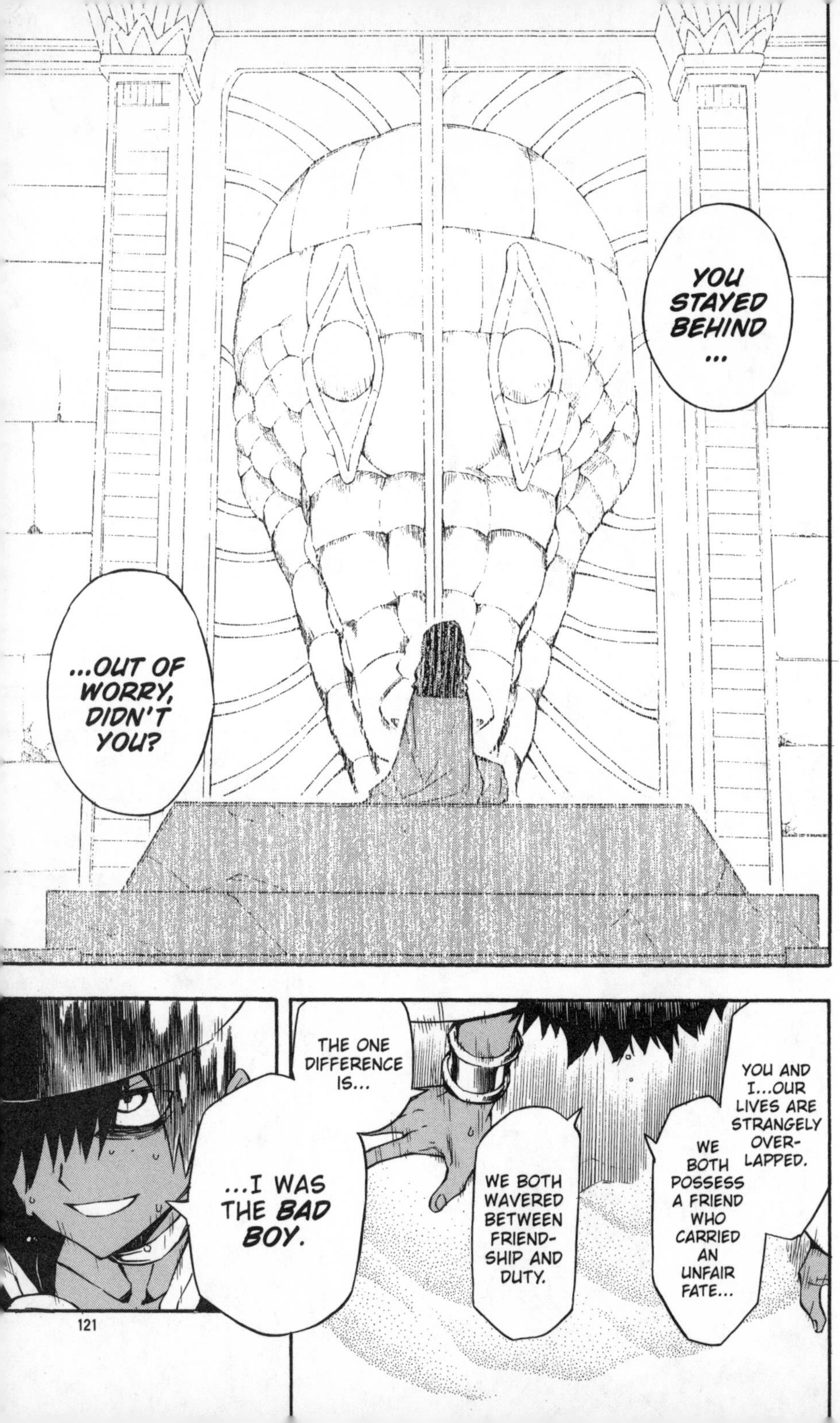
YOU STAYED BEHIND...
...OUT OF WORRY, DIDN'T YOU?
YOU AND I...OUR LIVES ARE STRANGELY OVER-LAPPED.
WE BOTH POSSESS A FRIEND WHO CARRIED AN UNFAIR FATE...
WE BOTH WAVERED BETWEEN FRIEND-SHIP AND DUTY.
THE ONE DIFFERENCE IS...
...I WAS THE *BAD BOY*.

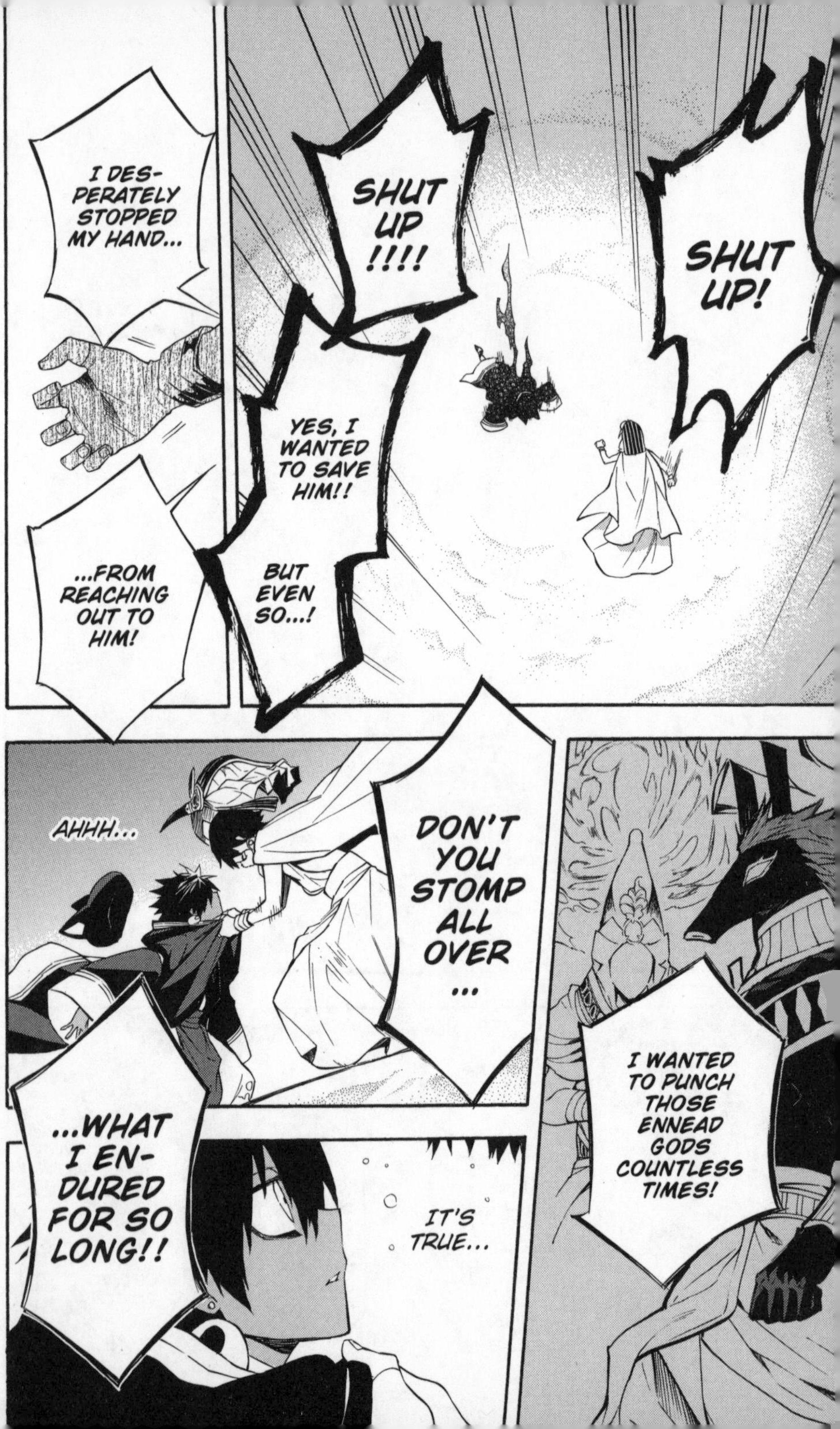

SHUT UP!
SHUT UP !!!!
YES, I WANTED TO SAVE HIM!!
BUT EVEN SO...!
I DES-PERATELY STOPPED MY HAND...
...FROM REACHING OUT TO HIM!
I WANTED TO PUNCH THOSE ENNEAD GODS COUNTLESS TIMES!
DON'T YOU STOMP ALL OVER ...
AHHH...
IT'S TRUE...
...WHAT I EN-DURED FOR SO LONG!!

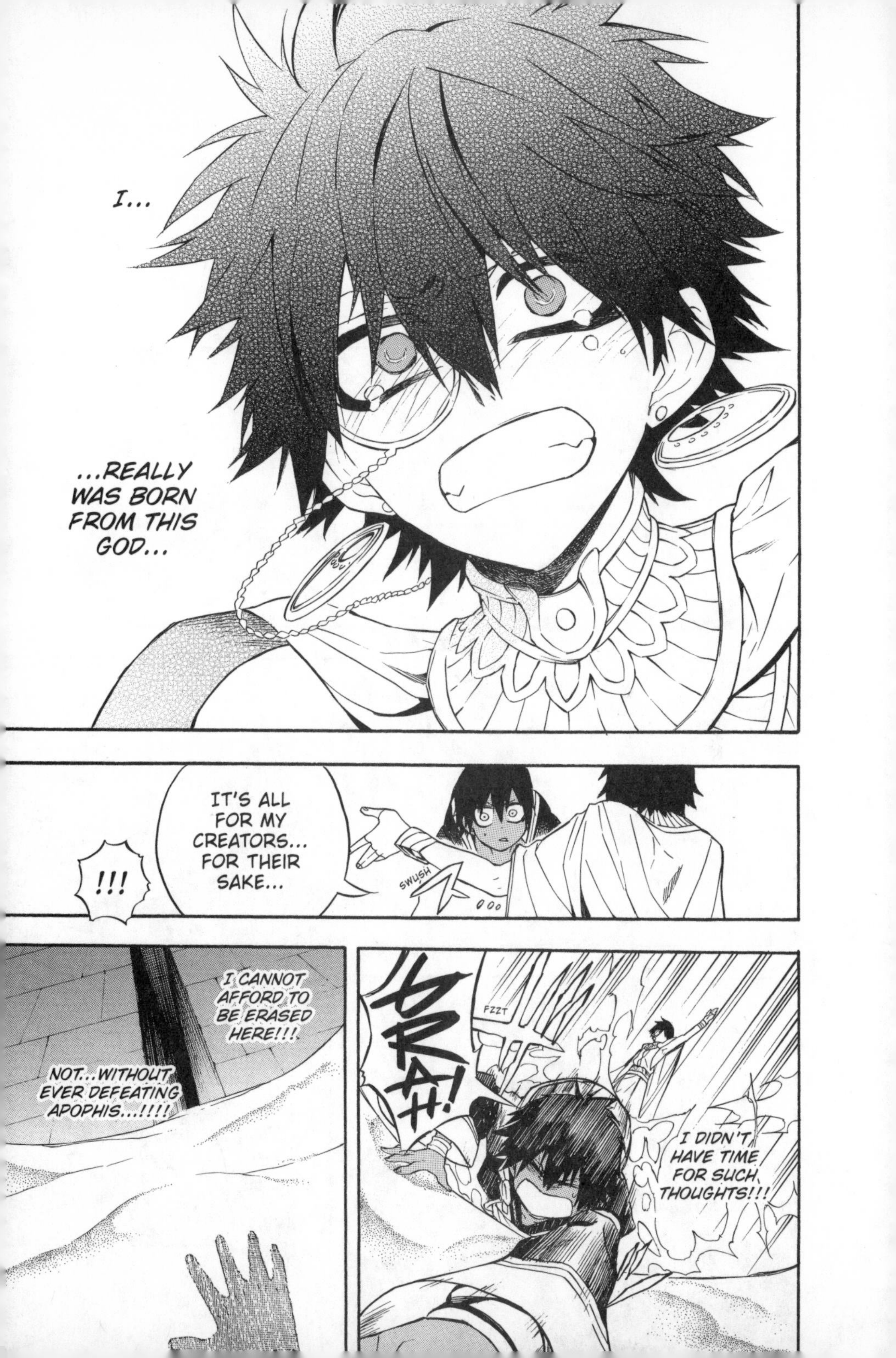
I...
...REALLY WAS BORN FROM THIS GOD...
IT'S ALL FOR MY CREATORS... FOR THEIR SAKE...
SWUSH
!!!
GRAH!
FZZT
I DIDN'T HAVE TIME FOR SUCH THOUGHTS!!!
I CANNOT AFFORD TO BE ERASED HERE!!!
NOT...WITHOUT EVER DEFEATING APOPHIS...!!!!

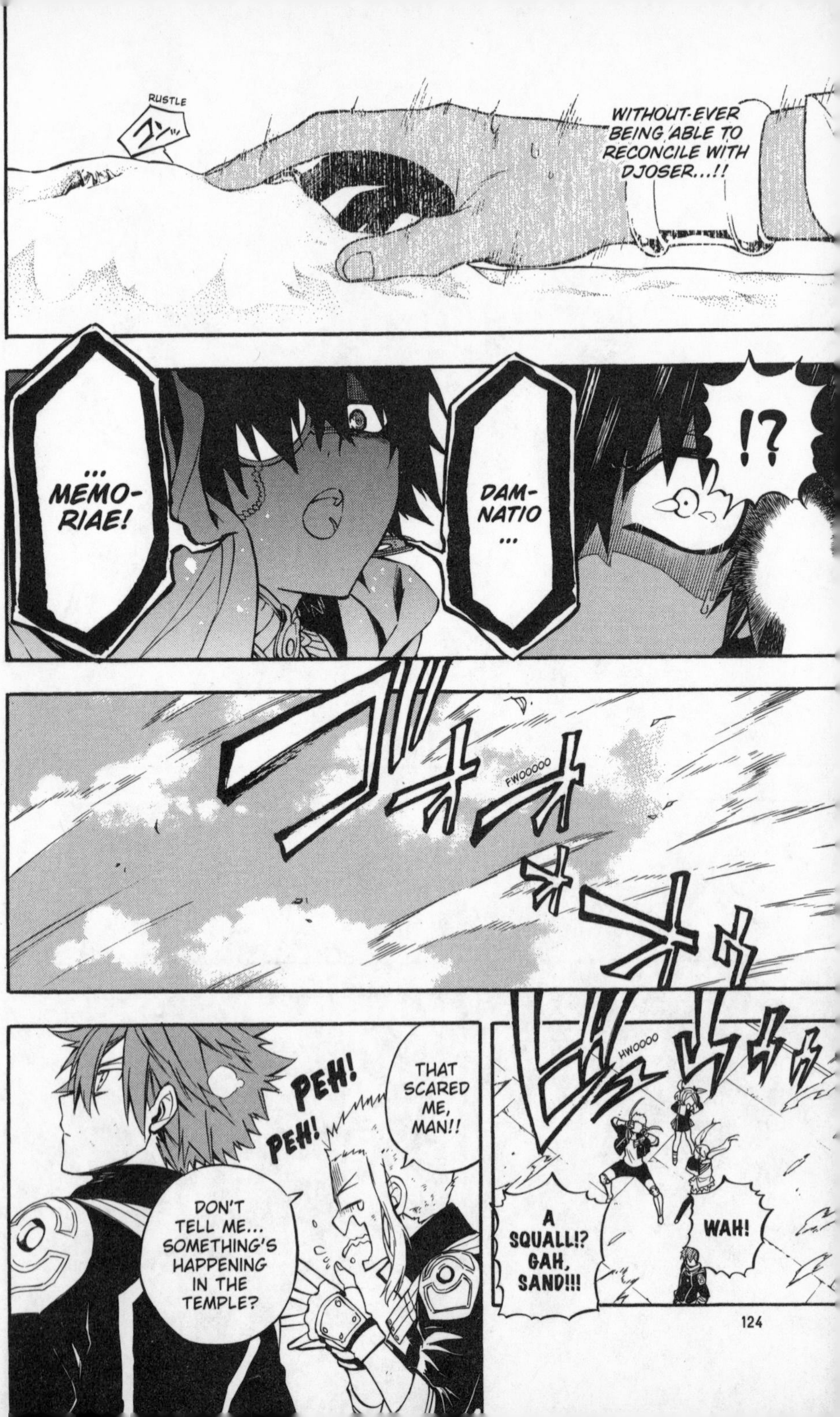
WITHOUT EVER BEING ABLE TO RECONCILE WITH DJOSER...!!
RUSTLE
!?
DAM-NATIO ...
... MEMO-RIAE!
FWOOOOO
HWOOOO
WAH!
A SQUALL!? GAH, SAND!!!
THAT SCARED ME, MAN!!
PEH! PEH!
DON'T TELL ME... SOMETHING'S HAPPENING IN THE TEMPLE?

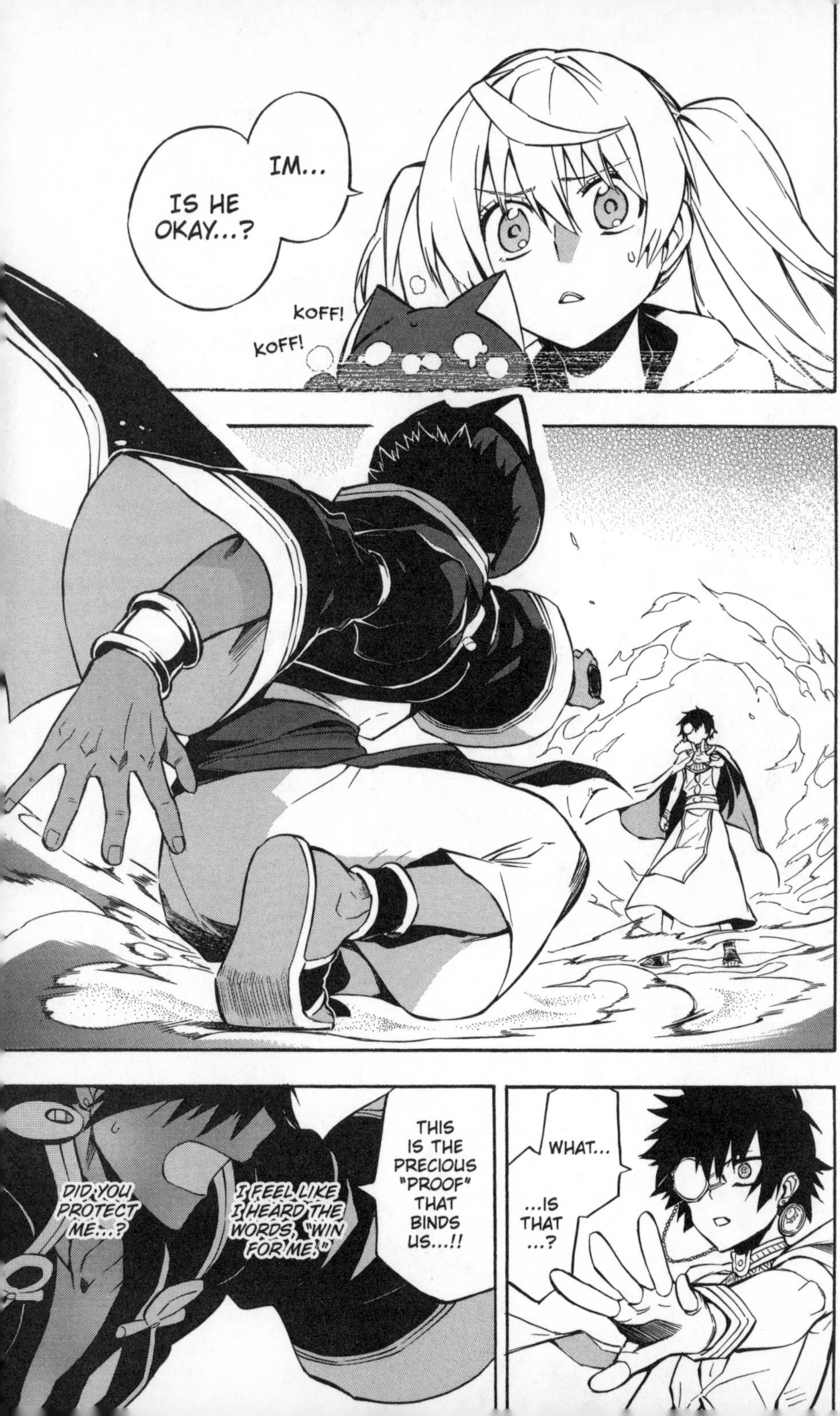
IM...
IS HE OKAY...?
KOFF!
KOFF!
WHAT...
...IS THAT ...?
THIS IS THE PRECIOUS "PROOF" THAT BINDS US...!!
I FEEL LIKE I HEARD THE WORDS, "WIN FOR ME."
DID YOU PROTECT ME...?

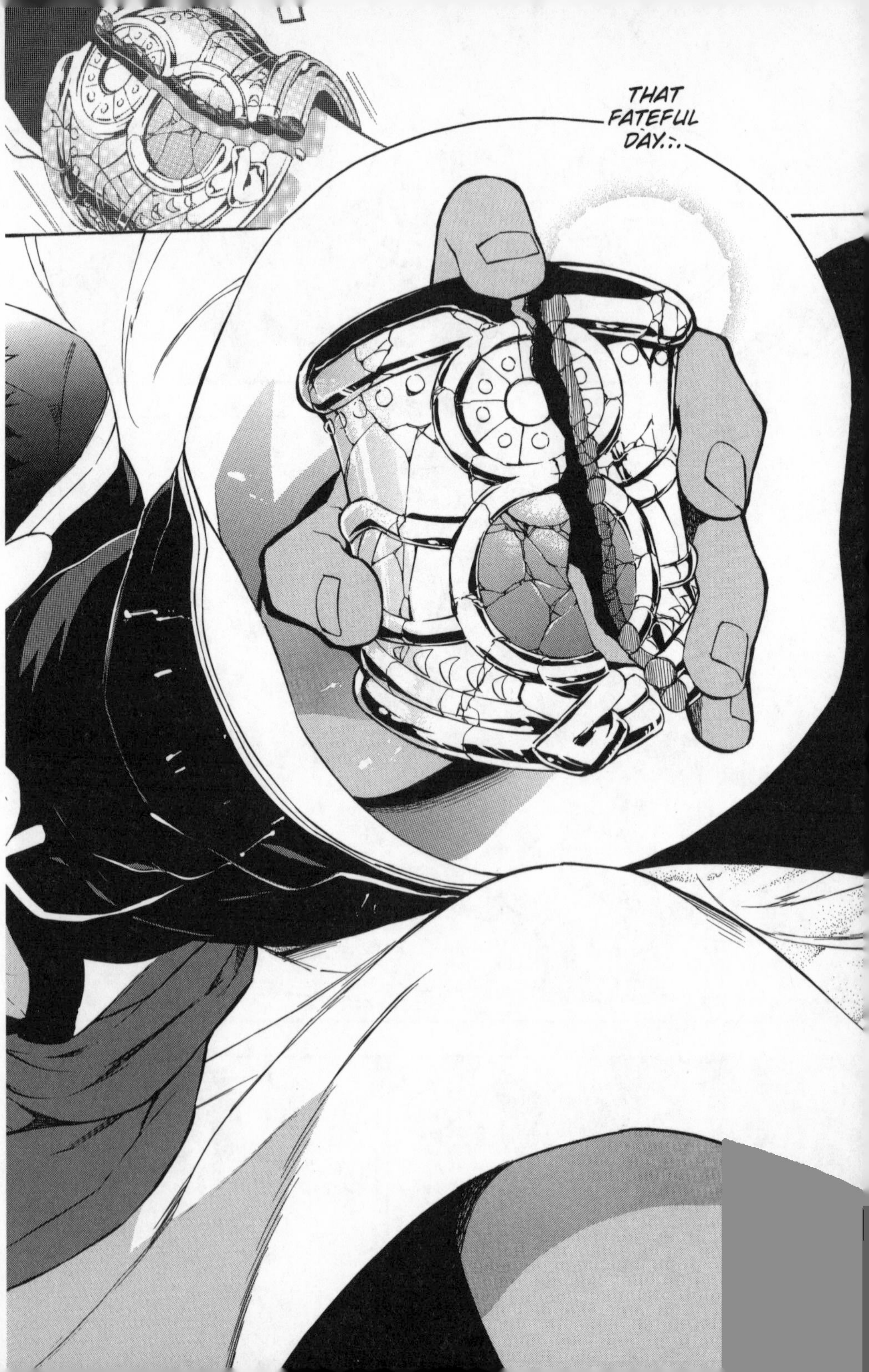
THAT FATEFUL DAY......

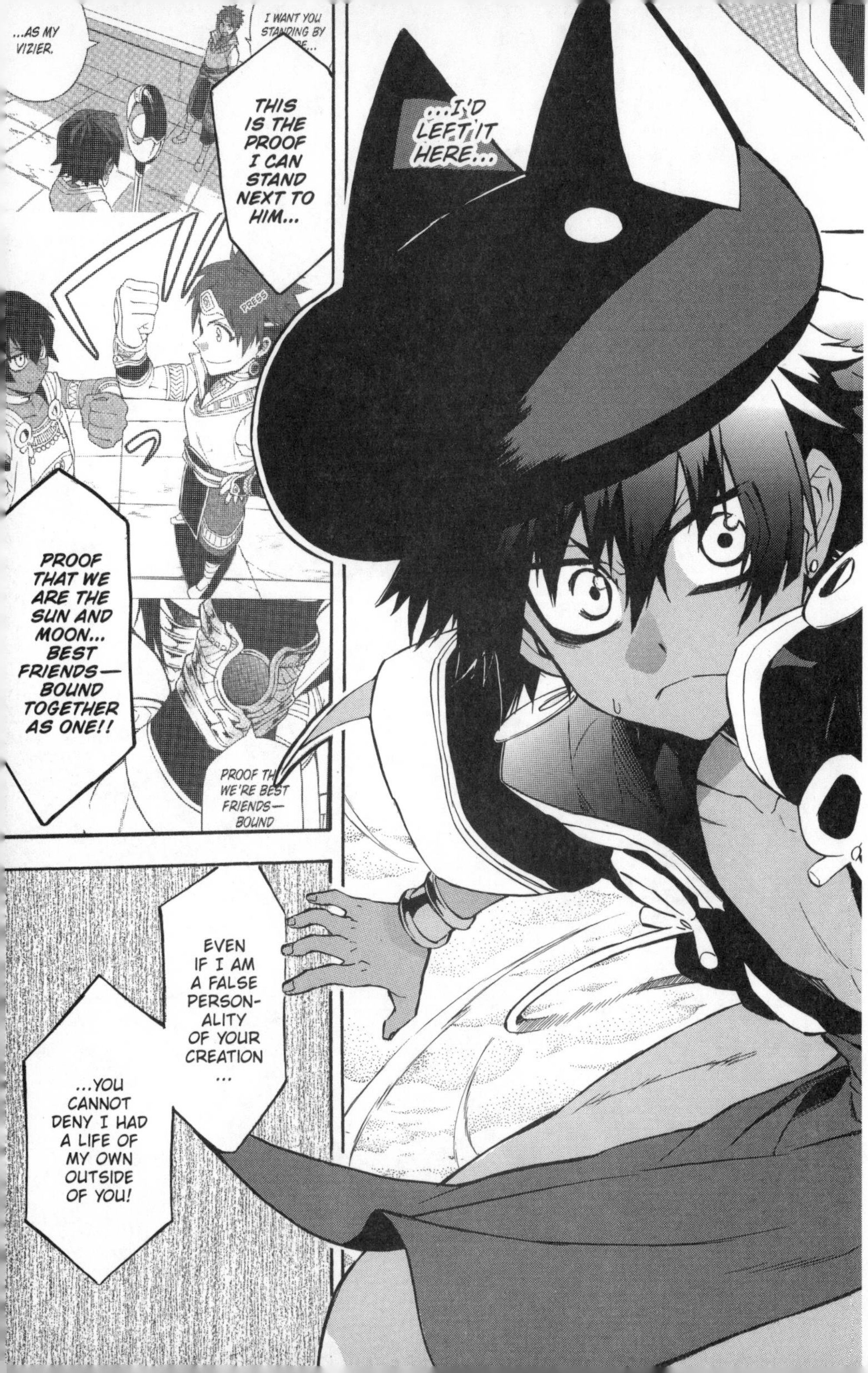

...I'D LEFT IT HERE...
I WANT YOU STANDING BY
...AS MY VIZIER.
THIS IS THE PROOF I CAN STAND NEXT TO HIM...
PRESS
PROOF THAT WE ARE THE SUN AND MOON... BEST FRIENDS—BOUND TOGETHER AS ONE!!
PROOF TH WE'RE BEST FRIENDS—BOUND
EVEN IF I AM A FALSE PERSON-ALITY OF YOUR CREATION...
...YOU CANNOT DENY I HAD A LIFE OF MY OWN OUTSIDE OF YOU!

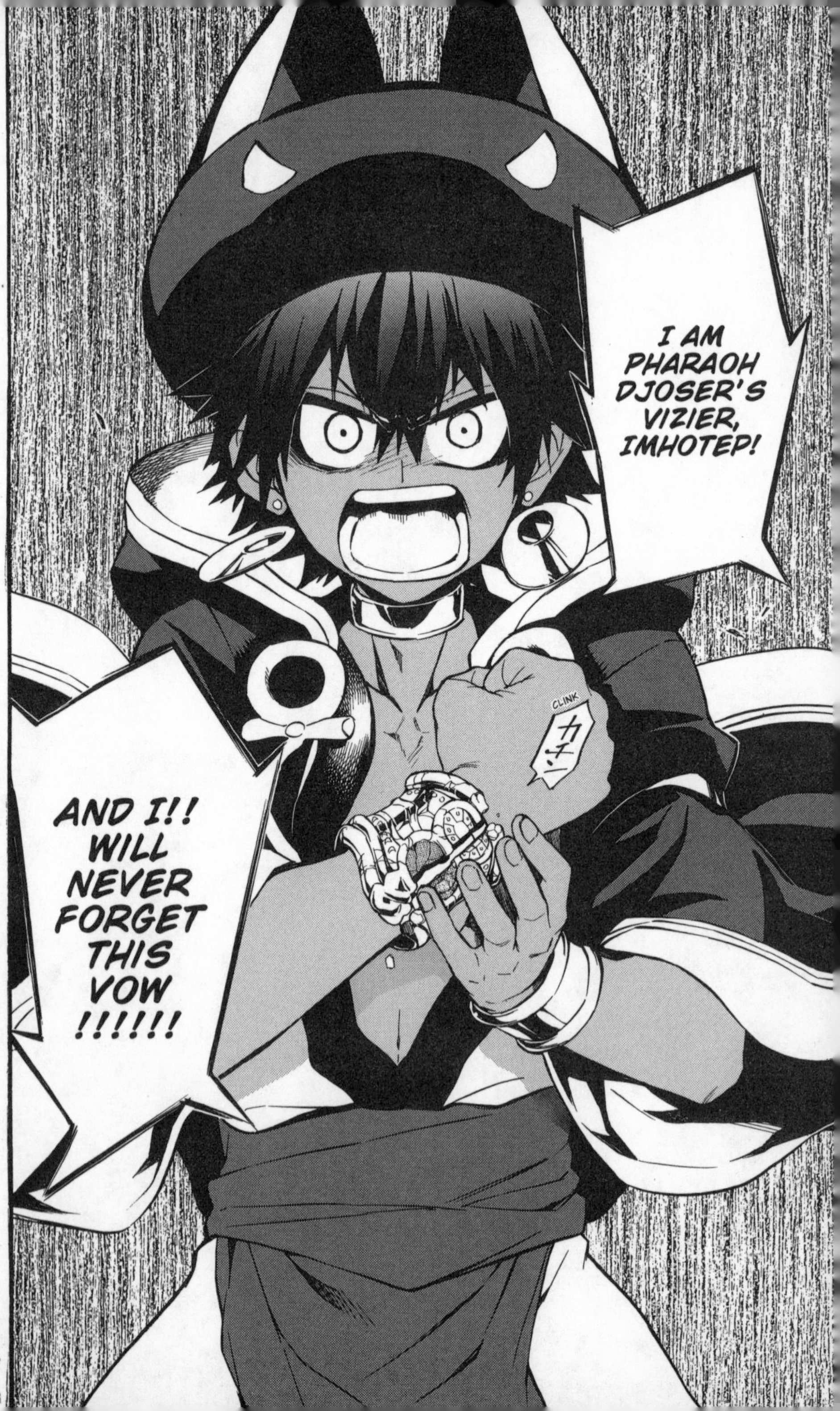
I AM PHARAOH DJOSER'S VIZIER, IMHOTEP!
CLINK
カチン
AND I!! WILL NEVER FORGET THIS VOW !!!!!!

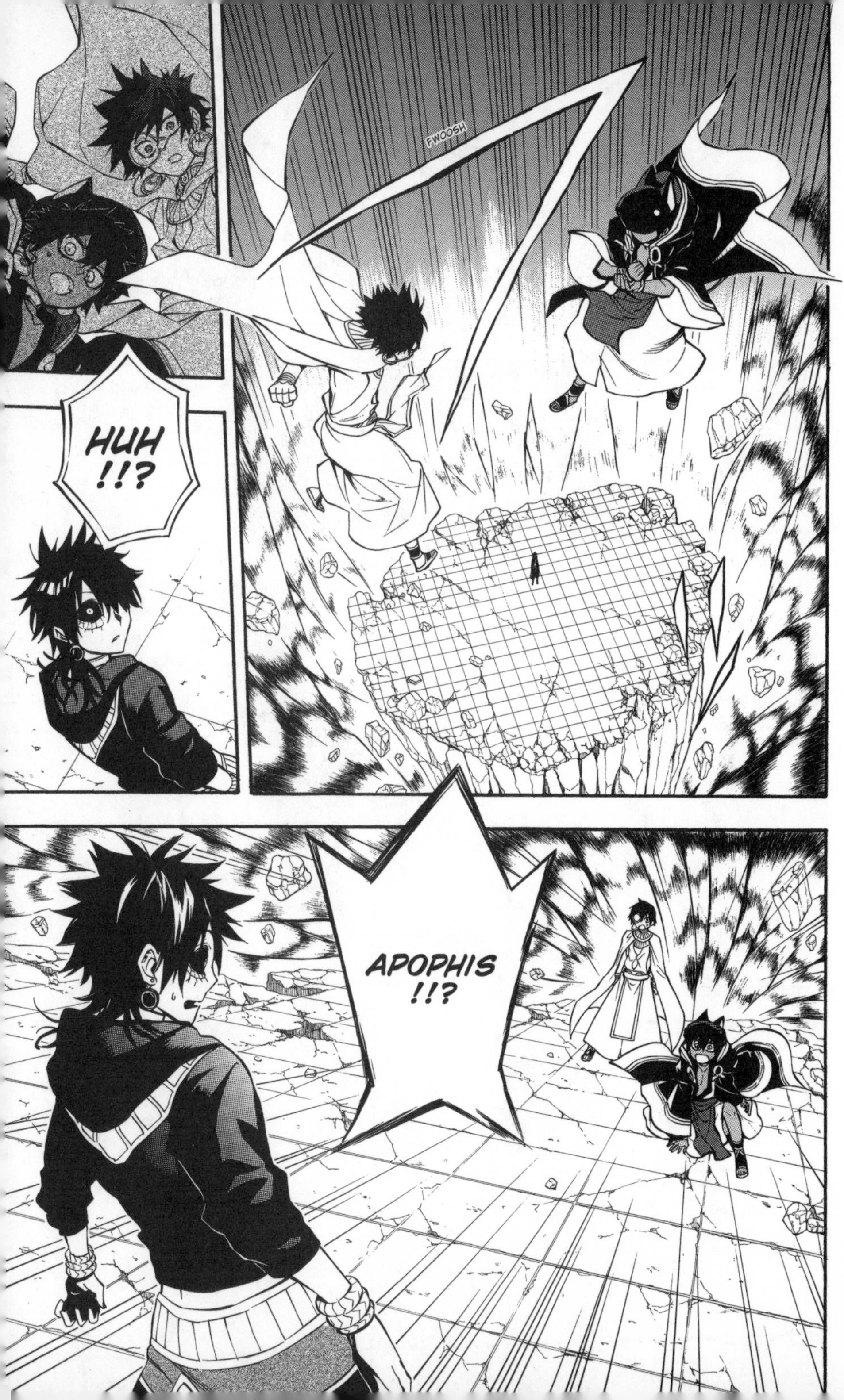
FWOOSH
HUH !!?
APOPHIS !!?

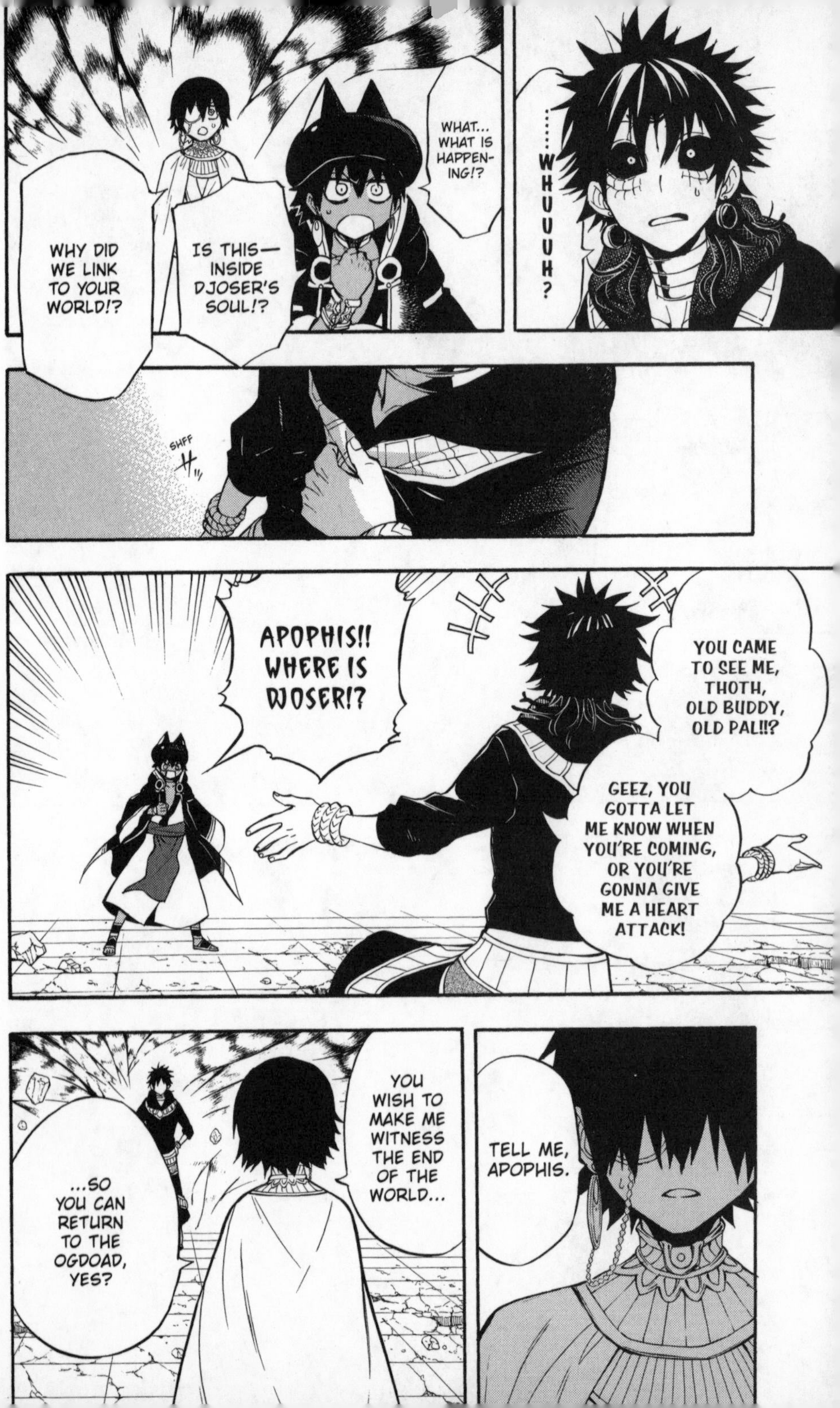
......WHUUUUH?
WHAT... WHAT IS HAPPENING!?
IS THIS— INSIDE DJOSER'S SOUL!?
WHY DID WE LINK TO YOUR WORLD!?
SHFF
YOU CAME TO SEE ME, THOTH, OLD BUDDY, OLD PAL!!?
GEEZ, YOU GOTTA LET ME KNOW WHEN YOU'RE COMING, OR YOU'RE GONNA GIVE ME A HEART ATTACK!
APOPHIS!! WHERE IS DJOSER!?
TELL ME, APOPHIS.
YOU WISH TO MAKE ME WITNESS THE END OF THE WORLD...
...SO YOU CAN RETURN TO THE OGDOAD, YES?

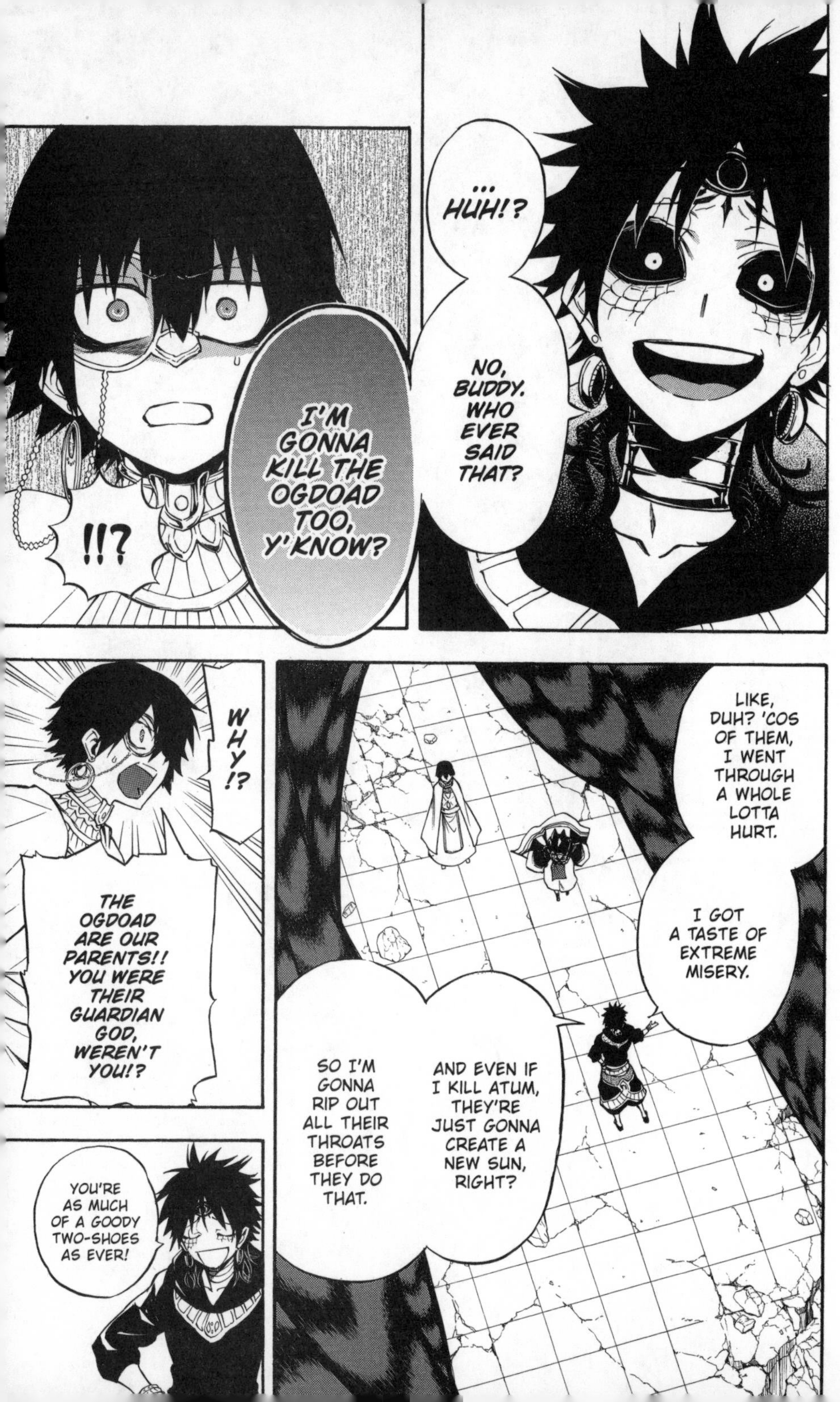
...HUH!?
NO, BUDDY. WHO EVER SAID THAT?
I'M GONNA KILL THE OGDOAD TOO, Y'KNOW?
!!?
LIKE, DUH? 'COS OF THEM, I WENT THROUGH A WHOLE LOTTA HURT.
I GOT A TASTE OF EXTREME MISERY.
AND EVEN IF I KILL ATUM, THEY'RE JUST GONNA CREATE A NEW SUN, RIGHT?
SO I'M GONNA RIP OUT ALL THEIR THROATS BEFORE THEY DO THAT.
WHY!?
THE OGDOAD ARE OUR PARENTS!! YOU WERE THEIR GUARDIAN GOD, WEREN'T YOU!?
YOU'RE AS MUCH OF A GOODY TWO-SHOES AS EVER!

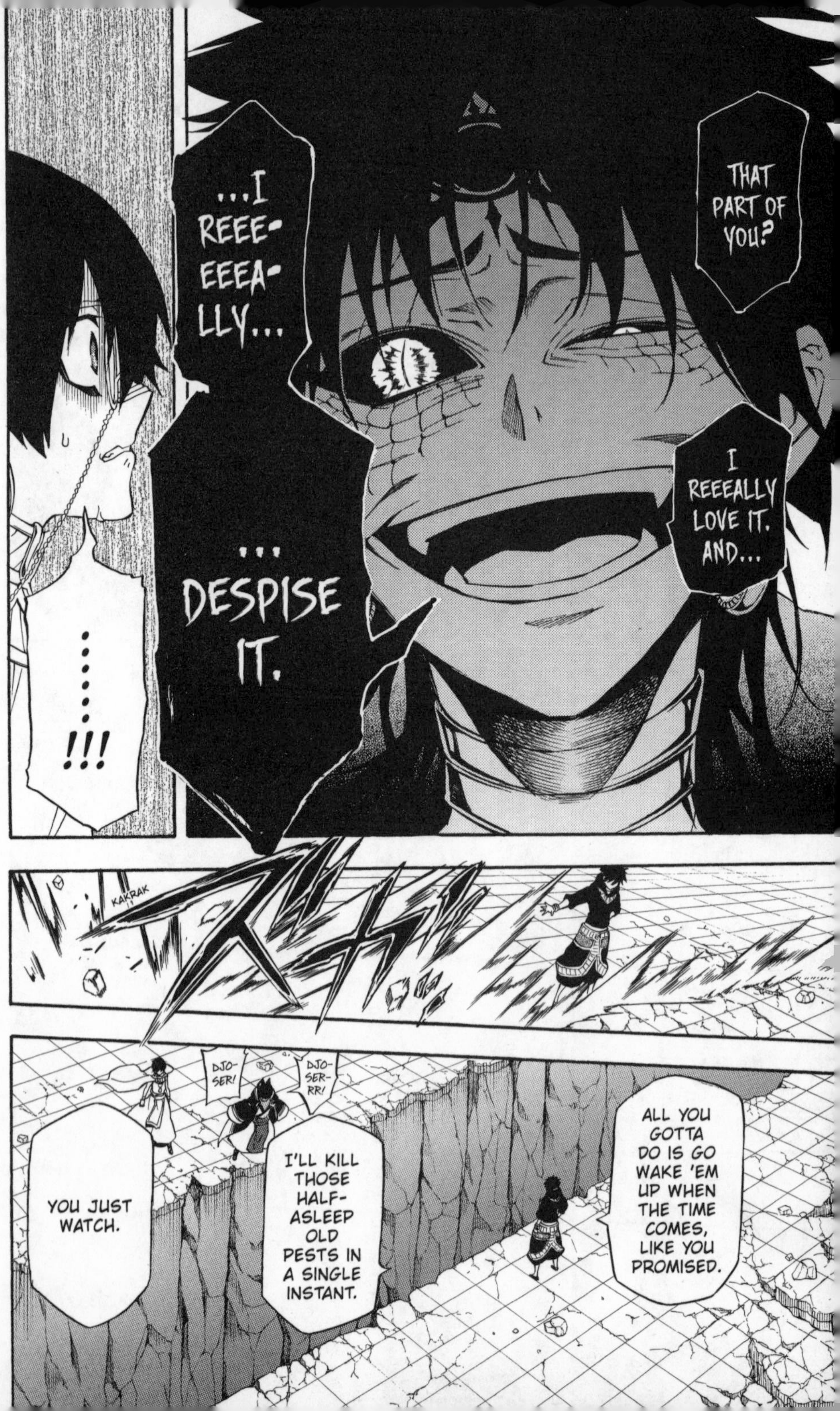
THAT PART OF YOU?
I REEEALLY LOVE IT. AND...
...I REEE-EEEA-LLY...
... DESPISE IT.
......!!!
KAKRAK
ALL YOU GOTTA DO IS GO WAKE 'EM UP WHEN THE TIME COMES, LIKE YOU PROMISED.
DJO-SERRR!
DJO-SER!
I'LL KILL THOSE HALF-ASLEEP OLD PESTS IN A SINGLE INSTANT.
YOU JUST WATCH.

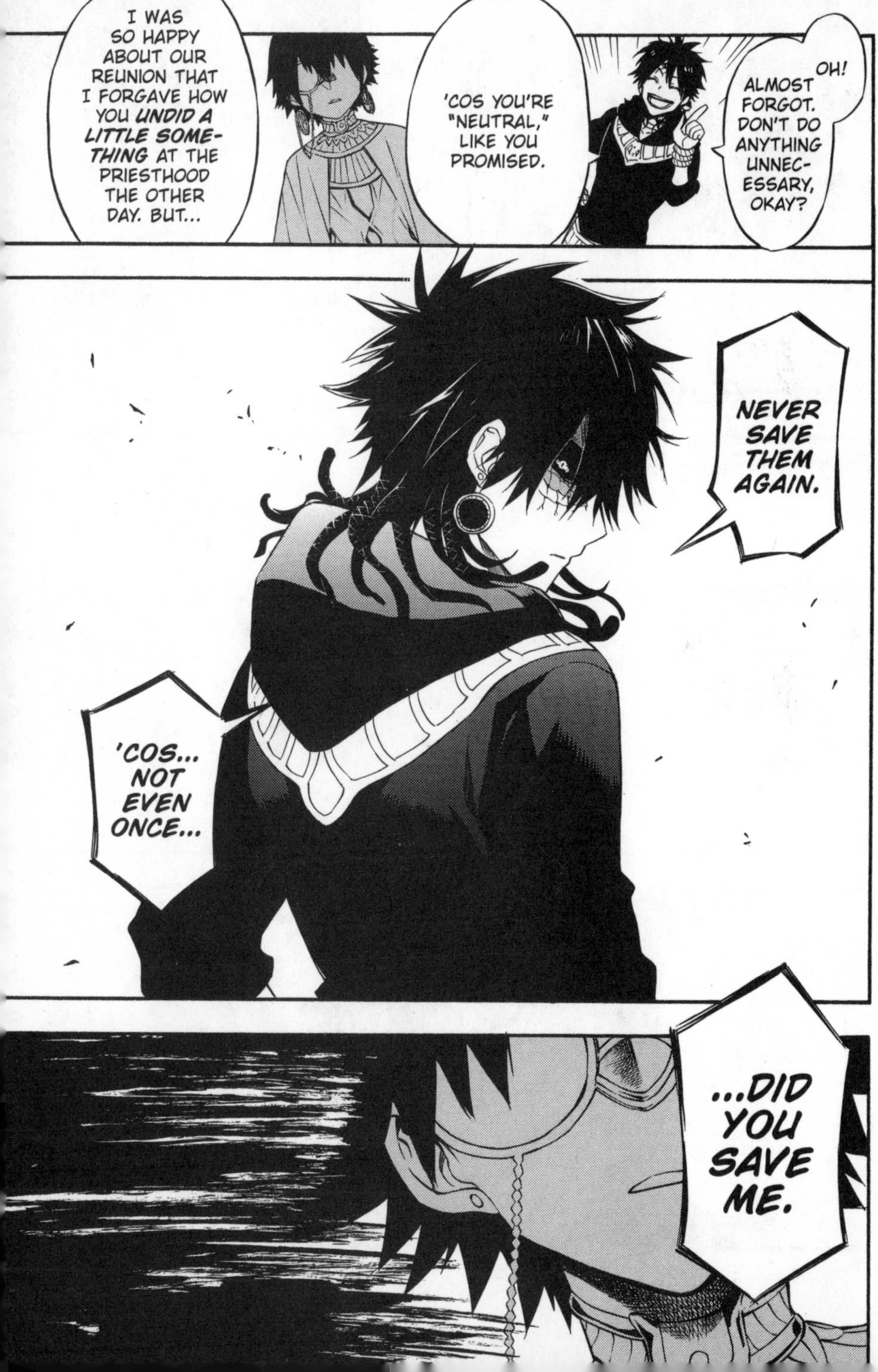
OH! ALMOST FORGOT. DON'T DO ANYTHING UNNEC-ESSARY, OKAY?
'COS YOU'RE "NEUTRAL," LIKE YOU PROMISED.
I WAS SO HAPPY ABOUT OUR REUNION THAT I FORGAVE HOW YOU *UNDID A LITTLE SOME-THING* AT THE PRIESTHOOD THE OTHER DAY. BUT...
NEVER SAVE THEM AGAIN.
'COS... NOT EVEN ONCE...
...DID YOU SAVE ME.

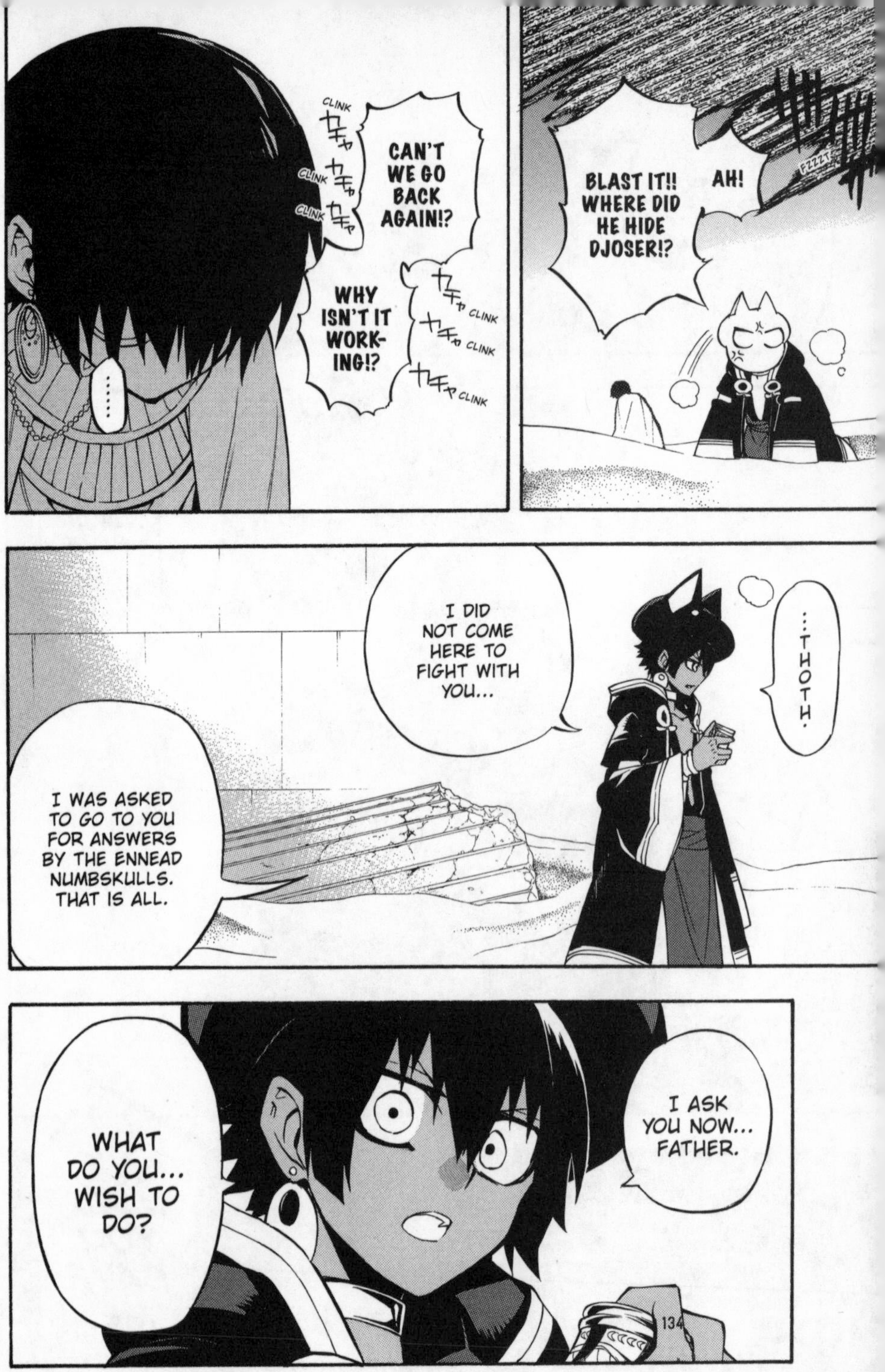
FZZZT
AH!
BLAST IT!! WHERE DID HE HIDE DJOSER!?
カチャ CLINK
カチャ CLINK
カチャ CLINK
CAN'T WE GO BACK AGAIN!?
カチャ CLINK
カチャ CLINK
カチャ CLINK
WHY ISN'T IT WORKING!?
......
...THOTH.
I DID NOT COME HERE TO FIGHT WITH YOU...
I WAS ASKED TO GO TO YOU FOR ANSWERS BY THE ENNEAD NUMBSKULLS. THAT IS ALL.
I ASK YOU NOW... FATHER.
WHAT DO YOU... WISH TO DO?

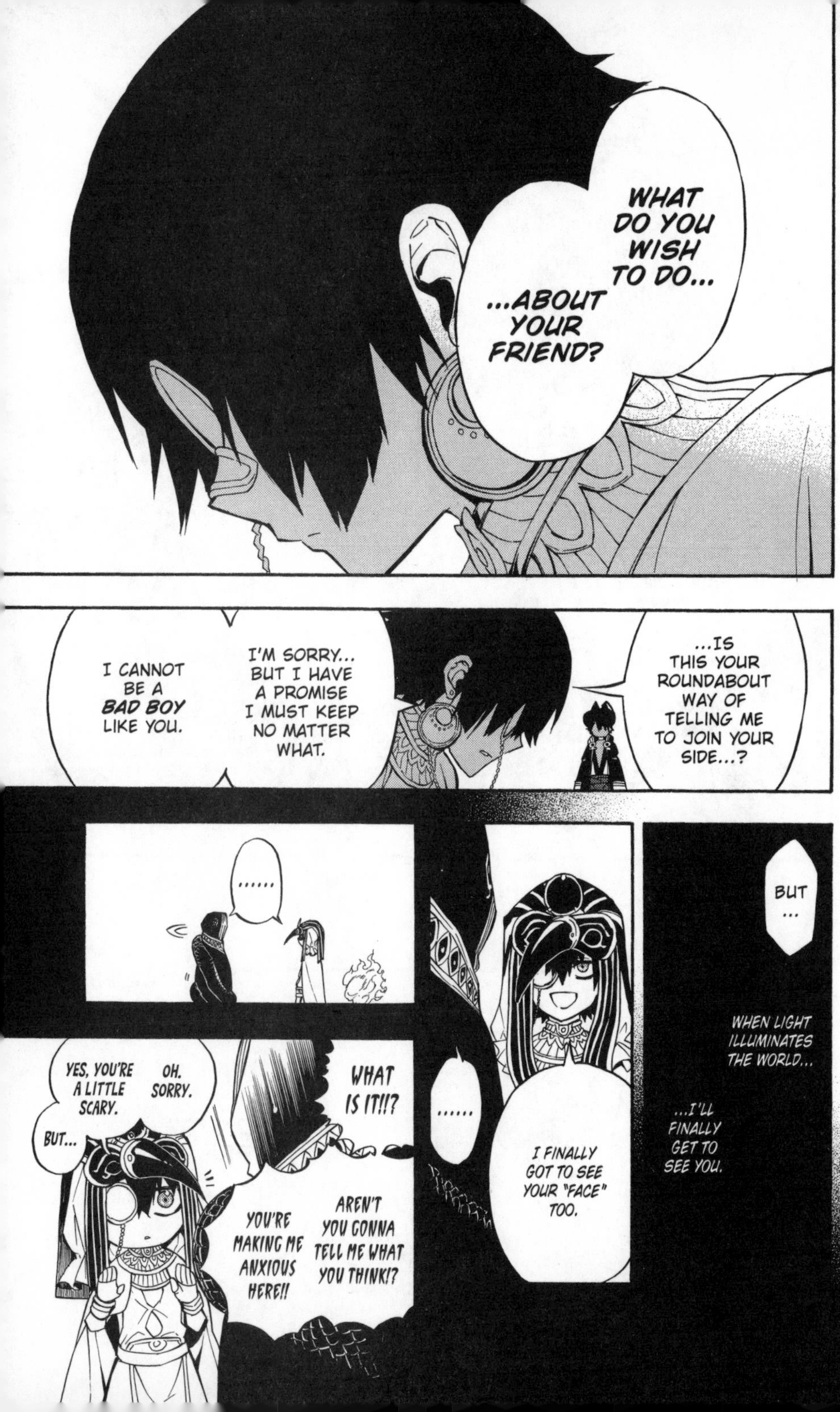
WHAT DO YOU WISH TO DO...
...ABOUT YOUR FRIEND?
...IS THIS YOUR ROUNDABOUT WAY OF TELLING ME TO JOIN YOUR SIDE...?
I'M SORRY... BUT I HAVE A PROMISE I MUST KEEP NO MATTER WHAT.
I CANNOT BE A BAD BOY LIKE YOU.
BUT ...
WHEN LIGHT ILLUMINATES THE WORLD...
...I'LL FINALLY GET TO SEE YOU.
......
I FINALLY GOT TO SEE YOUR "FACE" TOO.
......
WHAT IS IT!!?
AREN'T YOU GONNA TELL ME WHAT YOU THINK!?
YOU'RE MAKING ME ANXIOUS HERE!!
OH. SORRY.
YES, YOU'RE A LITTLE SCARY.
BUT...

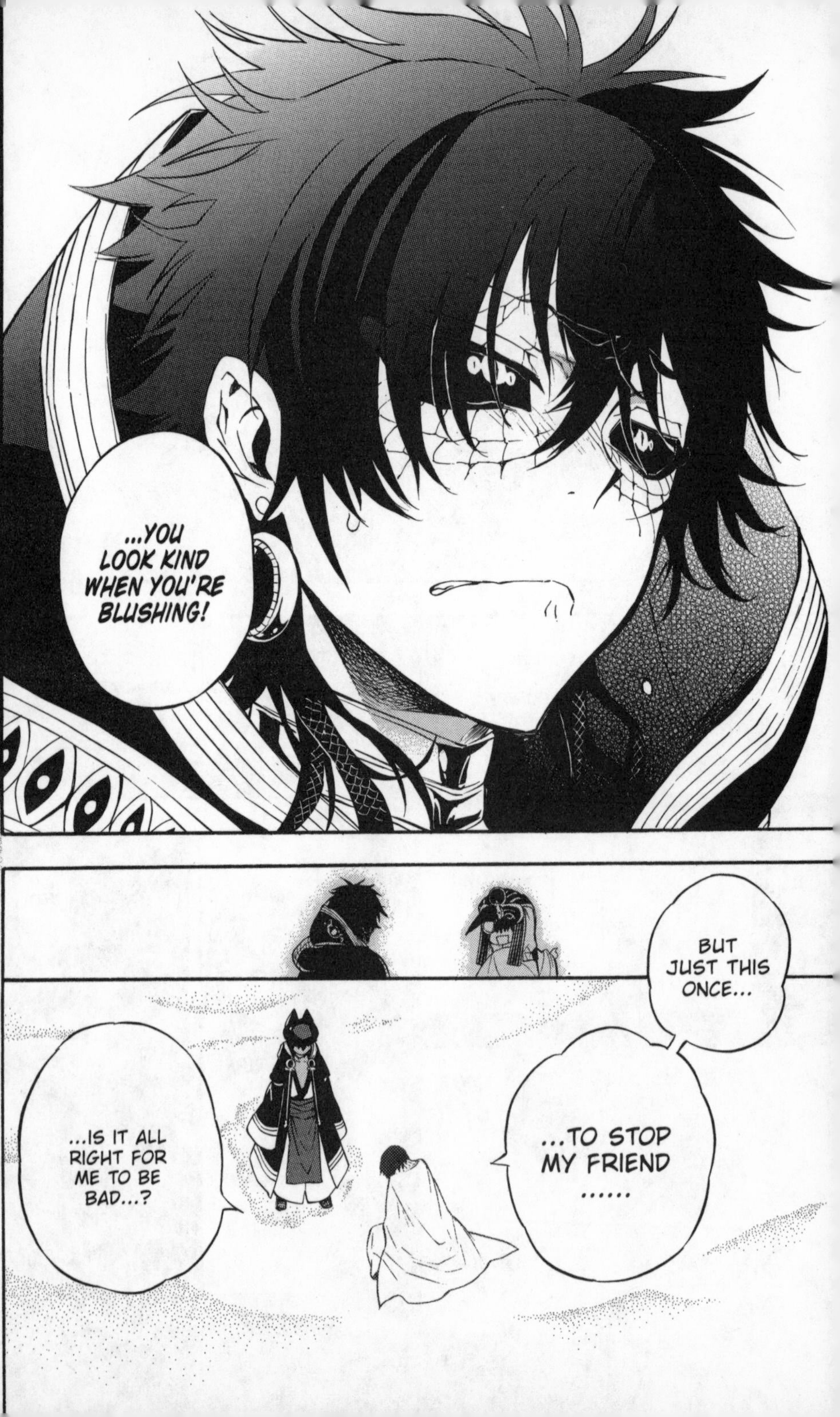
...YOU LOOK KIND WHEN YOU'RE BLUSHING!
BUT JUST THIS ONCE...
...TO STOP MY FRIEND ......
...IS IT ALL RIGHT FOR ME TO BE BAD...?

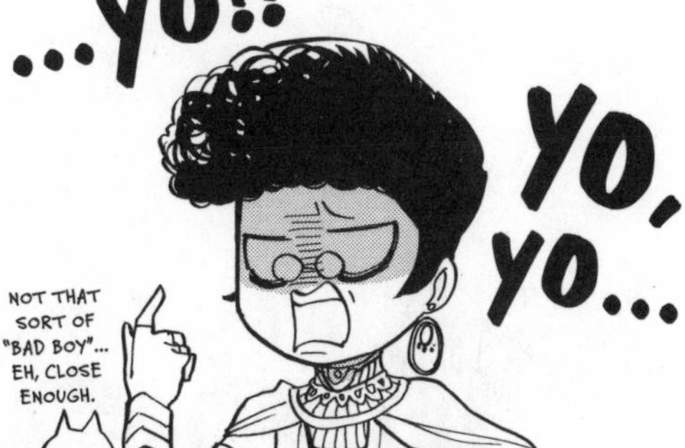

...YO!!
YO, YO...
NOT THAT SORT OF "BAD BOY"... EH, CLOSE ENOUGH.
BAD BOY

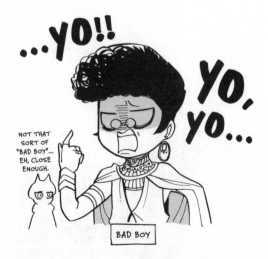

Great Priest Imhotep

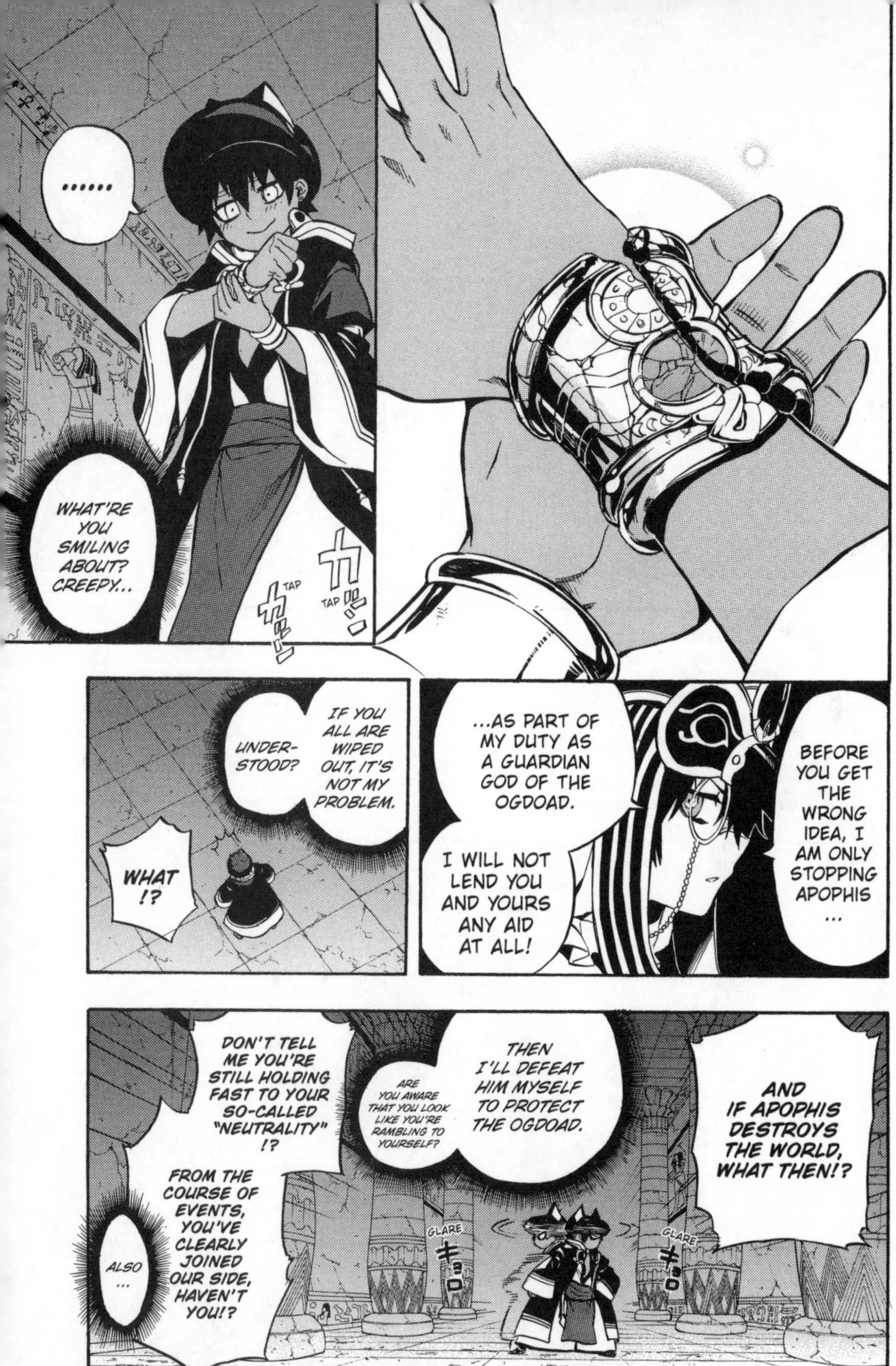
......
WHAT'RE YOU SMILING ABOUT? CREEPY...
TAP
TAP
BEFORE YOU GET THE WRONG IDEA, I AM ONLY STOPPING APOPHIS ...
...AS PART OF MY DUTY AS A GUARDIAN GOD OF THE OGDOAD.
I WILL NOT LEND YOU AND YOURS ANY AID AT ALL!
IF YOU ALL ARE WIPED OUT, IT'S NOT MY PROBLEM.
UNDER-STOOD?
WHAT !?
AND IF APOPHIS DESTROYS THE WORLD, WHAT THEN!?
THEN I'LL DEFEAT HIM MYSELF TO PROTECT THE OGDOAD.
ARE YOU AWARE THAT YOU LOOK LIKE YOU'RE RAMBLING TO YOURSELF?
DON'T TELL ME YOU'RE STILL HOLDING FAST TO YOUR SO-CALLED "NEUTRALITY" !?
FROM THE COURSE OF EVENTS, YOU'VE CLEARLY JOINED OUR SIDE, HAVEN'T YOU!?
ALSO ...
GLARE
GLARE

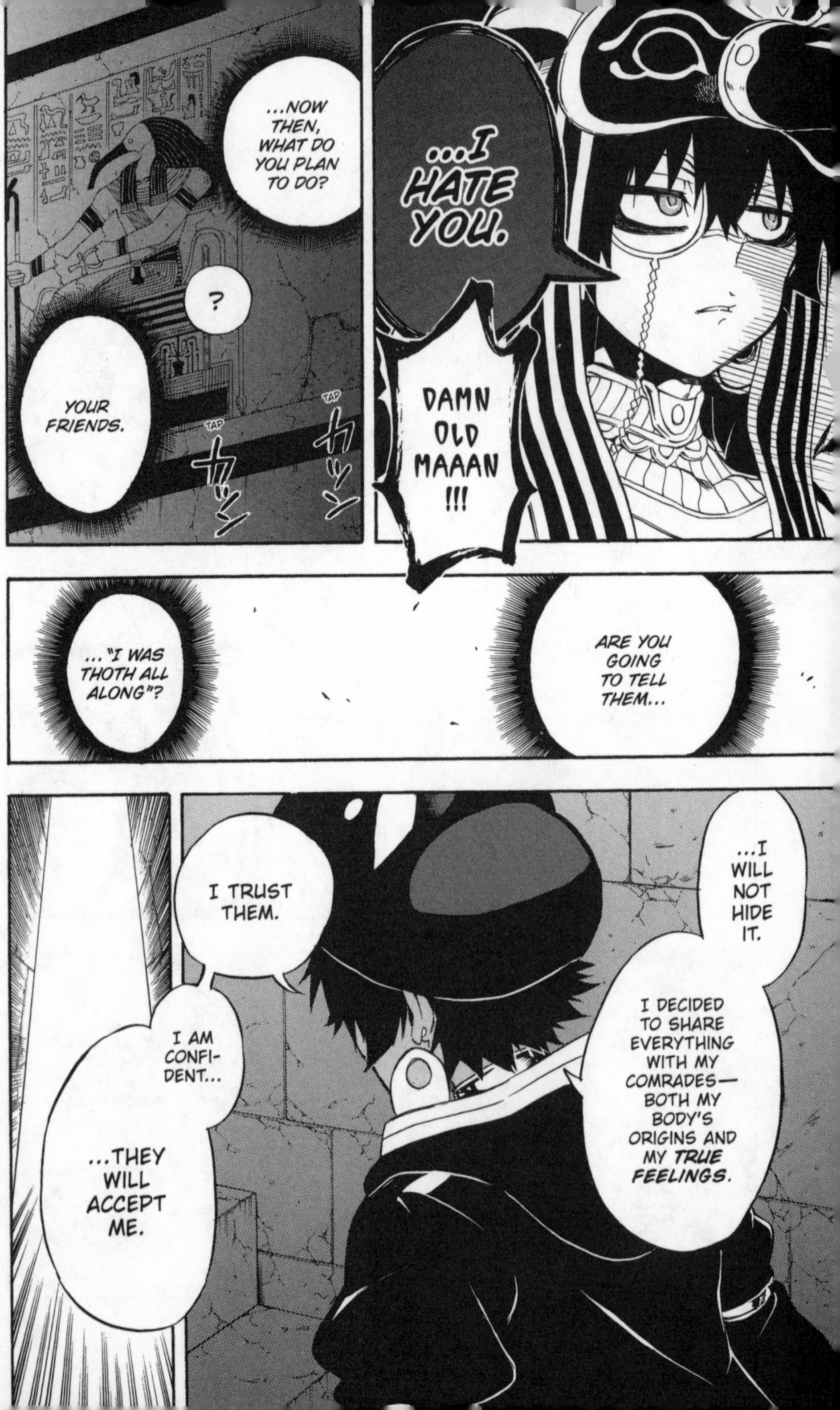
...I HATE YOU.
DAMN OLD MAAAN!!!
...NOW THEN, WHAT DO YOU PLAN TO DO?
?
YOUR FRIENDS.
TAP
TAP
ARE YOU GOING TO TELL THEM...
..."I WAS THOTH ALL ALONG"?
...I WILL NOT HIDE IT.
I DECIDED TO SHARE EVERYTHING WITH MY COMRADES—BOTH MY BODY'S ORIGINS AND MY TRUE FEELINGS.
I TRUST THEM.
I AM CONFIDENT...
...THEY WILL ACCEPT ME.

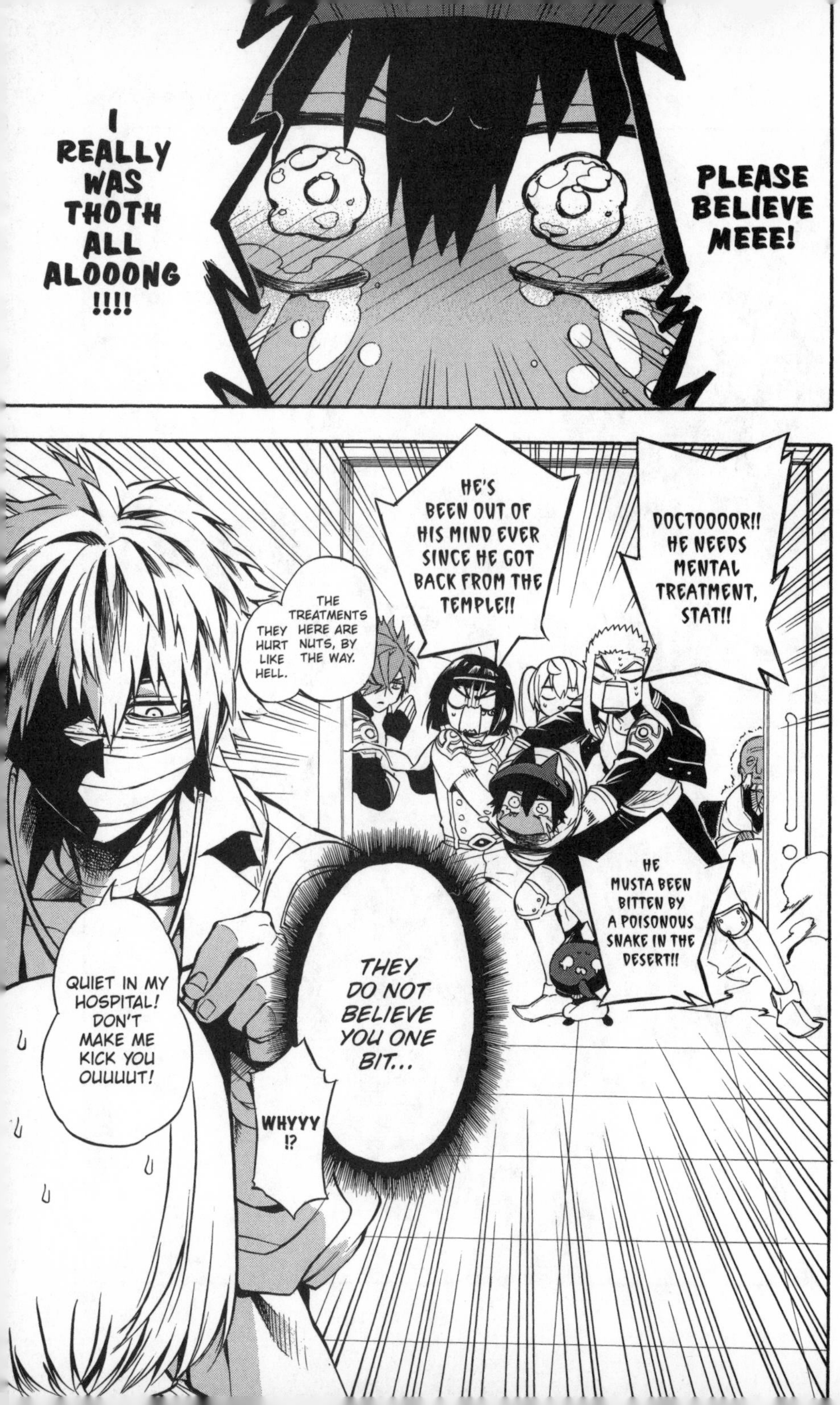
PLEASE BELIEVE MEEE!
I REALLY WAS THOTH ALL ALOOONG!!!!
DOCTOOOOR!! HE NEEDS MENTAL TREATMENT, STAT!!
HE'S BEEN OUT OF HIS MIND EVER SINCE HE GOT BACK FROM THE TEMPLE!!
THE TREATMENTS HERE ARE NUTS, BY THE WAY. THEY HURT LIKE HELL.
HE MUSTA BEEN BITTEN BY A POISONOUS SNAKE IN THE DESERT!!
THEY DO NOT BELIEVE YOU ONE BIT...
QUIET IN MY HOSPITAL! DON'T MAKE ME KICK YOU OUUUUT!
WHYYY!?

SCROLL 35: OUR COMPLICATED CONFESSIONS

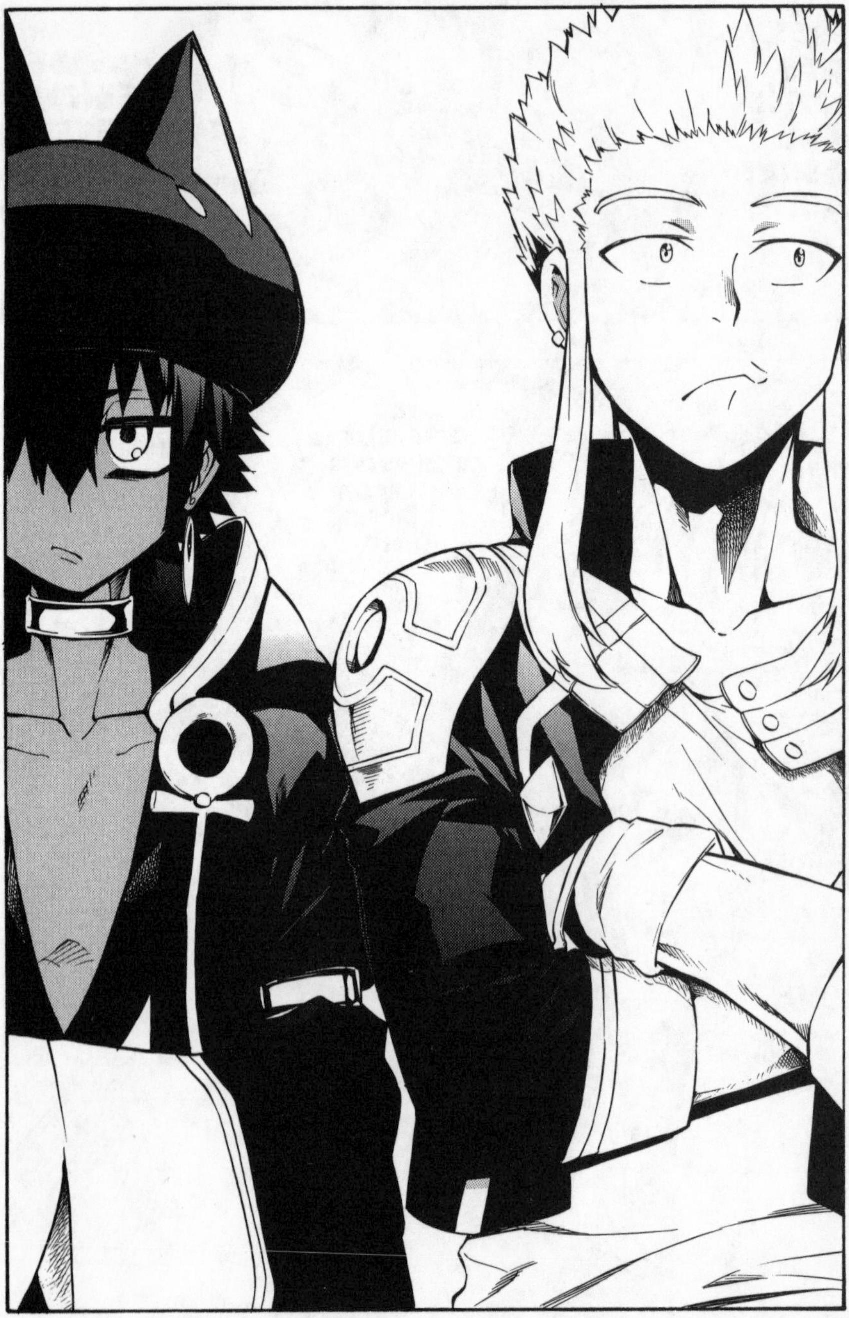

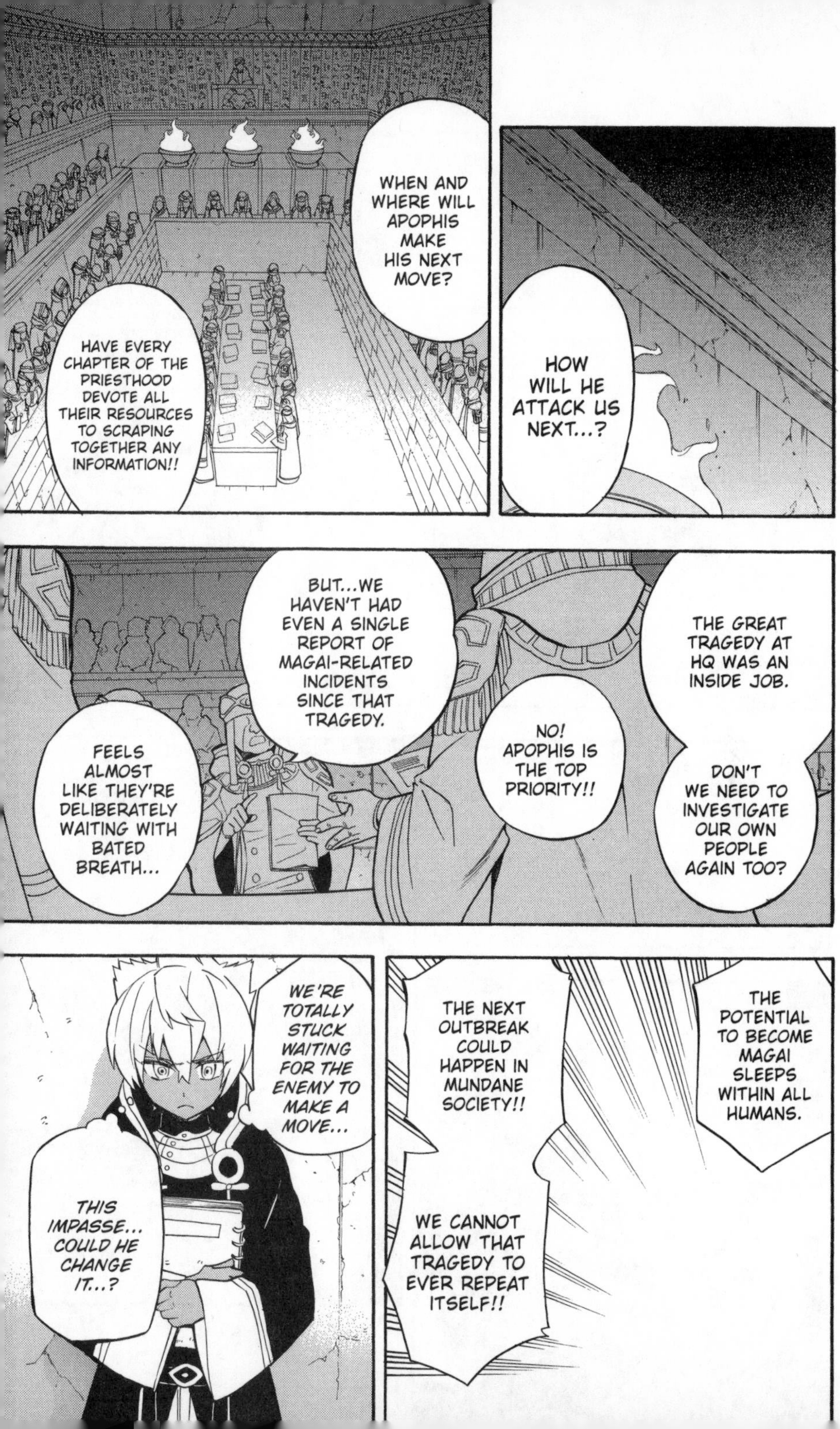
WHEN AND WHERE WILL APOPHIS MAKE HIS NEXT MOVE?
HOW WILL HE ATTACK US NEXT...?
HAVE EVERY CHAPTER OF THE PRIESTHOOD DEVOTE ALL THEIR RESOURCES TO SCRAPING TOGETHER ANY INFORMATION!!
THE GREAT TRAGEDY AT HQ WAS AN INSIDE JOB.
DON'T WE NEED TO INVESTIGATE OUR OWN PEOPLE AGAIN TOO?
NO! APOPHIS IS THE TOP PRIORITY!!
BUT...WE HAVEN'T HAD EVEN A SINGLE REPORT OF MAGAI-RELATED INCIDENTS SINCE THAT TRAGEDY.
FEELS ALMOST LIKE THEY'RE DELIBERATELY WAITING WITH BATED BREATH...
THE POTENTIAL TO BECOME MAGAI SLEEPS WITHIN ALL HUMANS.
THE NEXT OUTBREAK COULD HAPPEN IN MUNDANE SOCIETY!!
WE CANNOT ALLOW THAT TRAGEDY TO EVER REPEAT ITSELF!!
WE'RE TOTALLY STUCK WAITING FOR THE ENEMY TO MAKE A MOVE...
THIS IMPASSE... COULD HE CHANGE IT...?

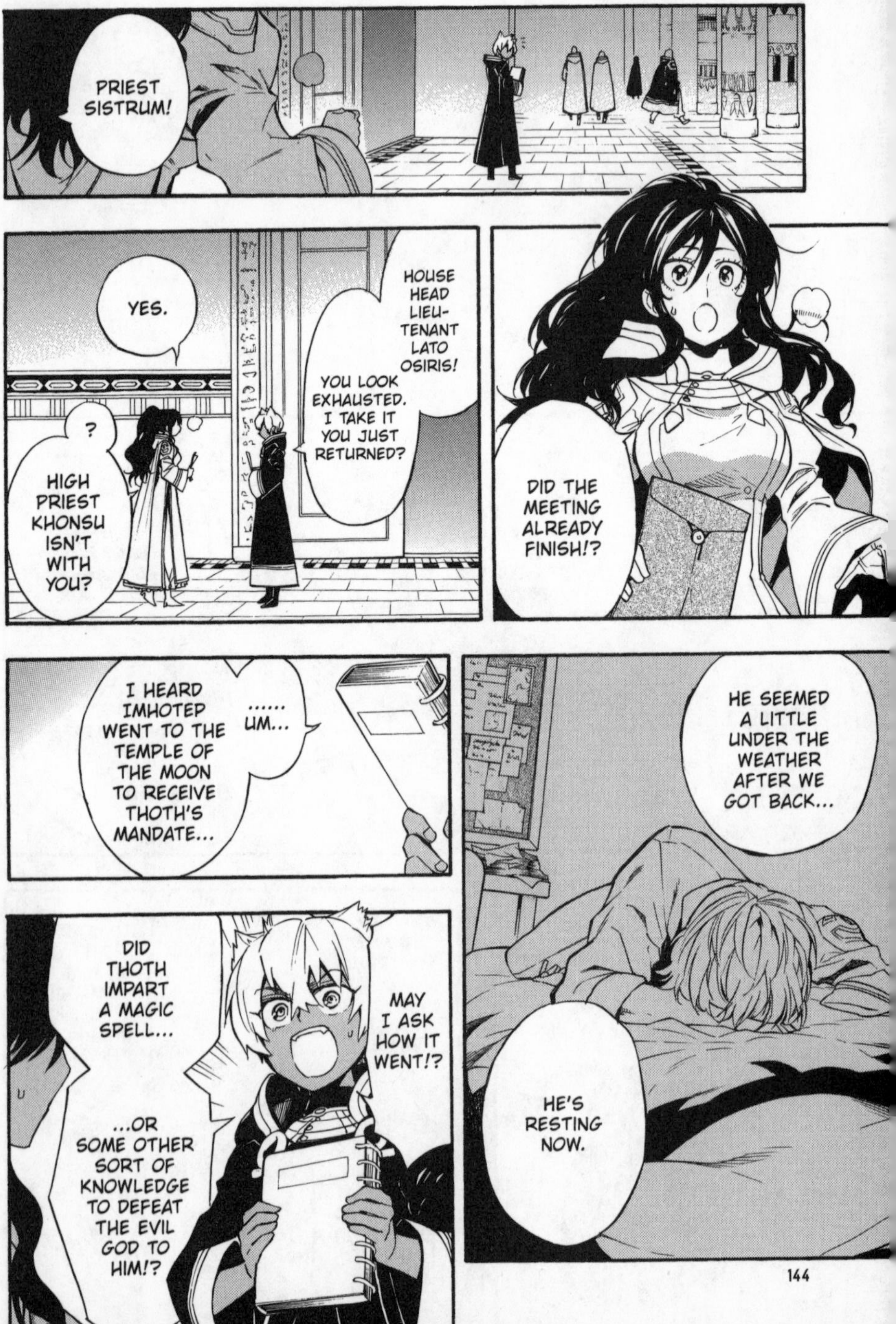
PRIEST SISTRUM!
DID THE MEETING ALREADY FINISH!?
HOUSE HEAD LIEU-TENANT LATO OSIRIS!
YES.
YOU LOOK EXHAUSTED. I TAKE IT YOU JUST RETURNED?
?
HIGH PRIEST KHONSU ISN'T WITH YOU?
HE SEEMED A LITTLE UNDER THE WEATHER AFTER WE GOT BACK...
HE'S RESTING NOW.
...... UM...
I HEARD IMHOTEP WENT TO THE TEMPLE OF THE MOON TO RECEIVE THOTH'S MANDATE...
MAY I ASK HOW IT WENT!?
DID THOTH IMPART A MAGIC SPELL...
...OR SOME OTHER SORT OF KNOWLEDGE TO DEFEAT THE EVIL GOD TO HIM!?

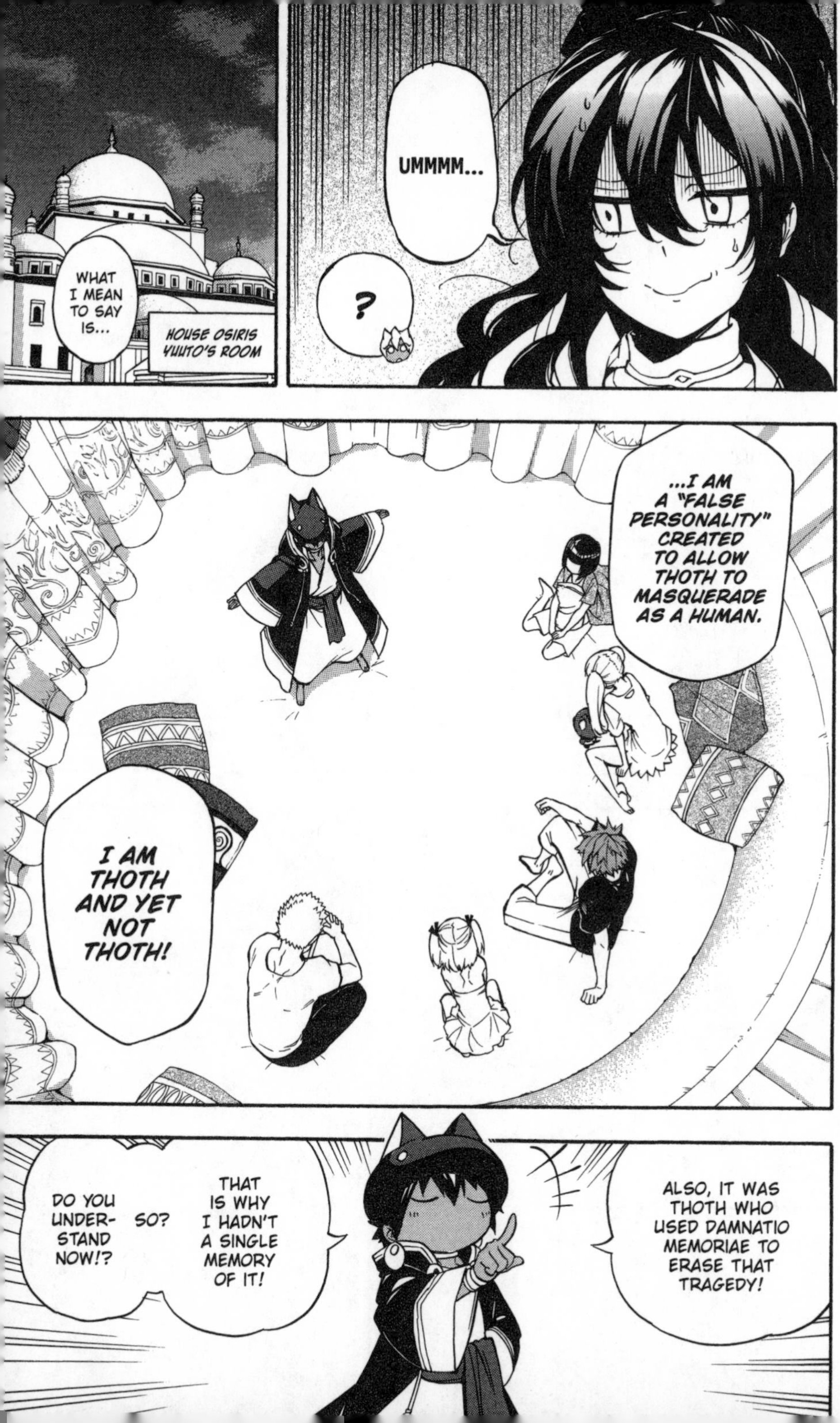
UMMMM...
?
HOUSE OSIRIS YUUTO'S ROOM
WHAT I MEAN TO SAY IS...
...I AM A "FALSE PERSONALITY" CREATED TO ALLOW THOTH TO MASQUERADE AS A HUMAN.
I AM THOTH AND YET NOT THOTH!
ALSO, IT WAS THOTH WHO USED DAMNATIO MEMORIAE TO ERASE THAT TRAGEDY!
THAT IS WHY I HADN'T A SINGLE MEMORY OF IT!
SO?
DO YOU UNDER-STAND NOW!?

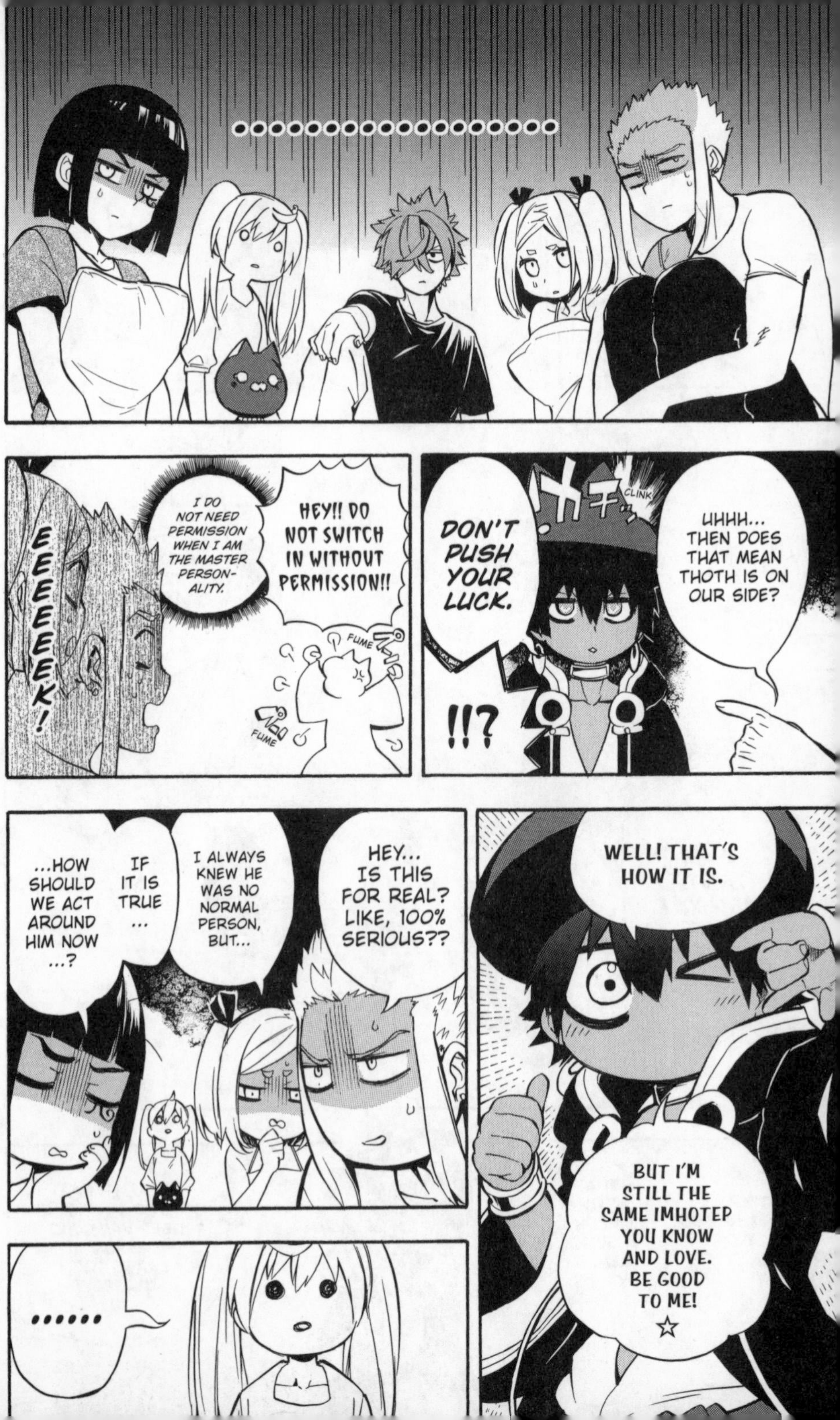
OOOOOOOOOOOOOOOOOOOO
UHHH... THEN DOES THAT MEAN THOTH IS ON OUR SIDE?
CLINK
DON'T PUSH YOUR LUCK.
!!?
HEY!! DO NOT SWITCH IN WITHOUT PERMISSION!!
I DO NOT NEED PERMISSION WHEN I AM THE MASTER PERSONALITY.
FUME
FUME
EEEEEEEK!
WELL! THAT'S HOW IT IS.
BUT I'M STILL THE SAME IMHOTEP YOU KNOW AND LOVE. BE GOOD TO ME! ☆
HEY... IS THIS FOR REAL? LIKE, 100% SERIOUS??
I ALWAYS KNEW HE WAS NO NORMAL PERSON, BUT...
IF IT IS TRUE ...
...HOW SHOULD WE ACT AROUND HIM NOW ...?
......

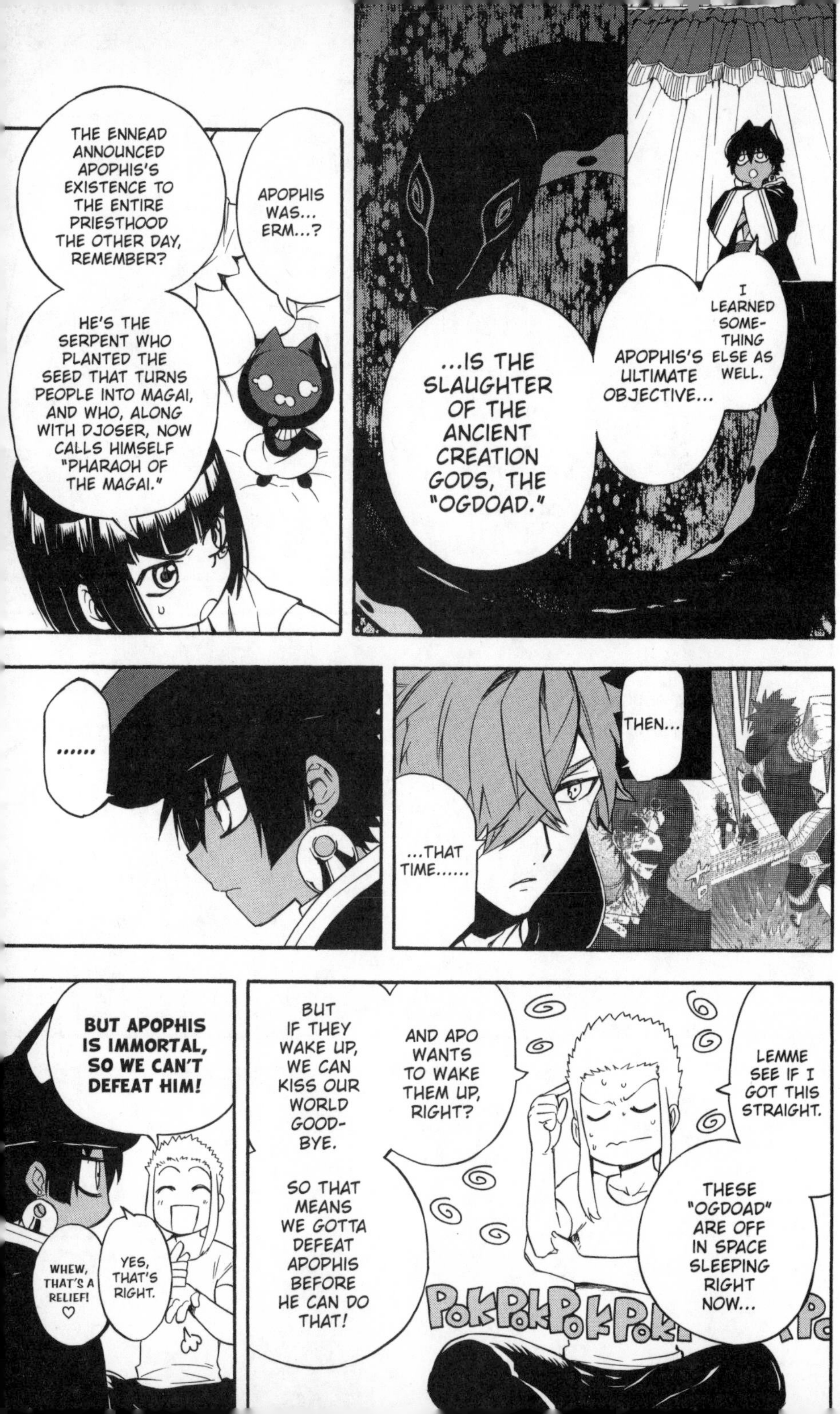
I LEARNED SOME-THING ELSE AS WELL.
APOPHIS'S ULTIMATE OBJECTIVE...
...IS THE SLAUGHTER OF THE ANCIENT CREATION GODS, THE "OGDOAD."
APOPHIS WAS... ERM...?
THE ENNEAD ANNOUNCED APOPHIS'S EXISTENCE TO THE ENTIRE PRIESTHOOD THE OTHER DAY, REMEMBER?
HE'S THE SERPENT WHO PLANTED THE SEED THAT TURNS PEOPLE INTO MAGAI, AND WHO, ALONG WITH DJOSER, NOW CALLS HIMSELF "PHARAOH OF THE MAGAI."
THEN...
...THAT TIME......
......
LEMME SEE IF I GOT THIS STRAIGHT.
THESE "OGDOAD" ARE OFF IN SPACE SLEEPING RIGHT NOW...
AND APO WANTS TO WAKE THEM UP, RIGHT?
BUT IF THEY WAKE UP, WE CAN KISS OUR WORLD GOOD-BYE.
SO THAT MEANS WE GOTTA DEFEAT APOPHIS BEFORE HE CAN DO THAT!
PokPokPokPok
BUT APOPHIS IS IMMORTAL, SO WE CAN'T DEFEAT HIM!
YES, THAT'S RIGHT.
WHEW, THAT'S A RELIEF! ♡

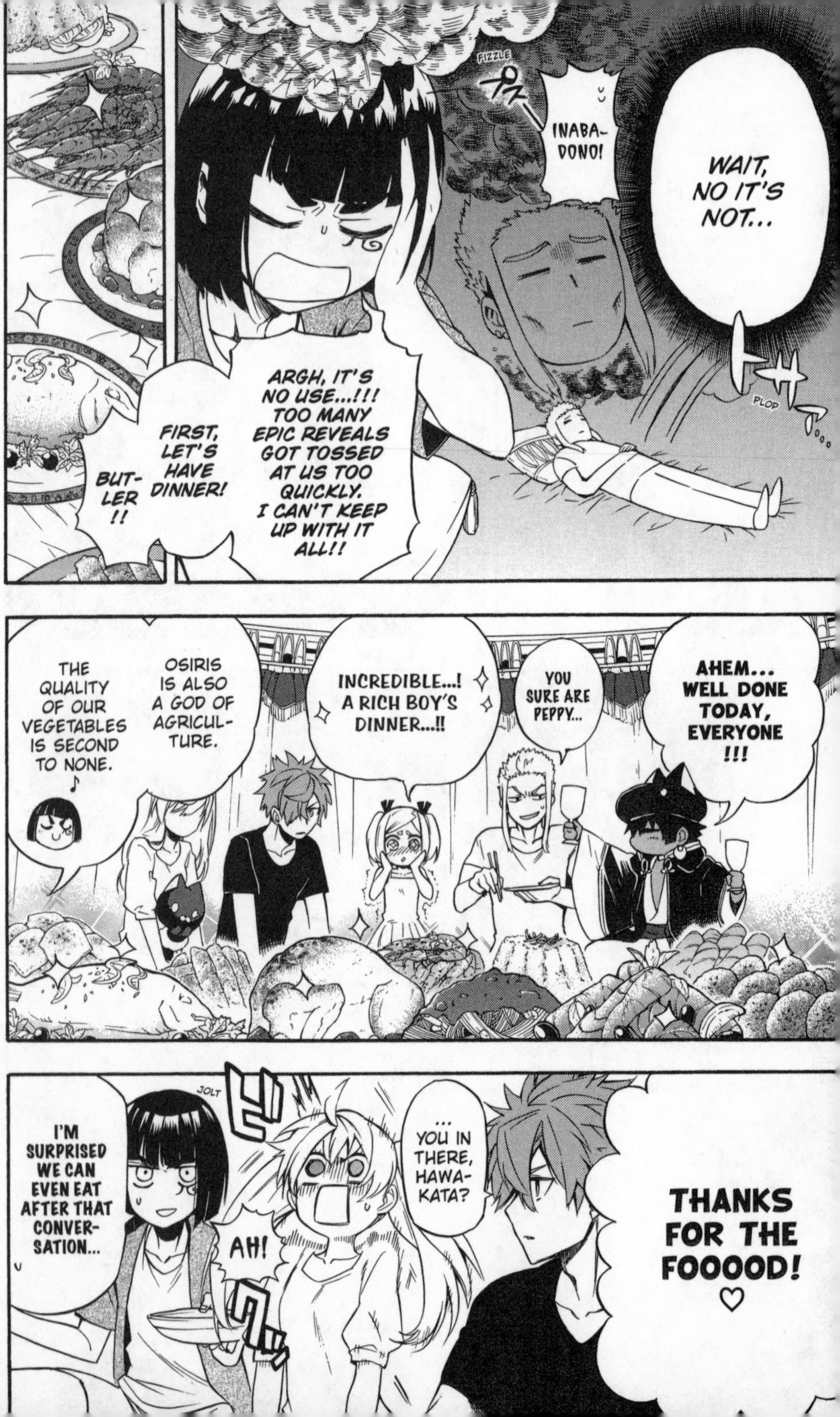
WAIT, NO IT'S NOT...
INABA-DONO!
FIZZLE
PLOP
ARGH, IT'S NO USE...!!! TOO MANY EPIC REVEALS GOT TOSSED AT US TOO QUICKLY. I CAN'T KEEP UP WITH IT ALL!!
FIRST, LET'S HAVE DINNER!
BUT-LER!!
AHEM... WELL DONE TODAY, EVERYONE!!!
YOU SURE ARE PEPPY...
INCREDIBLE...! A RICH BOY'S DINNER...!!
OSIRIS IS ALSO A GOD OF AGRICUL-TURE.
THE QUALITY OF OUR VEGETABLES IS SECOND TO NONE. ♪
THANKS FOR THE FOOOOD! ♡
... YOU IN THERE, HAWA-KATA?
AH!
JOLT
I'M SURPRISED WE CAN EVEN EAT AFTER THAT CONVER-SATION...

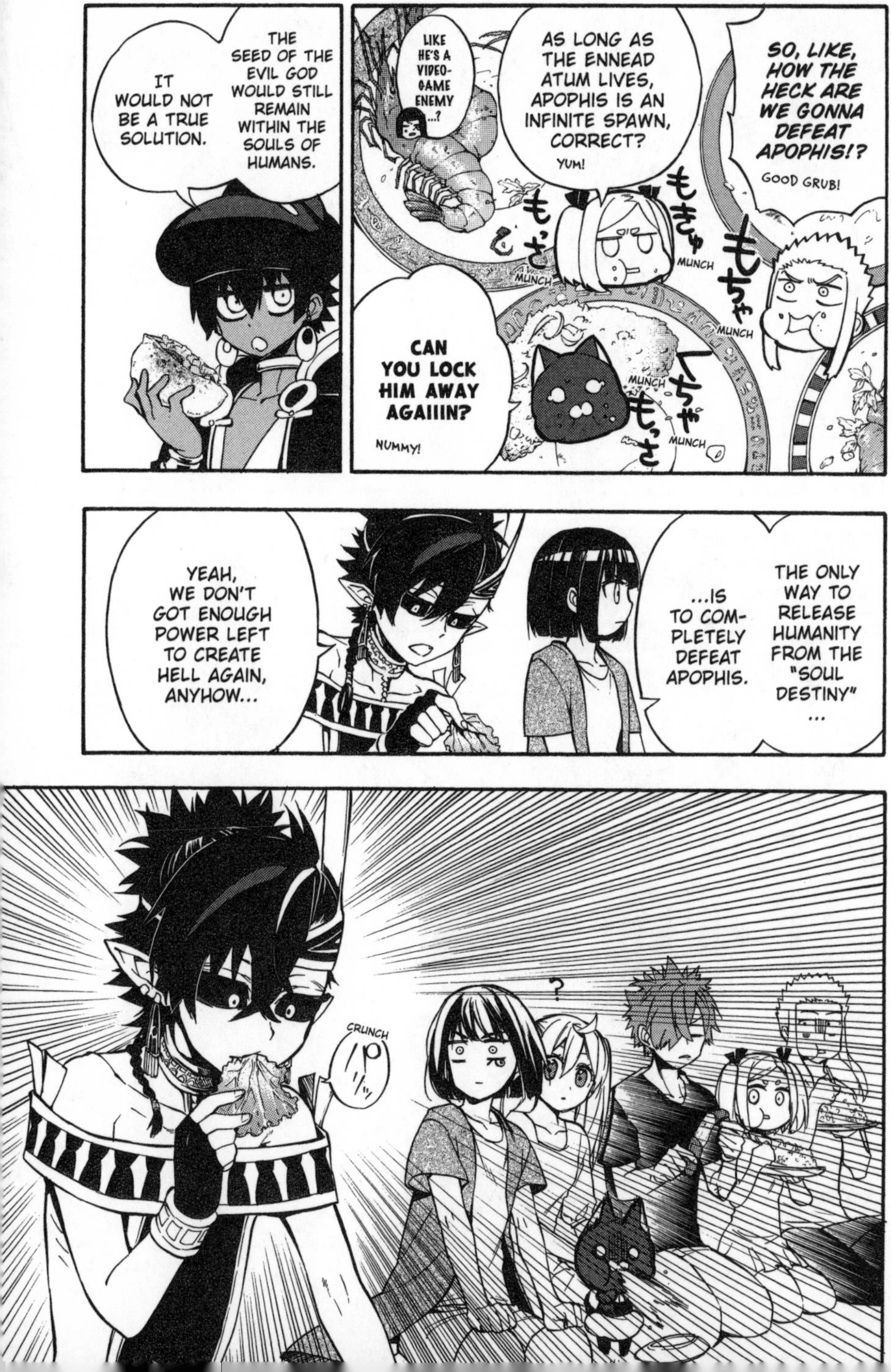
SO, LIKE, HOW THE HECK ARE WE GONNA DEFEAT APOPHIS!?
GOOD GRUB!
もちゃ
MUNCH
AS LONG AS THE ENNEAD ATUM LIVES, APOPHIS IS AN INFINITE SPAWN, CORRECT?
YUM!
もきゅ
MUNCH
LIKE HE'S A VIDEO-GAME ENEMY ...?
もさ
MUNCH
CAN YOU LOCK HIM AWAY AGAIIIN?
NUMMY!
くちゃ
MUNCH
もっさ
MUNCH
THE SEED OF THE EVIL GOD WOULD STILL REMAIN WITHIN THE SOULS OF HUMANS.
IT WOULD NOT BE A TRUE SOLUTION.
THE ONLY WAY TO RELEASE HUMANITY FROM THE "SOUL DESTINY" ...
...IS TO COMPLETELY DEFEAT APOPHIS.
YEAH, WE DON'T GOT ENOUGH POWER LEFT TO CREATE HELL AGAIN, ANYHOW...
?
パリッ
CRUNCH

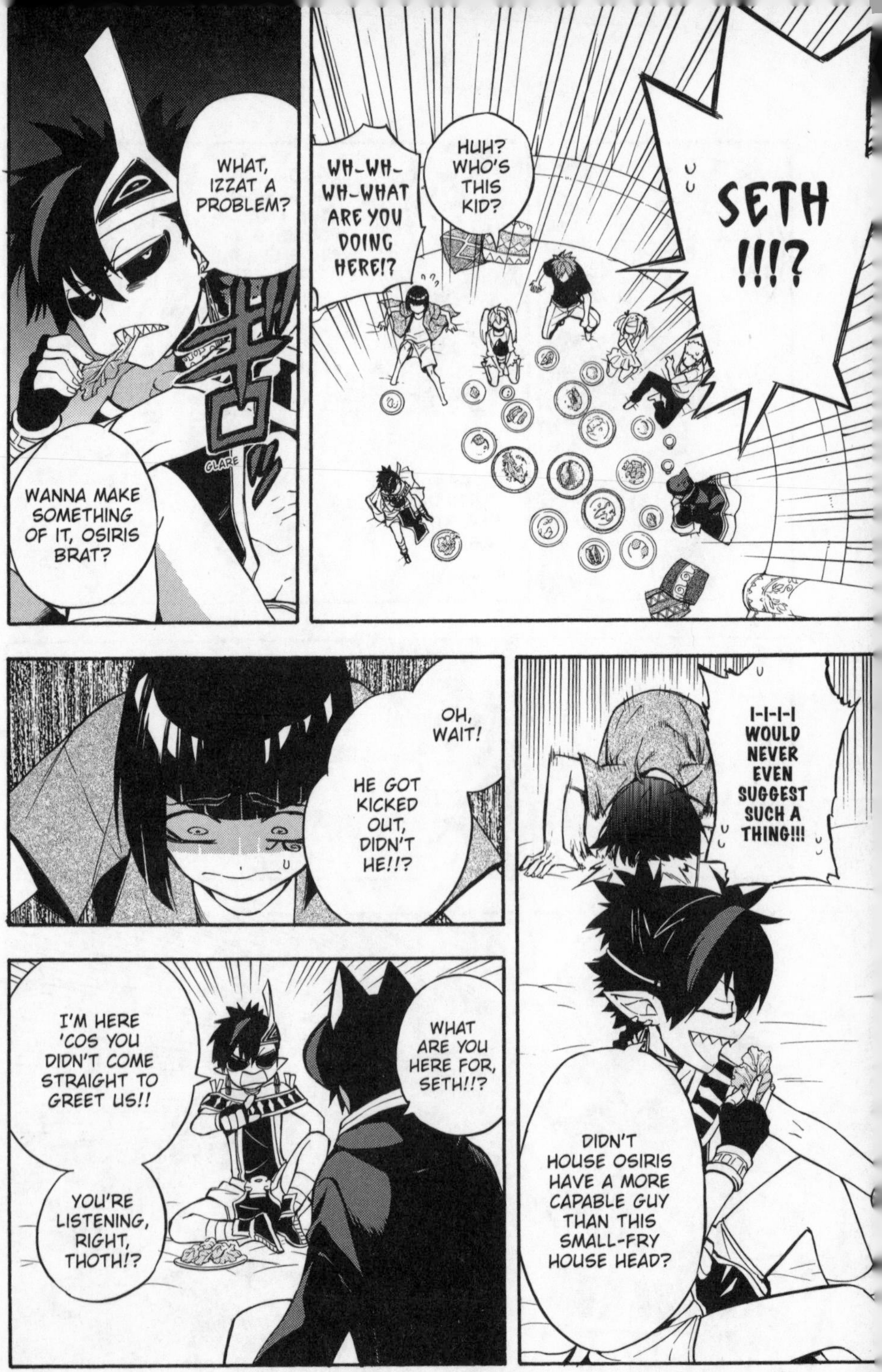
SETH !!!?
HUH? WHO'S THIS KID?
WH-WH-WH-WHAT ARE YOU DOING HERE!?
WHAT, IZZAT A PROBLEM?
GLARE
WANNA MAKE SOMETHING OF IT, OSIRIS BRAT?
I-I-I-I WOULD NEVER EVEN SUGGEST SUCH A THING!!!
DIDN'T HOUSE OSIRIS HAVE A MORE CAPABLE GUY THAN THIS SMALL-FRY HOUSE HEAD?
OH, WAIT!
HE GOT KICKED OUT, DIDN'T HE!!?
WHAT ARE YOU HERE FOR, SETH!!?
I'M HERE 'COS YOU DIDN'T COME STRAIGHT TO GREET US!!
YOU'RE LISTENING, RIGHT, THOTH!?

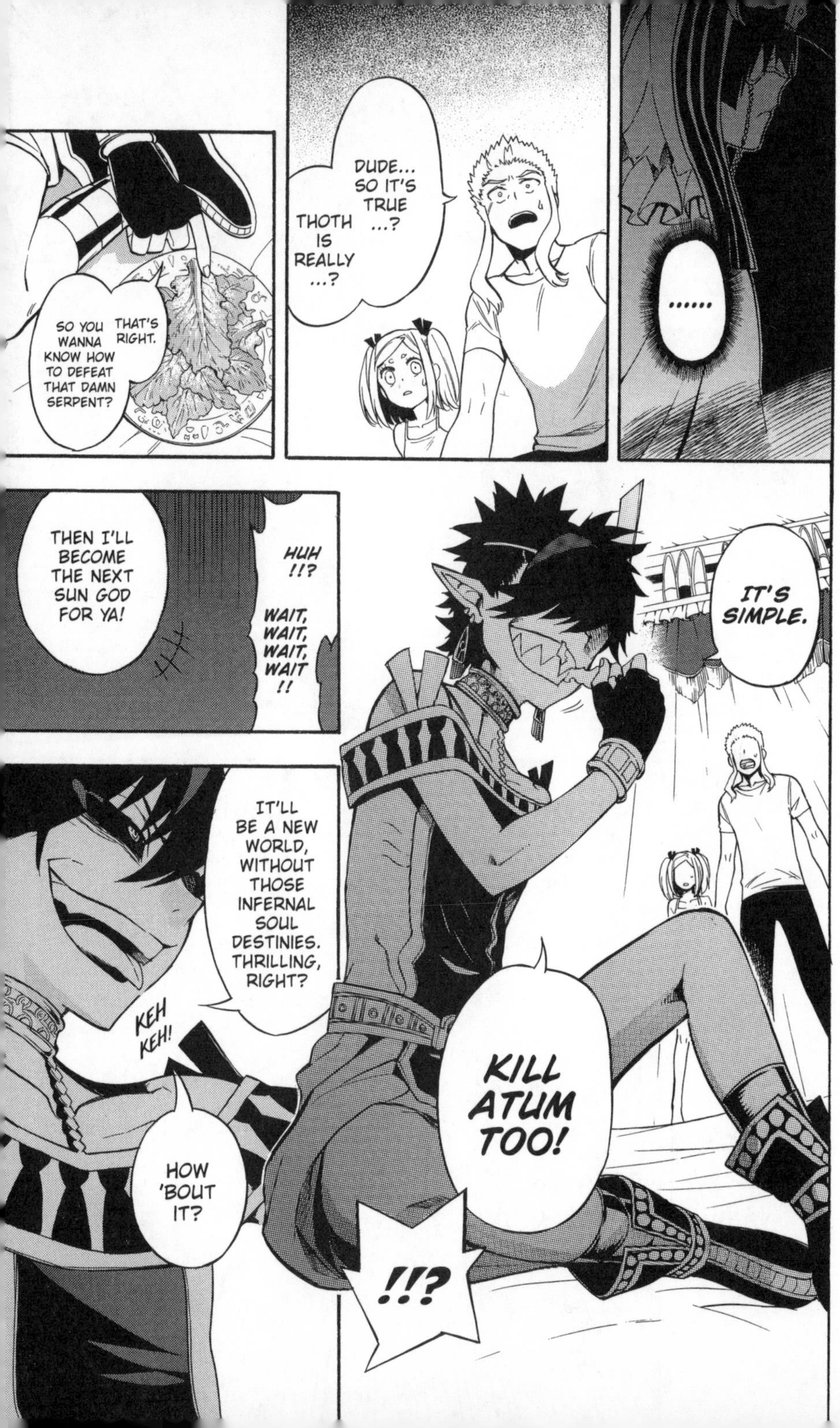

......
DUDE... SO IT'S TRUE ...?
THOTH IS REALLY ...?
THAT'S RIGHT.
SO YOU WANNA KNOW HOW TO DEFEAT THAT DAMN SERPENT?
IT'S SIMPLE.
KILL ATUM TOO!
!!?
THEN I'LL BECOME THE NEXT SUN GOD FOR YA!
HUH !!?
WAIT, WAIT, WAIT, WAIT !!
IT'LL BE A NEW WORLD, WITHOUT THOSE INFERNAL SOUL DESTINIES. THRILLING, RIGHT?
KEH KEH!
HOW 'BOUT IT?

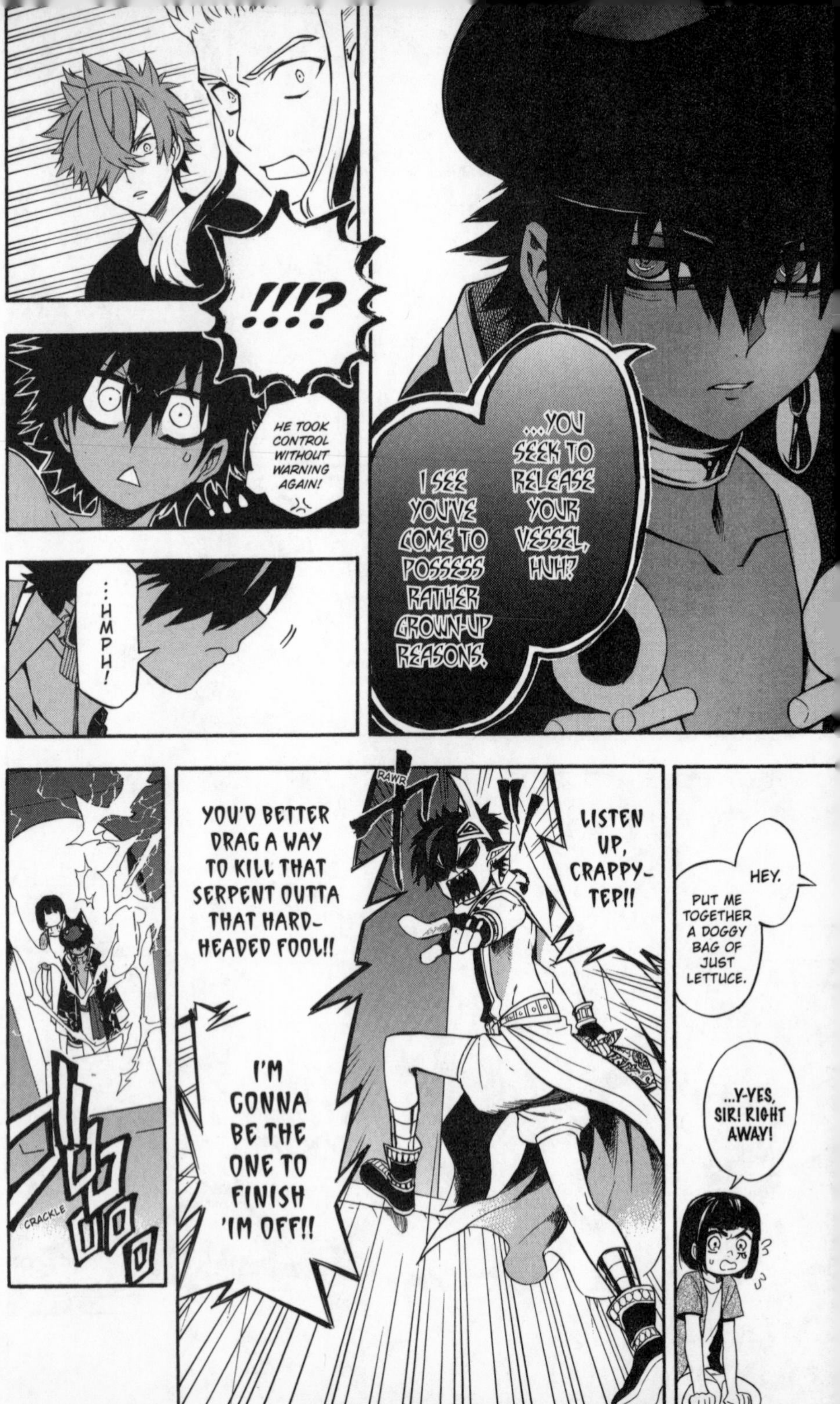
...YOU SEEK TO RELEASE YOUR VESSEL, HUH?
I SEE YOU'VE COME TO POSSESS RATHER GROWN-UP REASONS.
!!!?
HE TOOK CONTROL WITHOUT WARNING AGAIN!
...HMPH!
HEY.
PUT ME TOGETHER A DOGGY BAG OF JUST LETTUCE.
...Y-YES, SIR! RIGHT AWAY!
RAWR
LISTEN UP, CRAPPY-TEP!!
YOU'D BETTER DRAG A WAY TO KILL THAT SERPENT OUTTA THAT HARD-HEADED FOOL!!
I'M GONNA BE THE ONE TO FINISH 'IM OFF!!
CRACKLE

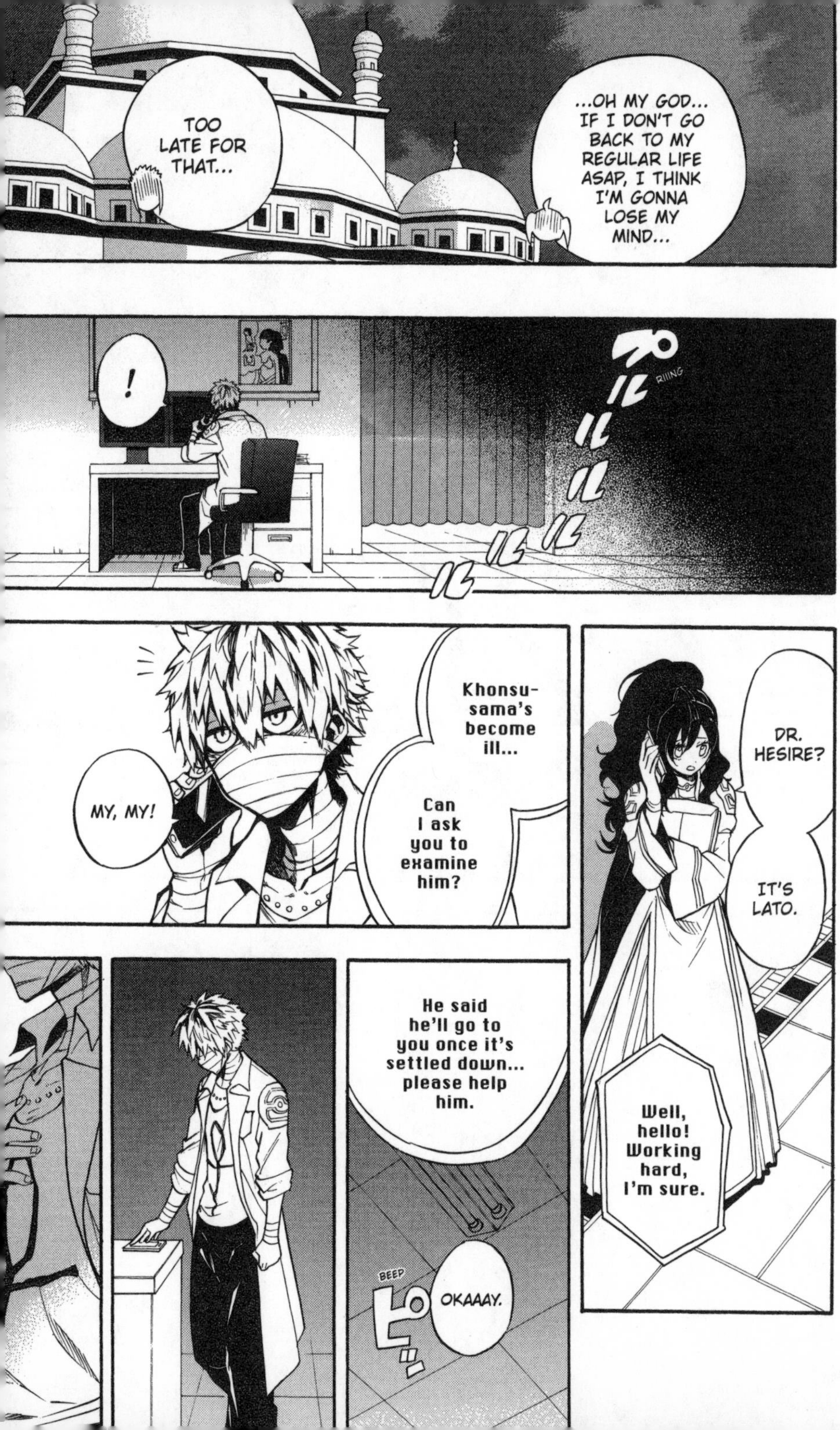
...OH MY GOD... IF I DON'T GO BACK TO MY REGULAR LIFE ASAP, I THINK I'M GONNA LOSE MY MIND...
TOO LATE FOR THAT...
RIIING
!
DR. HESIRE?
IT'S LATO.
Well, hello! Working hard, I'm sure.
Khonsu-sama's become ill...
Can I ask you to examine him?
MY, MY!
He said he'll go to you once it's settled down... please help him.
BEEP
OKAAAY.

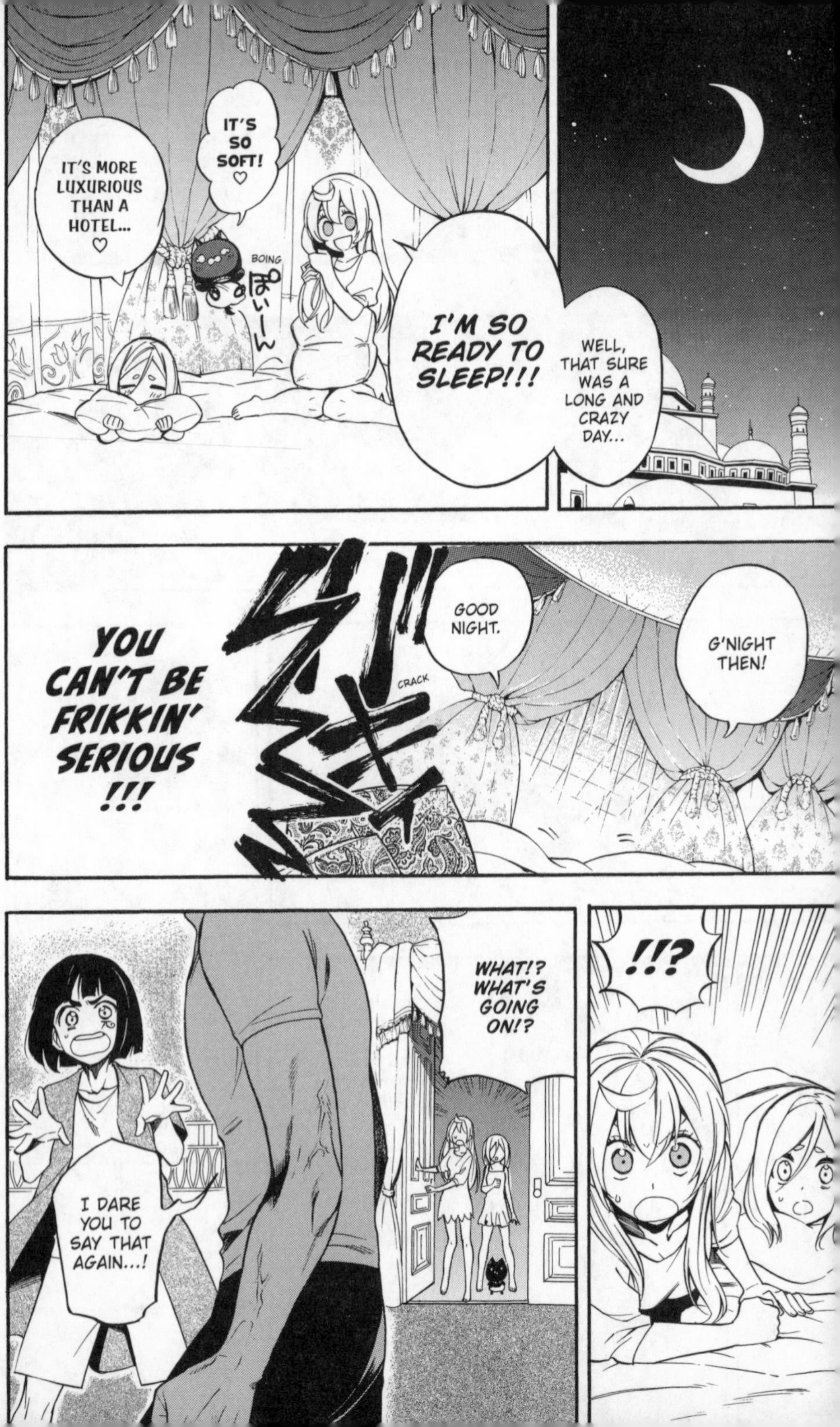
WELL, THAT SURE WAS A LONG AND CRAZY DAY...
I'M SO READY TO SLEEP!!!
IT'S SO SOFT! ♡
BOING
ぽいーん
IT'S MORE LUXURIOUS THAN A HOTEL... ♡
G'NIGHT THEN!
GOOD NIGHT.
CRACK
YOU CAN'T BE FRIKKIN' SERIOUS!!!
!!?
WHAT!? WHAT'S GOING ON!?
I DARE YOU TO SAY THAT AGAIN...!

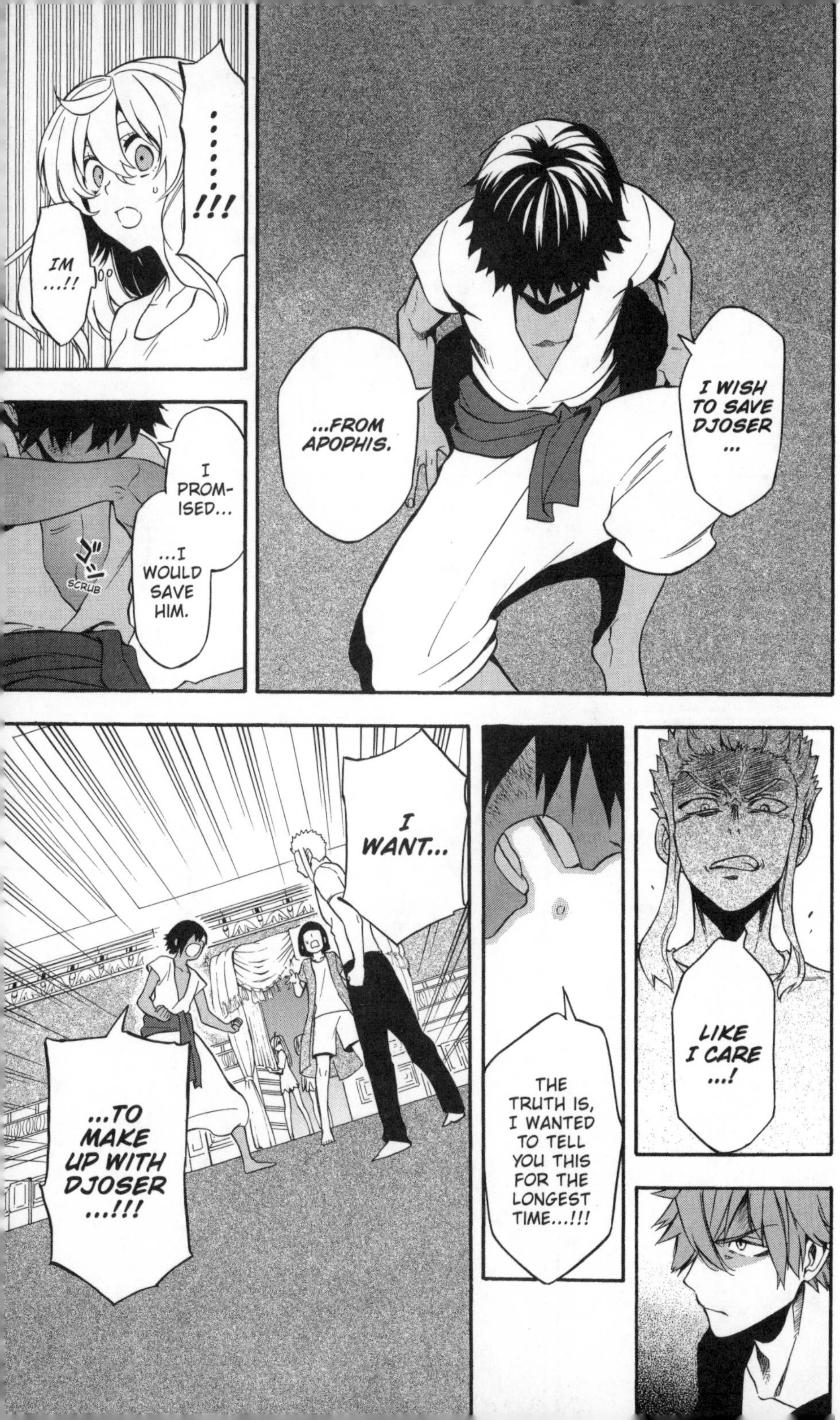
I WISH TO SAVE DJOSER ...
...FROM APOPHIS.
......!!!
IM ...!!
I PROMISED...
...I WOULD SAVE HIM.
SCRUB
LIKE I CARE ...!
THE TRUTH IS, I WANTED TO TELL YOU THIS FOR THE LONGEST TIME...!!!
I WANT...
...TO MAKE UP WITH DJOSER ...!!!

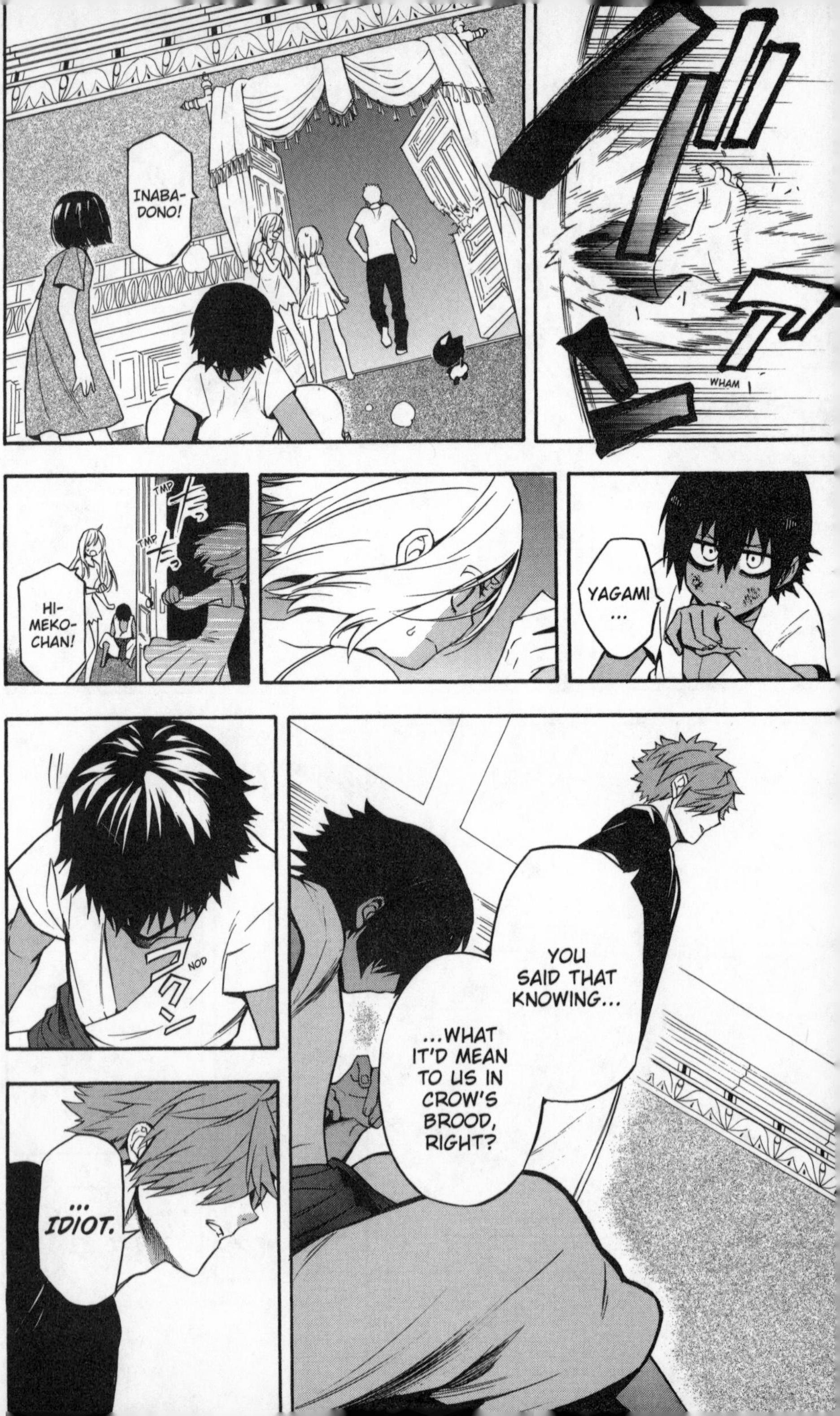
WHAM
INABA-DONO!
YAGAMI ...
TMP
TMP
HI-MEKO-CHAN!
YOU SAID THAT KNOWING...
...WHAT IT'D MEAN TO US IN CROW'S BROOD, RIGHT?
NOD
... IDIOT.

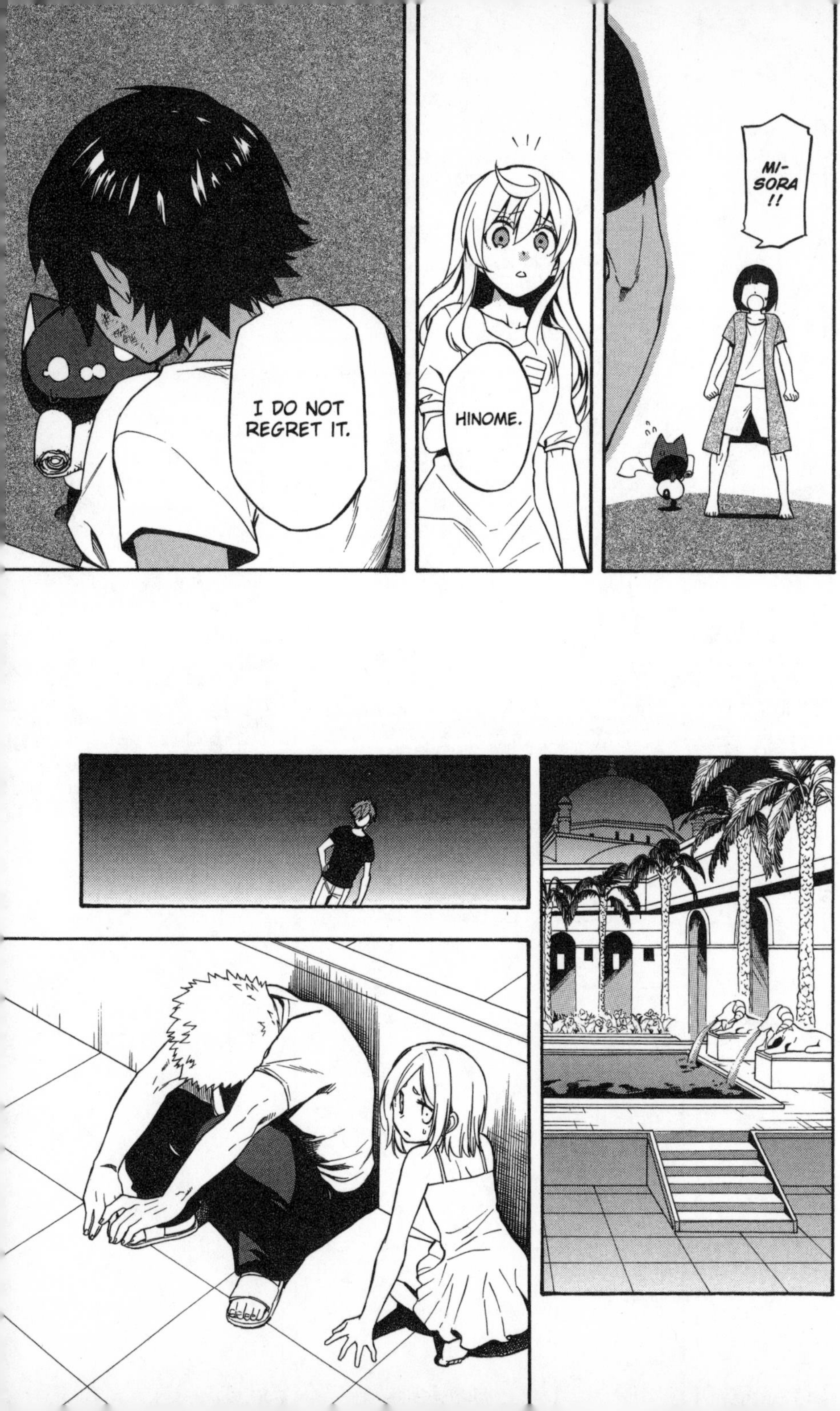
MI-SORA !!
HINOME.
I DO NOT REGRET IT.

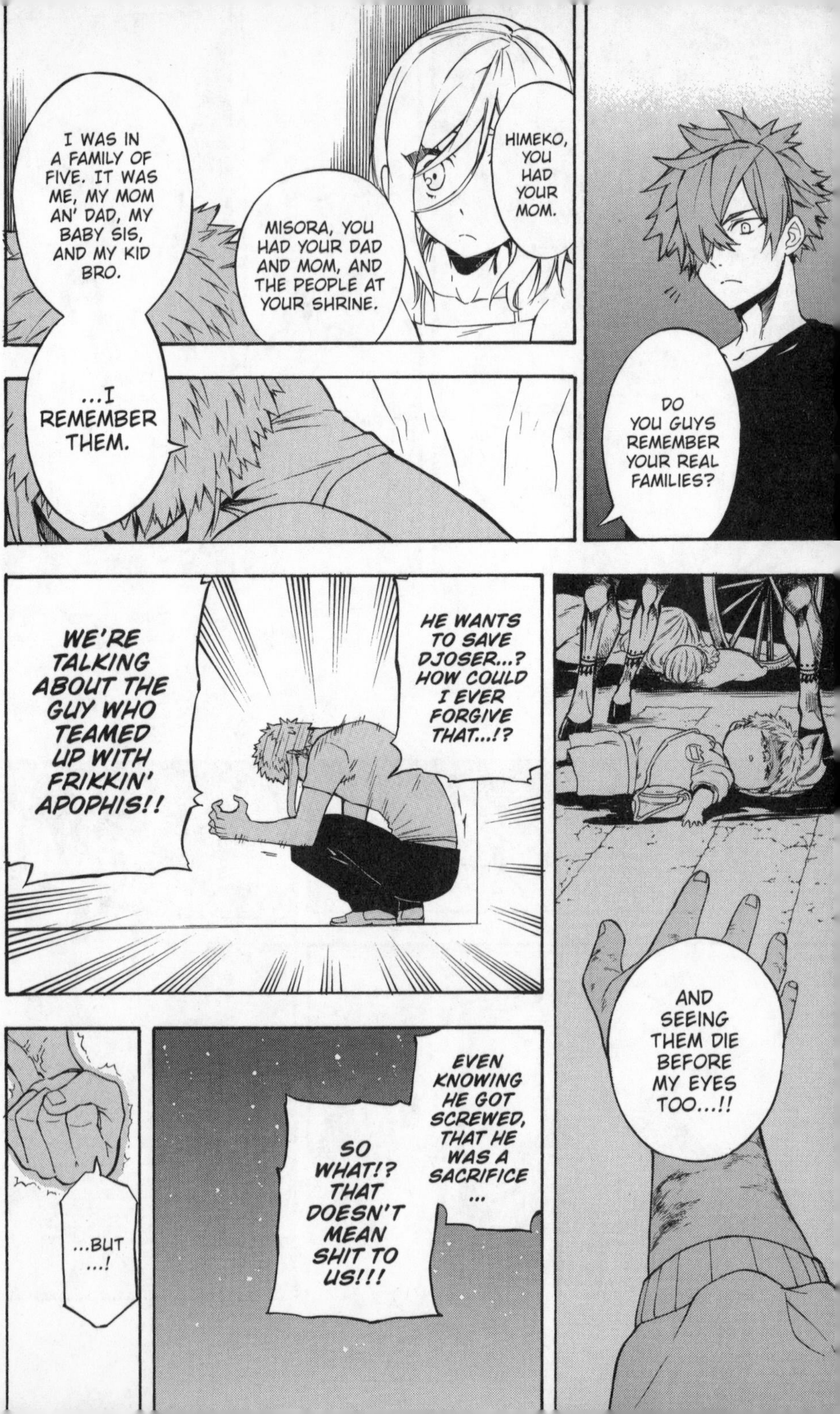

DO YOU GUYS REMEMBER YOUR REAL FAMILIES?
HIMEKO, YOU HAD YOUR MOM.
MISORA, YOU HAD YOUR DAD AND MOM, AND THE PEOPLE AT YOUR SHRINE.
I WAS IN A FAMILY OF FIVE. IT WAS ME, MY MOM AN' DAD, MY BABY SIS, AND MY KID BRO.
...I REMEMBER THEM.
AND SEEING THEM DIE BEFORE MY EYES TOO...!!
HE WANTS TO SAVE DJOSER...? HOW COULD I EVER FORGIVE THAT...!?
WE'RE TALKING ABOUT THE GUY WHO TEAMED UP WITH FRIKKIN' APOPHIS!!
EVEN KNOWING HE GOT SCREWED, THAT HE WAS A SACRIFICE ...
SO WHAT!? THAT DOESN'T MEAN SHIT TO US!!!
...BUT ...!

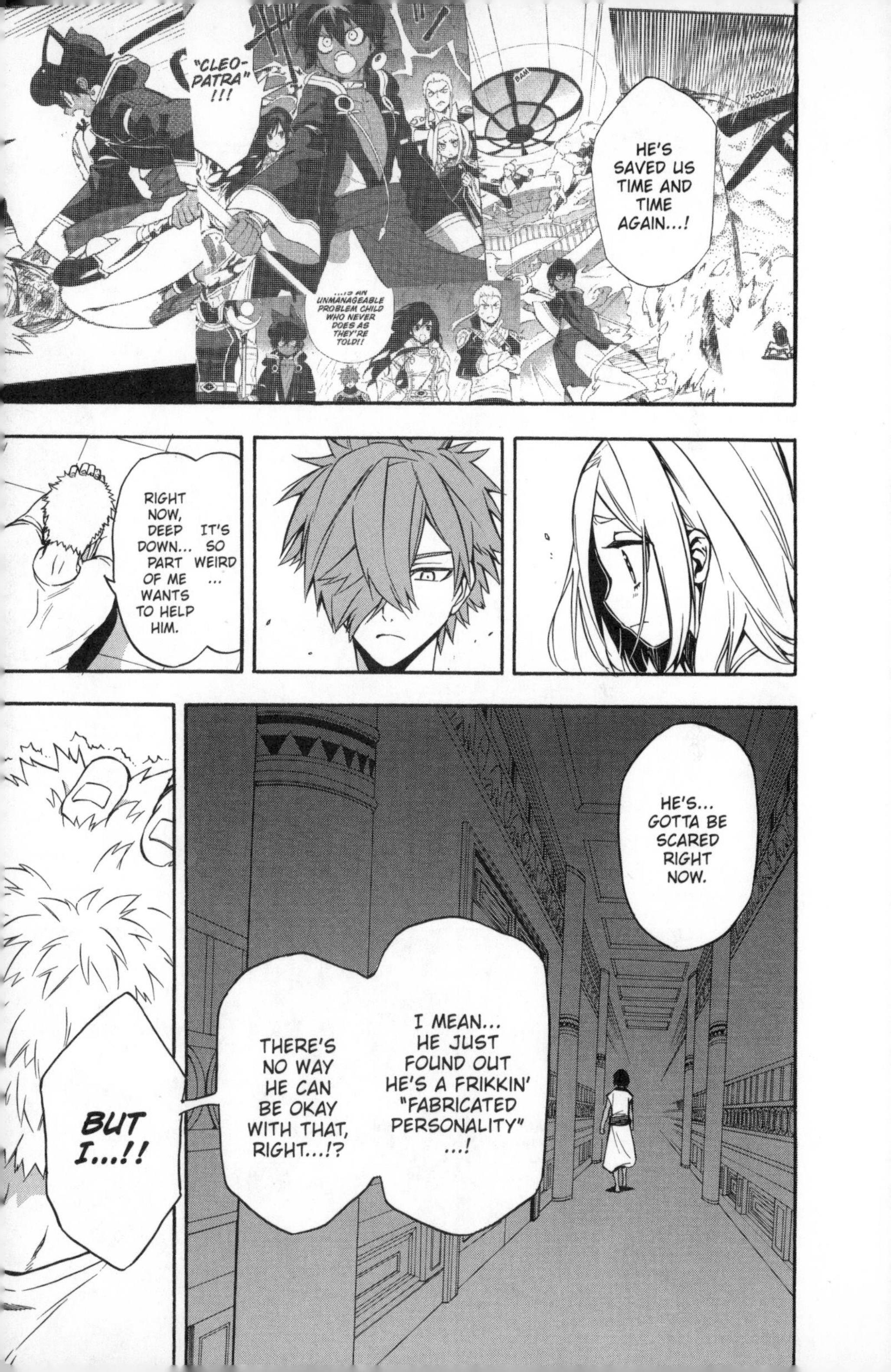
THOOOM
HE'S SAVED US TIME AND TIME AGAIN...!
BAM
...IS AN UNMANAGEABLE PROBLEM CHILD WHO NEVER DOES AS THEY'RE TOLD!!
"CLEO-PATRA" !!!
IT'S SO WEIRD...
RIGHT NOW, DEEP DOWN... PART OF ME WANTS TO HELP HIM.
HE'S... GOTTA BE SCARED RIGHT NOW.
I MEAN... HE JUST FOUND OUT HE'S A FRIKKIN' "FABRICATED PERSONALITY"...!
THERE'S NO WAY HE CAN BE OKAY WITH THAT, RIGHT...!?
BUT I...!!

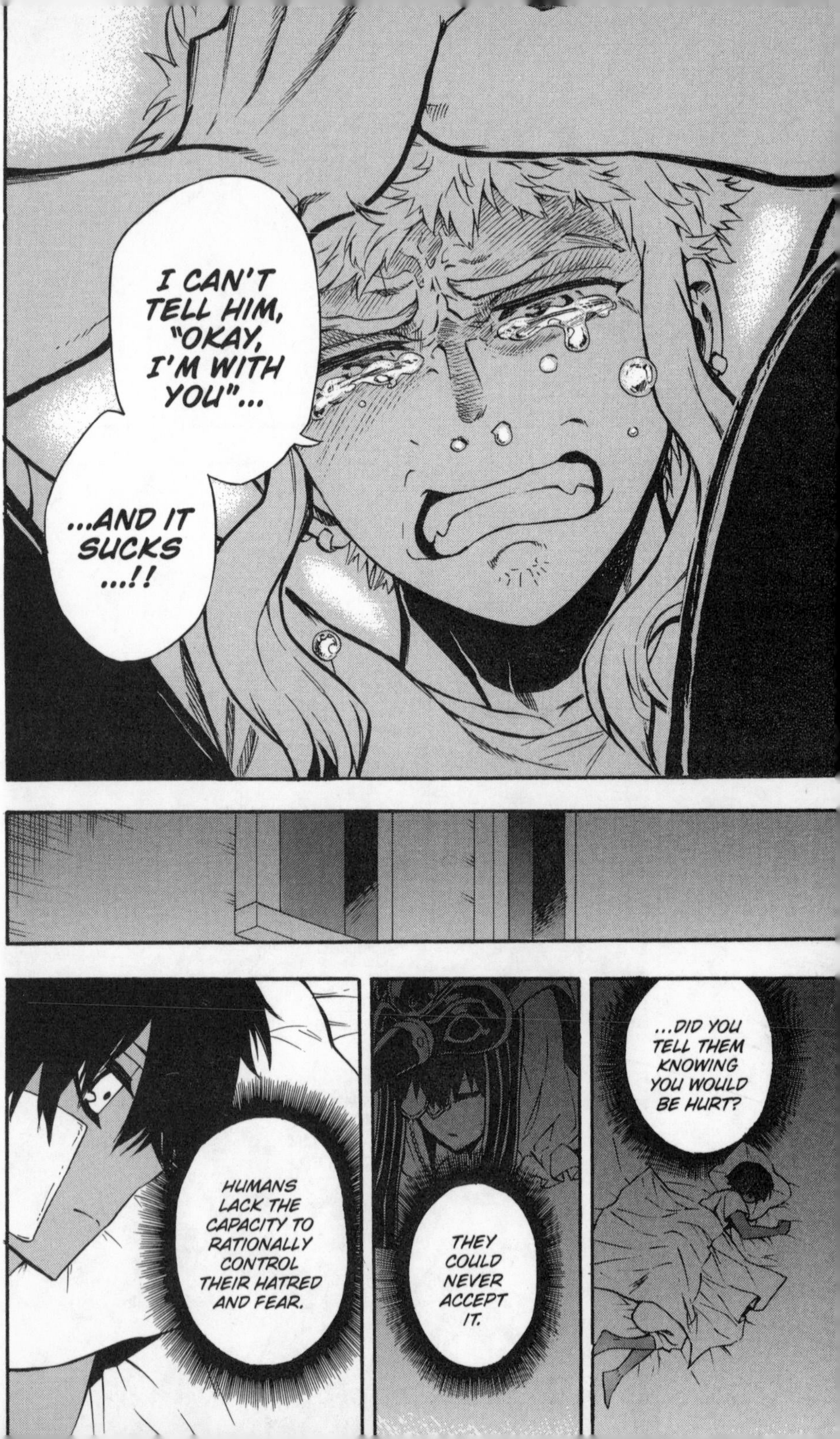
I CAN'T TELL HIM, "OKAY, I'M WITH YOU"...
...AND IT SUCKS ...!!
...DID YOU TELL THEM KNOWING YOU WOULD BE HURT?
THEY COULD NEVER ACCEPT IT.
HUMANS LACK THE CAPACITY TO RATIONALLY CONTROL THEIR HATRED AND FEAR.

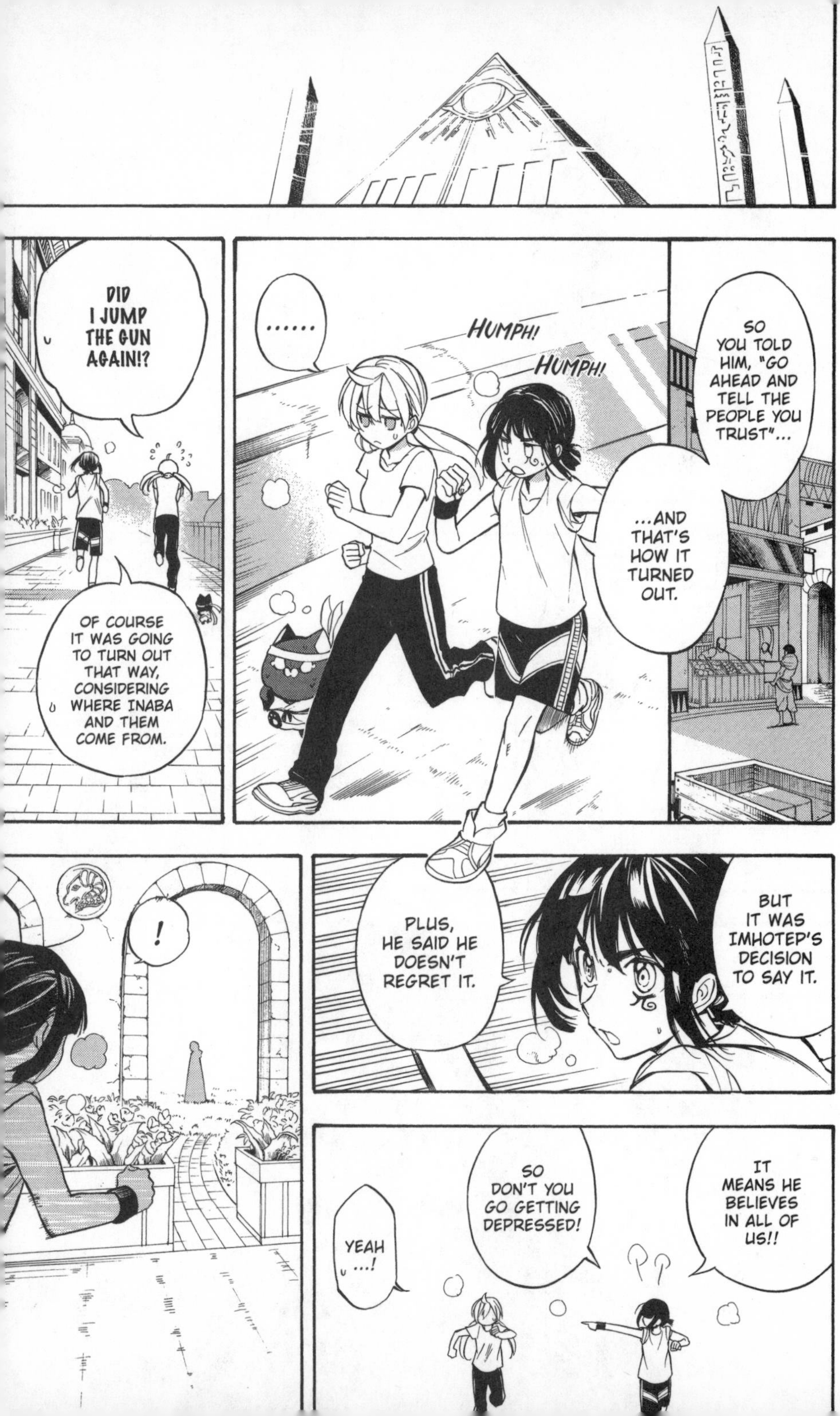
SO YOU TOLD HIM, "GO AHEAD AND TELL THE PEOPLE YOU TRUST"...
...AND THAT'S HOW IT TURNED OUT.
HUMPH!
HUMPH!
....
DID I JUMP THE GUN AGAIN!?
OF COURSE IT WAS GOING TO TURN OUT THAT WAY, CONSIDERING WHERE INABA AND THEM COME FROM.
BUT IT WAS IMHOTEP'S DECISION TO SAY IT.
PLUS, HE SAID HE DOESN'T REGRET IT.
IT MEANS HE BELIEVES IN ALL OF US!!
SO DON'T YOU GO GETTING DEPRESSED!
YEAH ...!
!

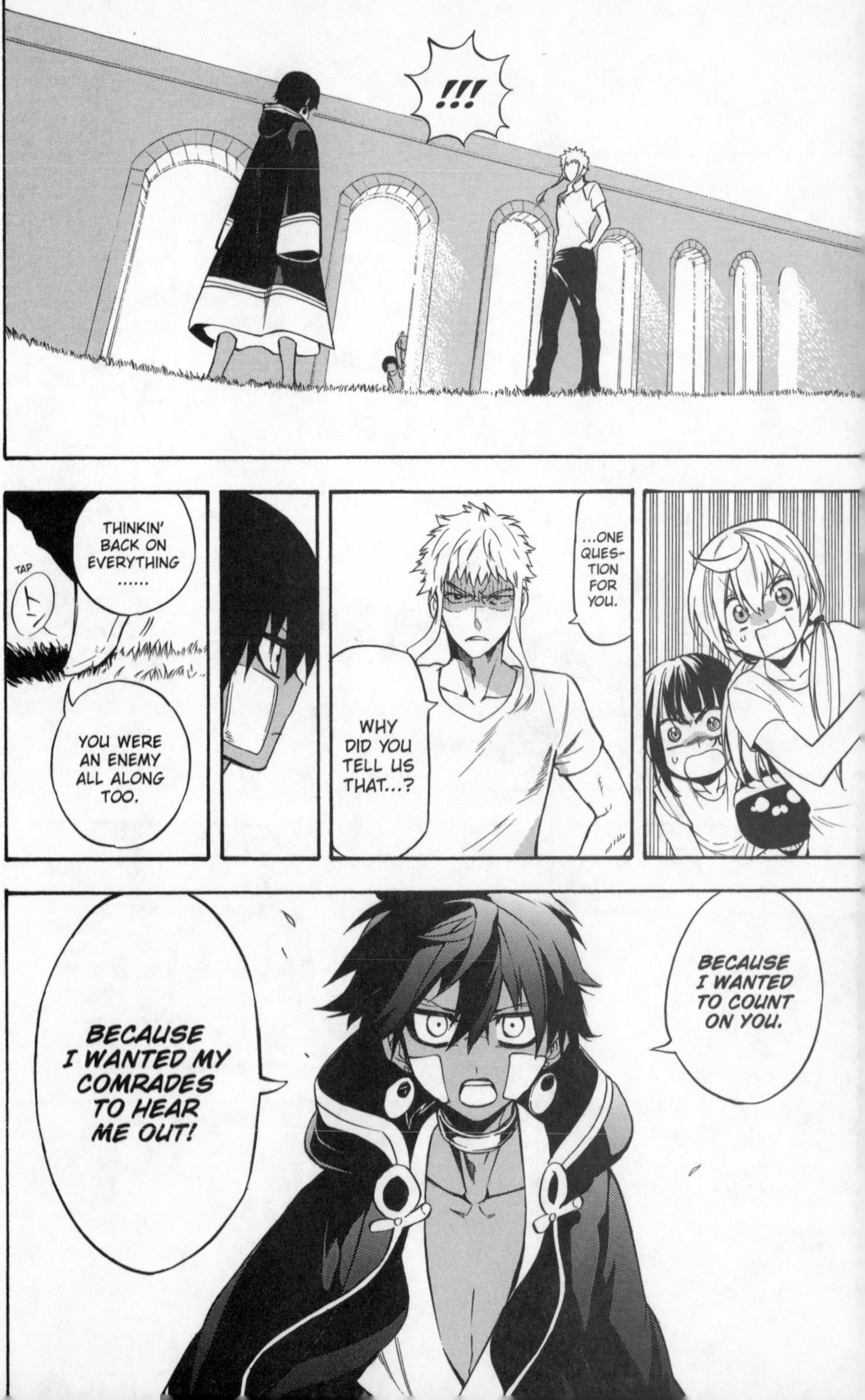
!!!
...ONE QUES-TION FOR YOU.
WHY DID YOU TELL US THAT...?
THINKIN' BACK ON EVERYTHING ......
TAP
YOU WERE AN ENEMY ALL ALONG TOO.
BECAUSE I WANTED TO COUNT ON YOU.
BECAUSE I WANTED MY COMRADES TO HEAR ME OUT!

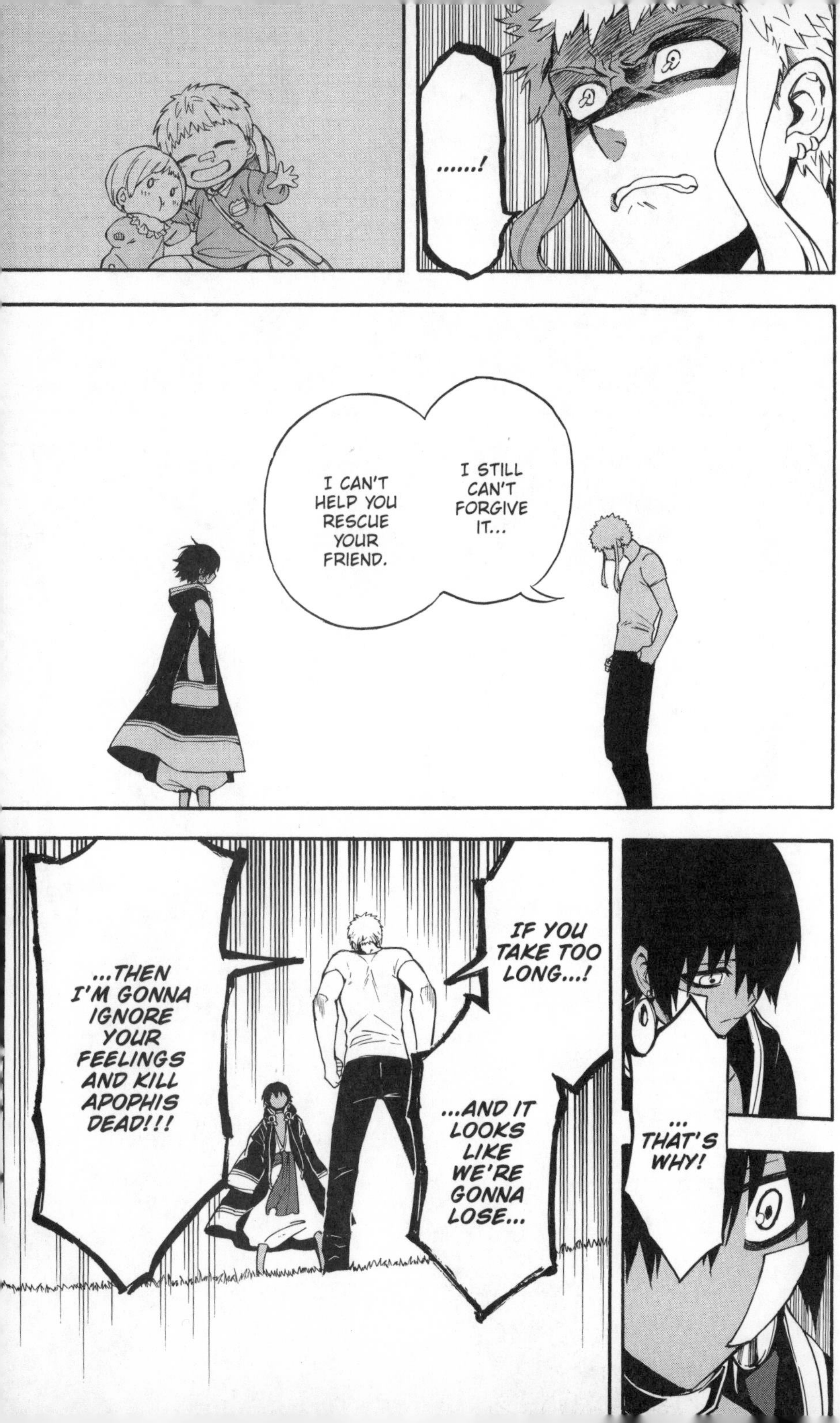
......!
I STILL CAN'T FORGIVE IT...
I CAN'T HELP YOU RESCUE YOUR FRIEND.
... THAT'S WHY!
IF YOU TAKE TOO LONG...!
...AND IT LOOKS LIKE WE'RE GONNA LOSE...
...THEN I'M GONNA IGNORE YOUR FEELINGS AND KILL APOPHIS DEAD!!!

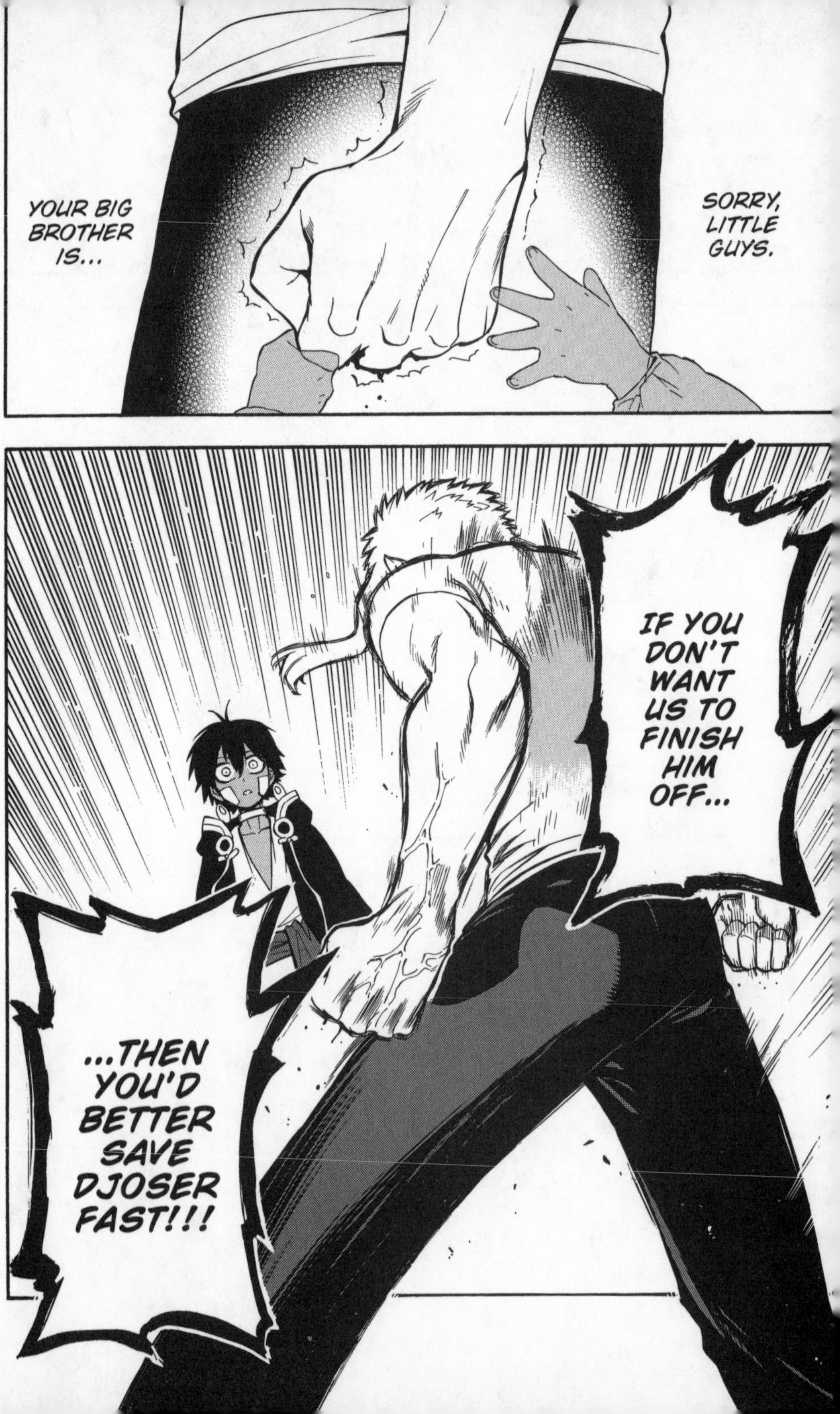
SORRY, LITTLE GUYS.
YOUR BIG BROTHER IS...
IF YOU DON'T WANT US TO FINISH HIM OFF...
...THEN YOU'D BETTER SAVE DJOSER FAST!!!

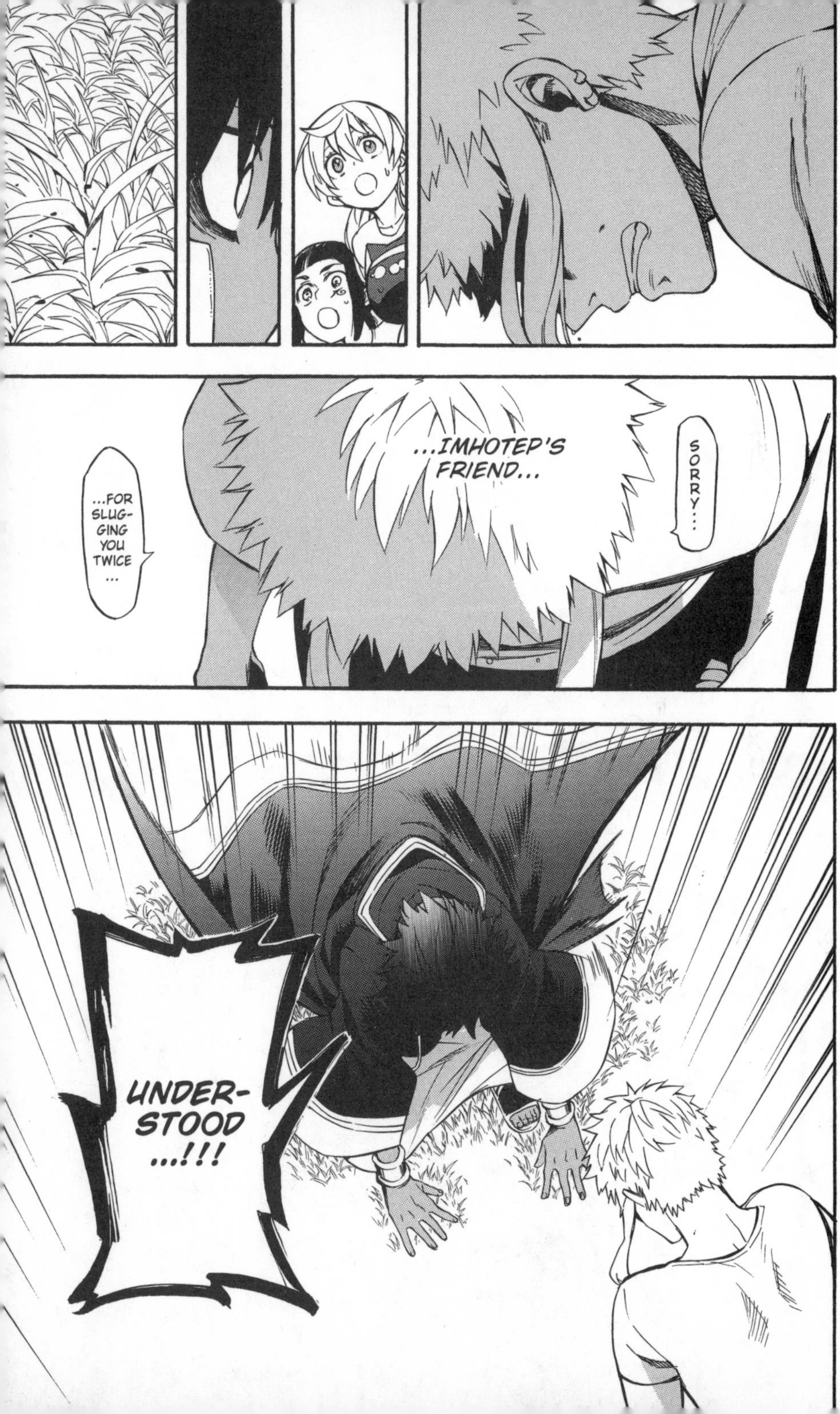
SORRY...
...IMHOTEP'S FRIEND...
...FOR SLUG-GING YOU TWICE...
UNDER-STOOD ...!!!

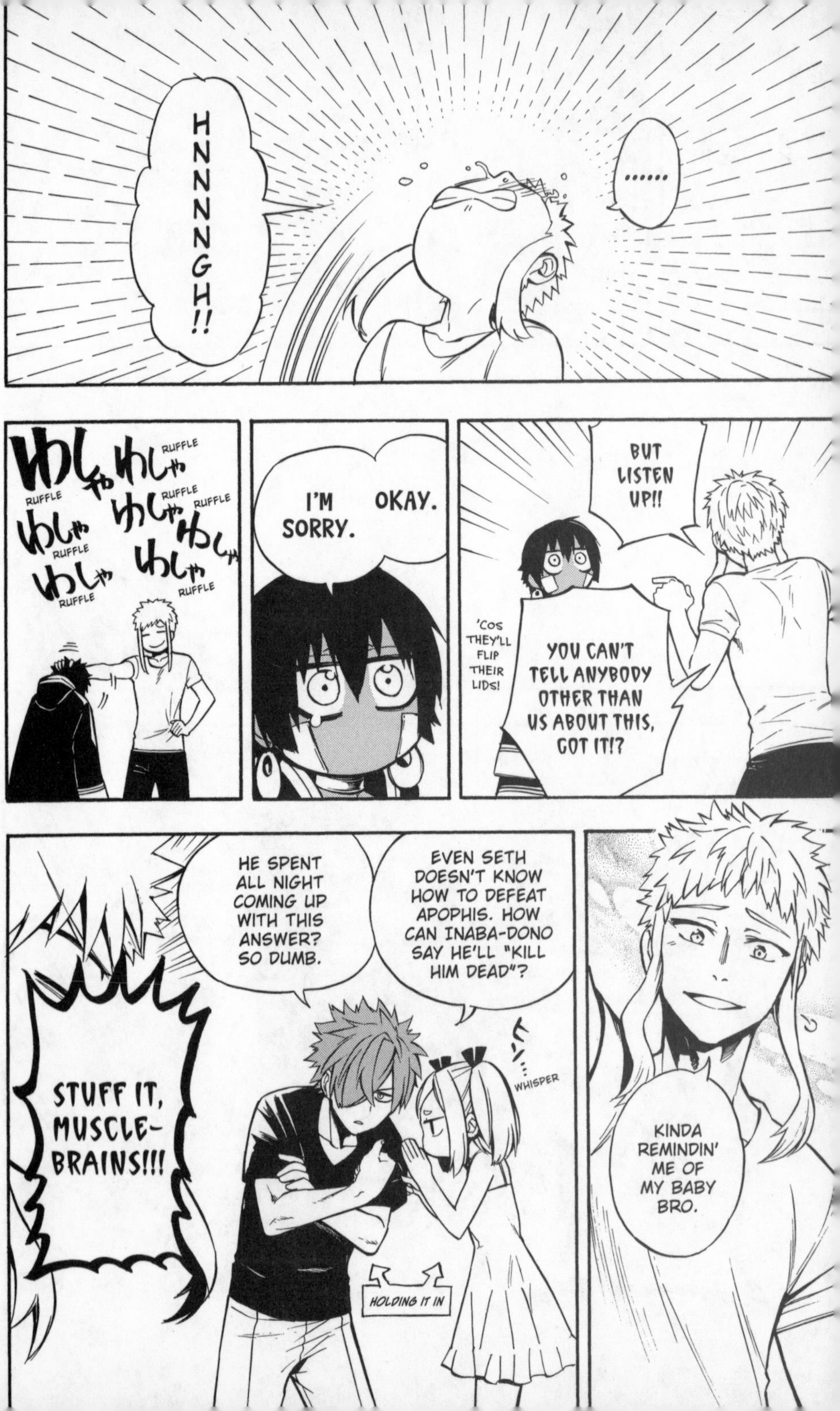
......
HNNNNGH!!
BUT LISTEN UP!!
YOU CAN'T TELL ANYBODY OTHER THAN US ABOUT THIS, GOT IT!?
'COS THEY'LL FLIP THEIR LIDS!
OKAY.
I'M SORRY.
わしゃわしゃ RUFFLE RUFFLE
わしゃわしゃわしゃ RUFFLE RUFFLE RUFFLE
わしゃわしゃ RUFFLE RUFFLE
KINDA REMINDIN' ME OF MY BABY BRO.
EVEN SETH DOESN'T KNOW HOW TO DEFEAT APOPHIS. HOW CAN INABA-DONO SAY HE'LL "KILL HIM DEAD"?
HE SPENT ALL NIGHT COMING UP WITH THIS ANSWER? SO DUMB.
WHISPER
HOLDING IT IN
STUFF IT, MUSCLE-BRAINS!!!

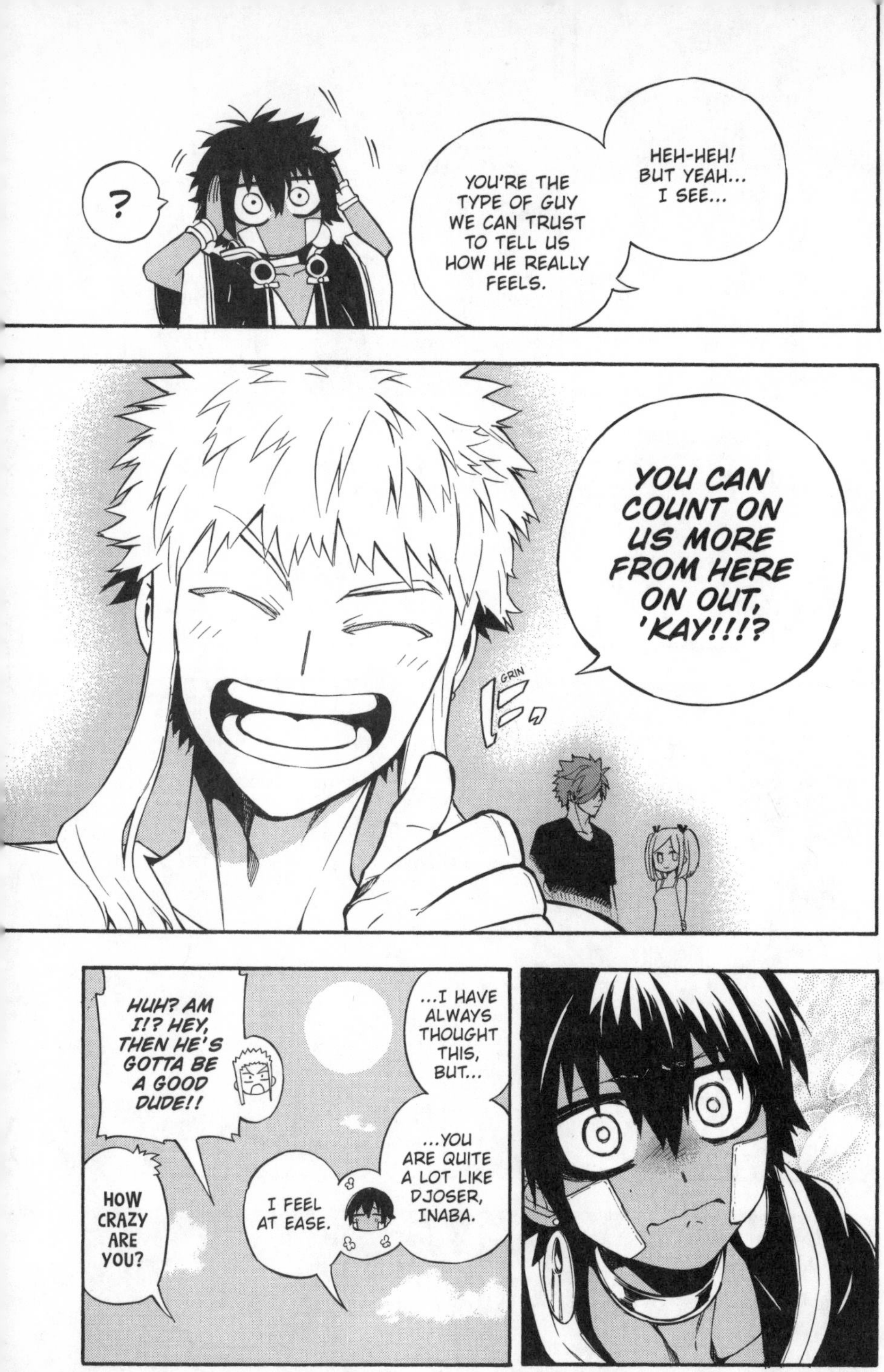
HEH-HEH! BUT YEAH... I SEE...
YOU'RE THE TYPE OF GUY WE CAN TRUST TO TELL US HOW HE REALLY FEELS.
?
YOU CAN COUNT ON US MORE FROM HERE ON OUT, 'KAY!!!?
GRIN
...I HAVE ALWAYS THOUGHT THIS, BUT...
...YOU ARE QUITE A LOT LIKE DJOSER, INABA.
HUH? AM I!? HEY, THEN HE'S GOTTA BE A GOOD DUDE!!
I FEEL AT EASE.
HOW CRAZY ARE YOU?

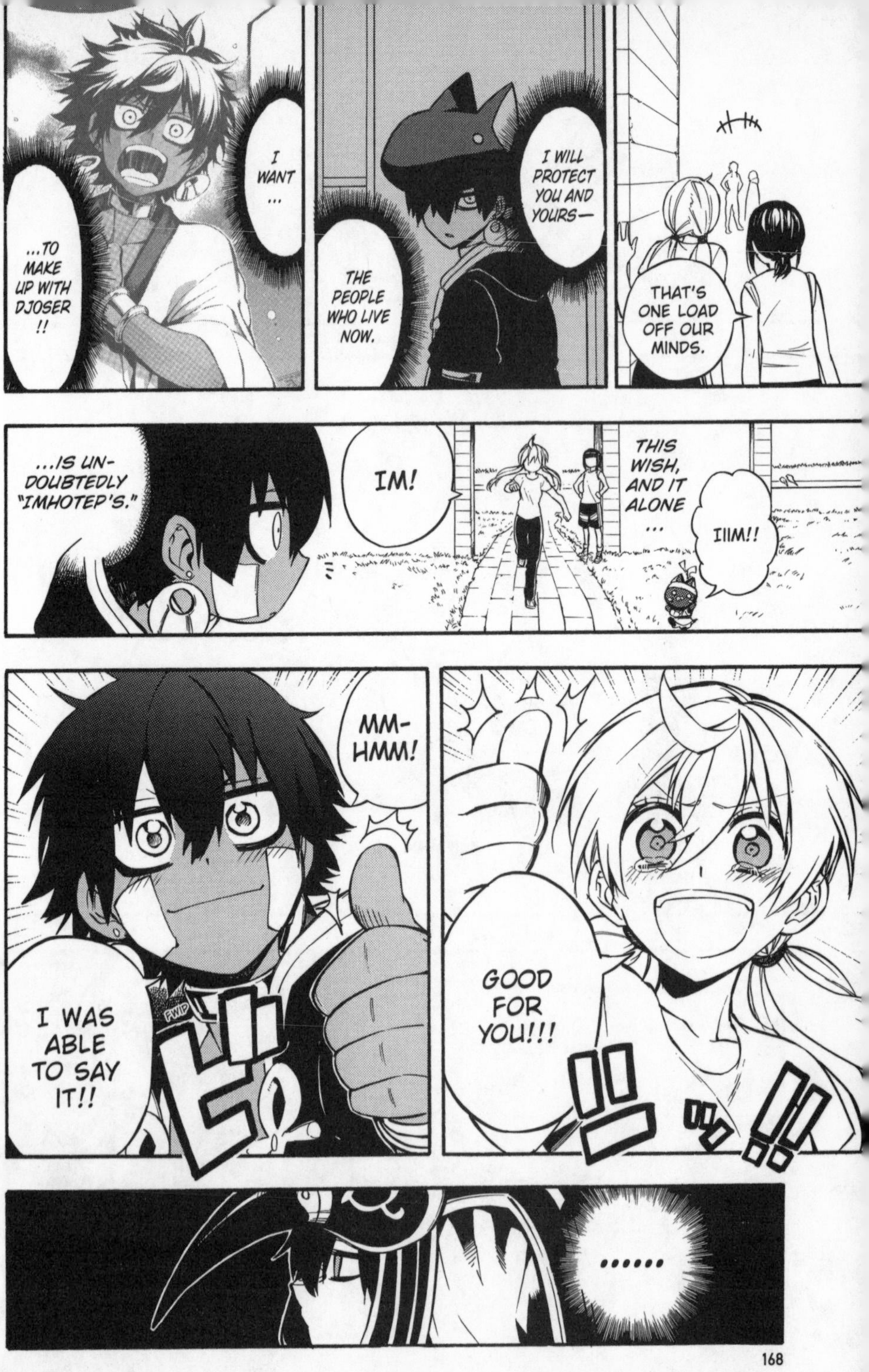
THAT'S ONE LOAD OFF OUR MINDS.
I WILL PROTECT YOU AND YOURS—
THE PEOPLE WHO LIVE NOW.
I WANT ...
...TO MAKE UP WITH DJOSER !!
THIS WISH, AND IT ALONE ...
IIIM!!
IM!
...IS UN-DOUBTEDLY "IMHOTEP'S."
GOOD FOR YOU!!!
MM-HMM!
I WAS ABLE TO SAY IT!!
FWIP
......

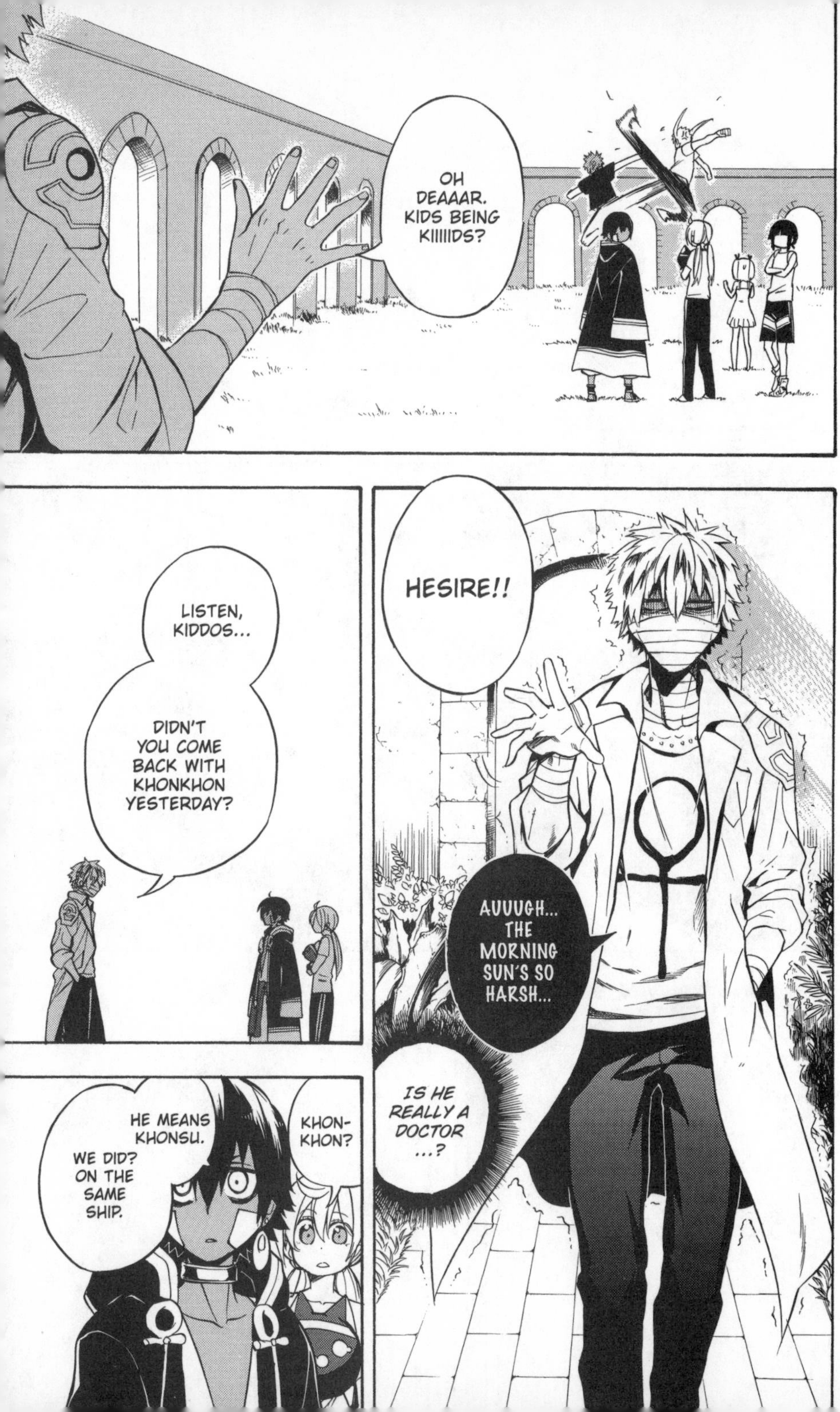
OH DEAAAR. KIDS BEING KIIIIIDS?
HESIRE!!
AUUUGH... THE MORNING SUN'S SO HARSH...
IS HE REALLY A DOCTOR ...?
LISTEN, KIDDOS...
DIDN'T YOU COME BACK WITH KHONKHON YESTERDAY?
KHON-KHON?
HE MEANS KHONSU.
WE DID? ON THE SAME SHIP.

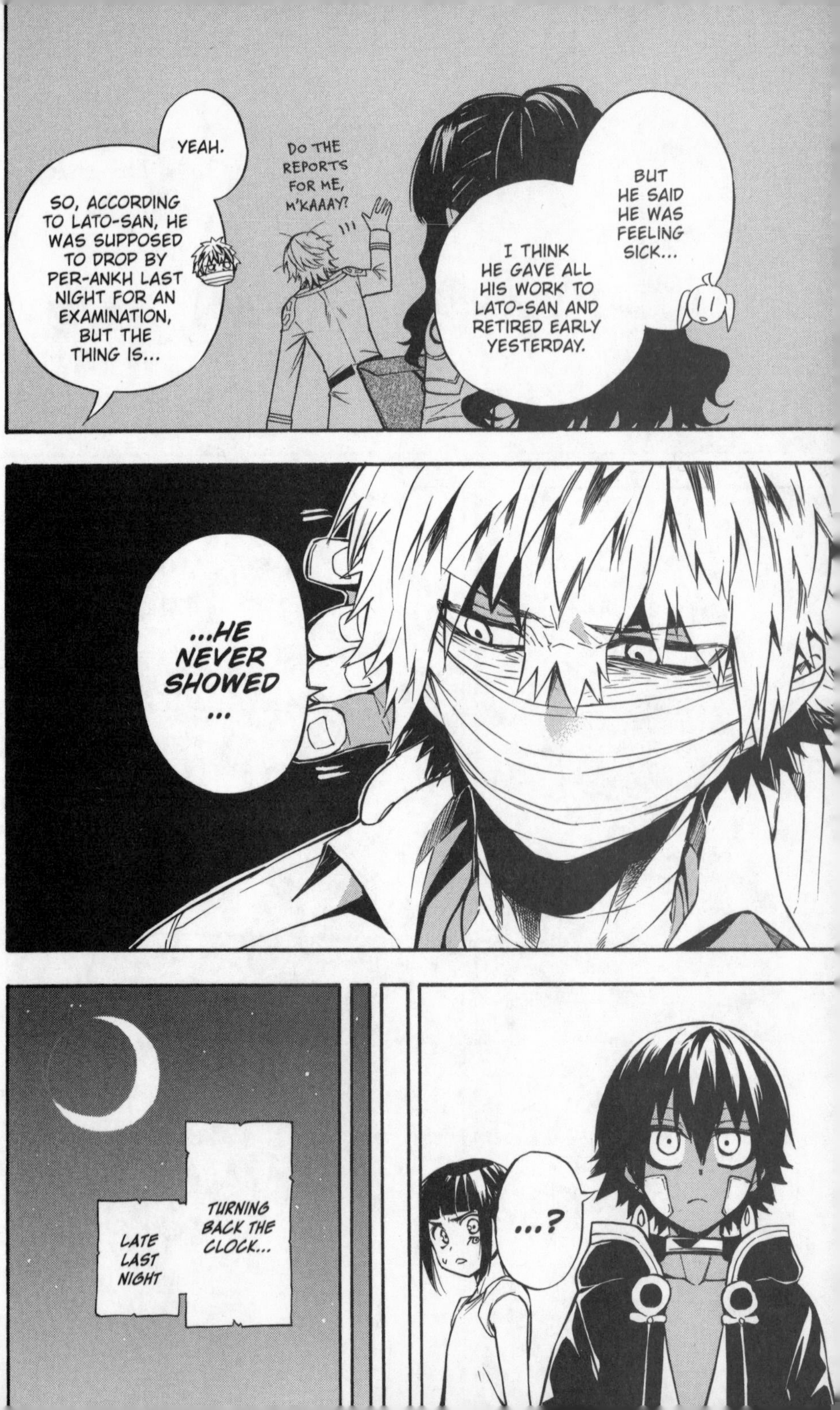
BUT HE SAID HE WAS FEELING SICK...
I THINK HE GAVE ALL HIS WORK TO LATO-SAN AND RETIRED EARLY YESTERDAY.
DO THE REPORTS FOR ME, M'KAAAY?
YEAH.
SO, ACCORDING TO LATO-SAN, HE WAS SUPPOSED TO DROP BY PER-ANKH LAST NIGHT FOR AN EXAMINATION, BUT THE THING IS...
...HE NEVER SHOWED...
...?
TURNING BACK THE CLOCK...
LATE LAST NIGHT

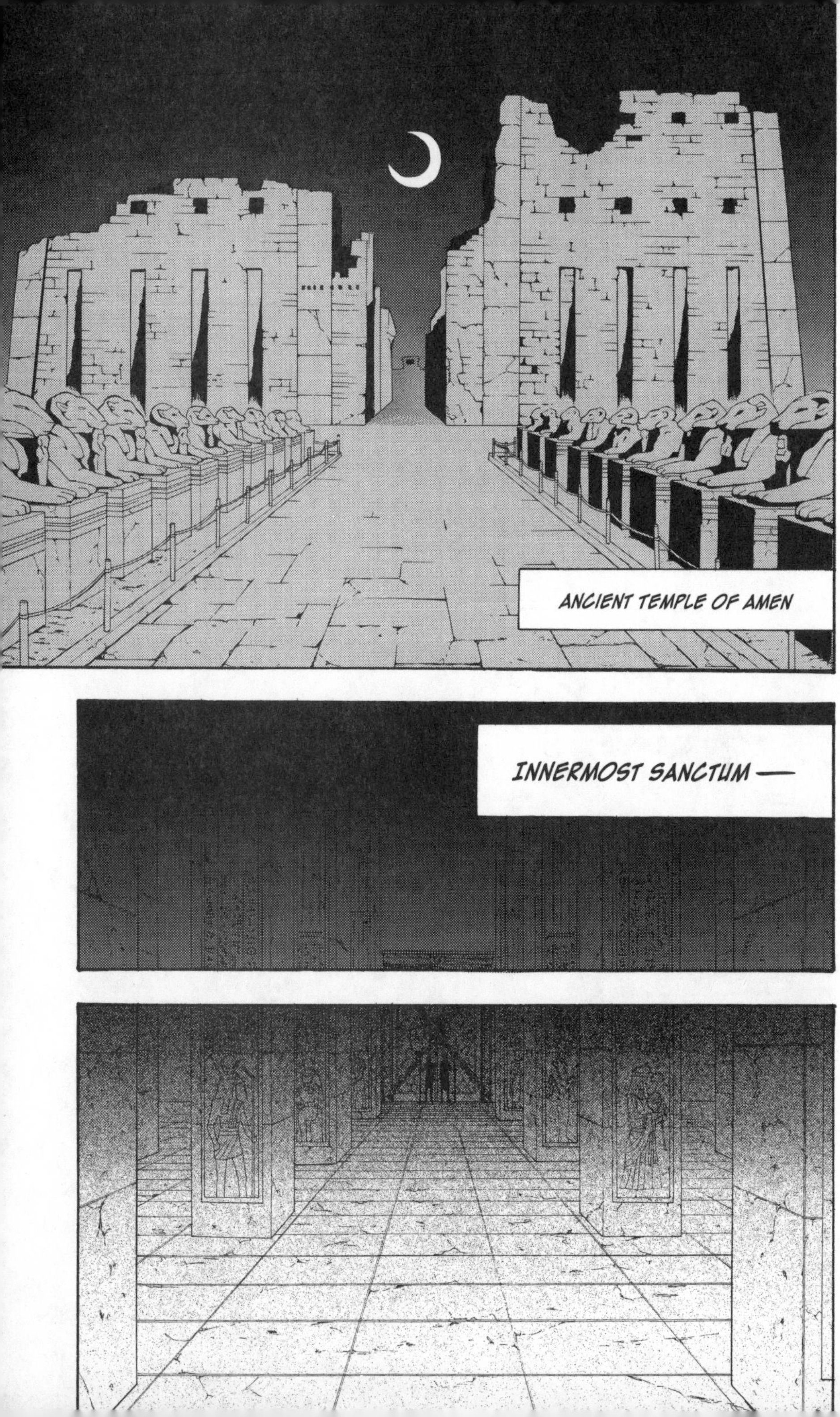
ANCIENT TEMPLE OF AMEN
INNERMOST SANCTUM —

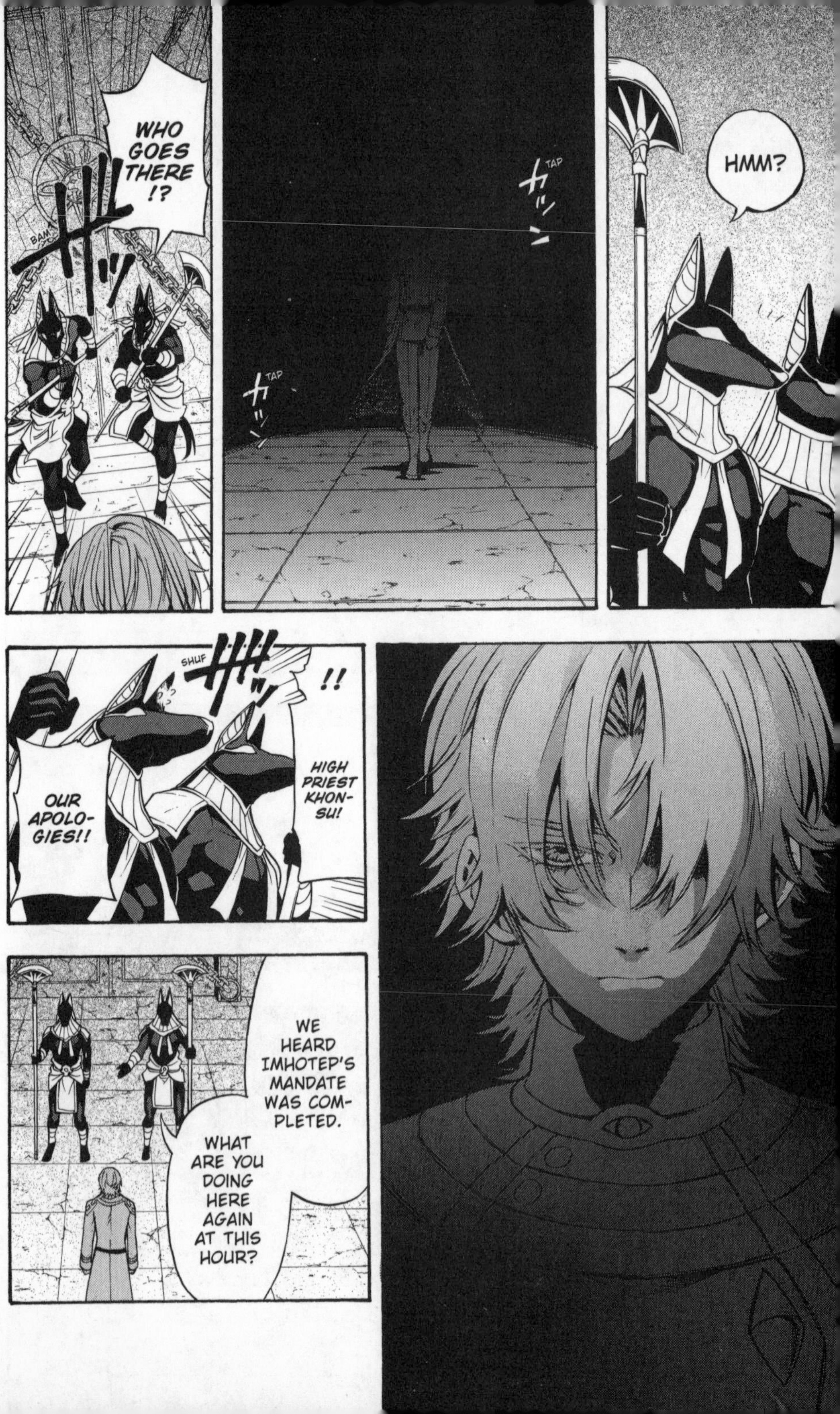
HMM?
TAP
TAP
WHO GOES THERE !?
BAM
!!
HIGH PRIEST KHONSU!
SHUF
OUR APOLO-GIES!!
WE HEARD IMHOTEP'S MANDATE WAS COM-PLETED.
WHAT ARE YOU DOING HERE AGAIN AT THIS HOUR?

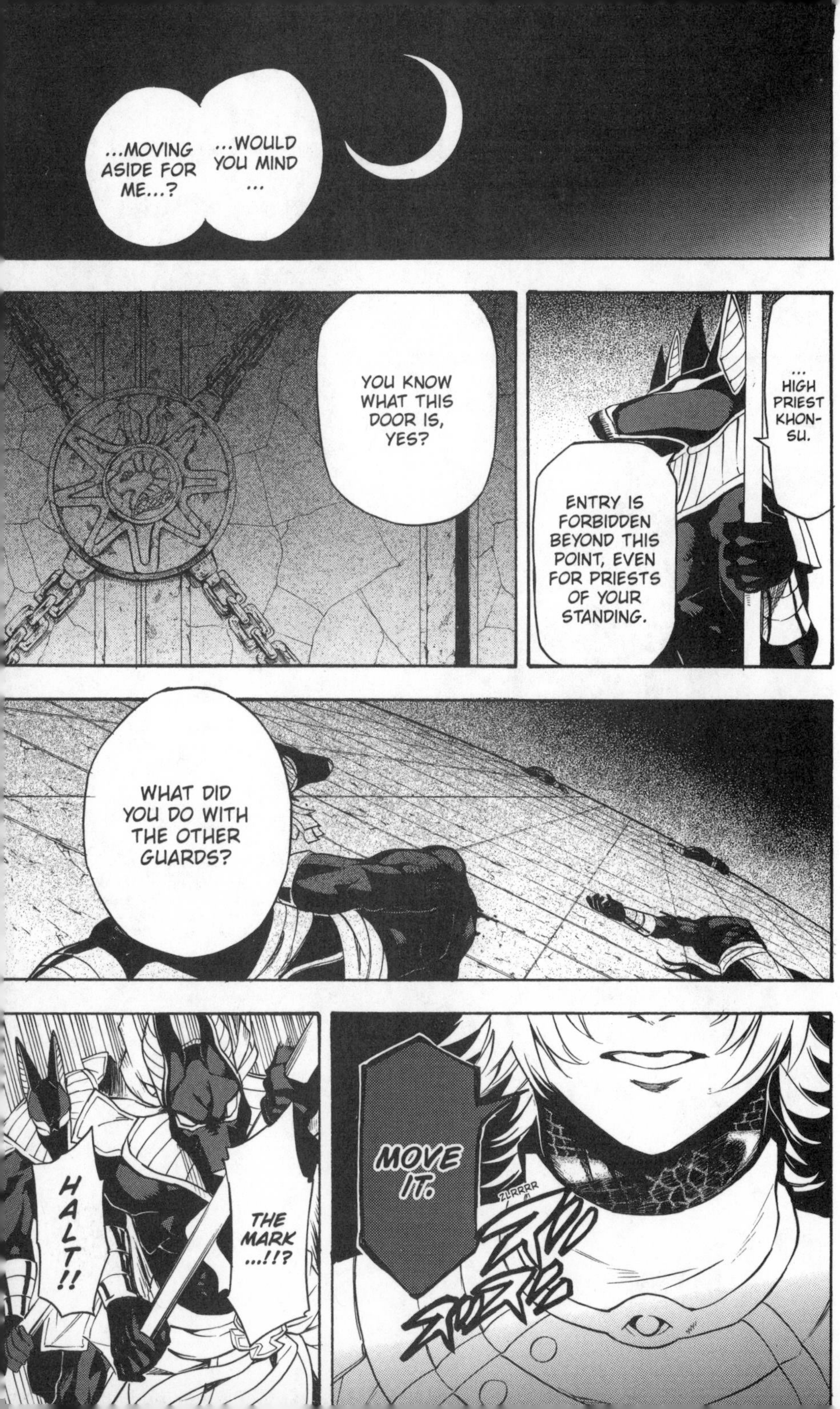
...WOULD YOU MIND ...
...MOVING ASIDE FOR ME...?
... HIGH PRIEST KHON-SU.
ENTRY IS FORBIDDEN BEYOND THIS POINT, EVEN FOR PRIESTS OF YOUR STANDING.
YOU KNOW WHAT THIS DOOR IS, YES?
WHAT DID YOU DO WITH THE OTHER GUARDS?
MOVE IT.
ZURRRR
THE MARK ...!!?
HALT!!

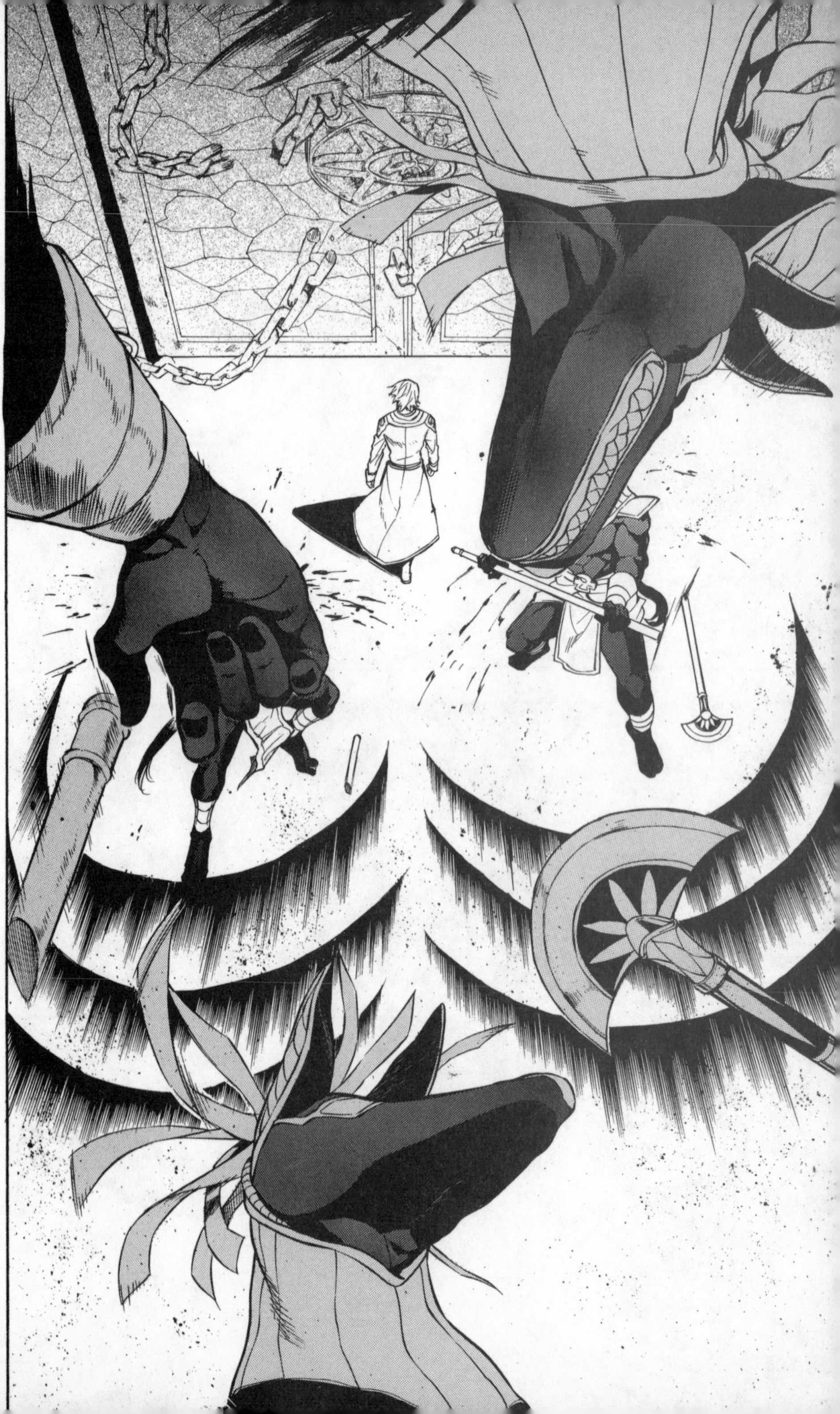

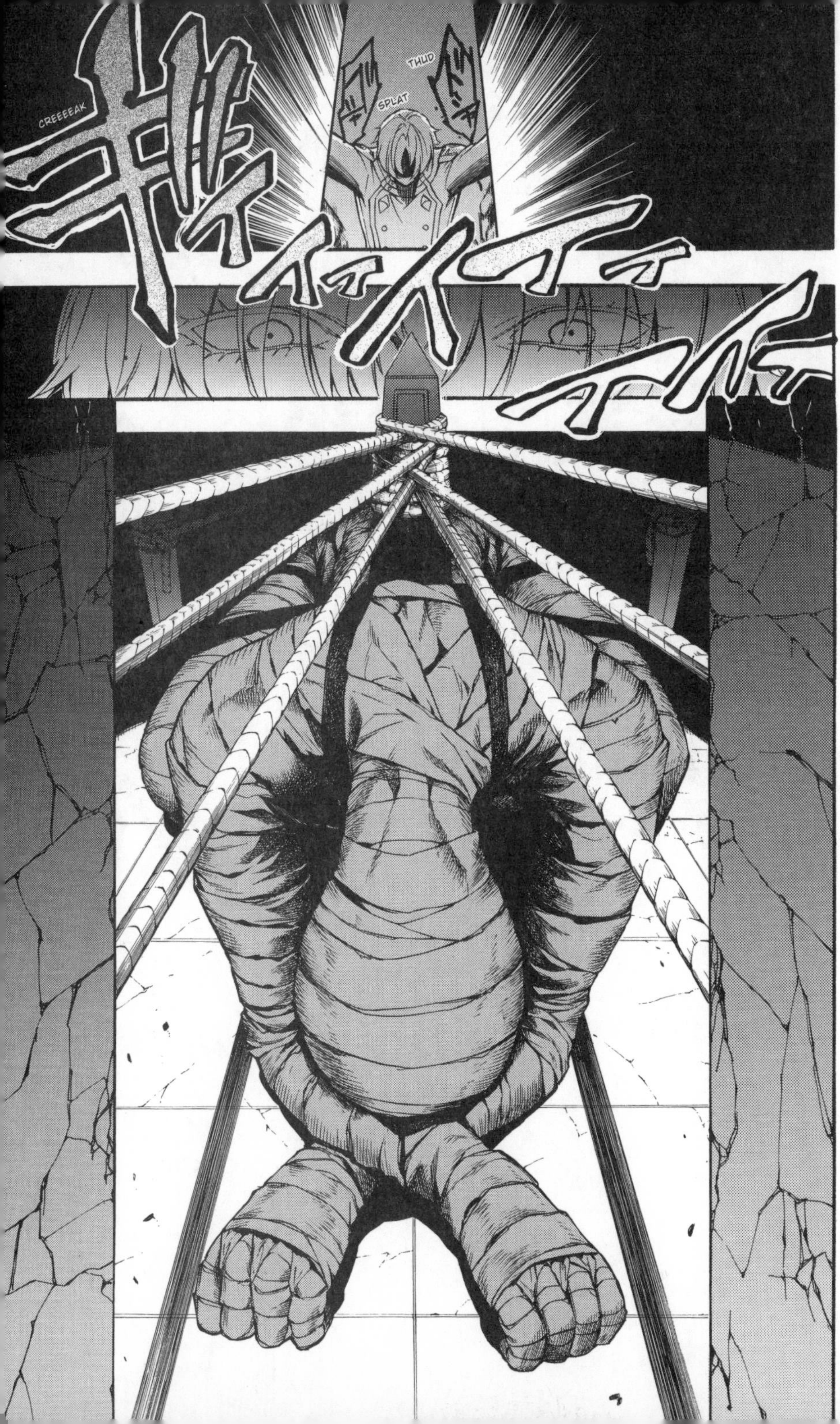
CREEEEAK
THUD
SPLAT

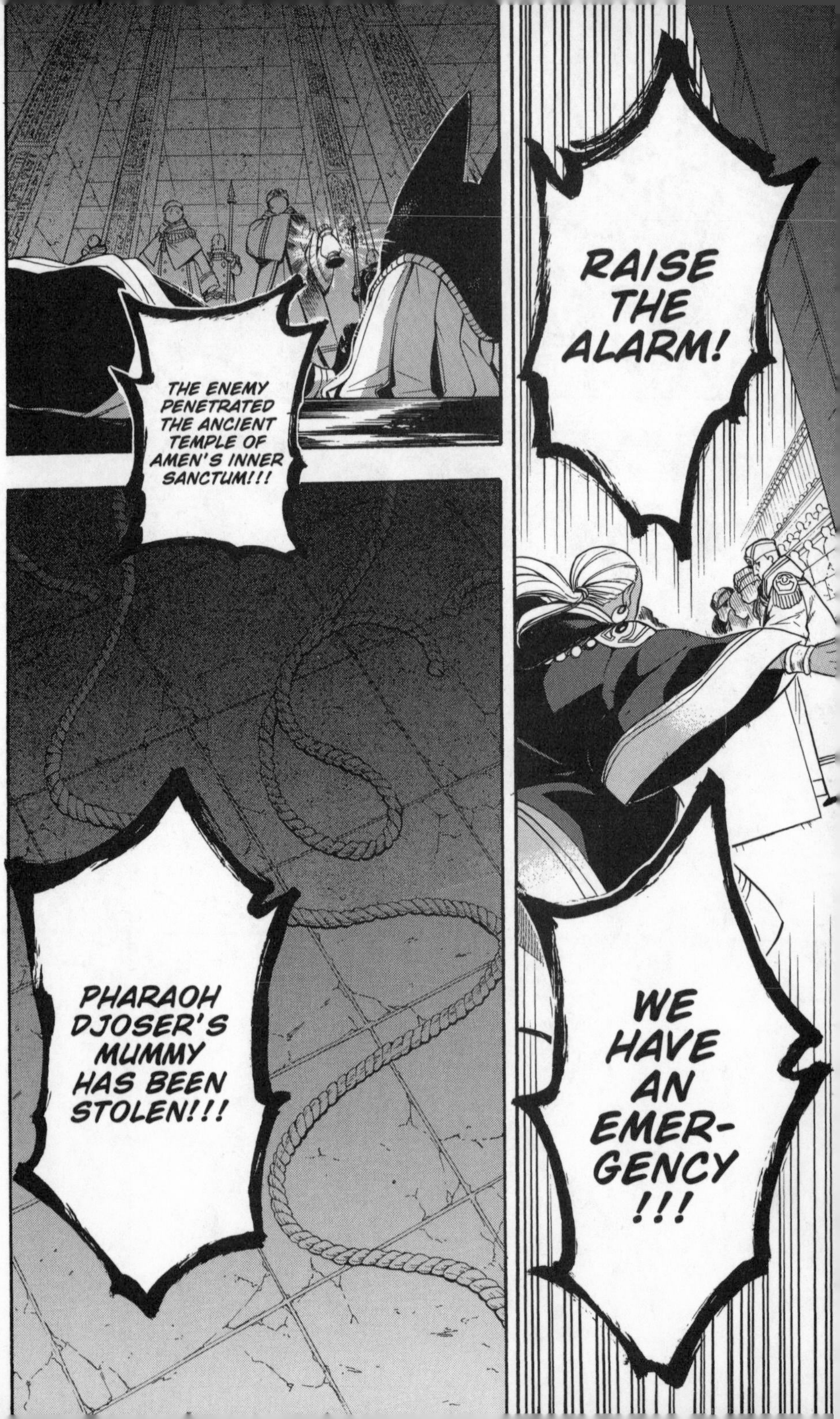
RAISE THE ALARM!
WE HAVE AN EMER-GENCY!!!
THE ENEMY PENETRATED THE ANCIENT TEMPLE OF AMEN'S INNER SANCTUM!!!
PHARAOH DJOSER'S MUMMY HAS BEEN STOLEN!!!

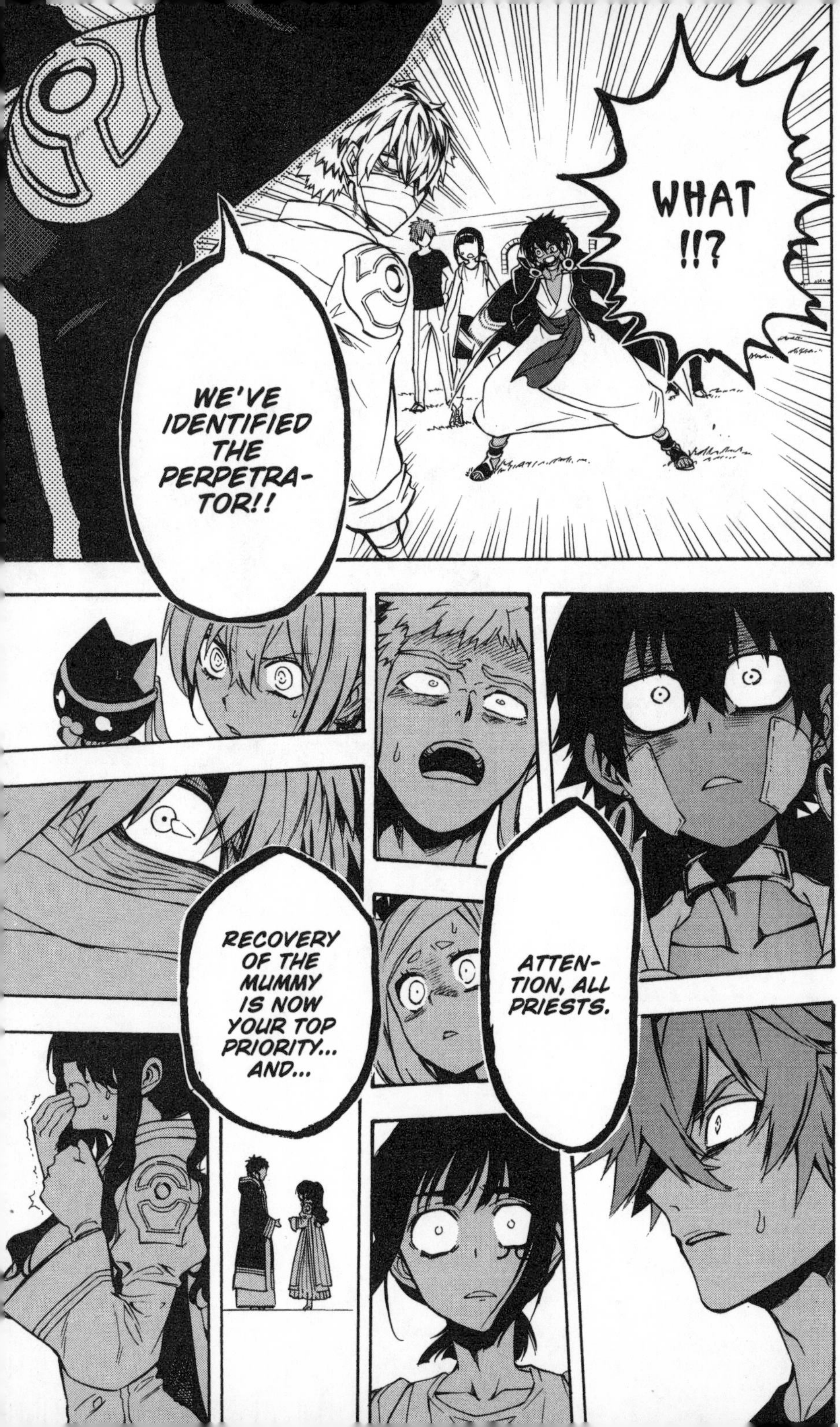
WHAT !!?
WE'VE IDENTIFIED THE PERPETRA-TOR!!
ATTEN-TION, ALL PRIESTS.
RECOVERY OF THE MUMMY IS NOW YOUR TOP PRIORITY... AND...

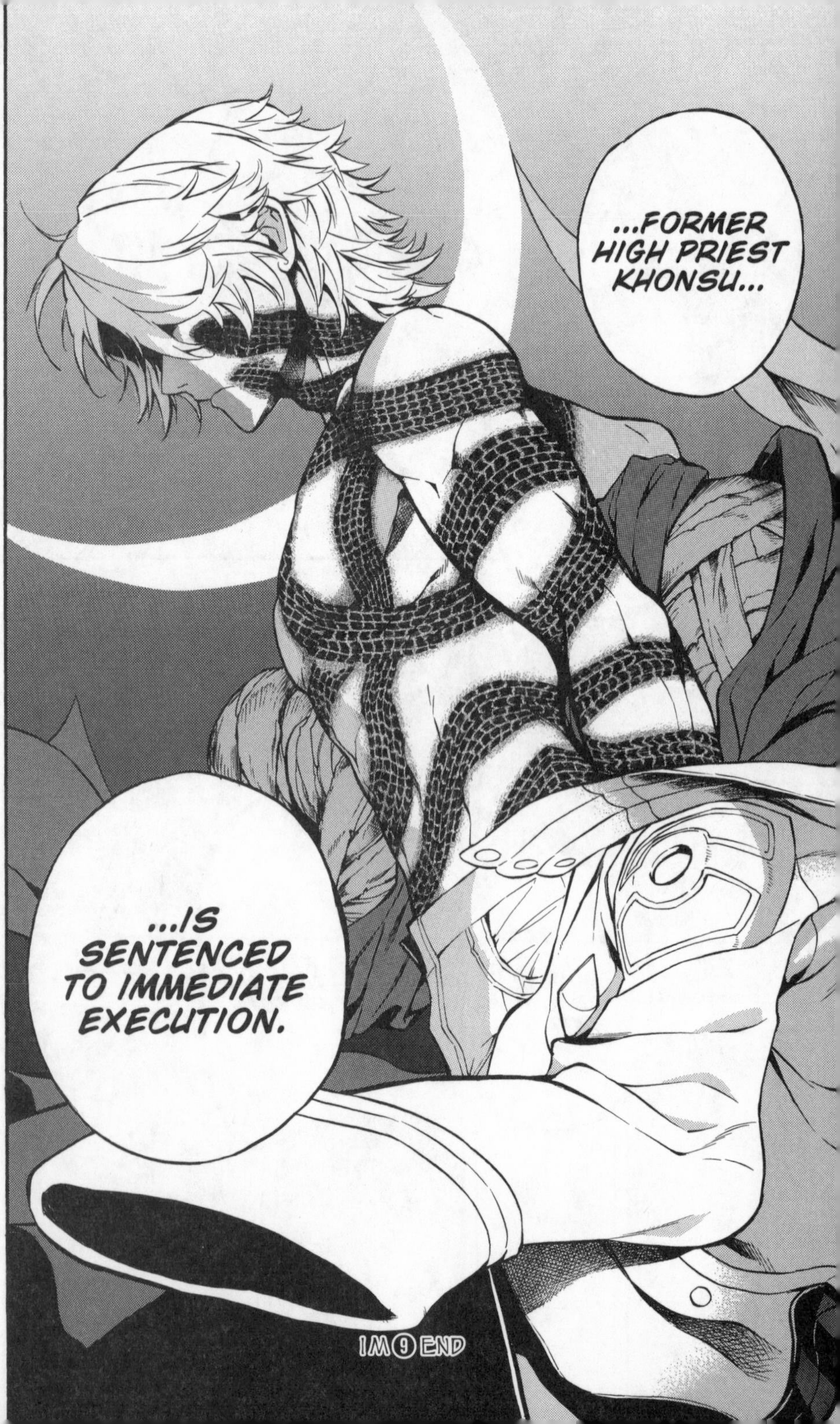
...FORMER HIGH PRIEST KHONSU...
...IS SENTENCED TO IMMEDIATE EXECUTION.
IM 9 END

Great Priest Imhotep

Great Priest Imhotep

BONUS MANGA

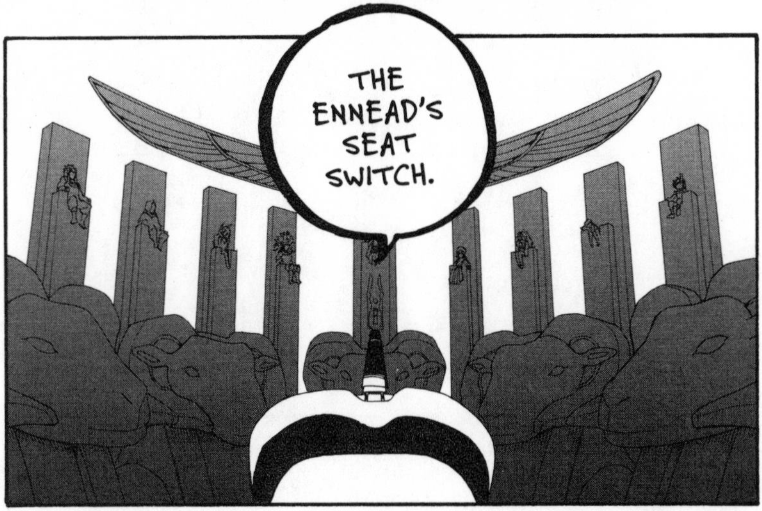
THE ENNEAD'S SEAT SWITCH.

HOW DID THEY END UP LINED UP LIKE THIS?

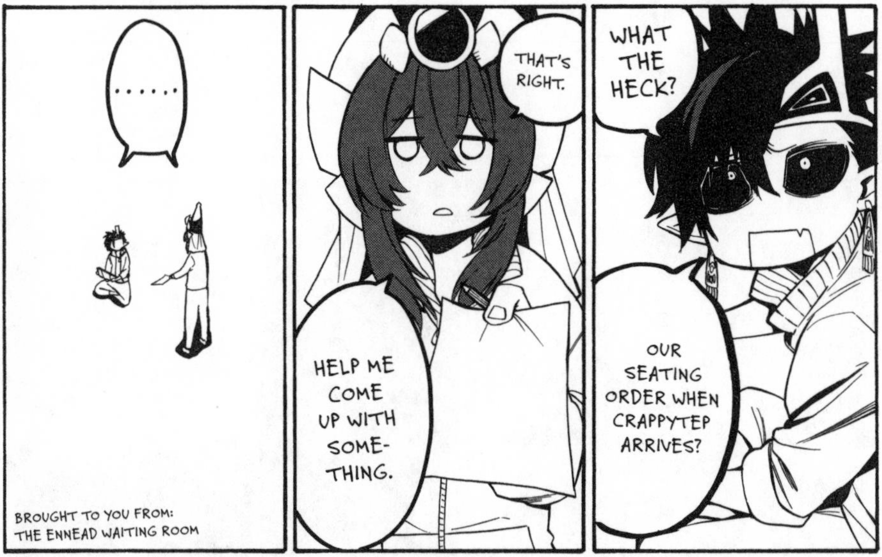
WHAT THE HECK?
OUR SEATING ORDER WHEN CRAPPYTEP ARRIVES?
THAT'S RIGHT.
HELP ME COME UP WITH SOME-THING.
......
BROUGHT TO YOU FROM: THE ENNEAD WAITING ROOM

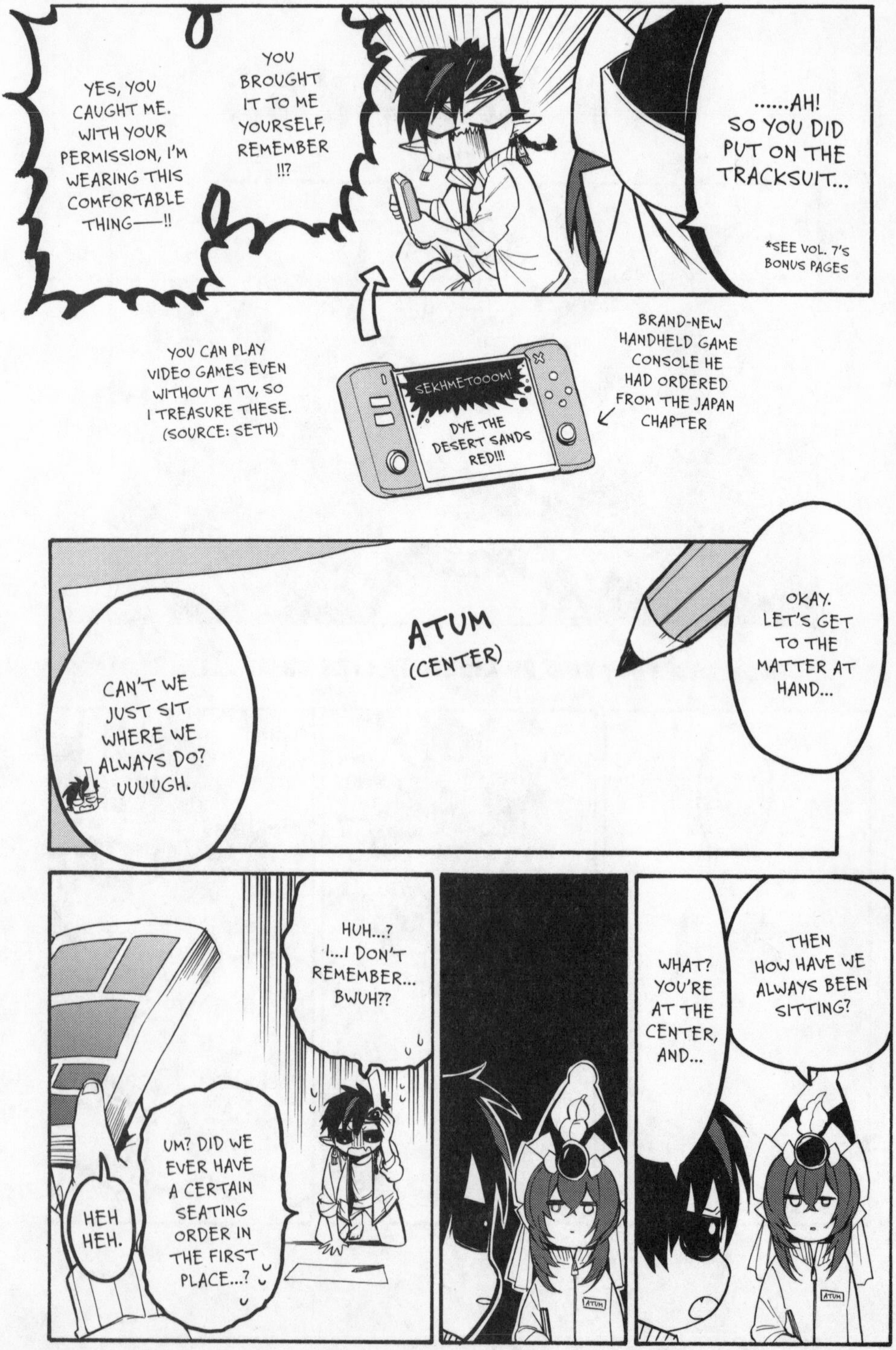
......AH! SO YOU DID PUT ON THE TRACKSUIT...
*SEE VOL. 7'S BONUS PAGES
YOU BROUGHT IT TO ME YOURSELF, REMEMBER !!?
YES, YOU CAUGHT ME. WITH YOUR PERMISSION, I'M WEARING THIS COMFORTABLE THING——!!
BRAND-NEW HANDHELD GAME CONSOLE HE HAD ORDERED FROM THE JAPAN CHAPTER
SEKHMETOOOM!
DYE THE DESERT SANDS RED!!!
YOU CAN PLAY VIDEO GAMES EVEN WITHOUT A TV, SO I TREASURE THESE. (SOURCE: SETH)
OKAY. LET'S GET TO THE MATTER AT HAND...
ATUM
(CENTER)
CAN'T WE JUST SIT WHERE WE ALWAYS DO? UUUUGH.
THEN HOW HAVE WE ALWAYS BEEN SITTING?
WHAT? YOU'RE AT THE CENTER, AND...
ATUM
ATUM
HUH...? I...I DON'T REMEMBER... BWUH??
UM? DID WE EVER HAVE A CERTAIN SEATING ORDER IN THE FIRST PLACE...?
HEH HEH.

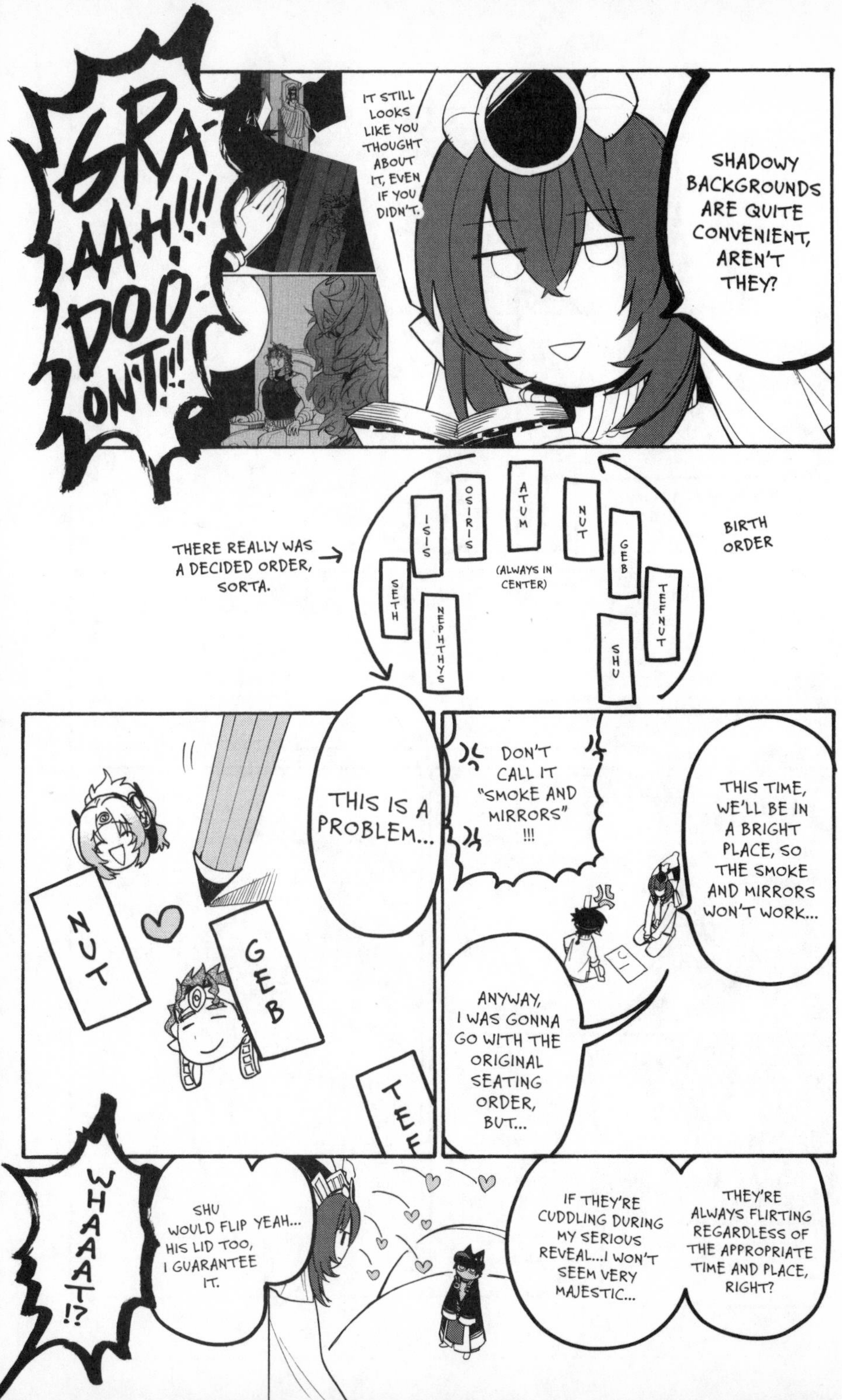
SHADOWY BACKGROUNDS ARE QUITE CONVENIENT, AREN'T THEY?
IT STILL LOOKS LIKE YOU THOUGHT ABOUT IT, EVEN IF YOU DIDN'T.
SRA-AAH!!! DOO-ON'T!!!
BIRTH ORDER
ATUM
(ALWAYS IN CENTER)
NUT
OSIRIS
GEB
ISIS
TEFNUT
SETH
SHU
NEPHTHYS
THERE REALLY WAS A DECIDED ORDER, SORTA.
THIS TIME, WE'LL BE IN A BRIGHT PLACE, SO THE SMOKE AND MIRRORS WON'T WORK...
DON'T CALL IT "SMOKE AND MIRRORS"!!!
ANYWAY, I WAS GONNA GO WITH THE ORIGINAL SEATING ORDER, BUT...
THIS IS A PROBLEM...
NUT
GEB
TEF
THEY'RE ALWAYS FLIRTING REGARDLESS OF THE APPROPRIATE TIME AND PLACE, RIGHT?
IF THEY'RE CUDDLING DURING MY SERIOUS REVEAL...I WON'T SEEM VERY MAJESTIC...
YEAH...
SHU WOULD FLIP HIS LID TOO, I GUARANTEE IT.
WHAAAT!?

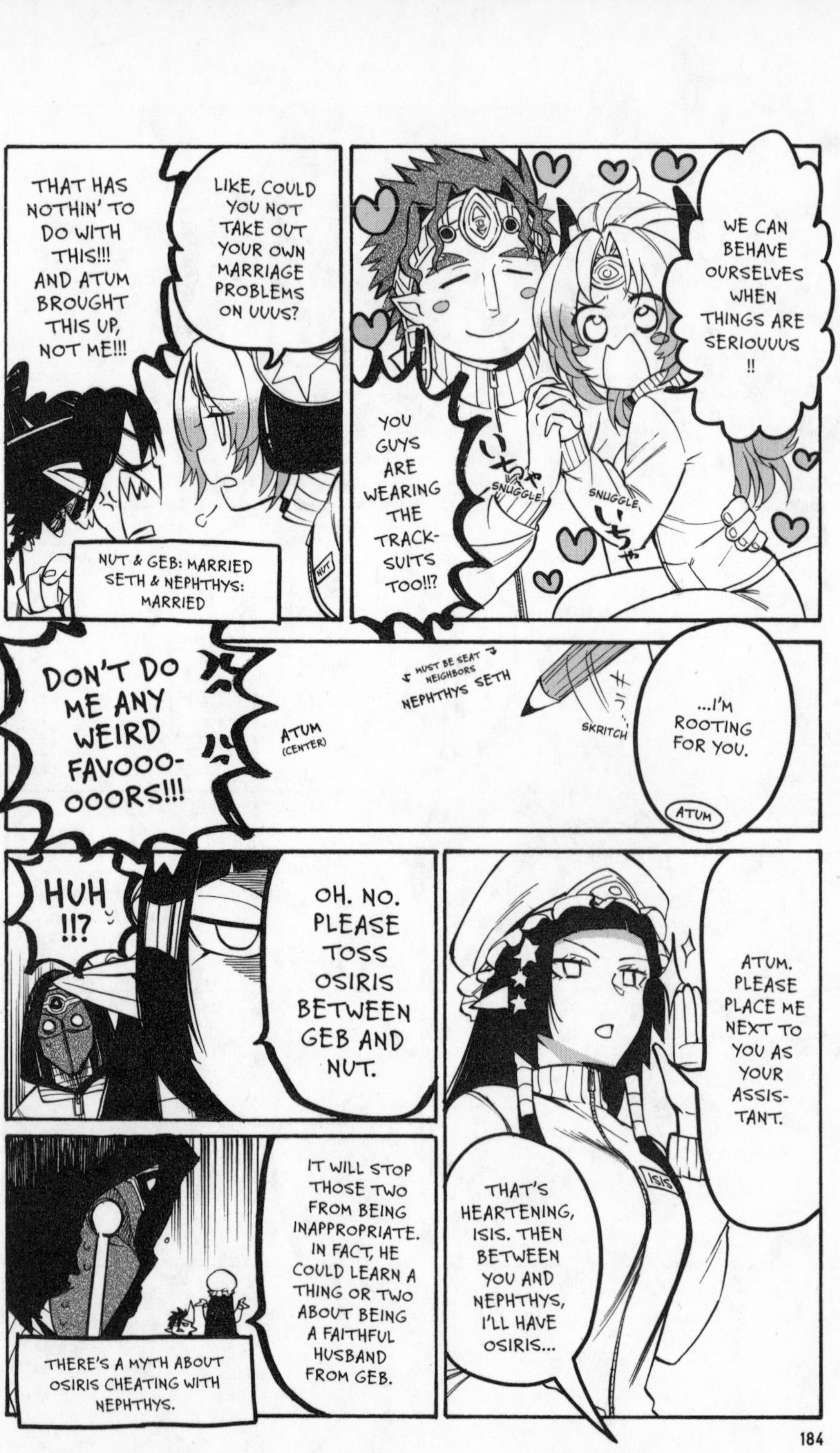
WE CAN BEHAVE OURSELVES WHEN THINGS ARE SERIOUUUS!!
SNUGGLE
SNUGGLE
YOU GUYS ARE WEARING THE TRACK-SUITS TOO!!?
LIKE, COULD YOU NOT TAKE OUT YOUR OWN MARRIAGE PROBLEMS ON UUUS?
THAT HAS NOTHIN' TO DO WITH THIS!!! AND ATUM BROUGHT THIS UP, NOT ME!!!
NUT
NUT & GEB: MARRIED
SETH & NEPHTHYS: MARRIED
...I'M ROOTING FOR YOU.
ATUM
SKRITCH
MUST BE SEAT NEIGHBORS
NEPHTHYS SETH
ATUM (CENTER)
DON'T DO ME ANY WEIRD FAVOOOOOORS!!!
ATUM. PLEASE PLACE ME NEXT TO YOU AS YOUR ASSISTANT.
ISIS
THAT'S HEARTENING, ISIS. THEN BETWEEN YOU AND NEPHTHYS, I'LL HAVE OSIRIS...
OH. NO. PLEASE TOSS OSIRIS BETWEEN GEB AND NUT.
HUH!!?
IT WILL STOP THOSE TWO FROM BEING INAPPROPRIATE. IN FACT, HE COULD LEARN A THING OR TWO ABOUT BEING A FAITHFUL HUSBAND FROM GEB.
THERE'S A MYTH ABOUT OSIRIS CHEATING WITH NEPHTHYS.

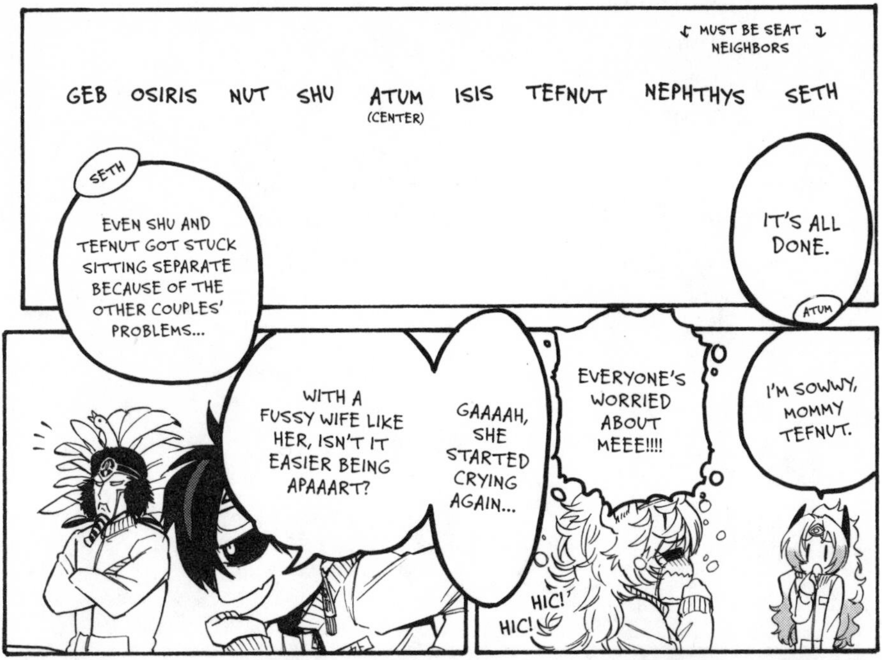
MUST BE SEAT NEIGHBORS
GEB OSIRIS NUT SHU ATUM (CENTER) ISIS TEFNUT NEPHTHYS SETH
IT'S ALL DONE.
ATUM
SETH
EVEN SHU AND TEFNUT GOT STUCK SITTING SEPARATE BECAUSE OF THE OTHER COUPLES' PROBLEMS...
I'M SOWWY, MOMMY TEFNUT.
EVERYONE'S WORRIED ABOUT MEEE!!!!
HIC! HIC!
GAAAAH, SHE STARTED CRYING AGAIN...
WITH A FUSSY WIFE LIKE HER, ISN'T IT EASIER BEING APAAART?

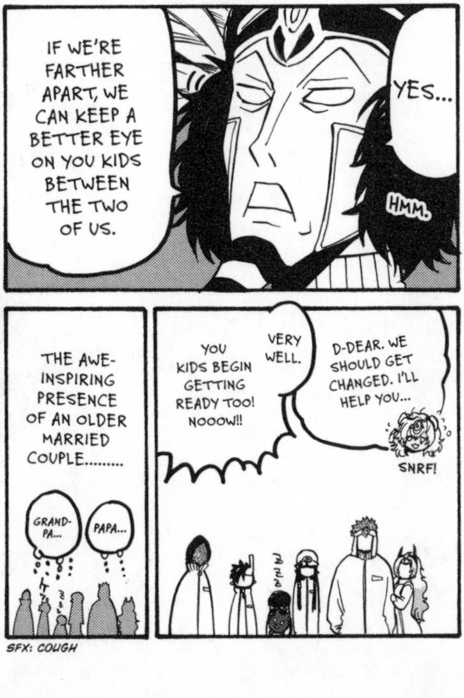
YES...
HMM.
IF WE'RE FARTHER APART, WE CAN KEEP A BETTER EYE ON YOU KIDS BETWEEN THE TWO OF US.
D-DEAR. WE SHOULD GET CHANGED. I'LL HELP YOU...
SNRF!
VERY WELL.
YOU KIDS BEGIN GETTING READY TOO! NOOOW!!
PAPA...
GRAND-PA...
THE AWE-INSPIRING PRESENCE OF AN OLDER MARRIED COUPLE.........

SFX: COUGH

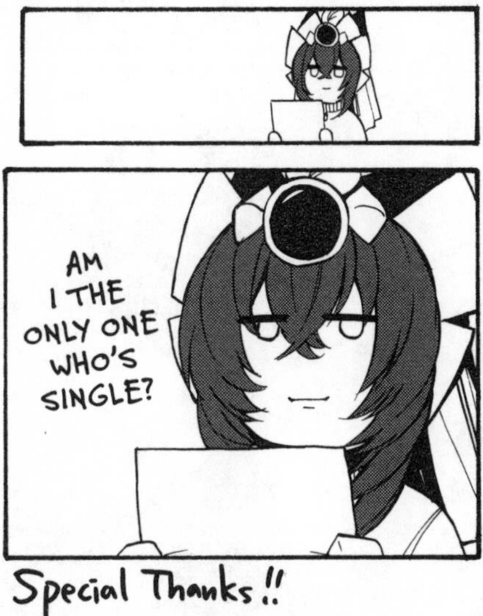
AM I THE ONLY ONE WHO'S SINGLE?

Special Thanks!!

ARISA YUKIMIYA, UI KIZUKI, MAI KUROZUKI

SPECIAL HELP FROM:
SHINONOME-SAN,
SHIKAMORI-SAN

MY EDITOR,
YUUICHI SHIMOMURA-SAMA

MAKOTO
MORISHITA

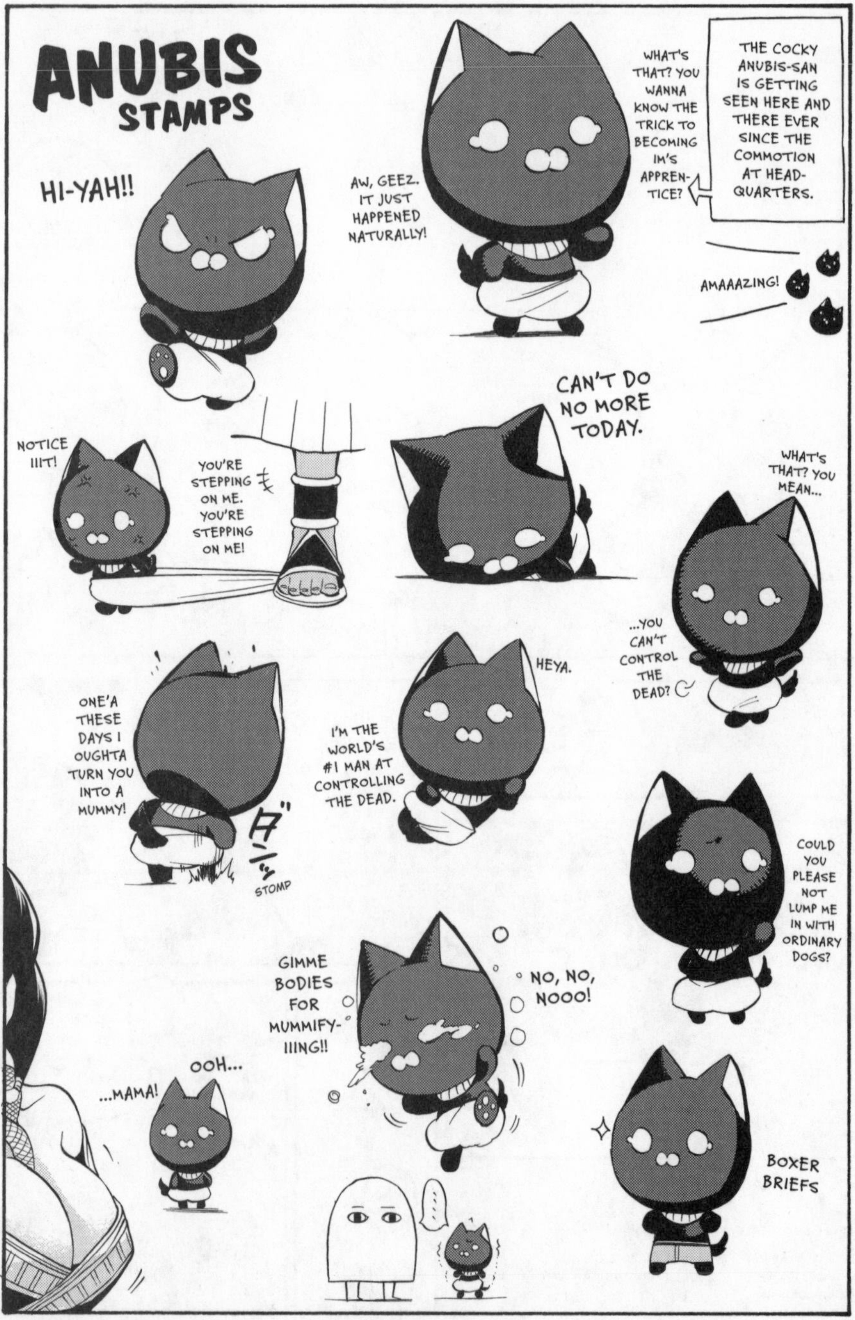
THE COCKY ANUBIS-SAN IS GETTING SEEN HERE AND THERE EVER SINCE THE COMMOTION AT HEAD-QUARTERS.
WHAT'S THAT? YOU WANNA KNOW THE TRICK TO BECOMING IM'S APPREN-TICE?
AW, GEEZ. IT JUST HAPPENED NATURALLY!
AMAAAZING!
ANUBIS STAMPS
HI-YAH!!
CAN'T DO NO MORE TODAY.
YOU'RE STEPPING ON ME. YOU'RE STEPPING ON ME!
NOTICE IIIT!
WHAT'S THAT? YOU MEAN...
...YOU CAN'T CONTROL THE DEAD?
HEYA.
I'M THE WORLD'S #1 MAN AT CONTROLLING THE DEAD.
ONE'A THESE DAYS I OUGHTA TURN YOU INTO A MUMMY!
STOMP
COULD YOU PLEASE NOT LUMP ME IN WITH ORDINARY DOGS?
NO, NO, NOOO!
GIMME BODIES FOR MUMMIFY-IIING!!
OOH...
...MAMA!
BOXER BRIEFS

NEW YEAR'S PARTY

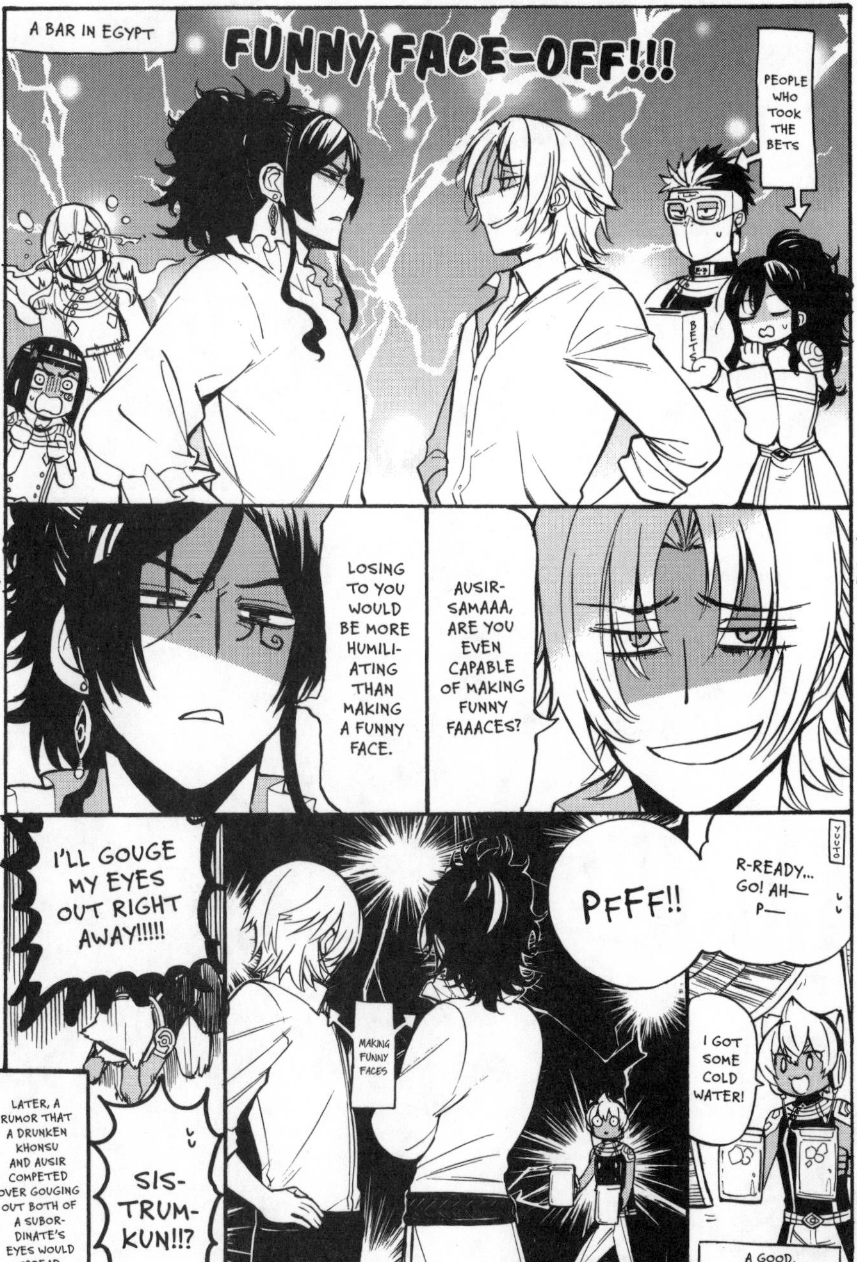
PEOPLE WHO TOOK THE BETS
FUNNY FACE-OFF!!!
A BAR IN EGYPT
BETS
STILL HIS REGULAR FACE
AUSIR-SAMAAA, ARE YOU EVEN CAPABLE OF MAKING FUNNY FAAACES?
LOSING TO YOU WOULD BE MORE HUMILIATING THAN MAKING A FUNNY FACE.
A LITTLE SLEEPY
YUUTO
R-READY... GO! AH— P—
PFFF!!
I GOT SOME COLD WATER!
A GOOD, PROACTIVE SUBORDINATE
MAKING FUNNY FACES
I'LL GOUGE MY EYES OUT RIGHT AWAY!!!!!
SIS-TRUM-KUN!!?
LATER, A RUMOR THAT A DRUNKEN KHONSU AND AUSIR COMPETED OVER GOUGING OUT BOTH OF A SUBORDINATE'S EYES WOULD SPREAD.

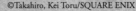

©Takahiro, Kei Toru/SQUARE ENIX

Akame ga KILL! ZERO

THEY BELIEVED THAT EVERY TIME THEY TOOK A LIFE, THEY BROUGHT HAPPINESS TO ANOTHER...

Before becoming Night Raid's deadliest ally, Akame was a young girl bought by the Empire and raised as an assassin whose sole purpose was to slaughter everything in her path. Because that's what makes people happy... right? Discover Akame's shocking past in *Akame ga KILL! Zero*, the prequel to the hit series *Akame ga KILL!*

FULL SERIES AVAILABLE NOW!

For more information, visit www.yenpress.com

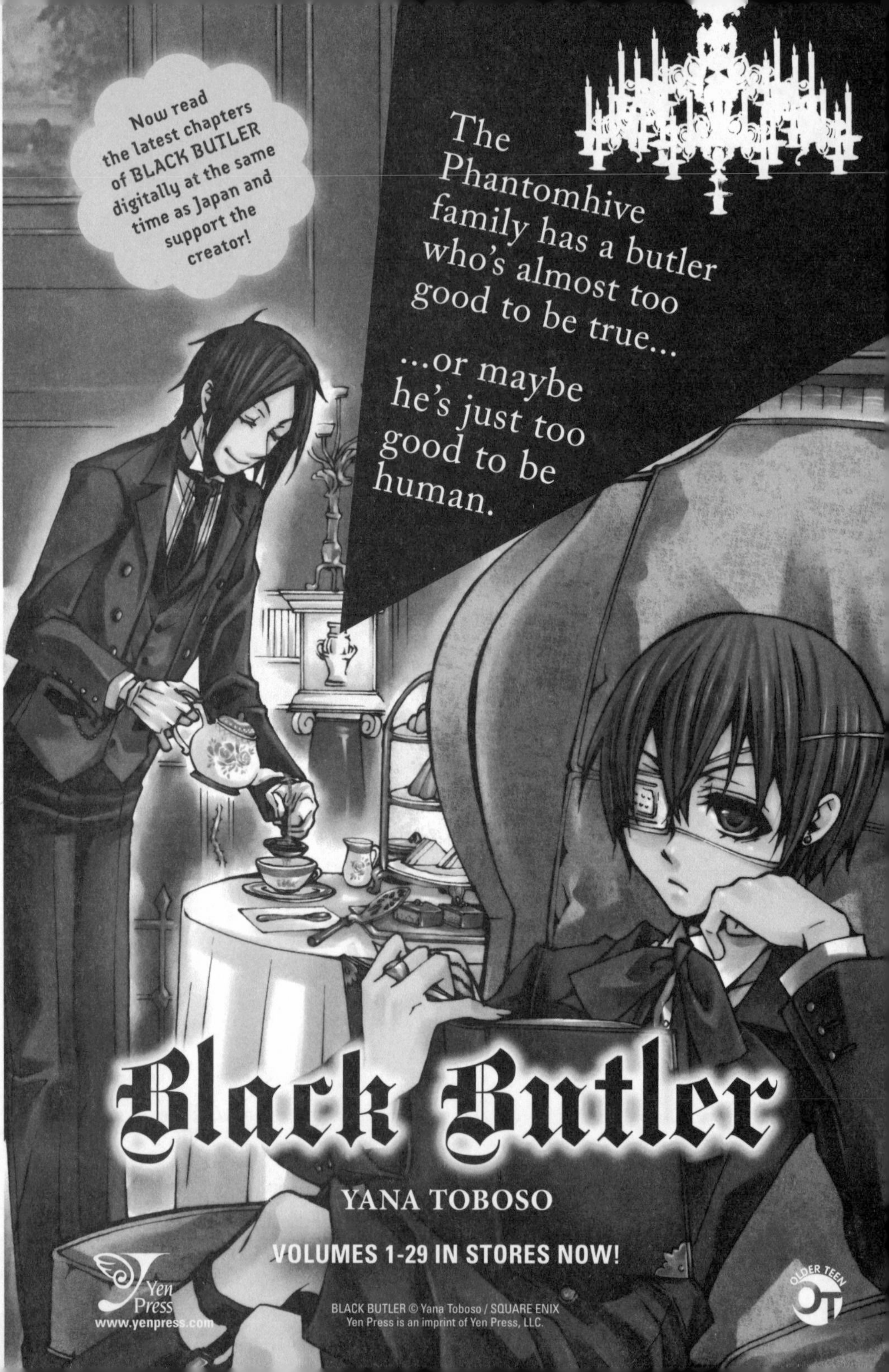
Now read the latest chapters of BLACK BUTLER digitally at the same time as Japan and support the creator!
The Phantomhive family has a butler who's almost too good to be true...
...or maybe he's just too good to be human.
Black Butler
YANA TOBOSO
VOLUMES 1-29 IN STORES NOW!
Yen Press
www.yenpress.com
BLACK BUTLER © Yana Toboso / SQUARE ENIX
Yen Press is an imprint of Yen Press, LLC.
OLDER TEEN
OT